338.91
M58e

65701

DATE DUE		
Oct 15 69		
Oct 29 69		
May 18 '72		
Mar 8 '73		
Mar 21 '73		
Apr 24 '77		
GAYLORD M-2		PRINTED IN U.S.A.

The Economics of
Foreign Aid

ALDINE TREATISES IN
MODERN ECONOMICS
edited by Harry G. Johnson
University of Chicago and
London School of Economics

The Economics of Foreign Aid

RAYMOND F. MIKESELL
University of Oregon

ALDINE PUBLISHING COMPANY / CHICAGO

First published 1968 by
Aldine Publishing Company
320 West Adams Street
Chicago, Illinois 60606

Library of Congress Catalog Card Number LC 67-27394
Designed by Bernard Schleifer
Printed in the United States of America

This book is dedicated to my mother
and to the memory of my father.

Foreword

The purpose of the Aldine Treatises in Modern Economics is to enable authorities in a particular field of economics, and experts on a particular problem, to make their knowledge available to others in the form they find easiest and most convenient. Our intention is to free them both from an insistence on complete coverage of a conventionally defined subject, which deters many leading economists from writing a book instead of a series of articles or induces them to suppress originality for the sake of orthodoxy, and from an obligation to produce a standard number of pages, which encourages the submergence of judgment of relevance in a pudding of irrelevant detail. The Aldine Treatises seek to encourage good economists to say what they want to say to their fellow economists, in as little or as much space as they consider necessary to the purpose.

The present volume treats of the economics of foreign aid. Its author, Raymond F. Mikesell, has had extensive experience in all aspects of the successive American aid programs. He has been a consultant to AID, the Treasury Department, the Department of Commerce, the Department of State, and the Organization of American States, and he has served with various presidential and congressional commissions on aid policy. This experience (which includes both the aid-giving and the aid-receiving process) has led him to be sceptical of the value of the formal mathematical models of development that have become so popular in academic theorizing about development—though as a conscientious scholar he has scrutinized ever ysuch model to determine what it may reveal of the ultimate essence of economic development and of the potential contribution of foreign aid to that process. In place of the spinning of elegant theoretical models of doubtful relevance, Professor Mikesell emphasizes the practical problems and possibilities of promoting development by means of foreign aid. And in place of the common tendency to single out some particular aspect of the development problem for detailed analysis, Professor Mikesell surveys comprehensively a large variety of writings from the point of view of their bearing on the aid-giving and aid-receiving processes.

The academic student of development will find herein a presentation and critical evaluation of formal theories of development and aid that is founded on profound common sense and extensive practical experience, the most difficult aspects of the economist's art to teach to students of the subject. The book should be equally useful to the expanding profession of aid administrators, who require a thorough grounding in relevant theory and a knowledge of the lessons of experience. For the benefit of both groups, Professor Mikesell draws together the results of his pragmatic scrutiny of aid theories and experience in proposals for an integrated aid policy which would enlist the lessons of the past in the service of the future.

As Editor of the Aldine Treatises in Modern Economics, I am extremely pleased that this first publication should exemplify so well what the series is intended to do: it treats authoritatively an important area of contemporary economic concern that cuts across the boundaries dividing fields of academic specialization, and it combines far-ranging academic scholarship with a willingness to assert personal judgment of what is important and what is not in the work that economists have been doing.

HARRY G. JOHNSON

Preface

THE PURPOSE OF this book is to set forth the major problems for economic analysis which arise in the formulation of foreign-aid policies and to review critically the theoretical approaches to these problems which are found in the literature and are frequently reflected in the policies of foreign-assistance agencies. This study is policy oriented in the sense that I am concerned mainly with the contribution of familiar economic growth models and other economic and social theories of development to foreign aid policies rather than with polishing existing theories or formulating new ones. Since policy is revealed more in practice than in the statements of foreign-aid administrators, I have drawn heavily on my experience with, and study of, the operations of United States' and international development assistance agencies.

The author acknowledges valuable comments by Jacob J. Kaplan who reviewed portions of my manuscript. I am especially indebted to Professor Harry G. Johnson whose penetrating criticism of the manuscript prevented my committing a number of sins of commission and omission. However the author alone is responsible for the errors and shortcomings that remain. Finally, this book could scarcely have been completed without Irene whose untiring efforts in the preparation of the manuscript and the reading of the galleys far exceeded the call of wifely duties.

Contents

List of Tables

The Economics of
Foreign Aid

CHAPTER ONE

The Objectives of
Foreign Economic Assistance

INTRODUCTION

STATEMENTS ON foreign-aid policy by political leaders and legislative
bodies are not sufficiently precise to meet the requirements of the social
scientist for a rigorous analysis of the means for achieving well-defined
ends. Motives, targets, and policy instruments tend to become confused in
the rhetoric of statements on public policy. In the United States, foreign-
aid doctrine has undergone several major shifts since World War II, but
basically aid is a means of carrying out national foreign-policy objectives.
However, foreign aid may serve several national objectives, ranging from
direct economic or security aims to the promotion of world peace and
stability, the relative importance of which not only differs in individual
situations, but may, individually, have a much greater appeal to certain
politically vocal groups than to others. Presidential foreign-aid messages
are directed to the public at large and seek to mobilize the broadest possible consensus for proposed programs. For the European colonial powers,
aid has been closely associated with national policy objectives relating to
former dependencies with which they continue to have special economic
and political ties. These policies tend to be influenced not only by considerations of national economic and political advantage but also by a
sense of responsibility for their former wards, who have been launched into
a national independence for which they were inadequately equipped.

Foreign-aid doctrine in the recipient countries, while often broadly in
accord with the immediate economic objectives of the donors, is usually
based on an entirely different philosophy of aid from that held by the
donors. Recipient countries regard aid as an *obligation* of rich countries,
a *right* of the recipients; they are frequently resentful or suspicious of the
donor countries' national objectives that are served by aid. Thus most recipient countries would prefer that aid be provided by United Nations'

agencies or by regional agencies largely controlled by developing countries, but financed by the developed, donor countries.

Goran Ohlin (1966a) suggests that there is a third approach, "the United Nations doctrine," which regards aid as a moral responsibility on the part of the advanced countries and an essential element in progress toward international peace and solidarity. None of these various aid doctrines are mutually exclusive and elements of the United Nations doctrine can be found among the national objectives of aid expressed by donor countries such as the United States and the United Kingdom.

Social scientists have sought to categorize and define more precisely public policy objectives in the field of foreign aid, but they have not been successful in dispelling confusion in the donor countries over the ultimate national objectives of aid or in relating specific economic and social targets to these ultimate objectives. Their principal contribution has been in analyzing the relationship between foreign aid and certain specific economic targets in the recipient countries. Within this limited area, the social scientist has had an enormous impact on public policy relating to foreign aid—even the specialized jargon of the economist, the sociologist, and the political scientist has crept into the highest-level policy statements. Thus the terms "transition to self-sustained growth," "economic planning and programing," "debt service capacity," "social and cultural change," "capital absorptive capacity," "economic integration," and "political maturity" have become familiar in foreign-aid policy statements. It should be emphasized that the social scientist, and particularly the economist, has played a strategic role in the shaping of foreign-aid policy as well as in its administration. This is not to say of course that all economists and other social scientists have been in agreement regarding U.S. and international economic policies and their implementation. But even in the light of the large amount of disagreement among economists, particularly with respect to the process of economic development, it is clear that economists representing certain schools of thought have played a predominant role in shaping foreign-aid policies, both in the United States and abroad, including the international agencies.

There are many forms of international economic assistance which do not involve resource transfers to poor countries. For example, the World Bank and the Export-Import Bank make loans to developed countries such as Australia and Japan, and the International Monetary Fund (IMF) provides stabilization credits to the United Kingdom.[1] In recent years a system of international stabilization credits available from the IMF and other sources has been organized as a kind of mutual insurance operation among a group of highly-developed countries, from which most developed

1. Where initials of organizations are relatively unfamiliar, the full name is given at the first mention. A Glossary is also provided.

countries—including the United States—have been direct beneficiaries. The World Bank is not only a source of development assistance for poor countries, but constitutes a supplement to the domestic supply of long-term capital for relatively opulent countries. It is not inconceivable that sometime in the coming decades the United States might arrange a long-term loan from the World Bank. Likewise, national export-credit and credit-guarantee institutions such as the Export-Import Bank of Washington and the German Reconstruction Bank promote the exports of their countries to importers in developed and underdeveloped countries alike. Many of these transactions involve more than one motive or ultimate objective and, thus, any definition of foreign aid is bound to be arbitrary and fuzzy at the edges.

The principal concern of this book is with official foreign economic assistance to poor countries, that which is granted primarily for promoting their economic and social development. Even this delimitation does not avoid a host of conceptual and definitional problems. For example, balance-of-payments credits from the IMF or the Eximbank may be designed to assist a country in restoring international equilibrium, but external equilibrium is of course also an important factor in economic growth. A reconstruction loan following an earthquake in Chile may enable that country to avoid diverting resources allocated to its development; in actual practice, proceeds from such loans or grants have been employed for new development, or other purposes, rather than for reconstruction as such. Supporting assistance (formerly called "defense support") by the Agency for International Development (AID) for Korea or Jordan may not increase their defense expenditures by an equivalent amount but rather may enable them to maintain a higher level of investment or consumption than otherwise. Resources, even in the form of military hardware, are fungible in the sense that their availability as supplements to a country's total resources may affect the level of productive investment. Likewise, economic development assistance will not necessarily increase investment expenditures by the amount of the assistance but may be partially absorbed in increased consumption or military or other noninvestment government expenditures.

NATIONAL OBJECTIVES OF FOREIGN ECONOMIC ASSISTANCE FROM THE STANDPOINT OF THE DONORS

National policies of donor countries with respect to foreign aid differ considerably, rooted as they are in political policies and historical relationships. In the case of the United States, the first developmental loans were made to a few Latin American countries during the late 1930's and early 1940's. This was an outgrowth of the Good Neighbor Policy inaugurated during the first Franklin D. Roosevelt administration and of the historical relationship which existed since the early part of the nineteenth century between the United States and the other Americas. The initial proposals for both the World Bank and the International Monetary Fund originated from rather well-advanced plans for inter-American financial institutions after America's involvement in World War II. The U.S. postwar bilateral development aid programs were closely related to the assumption of broad military and political responsibilities in the Cold War beginning in the late 1940's; U.S. political leaders became convinced that second only to the security of Western Europe was the maintenance of the independence of the developing countries by preventing internal and external Communist aggression, and that development assistance could play a critical role in realizing this objective. Just as the United States assumed the primary responsibility for the containment of Communism through political and military means, it also assumed the primary responsibility for promoting economic development throughout the Free World. However, the U.S. government has constantly found itself obliged to convince large portions of the American electorate of the relationship between foreign economic assistance and America's worldwide political goals.

The major Western European powers had a much different historical relationship to the developing world and have had neither the resources nor the same commitment to the Cold War as the United States. They were concerned with achieving security and prosperity through cooperation among themselves, together with the assistance from the United States, and in the case of the European colonial powers this concern was extended to their colonies and dependencies in the developing world. Economic aid to less-developed areas with which European countries had close political ties did not newly emerge with the far-reaching political and social developments of the postwar era.

The nineteenth-century attitude of the European powers toward their colonies as mainly sources of national economic gain or of military advantage gradually gave way to attitudes of responsibility for the well-being of dependencies and to the concept of a community of cultural, economic and political interests under the leadership of the metropolitan country. These attitudes carried over into the post-World War II period during which most of the former dependents became independent nations. The British Commonwealth of Nations and the French community are the best examples of this evolution. The vast bulk of French and British foreign aid is directed toward their respective communities of nations. Unlike the United States, Britain and France have not had to develop a special rationale in terms of either Free World security or universal humanitarianism for obtaining public support for their aid programs. Political, cultural, economic, and humanitarian objectives are merged with a feeling of mutual interest based on a long association between the European powers and the developing areas over which they have had sovereignty. This feeling has been enhanced by the close personal contacts arising from the large numbers of British and French citizens who have lived, or are living, in other members of their communities.

U.S. FOREIGN-ASSISTANCE OBJECTIVES

The U.S. national foreign-assistance objectives that are usually stressed in official policy statements may be divided into three categories: (1) national security; (2) humanitarian; and (3) national economic benefit. The weight which is given to these objectives differs with the type of program in the recipient country, but all three need to be carefully examined as a basis for analyzing the probable relationship between aid and the ultimate objectives.

The national security objective is perhaps clearest in the case of countries such as Vietnam, Korea, Thailand, and Formosa, to each of which the United States has provided large amounts of assistance designed to enable the recipient countries to maintain a military establishment capable of dealing with actual or threatened aggression which would lead either to foreign domination, or to domination by a group under foreign influence, regarded as inimical to U.S. political and security interests. For some of these countries, "defense support" has been the major category of U.S. economic assistance, but it was intended that this assistance should raise both consumption levels and productive investment as a contribution to defense capabilities. In recent years an effort has been made on the part of AID to program a portion of the aid which is currently called "supporting assistance" (formerly "defense support") with a view to making a contribution to long-run economic and social progress. Thus a portion of U.S. "supporting assistance" must be regarded as much the same as any other economic assistance directed toward economic development and stability. Moreover, the ability of a country to ward off both internal and external aggression inimical to the U.S. may depend more upon the political attitudes of its people as affected by the economic and social structure, than by the size and equipment of its military forces. Thus, we are forced to consider the relationship between economic assistance and the creation of a political and social environment which will support the political and security objectives of the donor country. This is especially evident in Vietnam where none of the series of governments which have been organized over the past few years has been able to secure the confidence and support of the majority of the populace.

The objectives of U.S. foreign economic assistance programs are frequently stated in terms of a combination of national security and humanitarian or "responsibility for our fellow men" motivations. Thus, in his Foreign Aid Message to Congress of January 14, 1965 (New York Times, Jan. 15, 1966, p. 12), President Johnson said:

For our own security and well-being, and as responsible free men, we must seek to share our capacity for growth, and the promise of a better life, with our fellow men around the world. That is what foreign aid is all about.

Similarly, in his messages on foreign aid, President Kennedy, drawing heavily on the language of the social scientist, emphasized a combination of security and worldwide responsibility in outlining our national objectives for foreign aid. In his Foreign Aid Message of March 22, 1961 (U.S. Dept. of State Bulletin, April 10, 1961), he stated:

The 1960's can be—and must be—the crucial "decade of development" —the period when many less-developed nations can make the transition into self-sustained growth—the period in which an enlarged community of free, stable, and self-reliant nations can reduce world tensions and insecurity. . . . For we are launching a "decade of development" on which will depend, substantially, the kind of world in which we and our children will live.

While the national security objective was more overtly emphasized during President Eisenhower's administration throughout much of the 1950's—and the bulk of U.S. economic assistance under the Mutual Security Program took the form of "defense support"—the administration nevertheless gave substantial weight to humanitarian objectives. Thus, in President Eisenhower's letter transmitting his Annual Report to the Congress on the Mutual Security Program for the Fiscal Year 1960 (AID, 1961), he stated that:

We have had as our goal the promotion of peaceful change for millions of people in Latin America, Asia, and the Middle East who are seeking domestic tranquility and a better way of life. We have responded to the hope of these millions for a decent future for themselves and their children through well-conceived programs of economic and technical assistance. . . . Our common safety has been of equal concern and it has been our purpose to unite the free people of the world in a sustained common defense against overt attack or suppression of liberty. . . .

These and many other official statements regarding U.S. national foreign-aid objectives constitute a welding or an identification of short- and long-run national security objectives on the one hand, and of humanitarianism, or the acceptance of world responsibility for the welfare of the peoples of other nations, on the other. The idea of public responsibility for promoting individual welfare, which as a responsibility of the federal government has only become accepted in the United States with respect to all American citizens over the past three or four decades, is gradually being expanded to include the people of the world. However, by and large, governments deal with other governments, and when President Nasser pursues policies inimical to those of the United States, the debate over whether or not surplus wheat shipments to the United Arab Republic shall be terminated rarely if ever includes a reference to that country's poverty-stricken fellahin. Thus, by denying aid to people who live under governments which are believed to constitute a threat to the security of the United States, the United States is somewhat parochial in its broad humanitarian objectives.

The breaking up of monolithic Communism centered in the Soviet Union, and the existence of Communist countries with varying degrees of independence from the two major security threats, Russia and mainland China, together with the varying shades of neutralism and the foreign interventionist policies of countries such as the U.A.R. and Indonesia, have greatly complicated the problem of identifying countries or governments that threaten U.S. security interests. Countries like Poland may be regarded as security risks for one purpose, and candidates for the receipt of aid for another purpose. In a number of borderline cases, aid or credits to countries for the purchase of U.S. exports may be regarded either as a means of influencing their external policies and of increasing their degree of independence from one of the two major Communist powers, or as a contribution to Communist capacity for aggression. Likewise, foreign aid to right-wing dictatorships may be regarded as a means of influencing policies for social reform and a contribution to development, or as shoring up governments whose very existence is embarrassing to the United States if not a direct threat to its security, and whose continuation in power will not only delay the creation of conditions for economic progress, but will make a violent, Communist-dominated revolution more likely.

Such problems as these not only cast doubt on the identification of national security and humanitarian objectives governing foreign-aid programs, but they also reflect the essentially political nature of public foreign aid. We can honestly desire to extend a helping hand to every individual in the world, and to provide greater opportunities for economic and social improvement for all peoples, but aid must be extended through governments and institutions reflecting the will of government and it is at this point that political and security considerations become predominant. Even under conditions of hot or cold war in relation to a particular country, say Cuba or mainland China, the U.S. government has continued to make it clear that we are at war with governments and their ideologies and not with the masses of people themselves—though not even CARE packages can be sent to people living under Chinese Communism.

While the compatibility of national security and humanitarian objectives is perhaps mainly a political question which must be decided on the basis of political strategies, the complementarity of these two objectives—in the sense that economic welfare promotes our political objectives in aid recipients—is a question which requires the most penetrating social, political, and economic analysis on a case-by-case basis. This complementarity depends upon how societies will react to the achievement of certain economic objectives (assuming foreign aid is successful in realizing or helping to realize these objectives) and upon the impact of these social reactions in turn on the character and policies of their governments. U.S. public officials and most social scientists have tended to accept more or less on faith the proposition that economic and social development along with economic stability will actively promote either the maintenance in power of governments whose policies are in accord with the political objectives of the United States (or are at least not inimical to them), or will help to avoid violent revolution and political extremism of the right or the left which may be contrary to U.S. political and security objectives.

According to Edward Mason (1964, p. 51), the rationale for foreign-aid programs should be "the demonstrated facts (1) that in at least a large part of the less-developed world foreign aid can make and has made an effective contribution to economic development; and (2) that most countries, developed and underdeveloped, desperately want to be independent of external control." Few would deny that foreign aid has contributed to economic development, but to date the success stories on foreign aid for development must be limited to a rather small proportion of the developing world. As to the desire of developing countries for independence from external controls, I see no obvious correlation between the realization of this desire and the provision of foreign aid.

John P. Lewis, in his *Quiet Crisis in India* (1962), separates the national security objective from the current cold war situation by stating that:

Even if all Communist organizations were wiped from the face of the earth, the very poverty of the underdeveloped countries would present a fundamental long-run threat to the security of rich countries, including, especially, the richest, now that the poor nations have become self-determining and have acquired massive appetites for material improvement. This threat, it is recognized, will grow at least as long as the welfare gap between the economically advanced and the economically backward countries continues to widen rather than narrow (p. 6).

Lewis emphasizes not only the poverty, but also the growing disparity in economic welfare between the rich and the poor nations as constituting a long-run threat to the security of rich nations. While this general view is widely held by social scientists, the underlying hypotheses need to be clearly stated and, if possible, substantiated by empirical evidence. Does social instability arise more from inequality within countries or from inequality of per capita incomes among countries? What evidence do we have of a correlation between poverty and aggression or between opulence and nonaggression? Even if it be admitted that economically frustrated peoples cannot have stable or viable political systems and will be subject to continual revolutions involving the establishment of extremist political dictatorships of the right or the left, how does this constitute a threat to U.S. security, assuming that the U.S. continues to have overwhelming military power? One source of threat, of course, would be the tendency of irresponsible dictatorships to launch aggression against neighboring states which the United States feels bound to support. Such actions could involve us in disputes with other great powers (whether Communist or not) which have alliances with the states initiating aggressive action. History is full of examples in which wars between great powers are generated by conflicts between minor ones. Certainly all of these possibilities need to be thought through and spelled out as a basis for statements relating foreign economic aid to national security.

Even if a positive relationship between economic and social progress and the maintenance of government policies in line with U.S. political and security interests is accepted, either on faith or on the basis of political and social analysis bolstered by empirical findings, we are still left with such questions as what kinds of economic and social change (or avoidance of instabilities) are most conducive to the desired political results? what types of foreign aid programs are most effective in achieving the economic and social objectives of the developing countries? and, given limited resources available for foreign aid, how should they be allocated among countries and regions? Undoubtedly different types of aid programs can be associated with achieving different results in terms of specific welfare objectives or of political objectives important to the donor country. Thus foreign-aid policy may be faced with a joint maximizing problem which includes both political and welfare objectives, with each welfare objective having a different value in terms of political impact. Given certain minimum political objectives, and a variety of welfare functions which include levels of living, social services, unemployment levels, and rates of growth, we might want to determine certain marginal payoffs in the allocation of aid as between welfare and national security. The social scientists haven't gone very far even in conceptualizing the problem of allocating aid in terms of these payoffs, although as we shall see, Charles Wolf, Jr. (1960), has done some interesting work on aid allocation from the standpoint of maximizing U.S. political objectives.

Considerable work has been done by social scientists in analyzing the relationship between political and economic development in emerging countries, but there is insufficient empirical evidence to give us a great deal of confidence regarding the basic political assumptions underlying foreign aid or even to suggest reliable guidelines for the allocation and administration of aid in a way which would maximize payoffs in terms of our political objectives (Wriggins, 1962). In relating instances of political development for Latin American countries to economic indicators, Charles Wolf, Jr. (1965), finds a significantly positive correlation between per capita GNP and the level of political development and between per capita gross investment and the political level. However, he finds that the rate of growth of GNP is not significantly correlated with the political level, and that the rate of growth in per capita GNP is just barely significantly correlated with political level. He also finds that there is no significant relationship between per capita economic aid and political level. In six of his nine comparisons between political change and the economic variables, no significant relationship appears to exist. Thus, an increase in the relative degree of political democracy as evidenced by a rise in the rank of a country in comparison with its other Latin American neighbors does not appear to be associated with the rate of growth of GNP, or per capita economic aid.

The sweeping claims made for aid to developing countries as a contribution to world peace and security are regarded by many serious scholars as little more than clichés, or at least not based on evidence. Thus a number of highly respected social scientists such as Edward C. Banfield (1963), Hans Morgenthau (1962), Milton Friedman (1958), and David McCord Wright (1959), deny that foreign aid is likely to promote development, that development will produce free and democratic or stable governments, and that aid with or without development will enhance the security of the United States. One can, of course, cite a number of cases in which aid has contributed to development and has been accompanied by (though not necessarily caused) greater political stability and a movement toward democracy. Just as it is difficult to prove that foreign aid can save the world for democracy, it is also difficult to prove that it will *not* make a contribution to world stability and security. A decision to provide foreign economic assistance, like most foreign-policy decisions, must be made on something other than the kind of evidence which constitutes acceptable proof of a hypothesis for the social scientists.

It may be that few if any generalizations regarding the impact of economic change on political developments which apply to all or most countries at a particular stage of development are possible. In the field of welfare, we are also in the dark regarding many essential questions relating to economic change. However, we would seem to be on sound ground in assuming that having enough to eat to keep people healthy, adequate clothing and shelter to avoid misery from the elements, and the availability of medical care constitute elemental conditions for happiness. But when we look to rates of economic growth which imply different rates of social time preference and differing allocations of investment in facilities for the production of personal and social goods, we are on far less sure footing with respect to welfare. Even at a low level of personal consumption, social preference for public buildings, monuments, modern highways, and even industrial production itself as a collective consumption good yielding social satisfaction independent of that derived directly from the industrial products—all these may yield high increments of social welfare relative to that derived from additional personal consumption (H. G. Johnson, 1965).

A third national objective of foreign aid is the promotion of national economic interests. This objective is frequently referred to by U.S. public officials in terms of the contribution of foreign aid to the financing of U.S. exports. Very often, U.S. aid-financed exports are broken down by states of origin. In its most unsophisticated form, this type of argument for foreign aid is not only spurious, but cheap and deplorable, since it does not reflect the national interest but, rather, sectional and industrial interests promoted at the expense of the taxpayer. Resources supplied on a grant basis or on loan terms which do not reflect the social opportunity cost of the capital in domestic employment certainly do not contribute to the national economic interest. A variant of this argument, which is frequently used in connection with U.S. Public Law No. 480 (PL 480) surplus agricultural commodity shipments, is that they help to create foreign markets for U.S. agricultural products, or that such shipments really do not constitute a real cost since the commodities are in surplus anyway and their value is being eaten up by storage costs (Mikesell, 1958). We shall consider the economic burden of aid from the standpoint of donor countries in Chapter 8.

If there are any national economic benefits accruing to aid donors (other than from export credits), they are largely indirect, highly tenuous, and of such a long-term nature that their discounted value will almost surely be exceeded by present costs. AID reports and other government releases designed to elicit popular support for foreign aid not only emphasize the benefits of immediate export sales to various U.S. industries and regions, but point out that the "most important long-term benefits of the mutual development program . . . are those that stem from the expanding export markets that are the product of successful development" (AID and U.S. Dept. of Defense, 1965). Although there are no adequate means of measuring the gains from trade, the net benefits arising from an increase of some $8 billion per annum in imports and $12 billion per annum in exports between 1952 and 1964 surely cannot be commensurate with more than $40 billion in economic assistance (largely to the less-developed countries) by U.S. government agencies over the 1952-64 period. Moreover, most of the expansion in U.S. commercial trade has been with the developed countries rather than the developing countries of the world. It is conceivable, however, that some forms of aid could bring about a national economic gain through an improvement in U.S. terms of trade. For example, aid to a country for expanding its supplies of low-cost raw materials or petroleum, either directly or by subsidizing U.S. private foreign investment, might be accompanied by a substantial payoff in terms of lower import prices of these commodities. But little U.S. aid has gone for this purpose (Simpson, 1962).

Private foreign investments, particularly in resource industries, may well yield a net economic advantage as well as a balance of payments gain to the investing country through a combination of high returns and improved terms of trade. Hence, if we regard government guarantees and other devices for promoting private foreign investment as a form of foreign aid, there may very well be a net payoff to the capital exporting country which would justify the aid in terms of national economic advantage. The extension of long-term credits for promoting exports is also regarded as a form of aid which yields a net economic surplus to the donor country. Given the existing conditions of export credit competition in world markets, this form of aid might be justified on balance-of-payments grounds. At the same time, however, an alternative use of the long-term credits for domestic investment (and a lower level of imports) might very well yield higher net social returns. Certainly this argument for aid as a contribution to the national economic interest requires far more penetrating analysis than has been undertaken thus far.

The argument is made that since the United States has unemployed resources, the social opportunity cost of foreign assistance is overstated by the monetary value of the aid, and that by providing long-term loan assistance, we not only earn a return on our investment but also stimulate the economy to higher levels of output and employment. This argument is of course spurious unless one is convinced that our domestic policy makers are so inept or subject to such political constraints that the only way the country can have a high level of output and employment is to export capital or build pyramids. This of course may be true but the underlying reasons are political and not economic. Thus, except for special cases, the valid national objectives for foreign economic assistance must lie in the combination of national security and humanitarian or broad, world interests.

EUROPEAN FOREIGN AID OBJECTIVES [2]

As has been noted, British and French bilateral foreign aid programs are directed mainly to their respective communities of colonies and former dependencies, but there are significant differences in their approaches to foreign assistance. The only other large European donor, Germany, ceased to be a colonial power after World War I and Germany's objectives, while influenced by the Cold War and the desire to promote Western ideology in the developing countries, are to a considerable degree directed by her economic interest in promoting trade and foreign investment in the developing countries.

Official British statements on foreign aid tend to emphasize Britain's political and economic tie with the Commonwealth countries. However, British White Papers on foreign aid are somewhat restrained. They lack the dramatic appeal for public support found in U.S. official statements and they tend to shun both the expressions of alarm for the political consequences of failure to promote development through foreign aid on the one hand, and commitments to specific development goals in terms of rates of growth in per capita output and other economic and social goals, on the other (Great Britain, 1957, 1963). British official statements do recognize the problem of world poverty, and they affirm the obligation of Britain to cooperate with other industrialized countries in providing assistance to developing countries. But the British view of the development process is long range, one seen as likely to continue for decades. Moreover they emphasize the essential self-help nature of development (Great Britain, 1963, p. 5).

Throughout much of the twentieth century, British colonial policy has looked toward the eventual creation of independent states by its African, Asian and western hemisphere territories, following the paths of Australia, Canada, New Zealand and South Africa. Varying degrees of self-government were introduced as political conditions permitted and the dependencies were expected to finance their current governmental expenses out of local taxation and to obtain their external capital from private foreign investment or by borrowing in the British capital market. In recent decades, the British capital market was regarded not so much as a source of net capital outflow but as a financial intermediary into which there flow surplus funds, including currency reserves, from the outer sterling area, and from which long-term development capital might be obtained. The continuation

2. The discussion in this section draws heavily upon I. M. D. Little and J. M. Clifford, *International Aid* (Chicago: Aldine Publishing Company, 1966), pp. 30-45.

of this system depended upon the strength of sterling and the balance of payments of the sterling area as a whole.

Beginning with the Colonial Development Act of 1929, Britain initiated a modest program of official development aid in the form of grants and loans to the colonies, and in the postwar period new and larger sources of public development assistance became available for both the dependencies and the newly independent nations. However, Britain has avoided underwriting long-range development programs of the Commonwealth countries, at least on a unilateral basis, and has tended to favor aid in the form of loans for sound projects and to encourage Commonwealth members to seek assistance from international agencies such as the World Bank.

In her assistance programs, Britain has reflected a policy of easing the transition to independence. Teachers, technicians, and administrators tended to leave the former dependencies upon independence, thus creating a shortage of trained personnel. Frequently the newly independent nations were eager to nationalize their official services at a rate far more rapid than was warranted by their supply of trained nationals. Even where former British officials were permitted to remain in government service in the new nations, their pay and fringe benefits were not sufficient to retain them. In response to this problem, Britain inaugurated in 1961 the Overseas Service Aid Scheme (OSAS), designed to supplement the salaries of British officials electing to remain in the service of the new nations, as well as the salaries of British citizens newly recruited by these countries. The OSAS also assisted the new nations in recruiting overseas personnel.

Only about 10 per cent of British bilateral aid has gone to countries other than colonial territories and independent Commonwealth countries over the past few years (Great Britain, 1965, p. 15). Even much of this aid has gone to countries such as Jordan and the Sudan which had been British mandates or dependencies in the past, but are not members of the Commonwealth. Britain has been an enthusiastic supporter of multilateral assistance agencies and is also a member of several aid consortia organized by the World Bank.

French foreign aid has also been provided mainly for her colonies and former dependencies. Unlike Britain, France aimed at integrating her colonies into metropolitan France rather than readying them for eventual independence. Thus, prior to a colony's independence, France provided substantial amounts of budget support and technical assistance in the form of teachers, administrators, technicians and advisors. She also aided her colonies by supporting the prices of their commodities shipped to France. Although French plans for the integration of her colonial empire were thwarted, much the same type of assistance has been continued to the former French colonies after independence. While France lacked the formal organization represented by the British Commonwealth, it is evident that France seeks to maintain a French community of nations characterized by membership in the French franc area, the existence of the French language and culture, close economic relationships including preferential trade and financial arrangements, and a strong French influence over foreign policy. The blow to French national pride arising from the loss of Algeria and other French dependencies is softened by the maintenance of a French community of nations held together in part by heavy subsidies from the French treasury. Not only does French aid constitute the largest proportion of national income of any of the donor industrial countries, but much of this French aid takes the form of grants. It may also be noted that the special preferential trade treatment given by the European Economic Community (EEC) countries to the former African territories of the EEC members was established at the insistence of France.

In summarizing the British and French foreign aid objectives, we may say that while there exist elements of the same objectives that underlie U.S. aid policies, British and French objectives are dominated by their historical relationships with the principal recipients of their largess and are perhaps less concerned with global political strategies. On the humanitarian side, these countries take a longer-run view of development and are under less public pressure to establish a terminal date for aid in terms of the accomplishment of predetermined goals. But the view that economic objectives achieved through aid will achieve desired political results is common to both the U.S. and European donors.

THE RELATIONSHIP OF THE ECONOMIC OBJECTIVES OF AID TO NATIONAL POLITICAL AND SECURITY OBJECTIVES

Before tackling the question of the relationship of foreign aid to the realization of the economic objectives of aid, I want to consider further the relationship of possible economic objectives for the aid recipients to the national security and political objectives of the donors. In this discussion I can do little more than pose some of the problems involved in determining these relationships, which all too often have been asserted in rhetorical and emotional statements with virtually no analysis. I would agree with the position of many political scientists who argue that not enough attention has been paid to the nature of political development and to the forces moving individual and group attitudes toward revolution and political change. Thus Howard Wriggins (1962) states:

There is a widespread assumption that an increase in living standards will bring with it a political stability favorable to American interests. This is by no means assured. On the contrary, one can posit that rapid economic development can accelerate social, psychological and organizational changes that were necessary before economic development could get underway. This acceleration in itself will be disruptive, and these dislocations are bound to bring political disorder in varying degrees. The converse is also true. . . . It is because there is bound to be rapid political change, generally disruptive, whether there is economic development or not, that the matter of political development is of such importance. Economic development in itself does not create a public order, nor a viable political system (pp. 208-209).

Political development appears not to proceed from one stage to another in any special relationship to economic development, and in reviewing the political history of nations it is difficult to discern common patterns and stages of political development through which nations progress. Among the developed countries, the political history of Germany would seem to bear out both of these points, while in the case of Argentina, we are confronted with an economic and a political enigma which appears to defy any orderly progression in either economic or political development. Thus, K. H. Silvert (1963, p. 350) concludes that "Argentina's class-bound politics assume that no public measure can be good for almost everybody, that the benefit of one group is the automatic loss of all others. Life is an inelastic pie, and a bigger piece for *fulano* necessarily means a smaller piece for *sutano*." The conclusions which have been distilled from a number of penetrating case studies of political development published in *Expectant Peoples: Nationalism and Development* (sponsored by the American Universities' Field Staff) suggest that a certain level of political development, including a degree of freedom and political maturity

. . . may be a functional requisite for *self-sustaining* development. Authoritarian techniques of development have their capacities, of course; they can be used to build pyramids and factories, force savings and mobilize labor. We suggest, however, that it may be that when the course of the change nears contemporary modernism, then gratuitously unfree procedures cause breakdowns, being conducive to neither rational public decisions nor to the generation of the attitudes and values necessary for the chain reactions of the modern, empirical society. This line of reasoning linking freedom with efficiency and continuity is not a novel concept among philosophers of science (Silvert, 1963, pp. 435-36).

Put differently, instead of economic development or economic growth constituting the *sine qua non* for democratic and responsible government, a considerable degree of political maturity may be an essential condition for meaningful economic development.

It is in the context of the forces of political change that we must judge John P. Lewis' (1962) statement:

I see no reason to dispute the considered judgment of India's leadership that the attainment of a rate of growth in real per capita incomes of 3 to 4 per cent annually is essential if constitutional processes are to survive. This of course does not mean that the rural and urban masses have any direct comprehension of this statistic, but the figures indicate the expansion in production that will be needed to provide clearly perceptible, continuing, broadly distributed improvements in diet, clothing, public services, and other categories of private and public consumption. However, if the country *should* manage to achieve this kind of economic performance, it is very unlikely that it would abandon constitutional processes in the quest of still more accelerated performance. For one thing, the nation's leadership, present and foreseeable, would be hostile to such a choice, and the public, while perhaps largely unaware of the basic ideological decision it would be making, would tend to reinforce the constitutional growth process simply by participating in it (pp. 10-11).

Without disputing these views, it seems clear that judging the political consequences of various economic objectives—such as achieving a target rate of growth in output per capita for a country like Chile (which already has a higher level of living than India can hope to attain in the next 50 years)—requires a penetrating analysis of political conditions and forces within the individual countries. Broad generalizations such as a universal dependable relationship between a steady rate of growth in output per capita and the realization of political objectives are unwarranted. Moreover, the achievement of the economic objectives themselves are in many cases much more a function of the existing and future political structure than of any conceivable amount of foreign aid.

At a much less sophisticated level of analysis, is there a justification of foreign aid as a means of influencing governments in power or of providing them with financial support in order to prevent their overturn by political forces that we believe would follow policies inimical to those of the United States? The policy has not always worked in the past, although a substantial amount of foreign assistance has been made available on the basis of this type of short-run political analysis. It is usually assumed by political officers in our embassies that any political change can only be for the worse; more often than not, the opposite has been true. But governments that require continual emergency budget support in order to remain in power are usually doomed in any case, and this kind of support frequently makes difficult the establishment of working relationships with the new regime. This is not to say that there cannot be true emergencies such as those resulting from sudden shortfalls in export proceeds or natural disasters which call for special emergency assistance. But many governments, particularly in Latin America, prefer to live out their span in a chronic condition of emergency—to which the United States responds with a flow of assistance—often accompanied by promises of reform which they are incapable of delivering even if they had the will to do so. This is aid without meaningful economic objectives and is based on the premise of a direct relationship between the aid and political results. I shall deal with this question further when I take up the problem of conditions for aid as a means of assuring the contribution of aid to the achievement of economic objectives.

CHARLES WOLF'S THEORY OF POLITICAL VULNERABILITY

Perhaps the most ambitious attempt to relate economic objectives in developing countries to the national political interest of the donors through the application of the techniques of the social scientists has been made by Charles Wolf, Jr., in his *Foreign Aid: Theory and Practice in Southern Asia.* I shall not deal with Wolf's hypotheses having to do with the relationship between foreign aid and the achievement of economic objectives in developing countries since I shall be concerned with more sophisticated approaches to this problem in the following chapters. Wolf's standard or measure of the realization of U.S. (and Western European) political objectives is summed up in his index of political vulnerability, Pe. Pe is regarded as a measure of political vulnerability to extremist political behavior defined specifically in terms of committed support for internal and external Communism. Pe is a function of three complex variables which constitute the basic elements in Wolf's model: economic aspirations; the level of living; and economic expectations. Pe then varies directly with economic aspirations, and inversely with the current level of living and with economic expectations (Wolf, 1960, pp. 305-308). Economic aspirations are a function of per capita outlays for education, literacy, and the disparity between the level of living of the members of a particular subset and a larger group with which the subset has contact. The components of the level of living include per capita consumption, industrial wage rates, unemployment adjusted for underemployment, and land-owning cultivators as a proportion of the total agricultural population. The third basic element, economic expectations, is a function of the rate of change in the level of living and of current net per capita investment.

Wolf assumes that foreign aid will achieve an increase in per capita output, which in turn will reduce political vulnerability in all countries. Yet a consideration of the elements in his political vulnerability equations reveals that an increase in output, depending upon its composition and distribution, may have effects which tend to decrease or to increase political vulnerability. Thus the favorable level-of-living effects might be offset in part at least by an increase in economic aspirations arising from increased education and increased disparities in income. But the returns on foreign aid to the donor are not simply, according to Wolf, a contribution to the reduction in political vulnerability via increased output, but vary directly with the degree of political vulnerability for a particular country (or the size of Pe) and with the size and other measures of importance of the country itself. Thus Wolf sets up an allocation problem for maximizing the total returns to the United States (as donor) from aid to a region consisting of a number of countries, given a certain amount of available aid. The relevant variables in the maximizing problem for the total region (or for each of n countries) are the aggregate productivity of the aid in terms of annual output, the political vulnerability index, the population, the size of the country measured by parameters other than population, and the value of economic aid (Wolf, 1960, pp. 367-68).

It is easy to find shortcomings in Wolf's analysis, but his pioneering effort in this field can only be admired. We may question the universal applicability of any model for determining political vulnerability, and we may further question the relationship of Wolf's concept of political vulnerability to the returns to Western donors from aid to a country in terms of the realization of Western political objectives. In many situations, the objective is to bring about a desirable political change in an orderly fashion, and while the elements which determine political vulnerability may constitute those most likely to bring about political change, it is presumptuous to identify political vulnerability, as defined, with vulnerability to "extremist political change" and in particular to Communism, as opposed to a dictatorship of the right (Higgins, 1962, pp. 52-57). Conceivably, a broader definition of Wolf's index of political vulnerability, and some reformulation which would include not only political vulnerability to extremism, but political pressure for economic reforms as well, would be useful in relating economic to political objectives of Western aid programs. It would appear, for example, that we would not want to dampen some of the conditions (such as education and literacy) giving rise to increased economic aspirations in order to minimize political vulnerability. Also, the expectations function, as it relates both to the behavior of consumption and the character of investment, must be carefully analyzed from the standpoint of the achievement of both economic and political objectives. For example, certain social programs which raise the level of economic expectations may not—as a consequence of disappointed expectations—be conducive either to longer-run development or to longer-run political objectives.

In Wolf's model for the allocation of foreign aid in terms of maximizing returns related to reducing political vulnerability, it is worth under-scoring that the returns to aid are not measured solely in terms of its con-tribution to output in the recipient country, but also to a reduction of political vulnerability. Thus, conceivably, in the case of two countries, both with more or less the same level of living, aid might be given a rela-tively low priority for the country with a low political vulnerability index but with a strong outlook for high economic return from the aid, while the other country might have a high priority for aid with a far less favor-able outlook for its efficient use. This point is of interest because of the strong insistence on the part of the U.S. Congress and in the policy state-ments of foreign-assistance administrators that aid shall go to those countries with the most favorable preconditions for making productive use of aid in terms of contributing to output. The principle of "unto everyone that hath shall be given, and he shall have abundance . . . ," or to that country which has gained the political and social preconditions enabling it to formulate productive projects for the most efficient use of foreign cap-ital shall be given, may—according to Wolf—be in conflict with the ra-tional allocation of aid for the achievement of Western political and se-curity objectives. The clash between (short-run) political objectives and longer-run economic (and possibly political) objectives also arises in deci-sions regarding conditions to be attached to aid such as those relating to monetary and fiscal policies, tax and land reform, and so forth (Feis, 1964).

As a rule, political instability and vulnerability in the Wolfian sense go hand in hand with inability to achieve a satisfactory growth rate and development progress. Where countries have achieved the social and polit-ical conditions for economic progress, from whatever level of output they start, they may not need foreign aid other than access to hard loans from external lending agencies as a means of speeding up the growth process.

NATIONAL DEVELOPMENT OBJECTIVES AND
POLICIES OF AID RECIPIENTS

There are a number of differences between the development and for-eign-aid objectives of the developing countries and those of the Western donors, including the international agencies which the latter dominate. These differences arise from the approaches to development, including development policies, from the preferences with respect to forms, terms, and conditions of aid, and even from the attitudes toward aid itself. To begin with, the idea of growth and development is not indigenous in poor countries. Economic growth as a national policy dates from the late 1940's or early 1950's for most developing countries. Like nationalism, with which it is closely associated, the urge for development is an import from the Western world and is being disseminated mainly by individuals in underdeveloped countries that have had contact with the ideas of the West. The ideas relating to national economic progress grew out of the experience of Western developed countries during the nineteenth and early twentieth centuries. For the developing regions, development is basically a revolutionary—as opposed to an evolutionary—concept, the carrying out of which requires a radical change in social attitudes and institutions. This has meant social conflict within the developing countries, and it was inevitable that the approaches to development by the Western democracies would clash with those of many leaders in the developing countries. Western officials find themselves in conflict with Marxist-oriented leaders and economic thinkers in the less-developed countries, on the one hand, and with those who oppose change in the existing economic and social order, on the other.

Development in the Western democracies has been largely carried out by competitive private enterprise operating on a national and later on an international scale. The economizing principle of modern production has been applied in the West to manufacturing, agriculture, distribution, finance, service trades, and even government, and this has meant a continual change in economic and social behavior. The application of this principle to the underdeveloped countries requires not only a change in social attitudes but major changes in governmental policies at all levels. Thus, while the establishment of aggregative output goals and the formulation of broad development plans have been readily accepted, Western foreign-assistance agencies, including international aid institutions, have been far less successful in securing the adoption of those development policies which have proved successful in the West.

Aid, other than general-purpose loans or grants with no conditions attached, often constitutes an involvement by the donor in the internal policies of the recipients—an involvement that goes beyond normal relationships between sovereign states. This problem is perhaps less difficult where assistance is confined to the financing of specific projects designed in accordance with engineering specifications. But where the donor undertakes to finance a portion of a development program by means of program loans or perhaps a package of project loans, subject to the adoption of a variety of national policies relating to monetary controls, taxation, national budgets, foreign-exchange rates, import controls, foreign investment, and land reform, sometimes calling for specific legislation, there appears to be an interference with the national sovereignty even where the government in power is in full agreement with the policy conditions imposed by the donor. The concept that aid will be provided according to the measure of self-help on the part of the recipient, while seemingly a fair proposition to the donor, becomes in fact a threat of withdrawal of aid if policies imposed by the donor are not carried out.

The conflict over the attachment of conditions to aid is clearly related to a divergence of attitudes toward what might be called the ethical basis for aid. The more sophisticated spokesmen for the developed countries no longer look upon aid for development either as a means of attaining unique national economic and political advantages for the donor or as a unilateral act of charity. Rather, assistance to developing countries is more and more regarded as a joint responsibility of the developed countries reflecting a common interest in world security and stability as well as affording an opportunity for less fortunate people to enjoy the fruits of economic progress. On the other hand, foreign aid among the leaders of the developing nations has come to be regarded as an unconditional right. The amount of assistance to which spokesmen for developing countries say they are entitled is calculated in terms of that required to achieve certain per capita growth goals, with the ultimate objective of reducing the disparities in per capita income levels among the countries of the world. This attitude, which is shared by many individual social scientists in the developed countries, was reflected in the addresses and resolutions of the representatives of the developing countries at the 1964 U.N. Conference on Trade and Development in Geneva. While the spokesmen for the developing countries admitted an obligation to promote development within their own countries, they generally rejected the notion that the amount of overall assistance should be subject to conditions imposed by the donors with respect to performance. Developing countries also regard increased trade opportunities, including preferences, as a right which developed countries are obligated to accord them.

In part, these attitudes stem from the view that the developed countries exploited the developing nations while they were in the colonial status and thereby arrested their development. Even the Latin American countries, most of which have been independent for over a century, regard themselves as victims of exploitation by foreign investors and traders. Developed countries are regarded as somehow having grown rich at the expense of the peripheral nations.

While developing countries differ among themselves as to the specific directions in which their economic growth should take place and the priorities to be assigned to various economic sectors, an important source of conflict between donors and recipients arises from differences in economic objectives. Aside from the realization of overall growth targets, developing countries have assigned a high priority to industrialization and to infrastructure in support of their urban centers. Developing countries have in general tended to neglect or give a low priority to agriculture, have not been selective in the promotion of industries, especially from the standpoint of encouraging those industries which are potentially competitive in world markets, and in many cases have failed to promote broadly based social development.

While it may be argued that both high rates of growth and industrialization are necessary conditions for the realization of social and economic progress, these former objectives are not in themselves the most important from the standpoint of political and humanitarian objectives of the U.S. and other donor countries in providing foreign aid. There are numerous examples of satisfactory or even relatively high rates of growth of per capita GNP without a broadly based economic and social development. For example, Venezuela had an average annual per capita rise in real GNP of over 5 per cent over the 1950-58 period. Yet in 1957, 50 per cent of the total population received 11 per cent of total personal income, and 36 per cent of the total population received 6 per cent of total personal income (UN, 1964a). Liberia, which had an annual rate of growth in gross national product in excess of 10 per cent over the 1950-60 period, experienced little development which affected the lives of the vast bulk of the population during that decade (Clower, Dalton, Harwitz and Walters, 1966).

There are certainly alternative economic objectives which government officials and other articulate elements in developing countries might stress as their major goals. These include a raising of the levels of living of the poorest 50 per cent of the population, an expansion of social services, a rapid increase in agricultural output and productivity, and a combination of various elements of social progress, including education, housing and health. It is not enough to argue that an expansion of the real social product is necessary for the achievement of these objectives; the expansion of output must be directed toward these objectives.

Emphasis on social programs and internal governmental reforms for achieving them is of comparatively recent origin in U.S. foreign economic assistance policy. Prior to the establishment of the Social Progress Trust Fund and to the negotiation of the Charter of Punta del Este in 1961, the financing of social impact projects was not regarded as an entirely proper field for sound development financing. Officials of both the United States government and the World Bank held that development financing should be restricted to "productive" projects which would yield a measurable increment in GNP, and that while technical assistance for health, education, housing, etc. could properly be made available, both the initiative and the financing of social-impact projects should come from the developing countries themselves, in accordance with what they could afford to spend. Since 1961, however, there has been an increasing emphasis by both U.S. government and World Bank officials on foreign aid for education, health, housing and other types of social investment.

It is worth noting that the initiative for social legislation and the channeling of external assistance into social-impact programs has not come mainly from the governments of the developing countries themselves. The reasons for this are obvious. In the developing countries, economic progress has had a rather narrow social base. The impetus for growth has come from the middle and upper classes, and they have tended to see economic progress in terms of industrialization and the modernization of urban centers, with little concern for the vast agricultural hinterland other than a demand for higher prices for export crops. Social programs require more than just external financing; they involve tax reform, a large increase in government revenues, and a reallocation of these revenues from the major recipients—the army, public buildings, subsidies to government-owned power and transportation services, modern streets and highways, and social security services enjoyed by the industrial worker elite—to peasant agriculture, mass education, rural community services, etc. Moreover, they require legislation dealing with land reform, taxation, and, in some countries, the removal of social and economic discrimination which strikes at the heart of the income and opportunity inequality that characterizes so many of the developing countries. In other words, what the agencies have been demanding (and what many of the aid recipients have been little more than paying lip service to) is a speeding up of the process of social revolution.

Second only to growth as an important national objective among the developing countries is that of a steady growth of export receipts. Like growth, export earnings are regarded as determined mainly by external forces affecting the world demand for the primary commodity exports of the developing countries and their terms of trade. Given the heavy dependence of most developing economies on a few primary commodity exports, changes in the level of foreign exchange income have a heavy impact on domestic income and investment. During a period of rising exports and world demand, there is a corresponding increase in domestic income, at least in the market sector of the economy, which in turn leads to a heavy demand for imports, both for consumption and investment purposes. Government revenues also rise because of their heavy dependence on import and export duties, and there is a Parkinsonian expansion of government expenditures. However, a decline in income from exports does not result in a proportionate decline in domestic monetary income and expenditures; in fact, fiscal and monetary policy may well permit domestic monetary income to continue rising. Nevertheless, real income and investment are adversely affected by the shortage of foreign exchange, the demand for which is curtailed either by devaluation or import licensing or a combination of both.

Spokesmen for the developing countries have emphasized the relationship between high world market prices for their exports, and growth. Growth is considered to be in large measure a function of "the capacity to import" which in turn is regarded mainly as a function of the terms of trade. Thus, foreign aid and trade are more or less equivalent and not just complementary means of promoting economic growth. Delegates from the less-developed countries to the United Nations Conference on Trade and Development of 1964 gave special emphasis to trade measures as a means of increasing the real resources available to developing countries.[3] In fact, an important theme of the Conference might be expressed as "aid through trade," in the sense that discriminatory trade advantages favoring the developing countries, various measures for maintaining or raising prices of primary commodity exports, and the operation of schemes for compensating countries for decreases in their export earnings or in their terms of trade, should become the primary means of transferring resources for the promotion of economic development. I shall deal with the economics of "aid through trade" in a later chapter.

While I have stressed the relationship between foreign-exchange earnings and growth as expressed by the spokesmen for the developing countries, the maintenance and expansion of foreign-exchange income has a special significance for the objective of industrialization and also for the interests of the dominant political and economic elite in the developing countries. Industrialization has been mainly import-substituting rather than export-oriented. This is partly a consequence of over-valued exchange rates and partly a result of import policies that give special encouragement to the production of goods in which developing countries are not potentially competitive in world markets. Industrialization, together with overhead capital facilities such as power and transportation, are heavily dependent upon imports of capital goods and raw materials and fuels. So also is the maintenance and expansion of the upper- and middle-class urban economies characterized by automobiles and other durable goods and modern apartments, to the needs of which economic policy is so largely directed. It is this middle-class urban sector whose interests are mainly affected by world prices of export crops and minerals, since it is this group to which is directed the vast bulk of the foreign exchange. The subsistence farmers or even the producers of export crops, large and small, are largely insulated from world price movements through internal marketing arrangements of various kinds, and little foreign exchange is allocated to the agricultural sector.

In fairness it should be said that in many developing countries national

3. Perhaps the best statement of this policy was given by the Secretary-General of the U.N. Conference on Trade and Development, Dr. Raul Prebisch, in *Towards a New Policy for Development* (Report by the Secretary-General of the United Nations Conference on Trade and Development; Geneva: United Nations, 1964).

economic objectives are changing in favor of a more broadly based social and economic development, and there is increasing concern both for domestic agriculture and for the creation of industries capable of selling in world or regional markets. But changes in objectives are not enough; they must be accompanied by national policies designed to realize them. It is in the area of development policies that there arises the greatest conflict between aid donors and recipients.

CHAPTER TWO

The Foundations of Modern Aid Theories and Strategies: A Review of Development Theories

IT IS THE PURPOSE of this chapter to review briefly the formal economic growth models and the theories of economic and social change which constitute the foundations for foreign-aid theories and policies. Traditionally, growth models have presented an oversimplified analysis of the process of economic growth. However, in recent years these models have become more complex by the introduction of a larger number of economic and noneconomic factors and have borrowed heavily from theories dealing with the process of social and institutional change. In reviewing these contributions, we must keep in mind the distinction between economic growth on the one hand, and social and economic development on the other. As growth theories have been broadened to include more of the elements bearing upon economic change, they inevitably have moved closer to theories of social and economic development. This applies to investment as well as to the nature of the product. Thus, for example, when we begin to think in terms of human capital and investment in man, growth theories are transformed into analyses of the development process, in which the improvement of man becomes not only an objective, but the principal means, of expanding and enriching the social product.

PRE-WORLD WAR II GROWTH MODELS

Various growth models emphasize different strategic or limiting factors in the growth process, and these factors in turn suggest the relative importance of external inputs such as capital and technology in an open economy. Historically, growth models and less formal approaches to growth have reflected the major economic problems and policy issues of the period of writing, since it is these current questions which have directed the efforts of contemporary economists. Thus Adam Smith in disputing the doctrines of the mercantilists, sought to show that unhampered trade and competitive enterprise provided the conditions for maximum growth. Although Smith did not formulate a theoretical growth model, he stated clearly the major factors in growth—specialization and trade, capital accumulation, and increased productivity through technical advance. Ricardo's concern with foreign trade policy, and more specifically, with the removal of the Corn Laws, led him to emphasize the role of diminishing returns to land and the desirability of holding down the prices of agricultural produce by their free importation. Capital accumulation was for Ricardo the key to growth, but accumulation is motivated by the rate of profit, which as growth progresses tends to be depressed by the rise in wages resulting from higher food prices as a consequence of the combination of expanding population, the scarcity of arable land, and the operation of diminishing returns. For Ricardo, growth stopped with the advent of the stationary state where capital accumulation and population growth fall to zero and wages to subsistence. "Wealth increases most rapidly in those countries where the disposable land is most fertile, where importation is least restricted, and where, through agricultural improvements, production can be multiplied without any increase in the proportional quantity of labor, and where consequently the progress of rent is slow" (Ricardo, 1821, p. 40). Foreign investment by a country with a scarcity of land in another country with an abundance of land should provide a means of keeping down food prices and of raising the profit rate and accumulation (though Ricardo does not appear to reach this conclusion). Thus, growth should be enhanced by capital exports to primary commodity producing countries. On the contrary, Ricardo (1821, p. 232) appears to argue that the export of capital and increased trade will neither affect the rate of profit nor, presumably, the rate of capital accumulation.

For Karl Marx, growth under capitalism is also limited by a reduction of the rate of profit, but the decline in the profit rate occurs not as a consequence of diminishing returns, but rather of the declining rate of "surplus value": the villain in the piece is not the landlord, but the capitalistic system of distribution. The end of the process is neither the dismal stationary swamp of Ricardo, nor Mill's Platonian stationary state in which technological progress contributes to increased leisure. Rather, it is the Armageddon of socialist revolution. For Marx, capital exports to the less-developed countries were seen as a means of temporarily maintaining the rate of profit, but competition for colonies and markets leads to imperialistic wars which help to overthrow capitalism. Moreover, while trade and the export of capital expanded output in the developing countries, the beneficiaries were the foreign investors; capitalistic production is exploitation, not development. To Marx (1909) capital accumulation was both a fundamental condition of modern production and a barrier:

The barrier of capitalist production is capital itself. It is the fact that capital and its self-expansion appear as the starting and closing point, as the motive and aim of production; that production is merely production for *capital,* and not vice versa, the means of production mere means for an ever expanding system of the life process for the benefit of the society of producers. Thus, while the capitalist mode of production is one of the historical means by which the material forces of production are developed and the world market required for them created, it is at the same time in continual conflict with this historical task and the conditions of social production corresponding to it (Vol. III, p. 293).

Thus, while Marx had a tremendous respect for the productive capacity of capital, its accumulation under capitalism led to depressions, unemployment, subsistence wages, and eventually to the destruction of capitalism. However, the laws of history require the introduction of modern industrial techniques and the establishment of capitalism as a basis for material progress in traditional society. Once capitalism was established, presumably the most socially productive foreign-aid package which could be delivered to poor countries was socialism, not capital. But modern Marxists are seeking to export socialism to countries that have not reached the stage of capitalistic production.

By Alfred Marshall's time it was clear that modern industry could overcome both the Malthusian population trap and the law of diminishing returns, and—in line with Victorian optimism—indefinite economic and social progress was highly probable, if not assured. Unlike Ricardo and Marx, Marshall did not formulate a theory of economic growth. Returning to the Smithian tradition, Marshall set forth a number of fundamental determinants and factors influencing growth, both economic and noneconomic in nature (Youngson, 1956). Natural resources, climate, human character, and political freedom are for Marshall the fundamental determinants of growth; the willingness and ability to save, improved transport, external economies, increasing returns, and the existence of extensive markets are among the major influences on growth. The existence of a substantial middle class, efficient and honest government, education and social mobility were also mentioned by Marshall as contributing to growth. Thus, while Marshall does emphasize saving, which he links to opportunities for productive investment, his view of the conditions of growth and development cover a wide range of technological, social, and political influences.

Neo-Classical economics was not especially concerned with either growth or full employment; growth was a function of savings and technology, while full employment could be assured by flexible wage rates and the avoidance of financial excesses which led to booms and depressions. One of the first major economists to break with the Neo-Classical tradition, Joseph A. Schumpeter, was concerned with growth and development and denied the Neo-Classical propositions relating to growth and stability. In fact, for Schumpeter, growth and stability were contradictory and inconsistent concepts. In his *Theory of Economic Development* (the first German edition of which was published in 1912), Schumpeter defined "development" as "the carrying out of new combinations," such as the introduction of a new good, the introduction of a new method of production, the opening of a new market, conquest of a new source of supply of raw materials, and the carrying out of a new organization of industry (Schumpeter, 1949, pp. 65-66). For Schumpeter, the hero of the development story and the fundamental determinant of growth was neither savings nor capital, but the entrepreneur or innovator. Given access to a supply of credit as contrasted with *ex-ante* savings, the entrepreneur is able to command the factors of production which he devotes to new uses, employing a reservoir of unused technical knowledge and inventions for the expansion of output and new directions of production. Thus, Schumpeter would have had little sympathy for the view that development is limited by the supply of external capital or for the concept of a low-level equilibrium trap, but he certainly would have advocated a flow of direct foreign investment embodying entrepreneurship to the developing countries as the principal means of promoting growth by external action.

During the inter-war period, economists were mainly concerned with stability and full employment rather than growth. In fact, the interest in growth for Western industrial economies—which arose during the late 1930's—was perhaps less for its own sake than for a concern with the relationship between the rate of growth and full employment (Hansen, 1939). But out of the problems posed by the Keynesian revolution requiring a dynamic approach to the major determinants of full employment, there arose the basic elements of modern growth theories.

MODERN ECONOMIC GROWTH MODELS AND THEORIES [1]

Most economic growth models employed today are variants of, or a logical development from, the Cobb-Douglas production function (Douglas, 1934, p. 131 ff.) and the Harrod-Domar model (Harrod, 1939, 1948; Domar, 1946, 1947), both of which were formulated before World War II and for neither of which was maximum growth the primary objective. The Cobb-Douglas production function has the form

$$O = cL^b K^{1-b}$$

1. For a comprehensive survey of modern formal growth theories, see F. H. Hahn and R. C. O. Matthews, "The Theory of Economic Growth: A Survey," *The Economic Journal*, 74 (1964), 779-902.

where O, L, and K are *output, labor,* and *capital*, c is a constant, and b and $1\text{-}b$ indicate the margin efficiencies of labor and capital or the elasticities of output with respect to labor and capital, respectively. This function was formulated and tested empirically in response to a concern for the distribution of income between labor and capital and its relationship to the marginal productivities of the factors.

The Harrod-Domar model, the basic elements of which were developed independently by both economists, was a by-product of the Keynesian revolution in income and employment theory. Keynes had shown that short-run full employment is achieved when the volume of investment is equal to full employment savings. However, in the longer-run, investment creates additional capacity and full employment at that capacity requires an increase in investment. Harrod and Domar were concerned with the rate of growth that would just maintain full employment over time. This critical rate of growth was shown to depend upon the relationship between income and spending, on the one hand, and the additional output generated by the additional capacity created by the initial volume of investment, on the other. The additional income or output, dY_t, is a function of the incremental capital–output ratio, k, and the inital volume of investment, I_t. Since savings aand investment are equal, we have $I_t = sY_t$ at full employment, where s is the ratio of savings, S_t *to income*, Y_t, and

$$dY_t = \frac{1}{k} I_t,$$

with k assumed to be constant. Hence the rate of growth, g, may be expressed as

$$\frac{dY_t}{Y_t} = \frac{s}{k} = \frac{I_t/Y_t}{k},$$

or the ratio of the investment coefficient to the incremental capital–output ratio (ICOR).

Thus, if a country is investing 9 per cent of its national income and the ICOR is 3, its rate of growth will be 3 per cent. If the country receives a flow of external aid equal to 3 per cent of its national income, it can grow at a rate of 4 per cent per year. Therefore, with the help of external assistance, an economy can grow at a faster rate than that permitted by its domestic savings ratio alone. Moreover, if the marginal propensity to save is greater than the average propensity, the savings ratio will rise with the increased growth rate induced by the external capital supplement to investment. Thus, given the critical pattern of the flow of external capital, aid can be tapered off and a higher rate of growth can be sustained by internal savings alone. However, growth goals are generally stated in terms of rates of growth in income per capita so that the rate of population growth becomes another critical factor. If the rise in income induces a higher rate of population growth, both the growth in the savings ratio and the amount and time pattern of aid for achieving "self-sustained growth," at the target rate of increase in income per capita, will be affected.

The simple model outlined above implies that the ICOR remains stable and that it is equal to the average capital-output ratio. This assumption of fixed factor proportions is at variance with experience. Moreover, a constant ICOR denies any contribution of increased labor and other non-capital inputs to the growth process, which are not proportional to the increase in capital, and ignores the contribution of technology and other factors contributing to the productivity of inputs. The popularity of the Harrod-Domar model with those who regard growth as being mainly a function of external capital assistance is easy to see. It must be recalled, however, that this model was not initially formulated to deal with a developing economy in which the major problem is regarded as that of maximizing investment for growth. Rather, it was developed for explaining the delicate balance among income, savings, investment, and output in developed countries required to maintain steady growth and full employment income.

The Cobb-Douglas production function has in recent years served as a starting point for growth theories which allow for changes in the capital-output ratio, for the substitution of the productive factors, and for an analysis of the nature and contribution of technical progress to the rate of growth. The assumptions of variable factor proportions, of the equating of factor returns to their marginal productivities, and of constant returns to scale with increases in factor incomes from additional inputs just exhausting the increments to the total product, are more closely akin to the neo-Classical theory than to the Keynesian emphasis on capital formation as the key to income and output as reflected in the Harrod-Domar model. However, attaching such labels to growth models does not indicate that one is more modern and realistic than the other. There is a great variety of formal growth models, each of which employs a high level of abstraction. However, owing to the simplified assumption and artificial nature of the problems considered, most of them are incapable of empirical testing and are of limited value either for explaining actual phenomena or for policy guidance (Hahn and Mathews, 1964, pp. 88-89).

The simple Cobb-Douglas model, while eliminating fixed factor proportions as the bottleneck to growth, fails to include a number of important determinants of growth, such as technical progress, scale, the amount and quality of natural resources, and the social and cultural characteristics of an economy. Empirical studies showing the relationship between increases in inputs of labor and capital over time and the increase in the total product in the United States reveal a substantially larger percentage increase in output than the percentage increases in inputs of either capital or labor (for a review of these studies, see Nelson, 1964). Thus, a popular exercise among economists has been to advance hypotheses (and attempt empirical verification) for explaining the residual element in growth. These efforts include the relating of technical improvements to the rate of production of new capital instruments (Solow, 1960) and measuring improvements in the quality of the labor force resulting from increased education, reduction in the average work week, and other factors (see, for example, Bowman, 1964; Denison, 1962).

One approach is to assume that technological change represents that part of the growth of output which cannot be explained by the growth of capital and/or of labor. Thus, the rate of growth of output may be written as:

$$\frac{\Delta O}{O} = b\left(\frac{\Delta L}{L}\right) + (1-b)\left(\frac{\Delta K}{K}\right) + \frac{\Delta T}{T}$$

where $\Delta O/O$ is the relative rate of growth of GNP; $\Delta K/K$ and $\Delta L/L$ are the relative rates of growth of capital and labor inputs; $\Delta T/T$ is the relative rate of growth of total fact or productivity; and b and $1-b$ are the elasticities of output with respect to labor and capital respectively, which will in equilibrium indicate the shares of these factors in the total product. Modern growth theory has been in considerable measure concerned with the disaggregation of $\Delta T/T$ and in showing its relationship and interdependence with factor inputs K and L. Robert Solow (1962, 1964) has emphasized the complementarity between technical change and investment, and distinguishes between improvements which do not require new capital and those which do; the latter so-called "designed improvements" must be embodied in new capital equipment. Empirical tests of the contribution of the technology embodied in new capital equipment have been made on the basis of measuring the age distribution of capital over time. Thus it has been shown that a substantial portion of the variation in rates of growth in the United States between 1929 and 1960 may be explained by a combination of differential rates of growth of capital and labor, and of trends in the average age of capital, which in turn constitutes an indicator of the rate of "embodiment" of new techniques or in the quality of the capital stock (Nelson, 1964).

Edward Denison focuses attention on the improvement in the average quality of the work force in accounting for productivity; in fact, Denison

(1964) denies the importance of embodiment effects as employed by Solow in explaining the contribution of technical progress to growth. Denison attributes 23 per cent of the U.S. national income growth over the period 1929-57 to inputs of productive services derived from education alone. Denison's analysis suggests that improvements in labor quality account for about half of the growth in total factor productivity in the United States over the 1929-60 period. However, according to Solow, technical change embodied in new capital can be shown to account for the vast bulk of the growth of total factor productivity, thus virtually ruling out education (Nelson, 1964).

An interesting approach to the problem of capital which has relevance for the so-called "embodiment" question has been put forward by Harry G. Johnson (1964) in what he calls "a generalized capital accumulation approach" to economic development. Johnson suggests a Fisherian concept of capital "as including anything that produces a stream of income over time, and income as the product of capital." Thus, while the growth of income is the result of the accumulation of capital, or of investment, "investment" includes "such diverse activities as adding to material capital, increasing the health, discipline, skill and education of human population, moving labor into more productive occupations and locations, and applying existing knowledge or discovering and applying new knowledge to increase the efficiency of productive processes."

Johnson's concept of capital in terms of the discounted value of the net income from a broad range of investment activities appears to be incompatible with explanations of growth in terms of production functions involving discreet and measurable units of inputs—since the value of the investment inputs will only be determined by the results. Moreover, the income to be capitalized is a joint product of the investment embodied in labor, capital instruments, entrepreneurial activities, and applied technical knowledge. Indeed, it is difficult to distill out of the production process any pure noninvestment factors, such as primordial labor and natural resources, or to measure them in a production function.

Without dealing further with the explanations provided by various models for the growth in output which cannot be accounted for by rates of change in the factor inputs of labor and capital, it seems clear that a fully satisfactory growth model would have to take into account the interdependence between the productive factors themselves and the elements of technical knowledge and education, plus the complex of factors leading to organizational change. The contributions of each of a number of factors whose change has an effect upon output cannot be added up separately but must be considered as a highly complex interdependent function. Simple regression techniques will certainly miss these interdependencies. Moreover, with respect to the Cobb-Douglas function, there seems little justification for the assumption of constant elasticities of output with respect to the factors of production or for the assumption that they are independent of other determinants of growth and of the structure of the economy. As Nelson (1964, p. 597) has stated, "We know more about the process of economic growth than the factors and relationships treated formally by the aggregative growth models we use." When we come to studying underdeveloped as contrasted to developed economies, where the whole social structure is undergoing rapid transformation (or must do so if successful development is to take place), we have even less justification to rely heavily on aggregate production functions as a guide to the determinants of growth, even if we had the data for testing them.

We may avoid the constraints of the Cobb-Douglas production function and begin with a function of the type:

$$Y_t = f (L_t, \ K_t, \ T_t, \ R_t, \ S_t)$$

where capacity output, Y, during a short period of time, t, is a function of the productive labor force, L, the stock of capital, K, the technical knowledge, T, natural resources, R, and all of the social, cultural, political, and environmental conditions which determine the productivity of the economy as a whole, S (Bruton, 1965, p. 11). But such a formulation is not a theory of production; it is simply a listing of the factors which determine output. A theory of the growth of output requires an explanation of the effects of changes in each of the determinants upon the rate of growth in output, of the changes in the volume, quantity, and character of the determinants themselves as affected by output, and of the interdependence of the variables, including the environmental conditions. Quantification of the inputs, capital, and labor provide difficulties because of the many forms which they take and of the problems of capital evaluation. Technology, natural resources, and social, cultural, and governmental environment cannot be reduced to homogeneous units, although some combination of quantitative indicators of these determinants may be employed to construct indexes reflecting the direction and relative magnitude of changes, at least in certain components of these determinants.

It is also possible to analyze the impact of technological and organizational change on the possible combinations of productive factors, labor, capital, and natural resources required to produce a given output. This is important in growth analysis because with given technology, maximum output may not be consistent with full employment of labor under conditions where marginal productivity of labor has a significant positive value. Also, changing technology may make desirable a shift in the products consistent with maximum output, given the pattern of domestic and foreign demand.

Growth theories often assume fixed environmental factors or perhaps deal only with one or two of them, treating the others as exogenous. While something of value may be learned from an abstract treatment, there is the danger that interaction between the environment and the quantity and quality of the factor inputs themselves may be minimized. A good example of this is represented by the relationship between investment in education and output. Education may be of the wrong type for the existing pattern of production, or it may be of value only if there is a shift in production in response to an alteration in the production possibilities function made possible by the improvement in labor, education, and skills. Nevertheless, for a variety of environmental reasons, or perhaps a slow rate of investments, these shifts in production may never take place, or at least not fast enough to employ the educated and skilled labor in a way which would utilize their capacities. Changes in the social structure may affect the propensities to save and willingness to invest in productive enterprise. The nature and organization of the market will affect output through economies of scale and the realization of the gains from specialization and international trade. Finally, income distribution, the level and character of social services, and incentives to save and invest will be greatly affected by governmental policies, which in turn will react upon the entire production process.

Before concluding this section, mention should be made of intersectoral or interindustry growth models in which output and the production process is disaggregated into a number of sectors such as industry, agriculture, and economic and social overhead capital, and the factor and intermediate good inputs are related to the output of each of these sectors. Interindustry models are certainly more useful, both for understanding the economic process and as a guide to planning and the projection of requirements, than are aggregate growth models. In this connection, they are frequently employed as a basis for decisions regarding foreign-aid requirements and investment priorities (Chenery and Clark, 1959; Barna, 1963; Peacock and Dosser, 1959).

Assuming adequate data are available, interindustry models constitute a useful tool for certain types of problem-solving. However, as explanations of growth they are subject to much the same types of limitations as aggregate growth models; in fact, they must be based on growth models relating to factor inputs and conditions affecting factor productivity and their interdependence, and may be regarded broadly as disaggregated growth models. Although they provide a more detailed picture of the changes in the economic structure in terms of factor inputs and the employment of intermediate products, they can tell us very little about the inducement mechanism in the context of opportunities for technological innovations and market opportunities in a dynamic economy. Such models provide us with a better picture of the interaction between factors and goods and services, just as an X ray provides a picture of the processes of the body. However, X rays do not show us the functioning of the regulatory mechanisms or the forces which stimulate and direct growth and change in the whole body mechanism. In the case of an economy these prime movers and regulators are to be found in the social, cultural, and governmental structure, and no way has been found to inject these elements into the matrices and linear and nonlinear functions of the interindustry model builder.

Nevertheless, disaggregated pictures of the economy can, in addition to indicating requirements and bottlenecks for growth and alternative growth patterns, help in illuminating types of relationships which may stimulate or induce investment, assuming other environmental factors conducive to the exploitation of investment opportunities are present. Thus, growth theories have been constructed to explain how a "leading sector" or industry may induce an expansion of investment and output in other sectors, or how some industries have greater inducement or "linkage" effects than others (Hirschman, 1958). Such theories in combination with detailed studies of an economy are of value in foreign-aid policy by helping to identify strategic sectors to which emphasis should be given in development programs and aid supplements.

One of the disturbing things about modern growth theories for the economic planner or the foreign-aid policy maker is that economists have formulated a bewildering number of highly abstract models on the basis of stylized variables and assumptions regarding economic behavior and organization, while at the same time readily admitting that the character and evolution of the noneconomic framework may be the major determinant of growth. The introduction of one or two noneconomic factors into an economic growth model may provide a higher degree of realism, but may still be of limited usefulness for policy. The usefulness of growth models, even as partial approaches to reality, will require advances in our knowledge of incentives and the agents of change and the formulation of theories of motivation capable of empirical testing. This point is well stated in the concluding paragraphs of Hahn and Matthews (1964) in their survey of modern theories of economic growth:

While not disparaging the insights that have been gained, we feel that in these areas the point of diminishing returns may have been reached. Nothing is easier than to ring the changes on more and more complicated models, without bringing in any really new ideas and without bringing the theory any nearer to casting light on the causes of the wealth of nations. The problems posed may well have intellectual fascination. But it is essentially a frivolous occupation to take a chain with links of very uneven strength and devote one's energies to strengthening and polishing the links that are already relatively strong.

Two aspects may be singled out as requiring more attention in future work (without implying that there are not others). The motivation of economic agents needs analysis in a way that avoids the twin dangers of empty formulas and inconclusive anecdotes. And more thought should be given to the concept of the world as a whole as an underdeveloped economy, in which even the evolution of the advanced sectors may be impossible to understand properly in isolation from the sectors that are less developed (pp. 890-91).

HISTORICAL STAGE THEORIES

By and large, the growth models that we have been discussing were initially formulated with a view to explaining the growth process in developed countries where long-run growth is assured, but fluctuation in its rate is affected mainly by relationships between dynamic economic forces including business expectations, and by government, monetary, and fiscal policies. While changes in the social structure continue to take place, the fundamental conditions for steady growth—social mobility, education, individual initiative, incentives and opportunities to achieve economic and social goals, a reasonable degree of economic freedom, a stable government, a vast amount of directly productive and social and economic overhead capital, well-developed capital markets, and mobility of labor and of entrepreneurs—exist in one degree or another in Western non-Communist countries. Historians have long been aware of the existence of social, cultural, and other environmental prerequisites for economic progress. Thus, throughout the nineteenth and twentieth centuries, a number of economic historians have sought to identify stages of economic and social development to which specialized models explaining economic processes could be applied. For countries which had not reached the stage at which the fundamental conditions for growth were assured, the major problem was to show how countries moved from one stage to another. In the nineteenth century, Karl Marx and various economists of the German Historical School designated and described various stages in the economic and social evolution of society. The best known protagonist of the historical stage approach today is Walt W. Rostow, whose historical stage theory has not only an enormous influence on modern development economists, but who as much as any other economist has influenced public policy, especially as related to foreign aid.[2]

Virtually all economists are familiar with Rostow's (1960) five stages:

2. Rostow's original formulation appeared in "The Take-Off into Self-Sustained Growth," *Economic Journal,* 66 (March, 1956), 25-48.

(1) the traditional society; (2) the long period during which the economic and social preconditions for growth are evolved; (3) the relatively short period of the "take-off"; (4) the rapid drive to maturity; and (5) the era of high mass consumption, or alternatively, high social investment in military and space machinery for the achievement of a position of a world power (or both, as in the case of the United States, if the country can afford it). The most important and most controversial aspect of Rostow's theory relates to the take-off stage. The concept of "the take-off into self-sustaining growth" has become a part of the standard lexicon of foreign-aid policy makers and is generally employed in the literature of development economics, even by those who have serious doubts regarding the validity of the entire concept. It is difficult to think of any concept which has been subjected to a greated barrage of criticism (Rostow, 1963) and yet has not only survived in the literature, but continues to have an enormous impact on development policy.

From the standpoint of the impact of Rostow's stage theory on foreign aid policy, we shall consider the following: (a) the take-off into self-sustained growth, (b) the preconditions, and (c) the role of capital from both internal and external sources. A key issue in Rostow's theory arises from the concept of the "take-off" as a *unique* stage in historical development. Rostow defines the take-off as requiring the following three related conditions: (1) a rise in the rate of productive investment, say from 5 per cent or less to over 10 per cent of national income; (2) the development of one or more manufacturing sectors (including the processing of raw materials) with a high rate of growth; and (3) the existence (from the precondition stage) or rapid emergence of a political, social, and institutional framework conducive to the transmission of impulses to expansion throughout the economy, including the capacity to mobilize capital from domestic sources. This third condition is necessary for the growth process to be self-enforcing, since unless the income and savings from a leading sector, say raw material exports, can be transmitted to other sectors—particularly manufacturing, but also to the modernization of agriculture and of other sectors of the economy—there cannot be a general and sustained rise in productivity and output.

Few would quarrel with Rostow's description of the developments which must occur in the social and economic structure of a country before a broad and sustained development—in terms of output per capita and of social, cultural, and political progress—can take place. The principal criticism which has been leveled at the Rostowian theory relates to his assertion that the take-off period covering two to three decades is a unique and identifiable stage, either in the history of existing developed countries, or in countries that have not achieved what we generally regard as a condition of economic maturity. Rostow has induced criticism from economic historians by suggesting approximate take-off periods for a number of countries, such as Great Britain (1783-1802), the United States (1843-60), France (1830-60), Germany (1850-73), Japan (1878-1900), Sweden (1868-90), and Canada (1896-1914). Not only have economic historians quarreled with the dates chosen for these countries in terms of the take-off conditions set forward by Rostow and the unique "engine of transformation" which Rostow believes to have operated during the take-off in each particular country, but most of them fail to discover this uniquely identifiable period in the economic and social evolution of any country. Thus, for example, Phyllis Deane and H. J. Habakkuk (1963) state with reference to the take-off in Britain that:

> The conclusion which emerges from the above discussion, therefore, is that the changes in overall rates of growth in production functions or in rates of capital formation which took place during the period 1783-1802 (Rostow's take-off date for Britain) were not in themselves decisive enough to constitute a take-off as defined for the Rostow model. Indeed it is doubtful whether any period of two or three decades in British history could be cast in this mold of "a period when the scale of productive economic activity reaches a critical level and produces changes which lead to a massive and progressive structural transformation" in the economy and the society of which it is a part. . . . In the end it seems that the most striking characteristic of the first take-off was its gradualness. . . . The sustained rise in the rate of growth in total output probably dates back to the 1740's. If the 1780's be taken as a starting point for the revolutionary changes in industrial technique and organization, then it took about a century for the long-term rate of growth in average real incomes (measured over 30-year periods) to rise from about 1 per cent per annum to just over 2 per cent per annum (pp. 80-82).

Professor Kuznets (1963) is also highly critical of the concept of the take-off stage, both on statistical grounds—that is, the doubling of the rate of capital investment and the sharp acceleration in the rate of growth are not confirmed by the statistical evidence—and on analytical grounds. Since in part the conditions for the era of sustained growth are established both in the precondition period and during the take-off, Kuznets (1963) finds no valid basis for a distinction between the precondition and take-off stages, and, in addition, regards the concept of stage of self-sustained growth as a "misleading oversimplification." What Rostow is seeking to do is to describe a period during which the forces making for acceleration—the capacity to transmit impulses from the leading sectors to the rest of the economy, to exploit opportunity for technical change and increased productivity, and to increase saving for productive investment throughout the economy—overcome the decelerating forces of diminishing returns to land and population growth (Kuznets, 1963). But

Rostow has obviously failed to convince many economists and historians as to why this period should be both short and unique, or why modern developing countries should be expected to achieve a condition of sustained or self-sustaining growth, even though modern developed countries, except for periods of depressions, war devastation, or radical changes in governmental structure (Eastern Europe, for example), have had a pretty good long-term record.

Another point of controversy relates to the nature of the preconditions, and particularly the role of social overhead capital. This is perhaps an aspect of the fuzziness of the take-off period itself, since one of the characteristics of the take-off period as defined by Rostow (1961) is "the existence of quick emergence of a political, social, and institutional framework which exploits the impulses to expansion in the modern sector and the potential external economy effects of the take-off and gives to growth an ongoing character." In addition, much of the investment in both the precondition and the take-off periods must, according to Rostow, go into social overhead capital. From the standpoint of current development policy, a basic question arises as to whether countries must go through a long period, say a century or at least several generations, of structural change combined with large inputs of social overhead capital before they may hope to reach the self-sustaining growth stage (whatever that may mean), or whether steady progress in terms of broad social and economic development, including increase in output per capita, is possible for countries which are now at a relatively low level of development. In terms of external assistance policy, this question has implications regarding (a) the degree to which large inputs of external capital and technical assistance can speed up this process, and (b) what level and duration of external assistance for creating social overhead and for promoting the transformation of the social structure (education and technical training, for example) will be required. Should foreign aid policy be governed by assistance during the precondition stage, and if so, what should be its objectives and measures of success? Or should foreign aid be concentrated during the take-off into self-sustaining growth stage? Or, alternatively, should development be looked at as a continuous process without regard to stages from the standpoint of external assistance and its objectives?

This leads us to the role of capital formation and the rate of investment in the development process. Rostow was considerably influenced by the Harrod-Domar model in his definition of the take-off in terms of the critical rate of investment required for the achievement of a level of income and savings sufficient to assure self-sustaining growth. Although Rostow himself was careful to point out that several countries have achieved self-sustained growth without external capital or with external capital playing a very minor role, many development economists have re-

garded an external supplement to domestic savings as a principal means
of raising the level of investment to the critical level which would generate
sufficient income out of which domestic savings could provide a volume of
investment necessary for self-sustained growth.

A. K. Cairncross not only denies the relevance of the concept of the
take-off stage to modern underdeveloped countries, but is especially critical of the idea that capital formation plays a strategic and causal role
in the whole development process. Thus, Cairncross (1963) states:

> There is no invariable dependence of growth on a high rate of capital
> formation and it is easy to imagine circumstances in which efforts to increase
> capital formation may actually slow down the progress of the economy. More-
> over, there is some justification for turning the causal relationship the other
> way around. If income is growing fast, investment opportunities are likely
> to be expanding even faster, so that the growth in income draws capital ac-
> cumulation along behind it. The biggest influence on capital formation is
> market opportunity, and many types of capital accumulation are likely to be
> embarked on only when income is booming. If capital formation does not
> respond, its failure to do so will certainly act as a drag on expansion and
> output. But there is no reason why it should bring it to a halt, and, given a
> rearrangement of the investment pattern, income might grow a long way
> before the shortage of capital became acute. In the meantime, the rapid growth
> in income, particularly if it were accompanied by profits, would be likely to
> generate additional savings, and so mitigate any symptoms of capital shortage
> that manifest themselves. . . . Technical progress does not always involve a
> high net investment; indeed it may permit a *reduction* in the stock of capital
> or an expansion of output without any comparable investment. A change in
> the pattern of investment could also, by enforcing the continued use or over-
> loading of old types of plant, make possible a far more rapid construction of
> those newer types which bear the fruits of technical progress in greatest
> abundance (pp. 244-45).

While Cairncross admits difficulty in finding statistical evidence for
rates of savings and investment for modern developed countries during the
nineteenth century, he states that, "So far as they go, they imply that a
rise in the savings ratio follows, rather than precedes, the take-off" (1963,
p. 249). In other words, Cairncross finds a complex interdependence
among savings, the inducement to invest, the social and economic structure, productivity and the rate of growth in output, and regards a tendency to consider savings and capital investment as independent causal
factors in growth as a misconception of the development process. He also
casts doubt on the vital role of social overhead capital as a precondition
for growth and on the contribution of foreign assistance to social overhead projects in the establishment of the fundamental conditions for
growth.

Paul H. Cootner is even more critical of the argument that there must be a certain level of social overhead capital stock as a condition for the initiation of self-sustaining economic growth. Like Albert Hirschman, he sees the demand for overhead capital facilities inducing their creation, while he states that we must explain "why some countries with little or no initial endowment of social overhead capital simultaneously build such a stock of utilities *and* develop, while other countries with more overhead capital grow less rapidly or not at all" (1963, p. 268).

Finally, critics of the take-off theory as applied to the nineteenth century have cast considerable doubt on the role of foreign capital in promoting the take-off. Not only have quite a number of countries succeeded in doing without foreign capital in the early stages of their development, but in a number of cases, including those of the United States and Canada, substantial capital inflow took place *after* the development process was in full swing. Moreover, capital investment, both in the form of direct investment and in raw materials production, and in railroads and other overhead capital associated with raw materials exploitation, frequently failed to promote development, but succeeded only in creating export enclaves and an urban middle class with little impact on industrialization, agricultural productivity, or the transformation of the social structure (Berrill, 1963). The nineteenth and early twentieth centuries experience with foreign investment in such areas as India, Egypt, Latin America, and Africa, are cited as illustrations of this point.

SOCIOLOGICAL AND CULTURAL APPROACHES

There is a difference between describing noneconomic factors such as population motivation, social deviation, social structure and the nature of government, on the one hand, and introducing one or a combination of these noneconomic factors into a growth model or a partial theory, which is potentially capable of empirical testing, on the other. I do not believe that a realistic *general* model of economic and social development is possible, at least one which would be worth very much from the standpoint of prediction and control. On the other hand, an immense amount of useful work remains to be done by economists, social psychologists, political scientists, and other social scientists in formulating and testing partial theories or hypotheses explaining the relationships among sets of economic, social, and political data.

One of the most important fields where more statistical and analytical work is needed is that of population and its relationship to income, savings, investment, and various aspects of the social and economic structure. Social scientists are widely at variance regarding the role of population in growth. Elaborate development models are formulated on the assumption that growth induces population expansion, and that this expansion constitutes a barrier to a further rise in per capita income. On the other hand, Everett Hagen states that, "Nowhere in the world has population growth *induced by rising income* been sufficient to halt the rise in income" (1962, p. 48). Such questions are of immense importance for development planning and foreign aid policy.

We know very little about the psychological basis for savings and its relationship to income levels and social structure in developing countries. Nevertheless, our theoretical constructs assume that countries with low per capita incomes can do little net savings and that there is a sharply rising marginal propensity to save beyond a certain level of per capita income. However, international comparisons of savings ratios in relation to per capita incomes show only a small positive correlation and wide deviations among individual countries (Houthakker, 1962, p. 16). Certainly the studies I have seen do not provide an empirical basis for the savings functions postulated in most growth models. We need to know much more about savings functions and the behavior of different sources of savings with changes in income and other conditions in developing countries. While poor countries are assumed not to be able to save a sufficient portion of their income to support a level of investment necessary for sustained growth in per capita output, it is amazing to see the high proportion of their output that can be mobilized rather quickly for making war on their neighbors!

A growing number of social scientists view the wellspring of development in the personality characteristics which shape a given society and its values and aspirations. David McClelland (1961) regards development as a function of the number of individuals who behave in an entrepreneurial fashion and that communities differ in the average level of "achievement" motivation which will produce Schumpeterian entrepreneurs. Hence the promotion of development should place heavy emphasis on inculcating achievement motives in people, beginning at an early age. Achievement motivation can, of course, be directed in ways other than those best suited for effective entrepreneurial activities in a modern capitalistic society; achievement may be satisfied by advancement within an organization rather than creating new ones or by the pursuit of individual artistic excellence. Moreover, economic and social transformation requires more than a good stock of entrepreneurs, since, depending upon the environment in which they operate, entrepreneurs may confine their activities to zero-sum games. It should also be said that while McClelland and other social psychologists (for a review of other studies, see Higgins, 1965, pp. 296-301) have conducted studies for determining achievement levels in various countries, and have found reasonably good correlations between these levels and per capita income growth (after an interval of 13 to 25 years), Bauer and Yamey (1957, pp. 103-105) do not find a dearth of entrepreneurship even in primitive African economies. Immigrants from low-income countries, such as China, India, and Lebanon, have displayed remarkable entrepreneurial and innovating capacities when operating in a new environment with opportunities not present in their own countries.

Hagen's theory of economic growth relies heavily upon the emergence of creative and reformist personalities. The transition from a traditional society to one in which economic growth (or more broadly, development) is possible depends upon the emergence of innovators willing to adopt new values and seize upon available technical knowledge for promoting them. Along with the reformers, they promote and guide institutional changes favorable to technological advance and economic growth (Hagen, 1962, Ch. XI). Hagan admits that, "Whether or not a given set of changes in personalities in a society will lead to economic growth may depend on the state of knowledge at the time" (p. 237). He also regards the size of the market and the volume of savings available for investment as factors favoring the ability of personality change to "bring about continuing technological progress" (p. 238). However, he does not regard change in these economic variables "as a force causing economic growth to begin." Rather, the economic changes are "symptoms" of change rather than initiating forces (pp. 239-40). Similarly, other aspects of social, political, and economic change such as the creation of unified national states, urbanization, the development of a money economy, and the establishment of modern communications, while facilitating economic growth, are not the initial causal factors in change (pp. 250 ff.).

Without disparaging Hagen's brilliant insights into the psychology of personality change, we cannot be wholly satisfied with a search for first causes and explanations of continuing growth. The factors identified by Hagen must still be regarded as necessary, but not sufficient, causes of social and economic transformation. The process by which the ideals and motivations of a critical group of personalities is transferred to the larger community requires a more complex analysis of the interrelations within the social structure. Economic analysis in relation to the social and political environment has an important role to play here.

A major problem of developing societies today is the eager acceptance of new technology and organization required for productivity and growth in the modern urban sector, while leaving the remainder of the country, which holds the bulk of the population, in a traditional social and economic state. This situation, together with the failure to develop industrial exports, limits the growth of the modern sector because of restricted markets needed for overall growth. Moreover, a characteristic of a dualistic society is the drawing of the best human talent, including enterpreneurship and skills, from the traditional sector to the modern sector.

Raul Prebisch, while known for his emphasis on external capital and favorable terms of trade for promoting development, nevertheless regards the transformation of the social structure in Latin America (and in other developing countries as well) as the key to accelerating development. Thus he points out in his *Towards A Dynamic Development Policy for Latin America* (1963) that the existing social structure impedes

the emergence of the dynamic elements of society. . . . Modern production techniques have an ever increasing need of these dynamic elements, men of initiative, drive and resolution who are capable of taking risks and shoulder-ing responsibility. They are needed at a vast number of levels, ranging from skilled workers to top-level technicians and the organizers and administrators of all phases of the economic process. . . . The need for these dynamic ele-ments increases far more quickly than the rate of development itself. In other words, if development is speeded up, the singling out and training of such men would have to be pursued much more vigorously. . . . A considerable human potential (in Latin America) is untapped, since very few dynamic elements succeed in forcing their way from the lower and middle strata of society. . . . The lack of proper social mobility is a clear proof of social stratification (pp. 68-69).

Prebisch believes that the starting point for increased social mobility is education and investment in human resources; by expanding opportunities for education and training for all elements of society there would be brought about "a new order of things in which the dynamic elements that reach the upper strata would be proportionate to the numerical size of the social strata from which they come" (p. 70).

SOME DEVELOPMENT THEORIES AND STRATEGIES

In addition to the economic growth models and the historical stage and sociological approaches to development, there have been a number of development theories and strategies, usually dealing with specific types of situations in developing countries, which have had a very great impact on foreign aid policy and administration. In this section I shall discuss the following partial or specialized development theories: (a) the critical rate of growth or minimum effort thesis; (b) the balanced growth or "big push" thesis; (c) the absorption of surplus labor approach; (d) theories empha-sizing external trade and capital imports; and (e) theories of investment criteria.

THE CRITICAL RATE OF GROWTH OR MINIMUM EFFORT THESIS

The critical rate of growth approach is by and large an extension of the Harrod-Domar theory and its elaboration to fit certain conditions believed relevant for developing countries that have not achieved sustained growth in per capita output. In addition to such factors as the rates of investment and savings and the capital-output ratio, attention is given to the rate of population growth as an endogenous variable and to a number of socio-economic parameters, some of which work toward the retardation of the rate of growth, while others tend to promote growth. According to the approach formulated by Harvey Leibenstein and Richard Nelson, there is a critical minimum level of per capita income which must be reached in order for sustained growth to take place. At a low level of income, a small rise in per capita output brings into play forces tending to push down the level of income to an equilibrium point which has been characterized by some economists (Nelson, 1956) as the "low-level equilibrium trap." To escape the low-level equilibrium trap, per capita income must rise to a critical level or there must be, in the language of Leibenstein (1957, pp. 187-216), a "critical minimum effort" to raise per capita income to a point where the growth-inducing forces overcome the depressing forces. The depressing forces operating below the critical minimum rate of growth include (a) population growth and the reduction in available capital per worker, (b) a rise in the incremental capital-output ratio, (c) insufficient stimulus to entrepreneurial activity, and (d) resistance to new ideas, technical progress, and non-productive conspicuous consumption (Leibenstein, 1957, pp. 189-90). These forces operate as per capita income rises, but can be overcome if per capita income rises fast enough, given certain changes in the social-economic structure which will assure a continued rise in per capita income.[3] In both the Nelson and Leibenstein models, population growth is a function of income, the relationship being determined by the impact of income levels on both mortality and fertility rates. Savings are also a function of the income level but can be influenced by changes in the social structure and by government action. Both Nelson (1956, p. 897) and Leibenstein (1957, p. 191) hold that there will be little or no savings at a subsistence or near-subsistence per capita income. According to Leibenstein (1957, pp. 112 ff.), savings as a per cent of national income is a function both of the initial level of income and the rate of in-

3. R. R. Nelson (1956, pp. 901-902) lists the conditions conducive to "trapping" of an economy as: "(1) a high correlation between level of per capita income and the rate of population growth, (2) a low propensity to direct additional per capita income to increasing per capita investment, (3) scarcity of uncultivated arable land, and (4) inefficient production methods."

crease in national income. However, savings cannot be effective in the absence of investment demand, which is regarded as more sensitive to the income growth rate than is savings supply; in addition, investment demand is a function of a variety of elements in the socioeconomic structure.

In the short-run, investment can exceed the rate of savings corresponding to a particular level of income, and in fact, according to Leibenstein (1957, p. 201), "The excess investment demand in one period is one of the dynamic factors that stimulates the expansion of the economy in future periods." While savings and investment are, to a degree, interdependent and both are functions of the rate of growth in income which is in turn a function of the capital-output ratio, internal savings available for productive investment may well be a limitation on the achievement of the critical minimum effort or a rate of growth sufficient to escape the low-level equilibrium trap.

Both Leibenstein and Nelson stress the importance of the social structure, including investment in human capital and the application of improved production techniques which usually accompanies social and political change. Entrepreneurship is important, but it cannot achieve the critical minimum effort alone. For example, Leibenstein (1957, pp. 112 ff.) points out that entrepreneurs in underdeveloped countries frequently engage in "zero sum" games, that is, trading activities which do not raise national income. But unless "positive sum" activities are undertaken in sufficient volume to raise per capita income, profit expectations will be disappointed and entrepreneurial talents will be shifted toward "zero sum" activities.

The contribution of Leibenstein and Nelson may be regarded as an elaboration of Rostow's take-off thesis, since we find so many of the basic requirements for the minimum critical effort of "getting out of the trap" among Rostow's conditions for the take-off. Thus, for example, Nelson (1956) lists the following means (employed simultaneously) for escaping the low-level equilibrium trap: (1) a change in the social structure with greater emphasis on thrift and entrepreneurship and a government investment program, all directed toward shifting both the income growth and the population growth functions; (2) the application of better production techniques, and (3) capital imports. Nelson points out, however, that funds from abroad may have no lasting effect "unless accompanied by changing social-economic parameters" since otherwise the increase in income will be offset by a population increase (pp. 903-904).

One of the weakest aspects of the critical minimum effort thesis relates to the assumptions regarding population growth. In recent years, rates of growth have varied sharply, not so much in response to higher per capita income levels, as in response to a reduction in death rates from epidemics and improved public health and sanitation. In some Latin American countries the rates of population growth have been for a period of a decade or so well above what has been regarded as the long-run biological maximum of 3 per cent (which itself could change). Another factor is the success of birth control efforts in certain countries like Japan, and to an increasing degree, in India, which may greatly alter the pattern of population growth in developing countries. We simply do not know enough about population behavior to build an economic model which depends heavily upon a certain relationship between the income per capita and population growth. Another difficulty with the minimum effort thesis, which also applies to other take-off type models, has to do with the timed relationships among the variables such as investment, saving, population, technological progress, diminishing returns, and other factors affecting the capital-output ratio. The authors of these theories usually do not take account of time except in terms of artificial periods during which things are supposed to happen. How long does it take for a change in per capita income to affect population growth? Or for population growth to affect social overhead capital requirements? Or for the capital-output ratio to shift in response to changes in the social and economic structure? Without taking account of time, it may appear that some countries have reached or well exceeded the critical minimum effort only to find that the delayed reaction on population cancels out the gains. The essential condition for assuring continuous growth may lie in investment in human capital, which involves a substantial period of time with delayed results. The rate of population growth is of course an important factor in human investment because of its effects on the cost of schooling and the necessity of supporting a large nonproductive population for an additional period of years.

Although by and large the authors of the minimum critical effort thesis do not employ it as an argument for foreign aid, or even suggest that a certain amount of foreign aid could provide the minimum critical effort, particularly in the light of the various social conditions for growth embodied in their theories, foreign-aid advisors have employed a variant of the critical minimum effort approach in their arguments. For example, this is quite evident in the statement on "The Objectives of the United States Economic Assistance Programs," prepared by the Center for International Studies, Massachusetts Institute of Technology for a Senate Committee on Foreign Aid (1957):

There is a minimum level of resources that must be devoted to such a program if it is to have any chance of success. Launching a country into self-sustaining growth is a little like getting an airplane off the ground. There is a critical ground speed which must be passed before the craft can become airborne; to taxi up and down the runway at lower speeds is a waste of gasoline. Debate is possible as to precisely what level of aid is required to get a country over this minimum threshold. We suspect that for many countries it is above recent levels of development assistance—but not so far above as to raise serious doubts about the ability of the United States to sustain the effort (p. 70).

BALANCED-GROWTH OR BIG PUSH THEORIES

The general thesis that the initiation of sustained growth cannot take place slowly over a period of generations, but that there must be a period of rapid acceleration of investment, income, and savings, need not rest either on historical foundations or on a theory of population, as in the case of the critical minimum effort or low-level equilibrium trap thesis. The principle may be defended on purely economic grounds arising out of the principle of "balanced growth." Various elements of the balanced-growth theory have been recognized by economists for a long time. The inducement to invest involves complementarity of different industries, and investment in one industry depends upon the generation of demand by investment in other industries. An often quoted example is that of P.N. Rosenstein-Rodan in his 1943 article in *The Economic Journal* (p. 205), in which he assumed that 20,000 unemployed workers were put into a shoe factory where they received wages substantially higher than their previous subsistence income. While the workers spend a portion of their money income on shoes, they can only purchase a fraction of the total output of the shoe factory. However, if—instead—one million unemployed workers were taken off the land and put into a number of industries which produced a wide variety of goods constituting the bulk of the commodities on which workers spend their wages, there would be sufficient demand to purchase the output of all of the industries, while a shoe factory by itself would fail for lack of demand in a closed economy.

Ragner Nurkse (1957, pp. 4-5) emphasized the necessity of balanced growth as a condition for eliminating the vicious circle of poverty in developing countries. In poor countries there is a low capacity to save, as a consequence of low income, which in turn is a reflection of low productivity, due mainly to the lack of capital. Capital formation requires both savings and an inducement to invest, but the inducement to invest is low because of the low level of purchasing power, which again is a consequence of low productivity resulting from a small amount of capital, caused at least in part from the lack of inducement to invest. The way out of this circle, particularly for developing countries that do not find a growing world market for their primary commodity exports, is to be found in balanced growth; simultaneous investment in a number of industries enlarges the size of the market and creates additional inducements to investment.

Nurkse, of course, recognizes the difficulty of inducing a "wave of capital investments in a number of different industries" in poor countries. He indicates the need for foreign private investment, but points out that except for investment in resources industries, for the products of which there exist world markets, private firms in developed countries are not induced to invest in low-income countries because of the limitations of the market. However, he points out that the market limitation does not affect capital investments by governmental authorities in social overhead capital, and that the limitations on the domestic supply of savings for these "autonomous" investments can be overcome by foreign borrowing or foreign aid. Nurkse is careful to point out that external capital cannot make a significant contribution to growth without proper domestic policies which promote private investment and savings. Nor does Nurkse suggest that massive injections of foreign aid constitute the solution to the achievement of balanced growth.

The fundamental problem of the balanced-growth theory is how to induce a nearly simultaneous expansion of investment on all fronts, given the existence of imperfect knowledge with respect to the future level of demand. Moreover, because of certain indivisibilities in the production process, optimum size plants may be substantially larger than would be warranted by any conceivable level of demand for several years to come. Rosenstein-Rodan (1961a, pp. 57-67) has sought to show why balanced growth requires a very large volume of investment in a variety of fields over a relatively short period of time. He bases his theory of the "big push" on the existence of three categories of indivisibilities: (1) indivisibility in the production function or lumpiness of capital; (2) indivisibility of demand (complementarity of demand); and (3) indivisibility in the supply of savings. Indivisibility in the production function occurs particularly in the case of social-overhead capital such as power and transport, but exists in industry as well. According to Rodan, social-overhead capital such as power plants and railroads must precede directly productive investments such as factories and commercial farms. One cannot build a road or a power plant to satisfy the precise demand two or three years after it is built; it must be built to satisfy the demand ten or twenty years hence. Rodan does point out that international trade tends to reduce the critical size of the "big push" since world demand can be substituted in part for domestic demand. Foreign investment and aid can also overcome the indivisibility in the supply of savings, but a high marginal savings rate will tend to ease this problem.

Critics of the balanced-growth and "big push" doctrines, of whom Albert Hirschman (1958, Ch. III) is perhaps best known, deny both the necessity of balanced growth as a condition for growth and its feasibility and realism as a theory of development. Balanced growth at any point of time is not required, because there always exist some areas of unsatisfied demand or opportunities for investment in lower-cost facilities which could replace output supplied by high-cost production. There will always be some unsatisfied demand for social-overhead capital investment which should be "induced" rather than precede the development of industries which require its services. Growth proceeds by a process of induced investment, in which one sector of the economy or industry moves ahead in response to certain inducements, and in turn induces investment in other sectors or industries. The concept of a "big push" involving a simultaneous investment in a large number of industries and social-overhead capital on the expectation that each will create a demand for the other services is fraught with difficulties. First of all, how do you induce such an expansion of investment in the private sector since many, if not most, investments will not appear profitable? Rodan (1961, p. 58), who recognizes this problem, suggests that the answer lies in "programming." Calculated future demand and prices would then be communicated to potential investors. Just how credible these projections would be and what influence they would have on potential investors is highly questionable.

Hirschman believes that, in practice, the "big push" would be heavily weighted in favor of social-overhead capital projects which have little inducement or linkage effects on directly productive activities. He also suggests that the "big push" approach constitutes superimposing an entirely new economy upon the old. Not only is an economy produced in this way likely to involve all kinds of imbalances and waste (Hirschman obviously is not impressed with the omniscience of programmers), but he believes that the "big push" thesis misses the whole point of the development process, which depends heavily upon a change in the social and economic structure as an integral part of growth. How do you suddenly transform an economy by means of massive and simultaneous investments on all fronts without providing the skills, managerial experience and ability, changes in social structure and attitudes, and other concomitants of development? We might also note that investment in human capital, which requires a long gestation period, can scarcely be fitted into a "big push" framework. Without social development, after a few years of furious capital investment in factories and overhead capital, perhaps with the aid of massive doses of foreign capital and technical assistance, the economy would consist of a vast infrastructure and an industrial capacity with very little output. Factories would be operating at a low level of capacity because of supply shortages and imbalances and the inability to make repairs or obtain materials and spare parts. Breakdowns would be frequent because of untrained labor, and agricultural output, which certainly doesn't lend itself to a "big push," would be insufficient to sustain the population. Added to this, of course, would be the problem of foreign-exchange shortages since the process is not likely to achieve sufficiently high productivity in industry for competition in world markets.

All of this raises questions regarding the relationship between economic growth as such and the process of broad social and economic development. How fast can you push an economy, or must it be merely induced and permitted to develop at a rate determined by a complex of internal social and political forces?

THE ABSORPTION OF SURPLUS LABOR APPROACHES

The basic role attributed to capital in some development models is the expansion of industry in the capitalist sector of the economy in order to absorb surplus or "disguised" unemployed labor in the rural or subsistence sector. The best-known statement of this approach is that of W. Arthur Lewis (1963) in his article "Economic Development with Unlimited Supplies of Labor." Lewis argues that for most developing countries, the supply of (unskilled) labor will be perfectly elastic to industry at a wage rate which is determined by, but somewhat above, the subsistence level in the rural sector. According to Lewis, the draining of surplus labor from the rural sector will not affect agricultural output, since their marginal productivity is zero or negligible. Their subsistence income in the rural sector will be below their marginal productivity in industry. Thus, the transfer of labor from the rural or subsistence sector to industry will increase productivity and output. Now, in a closed economy, the level of employment in the industrial sector will depend upon investment, which in turn will depend upon savings out of profits in industry. Profits will increase with an expansion of industry and technical progress and the share of profits in the national income will rise with capital accumulation, since labor supply is perfectly elastic at the wage governed by the subsistence level in the rural sector. However a somewhat higher wage will be necessary to induce workers to move to the cities and to meet certain increased costs of conventional urban living. This process of capital accumulation, which governs the rate of industrial capital formation and the absorption of surplus labor, goes on until the labor surplus is exhausted and wages begin to rise. However, the process of capital accumulation can be halted or slowed down for other reasons, such as a decline in the terms of trade of the industrial sector vis-à-vis the agricultural sector, or because of a rise in productivity (and hence the real wage) in the subsistence sector not offset by an improvement in the terms of trade of the industrial sector (Lewis, 1963, p. 432). Capital imports into countries with surplus labor will of course expand the rate of industrialization, but will not increase real wages unless there is an increase in productivity in the production of wage goods (1963, p. 449).

There are a number of difficulties in the Lewis model. For example, his argument that increased productivity in the rural sector will reduce capital accumulation unless offset by reduced terms of trade of the rural sector in order to avoid any rise in real wages, seems inadmissible. Why cannot both real wages and profits rise with increased productivity? Lewis also minimizes the problem of training unskilled labor as a bottleneck to industrial expansion. In addition, many economists have pointed out that in the absence of technological improvements in the agricultural sector, the assumption that a reduction of the number of workers employed in agriculture will not affect total agricultural output is a dubious one, since frequently nearly all hands are required for at least a few weeks during the periods of planting and harvesting (Higgins, 1965, pp. 353-54).

Building on the initial assumptions of Lewis, Fei and Ranis (1964) have formulated a much more detailed and satisfactory model of the process of development in a labor surplus economy. Their assumptions regarding the determination of wages in the rural and industrial sectors are similar to those of Lewis. However, they place great stress upon the desirability of increasing productivity in the agricultural sector and in its commercialization, and develop the thesis that the agricultural sector not only supplies the manpower for industrial development (without loss to agricultural output), but a substantial proportion of the savings for the development process as well. This contribution to savings arises from the reduction in total consumption by agricultural workers which accompanies the movement of surplus workers to industry. This assumes that the remaining agricultural workers do not increase their consumption by an amount equal to that which was previously consumed by the departing surplus labor. Fei and Ranis also make the assumption that a good portion of the agricultural surplus arising from the transfer of surplus workers will accrue to the landlords who will save the surplus in ways which will make savings available to the industrial sector. They may also use some of the savings for increasing agricultural productivity, but this would tend to raise the surplus, since again it is assumed that the consumption of the agricultural workers will remain at the subsistence level so long as there is a surplus. (This may be questioned, but *some* rise in consumption by rural workers with increased productivity would not obviate the theory.) Industrial profits will constitute the major source of funds for industrial expansion and such profits will constitute an increasing share of the value of industrial output, since wage rates will not rise (Fei and Ranis, 1964, p. 19). However, this source of capital accumulation will be supplemented to a substantial degree by the agricultural surplus, provided institutions and incentives exist for channeling the savings of the landlords to the industrial sector.

External trade and foreign borrowing and grant assistance play only a facilitating and secondary role, rather than a decisive one, in the process of development as formulated by Fei and Ranis (1964, pp. 290 ff.). While emphasizing the role of capital in the promotion of industrialization, Fei and Ranis stress the interdependence of agriculture and industry in the evolution of a dual economy, and, in addition, recognize the importance of technological change and the structural factors which must accompany a shift from a dual to a mature economy.

Until recently, the assumption that there is a large amount of disguised unemployment in agriculture in developing countries, in the sense that under current conditions of production the marginal product of labor in agriculture is zero, has been widely accepted and employed as a basis for a number of development theories. For example, the United Nations report entitled *Measures for the Economic Development of Underdeveloped Countries* (1951), prepared by a group of experts including W. Arthur Lewis and Theodore Schultz, cited a number of earlier studies and added (pp. 8-9) that it seems "safe to assume that for many regions of India and Pakistan, and for certain parts of the Philippines and Indonesia, the surplus (rural population) cannot be less than the pre-war average for the Eastern European region," or 20 to 25 per cent of the number of people engaged in agriculture. The same U.N. report (p. 33) also cited an estimate of surplus labor for Egypt in 1937 as equal to about one-half of the farm population. Ragner Nurkse, Harvey Leibenstein, P. N. Rosenstein-Rodan, and others have also made the assumption based on casual empirical evidence that the industrial sector could grow by drawing on cheap rural labor without any significant reduction in agricultural output (Kao, Anschel, and Eicher, 1964, pp. 129-44). However, particularly since mid-1955, this assumption has been subjected to more rigorous empirical investigation by a number of agricultural economists, including Theodore Schultz (1964), B. F. Johnston (1962), Harry Oshima (1958), John Mellor and R. D. Stephens (1956), and Morton Paglin (1965), among others.

Since the surplus-labor hypothesis has played an important role in the arguments regarding the need for external assistance for raising output in developing countries, it is important at this point to indicate some of the criticisms of this hypothesis based on empirical studies of agricultural production in India, Greece, Japan, and other countries. The criticisms relate both to the assumption of zero marginal productivity of labor and of large disguised unemployment in agriculture under present methods of production in developing countries, on the one hand, and to the possibility of absorbing substantial numbers of agricultural workers by the use of more labor-intensive techniques through a transformation of agriculture, on the other. Morton Paglin, in an analysis of the data based on the extensive 17-volume *Farm Management Studies* of Indian agriculture, finds no evidence of zero marginal productivity of labor in Indian agriculture; on the contrary, additional hired labor inputs are positively correlated with increased output combined with the same quantity of other inputs on the same quality of land. In addition, there appears to be a considerable under-utilization of land on the larger holdings.

In his *Transforming Traditional Agriculture* (1964), Schultz states:

The conclusion with respect to the doctrine that a part of the labor working in agriculture in poor countries has a marginal productivity of zero is that it is a false doctrine. It has roots that make it suspect. It rests on shaky theoretical presumptions. It fails to win any support when put to a critical test in analyzing effects on agricultural production of the deaths in the agricultural labor force caused by the influenza epidemic of 1918-19 in India (p. 70).

Schultz states further that:

There is no longer any room for doubt whether agriculture can be a powerful engine for growth. But in acquiring such an engine it is necessary to invest in agriculture, and this is not simple because so much depends on the form the investment takes. Incentives to guide and reward farmers are a critical component. Once there are investment opportunities and efficient incentives, farmers will turn sand into gold (p. 5).

Of considerable significance are the findings based on Japanese and other experience that changes in land management and agricultural techniques and incentives, together with shifts in crops, permit substantial increases in agricultural output per worker with increases in the labor-land ratio. Moreover, much of the capital required for the transformation of agriculture to more labor intensive methods involves large amounts of labor inputs such as the creation of earth dams and the digging of irrigation trenches. The same is true in India and other areas of low agricultural productivity. Thus, for example, John P. Lewis (1962) states that

. . . Lack of outside capital is not the principal impediment to rapid expansion in production. . . . India's ability to achieve the expansion in farm output it needs for the 60's may therefore be said to depend on getting millions of cultivators to do a lot of comparatively little things differently. . . . In many cases, for example, the need is for better water use *and* better seed *and* more fertilizers *and* improved cultivating practices—and therefore, also for better credit facilities and improved availability of supplies (pp. 155-56).

Empirical evidence on actual and potential labor productivity in agriculture not only casts serious doubt on the possibility of expanding employment in industry without a loss of agricultural output, but also opens to question the desirability of emphasizing investment in industry as the best means of increasing output per capita. Given the shortage of food supplies and of agricultural raw materials for domestic use in most developing countries, may not the major contribution of the agricultural sector to industry be in the form of increased output of agricultural products rather than of released unskilled labor, the supply of which is already redundant in most industrial sectors? There is a growing belief that high cost, high foreign exchange content, import-substituting industry, which can only exist with a high level of protection, constitutes a gross misallocation of capital and other resources. Yet such industrialization is often defended on grounds that it provides employment for workers crowding into the cities from the farms. The same capital, technical talent, and governmental effort that goes into much of the industrialization and the overhead capital and expenditures for public services required for the giant metropolises found in Latin America and Asia very likely could yield substantially larger returns in both output and social welfare if they were devoted to a transformation of agriculture along more labor-intensive lines and the improvement and attractiveness of rural and village life generally.

APPROACHES EMPHASIZING EXTERNAL TRADE AND FOREIGN EXCHANGE

Some development economists formulate their growth theories in terms of a closed economy, leaving to the last chapter (or few paragraphs) some sketchy and uncoordinated suggestions as to how their model might be adjusted to the real world of international trade, foreign exchange and capital movements. Others like Raul Prebisch (1959), Gunnar Myrdal (1956), and Hans Singer (1950) give primary emphasis to external factors, and in fact make foreign trade and capital imports the principal determinants (or deterrents) in the development process. Nearly all developing societies have gone through, or are still in, a stage where the modern monetary or capitalist sector has been initiated by, and derives its support from, exports of primary commodities to world markets, and frequently investment and ownership in the export sector is dominated by foreign interests. This situation has usually led to technological and social "dualism" which has been reinforced by the industrialization of the urban centers, leaving the vast rural hinterland relatively untouched socially and economically. But the alternative to dualism was not balanced development (as some critics of "colonialist" policies seem to imply) but no development out of the traditional society.

One of the legacies of development initiated by the production of primary commodities for an external market has been continued dependence on world markets for these commodities and often on foreign investment as well. Since industrialization in developing countries has largely taken the form of production for the home market, the primary-product export industries have tended to provide the foreign exchange required for imports of both consumer goods and of capital goods and raw materials for industry. Thus, in analyzing the basic factors in the growth or stagnation of Latin American economies during the postwar period, the publications of the U.N. Economic Commission for Latin America have given preponderate weight to fluctuations in import capacity as determined by a combination of the volume of exports, terms of trade, and net capital imports (U.N., 1964a, pp. 8 ff.). It is held that this dependence on the export sector and on capital imports for growth can only be reduced by import substitution, but the capacity to import capital goods also affects the rate of import substitution. However, there are limits to import substitution arising from the limitations of the domestic market and the inability to produce a growing range of intermediate goods required in the industrialization process. Import substitution will not permit a decline in total import requirements with the growth of the economy—only a reduction in the proportion of imports to total output. Thus the problem of development policy as stated by the U.N. Commission for Latin America (1964a) is summarized as follows:

In conclusion, when the rate of increase or the absolute level of a country's external purchasing power decline, the possibility of changing the structure of imports and reducing the import coefficient, and the ability to do so, set the limits to the growth of the domestic product. The determination of how, and up to what point, it will be economically expedient to reduce the import coefficient, and the adoption of basic decisions with respect to the reallocation of resources so that exports may be expanded and diversified, with due consideration of the various alternatives for optimum use of resources, constitute the cornerstone of a development policy (p. 9).

Writings by Prebisch, Singer, and others have assumed that the long-run terms-of-trade will inevitably move against the exporters of primary products and that even the gains from technical progress both in industry in the developed countries and in primary production in the developing countries, will accrue to the industrial countries in their trade with the developing countries. The reasons (Kindleberger, 1956; Morgan, 1959) for this prediction were not based on history (since most economic historians have not found evidence for long-term declining terms-of-trade) but upon the relative price and income elasticities of demand for industrial and primary goods. The solution recommended by these writers during the 1950's was for the developing nations to move out of primary production into import-substituting industry as rapidly as possible, with the help of foreign assistance.

However, there has been a change in emphasis in the writings of spokesmen for developing countries during the past few years from an almost exclusive reliance on import-substituting industrialization to expanded export earnings from primary products through world output and price controls, improved access to world markets for both primary and industrial goods, and broadening the market for the industrial products of developing countries by means of regional economic integration. In fact, many spokesmen for the developing countries see opportunities for improved foreign-exchange earnings from trade as more important than economic assistance. This was especially evident during the proceedings of the United Nations Conference on Trade and Development (1964).

The emphasis on import capacity or foreign exchange as a preponderant determinant of growth raises questions relating to trade and aid policies (or aid through trade) which will be considered in a later chapter. At this point, however, I want to consider briefly the relationship of foreign exchange to growth, and how it differs from capital, whether from internal or external sources. There is the familiar textbook question of whether countries require foreign capital because they need foreign exchange to acquire capital goods from abroad or whether foreign capital should be regarded simply as a supplement to domestic savings. In terms of aggregative analysis, real capital imports make possible an increase in domestic investment over domestic savings, or $I_d = S_d + K$, where I_d and S_d are domestic investment and savings respectively, and K is real capital imports or $M - X$, where M and X are imports and exports respectively. Considered more broadly, capital imports constitute a supplement to total resources employed by the economy for consumption, C, investment, I_d, and government services, G, which we may call absorption, A. Thus $A = C + I_d + G = Y + K$, where Y is domestic output. Therefore an increase in capital imports may not constitute a net supplement to domestic investment, but may be used in part to increase consumption and government services.

Looked at in this way, an increase in foreign-exchange earnings as a consequence of shifting resources to export industries will not, in the absence of improved terms of trade, provide additional resources for domestic investment and consumption. However it would be wrong to conclude that because a country has ample domestic savings to carry out a target investment program, it does not need capital imports. Foreign and domestic resources are only partially substitutable either for investment or for consumption, and it may not be possible to export domestic goods in order to meet the rising requirements for foreign goods as investment and income expand. Therefore, in order to expand the volume of investment, a certain amount of foreign capital may be required in order to meet the increased foreign-exchange requirements associated with both investment and consumer demand. This question will be explored further when I discuss the savings and the foreign-exchange-gap approaches to foreign aid.

There are further contributions of imports and of foreign trade generally that are often overlooked in aggregative analysis. The employment of foreign equipment embodying advanced technology and the purchase of foreign materials increases efficiency and provides a wider range of opportunities for domestic investment than that provided by the use of domestic goods and services alone. The additional foreign exchange for this purpose need not be supplied by capital imports, provided a proper portion of domestic investment is directed toward exports. A redirection of investment may require capital imports in the short run, however. Participation in international trade makes available a new production function to the economy, which raises the level of efficiency and provides access to advanced technology abroad. Economists have also emphasized the inducement effects of export markets on investments. Rather than reducing resources available for domestic use, exports expand real resources, not simply through the process described in the analysis of the gains from trade, but through the utilization of foreign technology and the investment of savings that are induced by a broadening of the market (Fei and Ranis, 1964, Ch. 8).

INVESTMENT CRITERIA AND THE ALLOCATION OF RESOURCES

Theories of investment criteria and of the allocation of resources for achieving development goals constitute the foundation for development policy and strategy. They are of major significance for foreign-aid policy-makers and administrators, both because these people are anxious to allocate available foreign assistance to countries in a manner which will maximize returns, and because they seek to influence through foreign assistance and counsel the development programs and policies of aid recipients. The literature on development theories reveals a large variety of approaches to investment criteria, and I can only sketch the principal lines of thought. It will be noted, however, that differences in approaches to the allocation of resources arise partly from differences in underlying growth models employed by the authors and partly from differences in development goals, or the stress which is given to certain goals rather than others. Thus, some approaches tend to emphasize the achievement of maximum growth rates over relatively short periods of time, while others give special emphasis to employment of surplus labor, and still others are concerned with the effect of resource allocation on the long-run improvement of the productivity of labor through education and a change in social structure. It must also be recognized that the developing countries differ with respect to the relative scarcities of different types of resources such as land and other natural resources and foreign exchange, as well as capital and labor skills.

The emphasis on capital as the strategic factor in growth which is associated with development theories based on the Harrod-Domar model is reflected in certain theories of resource allocation. One simple criterion is to give preference to those investments characterized by a low capital-output ratio or, in other words, those with a high rate of capital turnover. This approach, however, has a number of well-known weaknesses, the most obvious of which is that it neglects the factor of time and the relationship between the annual output of an investment and the life of the investment as determined by its rate of depreciation. Hence, an investment in a hydroelectric project which has an expected life of 50 years, but a low rate of annual output, may produce a total output over its lifetime equal to several times that of the same amount of investment in a factory with a much higher annual output but an expected life of only 15 years. However minimization of the ratio of capital to lifetime output would be equally erroneous since the present value of future output is a function of the time pattern of that output. Hence the present values of the outputs of the hydroelectric project and of the factory could be compared by discounting the output streams at an appropriate rate of interest. The present value of an output of $100 per annum for 15 years at 10 per cent (compound interest) is $761, while the present value of $50 per annum for 50 years at the same rate of interest is only $496. Thus, total output of the hydroelectric project over a 50-year period may be substantially higher than the total output of the factory over a 15-year period, but the present value of the future output of the factory may be substantially greater than that of the hydroelectric project.

The capital-output ratio criterion also neglects the cost of other productive factors, which are assumed to be free. Yet the employment of nearly all productive factors involves some social cost. Even though there is a large amount of unemployed labor, certain skills may be in short supply and their social-opportunity costs quite high. Even the employment of unskilled labor involves a social cost although the marginal social cost may be less than the actual wage. Finally, investment criteria must take into account the pattern of demand and the complementary nature of production. Factories and farms with low capital-output ratios require power plants, roads, and irrigation systems which may have high capital-output ratios. Nevertheless, it may be argued that for the production of any particular commodity or service, labor-intensive as opposed to capital-intensive techniques should be employed if capital is a scarce factor. On the other hand it has been argued (Hirschman, 1958, pp. 146 ff.) that capital intensive techniques embodying modern technology may have an educational value in spreading the use of more advanced technical knowledge and skills.

In sum, investment decisions present complex problems for which there are no simple rules of thumb. Yet there must be some compromise between criteria which could only be applied if we had vast amounts of knowledge about the economy which could be fed into highly sophisticated programming models, on the one hand, and simple criteria which are likely to be both inadequate and misleading, on the other.

The problem of resource allocation is usually presented to planners and foreign-aid administrators in terms of (a) judging the economic feasibility of particular investments which yield a stream of benefits, and (b) establishing priorities among a number of alternative investments producing different types of goods or services or of alternative investments involving different combinations of the factors for producing the same good or service. There are also problems of the interrelations between complementary investments, but these must be taken into account in estimating the discounted values of the benefits flowing from particular investments viewed as parts of an investment program. One approach to the problem is to determine the social marginal productivity of alternative investments in order (a) to discover if the present value of the stream of benefits is at least equal to the amount of the investment expenditure when employing an acceptable rate of discount, and (b) to determine priorities among a group of feasible investments.

Following the method employed by Hollis B. Chenery (1953, pp. 76-96), we may define social marginal product (*SMP*) as the average annual increment to the national income, ΔY, plus the national income equivalent of any foreign exchange earning or saving, from the marginal unit of investment in a given productive use. Since the exchange rate in most developing countries tends to be overvalued, the net balance of payments effect of any investment, ΔB, multiplied by the average overvaluation of the currency, r, should be added to (or subtracted from) the social product. Thus

$$SMP = \Delta Y + r\Delta B \qquad (1)$$

SMP must take into account not simply private income and costs, but total social benefits, including external economies, and social costs. Thus, if the investment makes possible the utilization of unused resources such as unemployed labor, the cost to society of employing unemployed labor is not the full amount of the wages paid, but only the increase in consumption resulting from the employment of the labor. Likewise, the value of output should be adjusted for tariffs which raise the prices of domestic output over the cost of importing the same product and for subsidies paid to producers.

Chenery (pp. 82-83) then expands equation (1) as follows:

$$SMP = \frac{X + E - M_i}{K} - \frac{L + M_d + O}{K} + \frac{Br}{K} \qquad (2)$$

$$= \frac{V}{K} - \frac{C}{K} + \frac{Br}{K} \qquad (3)$$

$$= \left(\frac{V}{K}\right)\left(\frac{V - C}{V}\right) + \frac{Br}{K} \qquad (4)$$

where all variables (except K) are annual flows:

$K =$ increment to capital (investment)

$X =$ increased market value of output (after allowance for subsidies and tariffs)

$E =$ added value of output due to external economies

$M_i =$ cost of imported materials

$V =$ social value added domestically $= X + E - M_i$

$L =$ labor cost

$M_d =$ cost of domestic materials

$O =$ overhead cost (including replacement of capital)

$C =$ total cost of domestic factors $= L + M_d + O$

$B =$ total balance of payments effect

From equation (4) it may be seen that *SMP* is the product of the rate of capital turnover (V/K) and the percentage margin of social value over cost $\left(\dfrac{V - C}{V}\right)$, plus the balance of payments premium Br/K. Thus the *SMP* of an investment with a low capital turnover (high capital-output ratio) may be offset by a high percentage margin of social value over cost, as might be the case with a hydroelectric power plant. Investments with a high positive value of Br/K, the balance of payments effect, may yield a relatively high *SMP,* even though as is the case with many resource investments, they have a low capital turnover.

Chenery (1953, p. 84) has applied his *SMP* formula to industrial projects in Greece and agricultural projects in southern Italy, estimating the three ratios in equation (4). In the case of the industrial products in Greece, Chenery's data show no correlation between *SMP* and capital turnover, since in several cases projects with high capital turnover had negative balance of payments effects. This was the case with the glass and refractory industries, while the lignite mining and nitrogenous fertilizer industries had high positive balance of payments effects and high values for *SMP.*

The variables employed in Chenery's *SMP* formula might well be included in cost-benefit calculations, so as to reflect social benefits and costs and the balance of payments effects. In fact, the *SMP* formula is essentially a cost-benefit approach to investment criteria. (The use of cost-benefit analysis in the administration of foreign aid will be discussed in Chapter 5.)

There are a number of versions of the social marginal productivity criteria for resource allocation which was originally formulated by Alfred Kahn (1951), of which Chenery's model is a modification. Galenson and Leibenstein have criticized the Kahn-Chenery theory on the basis that it maximizes a discounted stream of income over time, rather than what they believe is a better criterion, the maximization of per capita income at some time in the future. Since Galenson and Leibenstein (1955) also doubt the ability of a government to affect the savings rate through fiscal measures, they have taken the position that the rate of savings and investment, and hence the maximization of future output, depend upon the profit rate per unit of capital invested. Thus the assumption that profits are reinvested while wages are largely spent forms the basis for the "marginal reinvestment quotient" as the principal criterion to be applied in judging alternative projects. Moreover, the most profitable projects are frequently those with the highest underlying capital-labor ratio, so that in order to maximize savings and investment and rate of growth, developing countries should select the most capital-intensive rather than labor-intensive techniques. (For criticisms of this approach, see Bator, 1957, and O. Eckstein, 1957.)

Otto Eckstein (1957) has sought to reconcile the Galenson-Leibenstein marginal investment approach with the Kahn-Chenery *SMP* approach by deriving a measure of the "marginal growth contribution" of a project, which embodies two elements: (a) the present value of the consumption stream (the efficiency term) and (b) the additional production to be achieved by reinvested earnings (the growth element). The relative weight to be given to the two terms depends upon the rate of discount applied to future consumption so that, for example, with a zero rate of discount we would seek to maximize income in the long term, and with a high rate of discount we would maximize income in the short term. While the rate of discount should reflect assumptions regarding social welfare (hopefully arrived at through democratic processes), we may certainly question whether the savings ratio is wholly or mainly related to the degree of capital intensity of the technology employed and whether the rate of growth is related to the volume of reinvestment in economic activities; in fact, the long-term rate of growth may be more related to the volume of investment in education and other human investment. (For a review of investment criteria, see Chenery, 1961.)

THE PROGRAMMING APPROACH TO INVESTMENT CRITERIA

The formulation of rules for the allocation of resources based on the social marginal productivity of capital, however defined, suffers from several weaknesses. First, by concentrating on capital as the one scarce factor, this approach tends to ignore or downgrade other restrictions and scarcities, such as those arising from certain types of labor skills and of management. As we have seen, some development theorists do not regard savings and capital investment as an effective constraint on growth in most developing countries today. But even if restrictions other than capital scarcity were included in the model from which rules regarding the priority of projects could be deduced, it is necessary to assign prices to the productive factors including foreign exchange and to the goods and services that are produced. The market prices of the factors may not reflect the social costs of the inputs, and market prices of the output may understate or overstate social values. There is also the problem of the internal consistency of a development program reflecting a set of rules for resource allocation. Given the structure of consumer and governmental demand and the possibilities for exporting, output must be balanced against demand and must be consistent with available resources for producing total output. However, a consistent program which seeks to achieve maximum efficiency in the realization of certain output goals must assume a set of prices which are by no means necessarily the same as existing prices. Thus Jan Tinbergen (1958), Hollis Chenery (1955, 1961), and others have suggested the use of "shadow" or "accounting" prices in determining investment priorities. These prices can then be employed in evaluating projects by *SMP* criterion or by the "simplex" criterion used in linear programming.

The determination of "accounting" prices by the employment of a mathematical programming model involves, among other things, the solution of a set of simultaneous equations, one for each production activity included in the program. Data for the programming model must be derived from an input-output matrix modified by varying assumptions regarding the use of alternative techniques. Chenery (1961) outlines a trial method for determining "accounting" prices for labor and other inputs and for foreign exchange, using a model containing a limited number of production and import activities in place of a complete programming model involving all commodities required for final use at a given level of income. The problem is to find the optimum solution to the submodel by linear programming, assuming different "accounting" prices for the inputs and outputs. As described by Chenery (1961), "The objective is to minimize the amount of capital required to supply the given final demands, with the use of labor and other 'inputs' valued at their opportunity costs in terms of capital" (pp. 35-36). The general procedure for solving a programming model of this type involves three steps: (a) finding a feasible program or set of activity levels that satisfies the supply-demand restriction; (b) calculating the shadow prices associated with the given program;

(c) using these prices to determine whether any improvement in the initial program is possible. This procedure is repeated as long as any further improvements can be made.

Thus, given the accounting prices, the social profitability of each activity may be calculated and the profitability of alternative techniques for producing the same good may be assessed. The programming method of determining the accounting prices corrects for the over evaluation of foreign exchange and of labor and for the under evaluation of capital. Given sufficient data and an expanded programming model, various indirect effects of a given investment such as external economies and additional costs of training and housing labor can be taken into account in evaluating projects.

While knowledge of a pattern of investment which will be consistent and optimal for achieving a target growth goal is certainly of value to the economic planner, in mixed economies, private investment decisions are made on the basis of actual or expected prices, and the ability of the government to influence prices and expectations by means of subsidies and taxes is limited. Even projects in the public sector not subject to a profit constraint must be selected on the basis of what is *likely* to happen in the economy rather than what *should* happen in an optimum program. Policy makers must also be concerned with inducing investments, which, even though they may not constitute an ideal pattern are better than no investments at all. Development strategists must operate in the real world over which they have only limited control. Policy instruments are by and large concerned with establishing an environment favorable to investment decisions which will promote growth goals; they do not determine particular decisions, nor can they guarantee that all the right decisions will be made. Finally, economic programs themselves are based on inadequate data in a world of constant and unpredictable change. Thus, in allocating credit, either domestic or foreign, or in deciding on inducements for certain investments or even in drawing up programs for public investment, the method of determining investment priorities cannot be based wholly or perhaps even largely on prices and other data derived from a programming model. What would be a high-priority investment in an optimum economic program might prove to be a misallocation of resources in the economy which actually emerges (for a discussion of this problem see Vernon, 1966).

RELEVANCE FOR FOREIGN AID MODELS

The foregoing summary of growth models and theoretical and historical approaches to growth and development reveal the wide divergence among economists with respect to both the process of growth and the strategic factors in the promotion of growth. Economists concerned with development have varying aims which their analysis is designed to serve. Some are concerned with the development process as a broad social and economic phenomenon, the determinants of which are neither quantifiable nor the parameters sufficiently reliable for use in building quantitative models. In other cases, the purpose is to analyze how an economy would grow under certain highly restrictive assumptions or "stylized" conditions, concentrating on the relationships among a few variables regarded as the sole determinants of growth. In still other cases, an effort is made to analyze the growth process in a disaggregated manner, employing empirical observations for determining by means of correlations and other statistical techniques, the relationships among a limited number of variables for individual countries with varying social, political, and economic structures.

Economists and other social scientists concerned with growth and development do not confine their differences simply to preferences with respect to methodology or to differences in aims. They differ widely in their conclusions regarding matters of critical importance for foreign-aid policy. Thus we have seen marked differences in views with respect to the role of capital and savings in growth, and in particular with respect to the importance of external capital, either historically or analytically. There is considerable difference in emphasis with respect to the factors making for the transition of economies to higher stages of development. The concept of the "take-off into self-sustaining growth," which has played such an important role in foreign-aid policy, has been rejected outright by some economists as having neither historical nor analytical validity. Parameters so designed that a rapid rise in investment over a relatively short period of time assures a condition of self-sustained growth constitute an integral part of the models of some economists, while denied by others as having no relevance for the real world.

Sharp differences exist among economists with respect to the behavior of parameters such as the marginal and average savings ratios and the incremental capital-output ratio. Despite the critical importance of these parameters, model builders often assign values to them based on very weak empirical evidence, or simply on a judgment which seems reasonable. Alternatively, they may permit the parameters to vary, but they are always exogenously determined. Critics of the models on the other hand, may regard the parameters as in fact endogenous variables. For example, instead of savings constituting a constraint on investment, many economists believe that for most developing countries productive investment in the private sector determines the amount of savings. Likewise, the ICOR which together with the investment or savings coefficient determines the rate of growth in the Harrod-Domar model is regarded by some as stable for pur-

poses of the operation of their model, while others have formulated dynamic models in which the ICOR shifts over time in some predictable way
but always as a consequence of exogenous factors. Still other economists
regard the ICOR as tautological and having no value in explaining growth
or as a planning instrument. Harvey Leibenstein (1966) has provided
rather convincing evidence that "the ICOR is really a function of growth,
rather than the other way around." Thus on the basis of data on growth
rates and ICOR's for 18 countries selected at random, he finds an inverse
relation between the growth rate and the change in ICOR in 129 out of
134 observations.

As is well known, over half of the increase in output in the United
States for historical periods must be attributed to an increase in the total
productivity of the factors of production rather than to increases in inputs.
But there has been sharp disagreement over the explanation of changes in
productivity and what weight to assign to technology embodied in capital
instruments, improvements in the quality of labor, or better economic
organization and administration. This debate has its counterpart in the
analysis of the growth process in developing countries and the determination of the strategic factors in growth as a guide to policy. Do we
concentrate on expanding capital stock, on better technology, or on
improving the quality of human beings as producers, administrators, and
entrepreneurs? The approaches to investment criteria in the debate over
balanced growth vs. induced growth, together with differences among economists with respect to the usefulness of linear programming in formulating
development plans, also present a confusing array of advice to policy
makers. Finally, it may be said that economists generally have not disaggregated growth sufficiently so as to make their conclusions relating to the
promotion of *growth* applicable to the promotion of broadly based economic and social development. Development involves many dimensions
which cannot be properly aggregated in a single parameter, such as the
rate of growth in GNP. On the other hand, social scientists dealing with
social, cultural, and political aspects of development have not been able
to relate their findings in a rigorous way to critical economic parameters
such as savings and investment propensities.

Social scientists have not formulated a general theory of growth or
development applicable to all countries and stages of development; nor
are they likely to do so. We have learned something about interrelations
among a few variables under certain assumed conditions which vary
widely from country to country. And we have learned something about the
growth process without fully understanding which are the determinant
variables. It would appear, therefore, that we are in no position to formulate a general theory of foreign economic assistance for development. Yet

as we shall see in the next chapter, general theories of foreign aid have been formulated on the basis of questionable or at least highly controversial generalized growth models. Moreover, the most widely known and accepted foreign-aid theories are based upon highly simplified growth models, and these aid theories have had a predominate influence upon current foreign-aid policies.

CHAPTER THREE

The Macroeconomics of Aid: Foreign Aid Theories

THE SUBJECT MATTER which I have called the macroeconomics of foreign aid deals with the application of aggregative economic analysis to foreign aid problems. This chapter presents a critical review of theoretical models for the determination of aid requirements for achieving quantitative growth goals. The next chapter examines the capital flow and debt service implications of different patterns of resource transfers to developing countries financed by loans under varying interest and repayments terms.

In Chapter 2 we noted the wide divergence among economists regarding the nature of economic growth, the criticisms of models giving a predominant role to capital, and the skepticism regarding the validity of the concept of self-sustaining growth. Nevertheless, most formal foreign-aid theories or models are based on the acceptance of a critical role for capital in the growth process and have as their objective the achievement of sustained economic growth by the recipient at some target rate of increase in output per capita. In support of this objective, aid theories provide an analytical framework for determining the amount and timing of the aid and the policies which must be followed by the recipient country for achieving a given target rate of growth which can be sustained without further external assistance. There are, however, other economic objectives of aid, such as that of maintaining minimum consumption levels in countries which because of military or political disturbances are not regarded as viable or capable of achieving the conventional development goal in terms of a sustained rate of growth in output. U.S. aid to such countries as Korea and Vietnam has been made available for these objectives in the past, but usually with the idea that it will be possible for the country to launch a development program with a specific growth target at some time in the future. Aid is also provided to countries that are making reasonably satisfactory economic progress but nevertheless have relatively low per capita incomes, simply as a means of supplementing their internal capital resources—without any specific development framework or target in mind.

Thus, the World Bank makes loans to such countries as Austria, Italy, and Japan, countries which are regarded in the developed category, without preconceived notions regarding the target rates of growth or of fitting assistance into a development program. Much the same is true in the case of loans to a number of developing countries, such as Mexico and Venezuela, which are regarded as having passed the threshold of "self-sustaining growth." With certain exceptions, aid provided to these countries takes the form of hard loans from such sources as the World Bank, Export-Import Bank, and the Ordinary Capital Resources window of the Inter-American Development Bank. On the other hand, aid on concessionary or soft-loan terms (frequently in combination with hard loans) is provided mainly to countries not regarded as having achieved self-sustained growth.

The underlying assumptions of aid theories based on the achievement of self-sustaining growth are (a) some minimum rate of growth is both the goal and the natural condition for a country in the modern world and (b) all aid programs must be self-terminating. The first is based on the recent history of the Western developed countries, while the second proposition stems from an aversion to external charity for an indefinite period of time or in perpetuity. Both propositions may be unrealistic and we may very well get used to the idea that foreign assistance is here to stay, although the countries being assisted may shift from time to time. At the time of the Bretton Woods Conference in 1944, it was unthinkable that the United States should ever draw on the resources of the International Monetary Fund, but U.S. cumulative drawings during 1963-66 were $1.6 billion.

During the discussion which follows I shall examine foreign-aid theories largely in terms of the goal of self-sustaining growth to be achieved by a finite amount of aid. However, the applicability of these theories depends on the realization of certain conditions, the absence of which may preclude the achievement of the self-generating goal. The question will then arise as to whether aid should be made available to countries where the realization of this goal is not possible. I shall also discuss the capital-absorption approach, which is not based on the self-generating growth thesis.

THREE BASIC APPROACHES TO FOREIGN AID REQUIREMENTS

There are three basic approaches to foreign-aid requirements for developing countries, either singly or in combination: (1) the savings-investment gap approach; (2) the foreign-exchange earnings-expenditure gap approach; and (3) the capital-absorption approach.

THE SAVINGS-INVESTMENT GAP APPROACH

In its simplest formulation, the savings-investment gap approach employs a variation of the Harrod-Domar model and assumes that the marginal savings ratio is significantly above the average savings ratio (Rosenstein-Rodan, 1961a). For any target rate of growth, r, required foreign aid in the initial year (F_o) is

$$F_o = I_o - S_o = Y_okr - Y_os_a = Y_o (kr - s_a)$$

where I_o and S_o are investment and savings respectively, Y_o is GNP in the initial year, k, the incremental capital-output ratio, and s_a, the average savings ratio in the initial year.
In year t,

$$I_t - S_t = Y_okr (1 + r)^t - S_o - s'Y_o (1 + r)^t + s'Y_o$$

If $t = 1$, in the second year required aid (F_1) is as follows:

$$F_1 = I_1 - S_1 = Y_okr (1 + r) - Y_os_a - Y_os'r = F_o + Y_or (kr - s')$$

where s is the marginal savings ratio at the initial year. If foreign aid is to decline so that $F_1 < F_o$, s' must be greater than kr, or the marginal savings ratio must be higher than the product of the ICOR and the target rate of growth.

For subsequent periods the formula becomes more complex.[1] A numerical example of the operation of the model over a number of years is given in Table 1. In Table 1, a country with an initial GNP of 1,000 and an initial average savings rate of .10 and a marginal savings rate of .20 grows at a rate of .05 and the incremental capital-output ratio is 3. The initial savings of 100 must be supplemented by capital imports of 50 (import surplus), in order to have an investment of 150. In the second year, GNP has grown to 1050 and savings to 110, but in order to achieve a further 5 per cent increase in GNP (assuming a one-year lag between investment and income), investment must be 158 and capital imports (the difference between investment and savings) fall to 48. By the fourteenth

---

1. The required amount of foreign aid for n years, $F_n = I_n - S_n$, is as follows:
$I_n = krY_o (1 + r)^n$
$S_n = s_a Y_o + s'rY_o (1 + r) \ldots s'rY_o (1 + r)^{n-1} = Y_o [s_a + s' (1 + r)^n - 1)]$
$F_o = Y_o [(kr - s') (1 + r)^n - (s_a - s')]$
For derivation see D. Avramovic and Associates, *Economic Growth and External Debt* (Baltimore: Johns Hopkins Press, 1964), pp. 188-89.

year, savings have risen to approximately 15 per cent of GNP so that thereafter no further external capital inflow is required to sustain the 5 per cent growth rate, and in addition there is a surplus available for debt service. (I shall consider the debt service problem in Chapter 4.)

THE FOREIGN-EXCHANGE EARNINGS-EXPENDITURES GAP APPROACH

The foreign-exchange earnings-expenditure gap approach to capital import requirements focuses on import capacity as the principal constraint on domestic investment and growth. In some models the rate of growth in exports is assumed to be higher than the rate of growth in import requirements so that net capital imports needed to fill the foreign-exchange gap gradually decline. Thus during the initial year foreign aid (F_o) required to cover the foreign exchange gap is

$$F_o = M_o - E_o = Y_o u - Y_o e = Y_o (u - e)$$

where M_o and E_o are imports and exports respectively during the initial year, and u and e are the average import and export ratios respectively, in the initial year. In the second year,

$$F_1 = M_1 - E_1 = Y_o (u - e) + Y_o ru' - Y_o re' = F_o + Y_o r(u' - e')$$

where u' and e' are the marginal import ratio and the marginal export ratio respectively, and r is the target rate of growth. Thus for aid to decline in the second year or $F_1 < F_o$, e' must be greater than u'.

Estimates of the aggregate foreigne-xchange earnings-expenditure gap for developing countries are derived from projection of exports in relation to foreign exchange requirements, based on relationships existing in an earlier period and adjusted for assumed changes in rates of growth. Some approaches provide alternative solutions to the foreign-exchange gap: capital imports, increased export opportunities, or import substitution. However, these solutions are obviously not identical in their economic impact. More comprehensive models combine the foreign exchange constraint with the savings-investment constraint.

In a formal sense, the savings-investment gap and the foreign-exchange gap approaches to the determination of capital import requirements for achieving a target rate of growth are identical.[2]

2. Bela Balassa argues that "under proper definitions" the trade gap and the capital requirements approaches "are complementary rather than competitive and, under proper definitions, they give identical results" ("The Capital Needs of the Developing Countries," *Kyklos,* 18(2) [1964], pp. 197-206).

TABLE 1

ILLUSTRATION OF EXTERNAL CAPITAL REQUIREMENTS: SAVINGS-INVESTMENT GAP
(See text for assumptions)

Year	GNP	Investment	Savings	Net Resource* Inflow (-Outflow)	Interest	Amortization	Gross Borrowing	Net Borrowing (-Prepayment)	Net Debt
0	1000	150	100	50	......	......	50	50	50
1	1050	158	110	48	2.5	2.5	52.5	50.5	100.5
2	1103	165	121	44	5.0	5.0	54	49	149.5
3	1158	174	132	42	7.5	7.5	57	49.5	197
4	1216	182	143	39	9.8	9.8	59	49	246
5	1277	192	155	37	12	12	61	49	295
6	1341	201	168	33	15	15	63	48	343
7	1408	211	182	31	17	17	65	48	391
8	1478	222	196	26	20	20	66	46	437
9	1552	233	210	23	22	22	67	45	482
10	1630	245	226	19	24	24	67	43	525
11	1712	257	242	15	26	26	67	41	566
12	1798	270	260	10	28	28	66	38	604
13	1888	283	278	5	30	30	65	35	639

14	1982	297	296	1				
15	2081	312	316	−4	32	32	65	33	
16	2185	328	337	−9	34	34	64	30	672
17	2294	344	359	−15	35	35	61	26	702
18	2409	361	381	−20	36	36	57	21	728
19	2529	379	406	−27	37	37	54	17	749
20	2655	398	431	−33	38	38	49	11	766
21	2788	418	458	−40	39	39	45	6	777
22	2927	439	485	−46	39	39	38	−1	783
23	3073	461	515	−54	39	39	32	−7	782
24	3227	484	545	−61	38	38	22	−16	775
25	3388	508	578	−70	38	38	15	−23	759
26	3557	534	611	−77	37	37	4	−32	736
27	3735	560	647	−87	34	34	−9	−43	704
28	3922	588	684	−96	33	33	−21	−54	661
29	4118	618	724	−106	30	30	−36	−66	607
30	4324	649	765	−116	27	27	−52	−79	541
31	4540	681	808	−127	23	23	−70	−93	462
32	4767	715	853	−138	18	18	−91	−109	369
33	5005	751	901	−150	13	13	−112	−125	260
34	5255	788	951	−163	7	7	−136	−143	135

* Net resource inflow is trade deficit, net resource outflow is trade surplus.

$$F = E - Y = I - S = M - X$$

where F is net capital imports, E is aggregate domestic expenditure, Y is national output, I is domestic investment, S is domestic savings, M is imports, and X is exports. Thus, net capital imports, or foreign aid, is equal to both the gap between imports and exports, and to that between domestic investment expenditures and domestic savings. However, the formal relationships expressed above are *ex post,* while in quantitative growth models, estimations of both the savings-investment and the foreign-exchange earnings-expenditure gaps are by their very nature *ex ante,* and there is no reason why the two *ex ante* gaps calculated on different bases should be the same. The foreign-exchange gap is calculated by partial equilibrium methods that are inconsistent with the savings-gap calculation. The justification for the concept of the two gaps rests on the lack of substitutibility of domestic and international resources, but in terms of aggregative analysis there can be but one gap. As will be discussed later on, a question is raised when the estimated amount of foreign aid required for achieving a given growth target is the larger of the two estimated gaps. Does filling the larger gap, which is frequently the foreign-exchange gap, constitute a misallocation of resources?

THE CAPITAL-ABSORPTIVE CAPACITY APPROACH

The capacity to absorb capital imports has been variously defined. Capital-absorptive capacity has been employed as a special constraint attached to the savings-investment gap approach or in combination with both the savings and the foreign-exchange constraints, or as a uniquely identified approach to capital requirements. It has a special appeal for economists and foreign-aid administrators who are not in sympathy with either the savings-investment gap or the foreign-exchange gap approaches to the determination of external capital requirements, and who prefer to view foreign aid in terms of specific capital projects or of measures designed to deal with specific limitations on economic growth. The capital-absorptive capacity approach regards capital requirements as being determined by the ability of an economy to employ both domestic and foreign capital productively in the sense that aid yields some minimum rate of return. One variant of this approach regards foreign capital as a means of overcoming internal obstacles to growth and as a catalyst for mobilizing domestic resources for increasing output and productivity. This approach tends to eschew models relating growth to the total volume of capital, and looks at savings and investment both as integral parts of the production process and not as independent variables.

SOME ESTIMATES OF AGGREGATE AID REQUIREMENTS FOR DEVELOPING COUNTRIES

THE U.N. EXPERTS REPORT OF 1951

One of the first post-World War II attempts to estimate external capital requirements of developing countries was made by a group of experts in a Report to the Secretary General of the United Nations. In this Report, issued in 1951, estimates of total capital requirements for all developing countries were made for the period 1950-1960; external capital requirements were the difference between total capital requirements and domestic savings. The total capital requirements of underdeveloped countries were estimated under two broad headings: (1) the volume of capital needed for industrialization assuming an annual transfer of 1 per cent of the total working population out of agriculture into nonagricultural employment; and (2) capital required for agricultural development. The amount of capital required for each person absorbed into nonagricultural employment, including outlays on research and training, was estimated at $2500. Under the second heading it was assumed that underdeveloped countries should spend annually an amount equal to 1 per cent of their national incomes on agricultural extension services and research, plus an additional 3 per cent per annum on agricultural investments. In this way total capital requirements for industrialization and agricultural development were estimated at $19 billion; this level of investment was expected to support an annual rate of growth in per capita national income of 2 per cent over the 1950-60 period. Of the total $19 billion required, some $5 billion could be covered by domestic savings, leaving about $14 billion as the requirement to be covered by foreign capital (UN, 1951, pp. 75-79).

It is interesting to note the degree to which this approach reflected the theoretical views of W. Arthur Lewis, since $15.3 billion, or 80 per cent of total capital requirements, was to be used for moving "surplus" agricultural labor into industry. The amount of capital needed for agriculture was estimated at less than $3.9 billion.[3] The relationship to the surplus agricultural labor thesis described in Chapter 2 is indicated in the following quotation from the group's Report:

We have assumed an annual shift of 1 per cent of the total working population into industry. This should originate national income to the extent

3. Theodore W. Schultz of the Department of Economics, University of Chicago, was also a member of the group. At that time Professor Schultz was a protagonist of the surplus agricultural labor thesis, but, as discussed earlier, he has since changed his position.

of about 2 per cent, after allowing for capital charges. In countries which
have surplus labor in agriculture this would be equivalent to an annual net
increase in the national income of 2 per cent. But, in other countries, the
net increase is equal only to the difference between the productivity of labor
in industry and the productivity of labor in agriculture from which it has
been withdrawn. We may assume that, over the underdeveloped world as a
whole, the shift might increase the national income by 1½ per cent per
annum (pp. 77-78).

THE MILLIKAN-ROSTOW APPROACH

A pioneering effort to estimate foreign aid requirements by means of
a combination of capital-absorptive capacity and the savings-investment
gap approaches is that by Max Millikan and W. W. Rostow in their *A
Proposal: Key to Effective Foreign Policy* (Millikan and Rostow, 1957,
Chs. V-VI; Center for International Studies, MIT, 1957, pp. 1-73). Millikan and Rostow view aid as a means of assisting countries to achieve a
condition of self-sustained economic growth. However, countries that are
in an early stage of development are likely to have a relatively low capital-absorptive capacity. Nevertheless, owing to their limited domestic resources, virtually all the additional capital needed to launch the growth
process must come from external sources. Depending upon such factors
as the existence of skilled labor, competent administrators, markets, basic
transportation, communication, and power facilities, additional foreign
capital requirements for these countries are estimated at 30 to 50 per cent
of their 1953 levels of gross capital formulation. Assuming a marginal-
savings ratio higher than the average, such additional external capital will
enable a country to mobilize sufficient savings out of the increases of its
income "to keep pace with a growing capacity to use capital." For
countries which have advanced beyond the early stages of development,
foreign capital requirements for achieving a target rate of increase in annual per capita income of 2 per cent would represent a much lower percentage of their 1953 capital formation. For example, the upper limit of
proposed annual per capita inflow for Latin America is given as 14 per
cent of the 1953 gross capital formation.

Assuming an incremental capital-output ratio of 3.5, which they believe to be conservative, Millikan and Rostow estimate that less-developed
countries would require $3.5 billion of external capital each year in order
to achieve per capita growth rates of 1 to 2 per cent. However, they believe that perhaps no more than 50 per cent of this amount could be
utilized effectively, at least for several years, on the basis of their estimates

of the capital-absorptive capacity at the time of writing (Millikan and Rostow, 1957, p. 155).

THE ROSENSTEIN-RODAN ESTIMATES

Perhaps the most ambitious attempt to estimate foreign aid requirements in developing countries is that of P. N. Rosenstein-Rodan, who also employs a combination of the absorptive capacity and the savings-investment gap approaches. Rosenstein-Rodan (1961b, pp. 108-109) determines absorptive capacity for virtually all developing countries in the Free World on the basis of three factors: (1) how much a country has succeeded in increasing its volume of investment during the past five or more years; (2) the degree to which the country has succeeded in maintaining or widening the difference between average and marginal rates of savings over the recent past; and (3) a judgment on the efficiency of the country's overall administrative and development organization. The estimated capital-absorptive capacity for each country is then reflected in the target rate of growth for each country. Rosenstein-Rodan calculates the capital inflow requirements for achieving the target growth rate for each country on the basis of its average and marginal savings rates, the initial GNP, and the estimated capital-output ratio (assumed in most cases to be 2.8 to 1). A summary of his estimates of annual foreign capital requirements for the underdeveloped countries is as follows (1961a, p. 137):

Period of Projection	Annual Foreign Capital Required (billions of dollars)	
	Est. I *	Est. II *
1961-66	5.7	5.5
1966-71	5.7	6.2
1971-76	3.8	4.8

* Estimate I is based on assumptions contained in India's Third Five-Year Plan. Estimate II is based on Rosenstein-Rodan's alternative assumptions for India.

By capital requirements Rosenstein-Rodan means "development capital" as distinguished from total capital flows. His definition of development capital is a special one which excludes three-fourths of U.S. "defense support," one-third of surplus agricultural products sold by the U.S. government under PL 480, and one-half of private investment in petroleum and minerals. Development capital requirements, as noted in the table above, decline in the third period 1971-76 as increased savings in the developing countries provide a larger share of the capital requirements for growth. Rosenstein-Rodan employs a savings-investment gap model for

determining capital requirements similar to that which I have discussed
in the preceding section of this chapter.[4]

THE U.N. SECRETARIAT AGGREGATE FOREIGN-EXCHANGE GAP ESTIMATES

In 1963 the United Nations Secretariat made a hypothetical projection
of the current account gap of the developing countries with the rest of the
world for 1970, assuming a 5 per cent rate of growth in aggregate gross
domestic product for the period 1960-70 for the developing countries. The
hypothetical level of imports was calculated on the basis of the relationships prevailing in the period 1950-60 between imports and GDP of the
developing countries; their commodity exports to the rest of the world
were calculated on the basis of the relationships prevailing in the 1950-60
period between imports by the developed countries from the developing
countries and the GDP of the developed countries, and assuming the same
rate of growth in GDP for the developed countries (3.7 per cent per
annum) as in the 1950-60 period (UN, 1964b, pp. 30-33). After adjusting the hypothetical trade gap for the payments on investment service and
other services (net), the calculated current-account gap is $20 billion. Net
capital imports are assumed to rise from $5 billion in 1960 to $9 billion
in 1970, based on trends during the period 1950-60. This gives a hypothetical gap for the developing countries on current and capital account
of $11 billion for 1970 (UN, 1964b, p. 30). This $11 billion hypothetical gap could, according to the U.N. report, be closed by a combination of
increased exports, increased import substitution, measures to improve the
net balance of service transactions, and increased capital imports.

Employing different methods of investigation, Bela Balassa arrived at
substantially lower estimates of the aggregate current account deficits of
the developing countries for 1970. Under his "most likely assumption"
with respect to world growth rates, Balassa (1964, pp. 104-105) estimates
a current account deficit for the developing countries of $9.4 billion for
1970; if target rates of growth for the world economy were to be achieved,
the 1970 deficit would be $10.5 billion; while if developing countries grow
at target rates and industrial countries at likely rates, the deficit is estimated to be $12 billion in 1970. Thus, his highest estimated deficit for

---

4. Rosenstein-Rodan's formula for determining required foreign capital inflow,
F, for a five-year period is:

$$F = (kr - b)\ \Sigma\ Y + 5Y_o\ (b - \frac{S}{Y_o})$$

where k is the capital-output ratio, r is rate of growth (assumed according to
estimated absorptive capacity), Y_o is GNP in the initial year, b is the marginal
savings rate, and S_o is savings in the initial year (1961a, p. 117).

1970, $12 billion, is $8 billion less than the current account deficit projected by the U.N. Secretariat for that year.

No special significance can be attached to differences among the absolute values of external capital requirements reflected in the studies I have just been discussing. The estimates were prepared at different times and for different time periods, and the country coverage is not the same for the different studies, nor is the definition of what constitutes foreign aid or capital inflow. The problem of defining and estimating foreign aid for promoting economic development will be discussed in a later chapter.

THE WORLD BANK ESTIMATE

Estimates of external financing requirements of developing countries on the basis of their capital-absorptive capacity are extremely difficult to make, both because of a certain vagueness in the concept itself and because of the absence of information needed for such estimates. Nevertheless, George D. Woods, President of the World Bank, did provide such an estimate in the course of an address to the Ministerial Meeting of the Development Assistant Committee (DAC) of the OECD on July 22, 1965.[5] According to Woods, a preliminary survey for each developing country, on the basis of judgments of the Bank's country specialists, "suggests that between now and 1970 the less-developed countries might productively use an additional 3 to 4 billion dollars a year" (p. 5). Since this was in addition to the approximately 10 billion dollars in annual net flow of public and private financial resources from DAC countries to developing countries, the total amount which the less-developed countries might "productively use" is of the order of the magnitude of 13 to 14 billion dollars per year. In establishing this figure, the Bank's staff reviewed the public investment programs of the developing countries and estimated the aggregate cost of aid projects and programs which in their judgment meet certain standards of technical and economic feasibility. In estimating the capital requirements for the private sector, the staff had to rely upon what they knew about projected investments in major industries and informed guesses as to the residual on the basis of past experience. They recognized, however, that expectations and intentions of private investors might be based on an overestimate of absorptive capacity. Once the total volume of public- and

5. The methodology and underlying data from which Woods' estimate was derived had not been made public by the Bank at the time of writing. The above discussion is based on conversations by the author with members of the World Bank staff. Woods' address was published by the World Bank in a pamphlet entitled *Statement of George D. Woods to the Ministerial Meeting, Development Assistance Committee, Organization for Economic Cooperation and Development* (Paris, July 22, 1965).

private-sector potential investment was determined, it was necessary to assess the resources available in the developing countries for implementing the investments. A combination of both the investment-savings gap and the import requirements-foreign exchange gap was employed to determine the *resource* gap in arriving at the figure of 3 to 4 billion dollars per year which could be productively employed by the developing countries.

Woods claims no precision for this estimate since he recognizes that capital-absorptive capacity can only be determined through actual experience. Moreover, the amount and nature of assistance, including technical assistance, may itself influence absorptive capacity. The purpose of the estimate was in considerable measure to dramatize Woods' "deep convictions that the present level of financing is wholly inadequate, whether measured by the growth rate which the advanced countries say they are willing to facilitate or in terms of the amount of external capital which the developing countries have demonstrated they can use effectively" (p. 5). Thus we have reflected in this statement two criteria for the determination of aid requirements; what developing countries can use effectively and what is needed to facilitate a target rate of growth.

COMPREHENSIVE FOREIGN AID THEORIES

THE CHENERY-STROUT MODEL

Several studies have appeared which set forth more elegant theories of foreign aid combining the three basic approaches—the savings-investment gap, the foreign-exchange gap, and capital-absorptive capacity. Perhaps the most comprehensive of these theories is that of Hollis B. Chenery and Alan M. Strout (1965, 1966) "Foreign Assistance and Economic Development." [6] I shall summarize portions of this document and refer to other studies employing similar models in the course of my analysis.

As in virtually all external assistance models, the objective of foreign aid as set forth by Chenery and Strout is to help a country achieve self-sustaining growth. The transition process is Rostowian in the sense that the preconditions must be established before the "take-off." However Chenery and Strout regard foreign assistance as being able not only to accelerate the rate of investment during the "take-off," but also to supply or to facilitate the creation of the basic requisites for the transition to self-

6. "Foreign Assistance and Economic Development" was originally prepared as an AID Discussion Paper. Since this chapter was written, a revised version of the Chenery and Stout paper was published under the same title in *The American Economic Review* (September, 1966), pp. 679-733. There are no essential differences in the model or in the assumptions in the two versions. However, for purposes of interpreting the authors' positions, I have employed both versions.

sustained growth, such as skills, the adoption of modern technology, a change in the composition of output and employment, the development of new institutions, etc. The authors analyze the transitional process in terms of three phases, each associated with a single limiting factor. The limiting factors are designated as (1) the skill limitation, (2) the savings limitation, and (3) the trade (or foreign exchange) limitation. Foreign assistance which can augment domestic resources for overcoming these limitations is divided into three categories: (1) the supply of skills and organizational ability; (2) the supply of investable resources; and (3) the supply of imported commodities and services (Chenery and Strout, 1966, p. 681).

The "skill limit" reflects "the skill formation required of managers, skilled labor and civil servants in order to increase productive investment" (p. 686). The authors state that their definition of the skill limit is closely related to the notion of absorptive capacity, but the method of measurement suggests a rather special concept of capital-absorptive capacity. The authors' measurement of absorptive capacity, or at least its upper limit, is given by the highest rate of increase in investment which a country has been able to achieve over a recent five-year period. During Phase I of their description of the development process, the skill limit does not permit a level of investment high enough for output to grow at the target rate. However, if investment can be increased at a rate which is higher than the target rate of growth, the rate of investment will eventually reach the level (kr) required to sustain the target rate of growth in GNP. Foreign aid during Phase I fills the gap between the increment in investment and increment in savings, until the rate of investment is high enough to sustain the target rate of growth. Thus if investment grows at the maximum rate, i, the amount of investment in any given year t, is $I_t = I_o + ki \, (Y_t - Y_o)$, where k is the incremental capital-output ratio. The required amount of aid in year t is

$$F_t = I_t - S_t = F_o + (ki - s')(Y_t - Y_o)$$

where $F_o = I_o - S_o$ in the initial year. In this equation the increment of investment in each period is a constant ratio (ki) to the increment of domestic output. Thus the increment of external capital $(F_t - F_o)$ finances the difference between the increment of investment and the increment of savings.

The authors (1966, p. 725) suggest that on the basis of their statistical studies, a rate of growth in investment of 10 to 12 per cent is a reasonable target for countries in Phase I where the initial investment level is below the required level for the target rate of growth. They state that Phase I should be completed by most countries within a decade if this rate of increase in investment (10 to 12 per cent) can be maintained with sufficient improvement in skills and organization to make effective use of the additional capital that becomes available. In the transition from Phase I to Phase II, the rate of increase in investment, once the level has been raised to a point where it can sustain the target rate of growth, can be permitted to decline toward the feasible target growth rate, say 6 to 7 per cent.

The principal function of foreign assistance during Phase I is to finance the difference between the increment in investment (up to the level permitted by the skill limit) and the increment in savings. Statistical studies of 31 countries by the authors show that the median value of the marginal savings'ratios is such that typically the increment of savings is well below the increment of investment permitted by the skill limit during Phase I. Thus, foreign capital fills the gap between savings and investment in both Phase I and Phase II, except that in Phase II the level of investment (as opposed to the rate of increase) has been raised to the point where it can sustain the target rate of growth in GNP (Chenery and Strout, 1966, p. 684, Table 1, and p. 687). The target rate of growth reflects the principle goal of development in developing countries. A realistic target must take into account the long-run capacity of the country to expand and to increase its rate of savings and its rate of export growth; the target must also reflect limitations on the availability of foreign assistance and the terms on external loans. The authors (p. 705) propose an investment criterion for Phase I to the effect that "the rate of growth of investment must be greater than the target rate of growth." Unless this criterion is met, Phase I could never be completed because the level of investment would never reach the point where it could sustain the target rate of growth.

Once the target rate of growth and corresponding level of investment are attained, foreign assistance is required to overcome the savings limit (Phase II) and the foreign exchange or trade limitation (which is characterized as Phase III [pp. 688-89]). Phase II normally begins at the end of Phase I, when investment reaches the level required to sustain the target growth rate, and ends when either (a) savings are equal to investment and the net flow of capital is reduced to zero or (b) when the trade limit becomes more restrictive (Phase III). Phase II is characterized by essentially the same kind of savings limitation which fits the conditions of the modified Harrod-Domar model for the achievement of a self-sustained target growth rate, discussed in my section on the investment-savings gap. External resource requirements will be determined in accordance with the familiar savings-limited sustained growth model (with net capital requirements eventually falling to zero) unless (a) the skill limit becomes more restrictive or (b) external assistance is not sufficient to cover minimum import requirements. But the appearance (or reappearance) of the skill limitation is simply another way of recognizing limited absorptive capacity. Phase II might conceivably come to a halt rather quickly because of the absence of opportunities for productive investment or failure of government to adopt appropriate policies and planning measures, including project formulation. It might also be brought to a halt by a decline in the marginal savings ratio. The basic performance criterion for Phase II (in terms of progress toward self-sustained growth at the target rate) is that the marginal savings rate must be greater than the target investment rate unless the average rate of saving is already above this level (p. 705).

I will now turn briefly to Phase III, which is defined as the condition in which foreign assistance needed to meet minimum import requirements exceeds the amount needed during a particular year under the operation of the Phase II condition. The trade limit is mainly a consequence of limited flexibility of the productive structure for expanding output for exports or for import substitution. Although avoidance of the trade limit is regarded as more amenable to policy measures (such as the elimination of over-valued exchange rates) than is the savings limit, the experience of developing countries suggests that in practice the trade gap is often "structural" in the sense that it can only be reduced over time without reducing the rate of growth, by a redirection of investment. The model for the determination of the amount of foreign capital required to fill the balance of payments gap employs the marginal import ratio, u', which is the average of the incremental ratios for different components of demand, and the rate of export growth, e. Assuming Phase III starts in the year j, GNP in year t is:

$$Y_t = Y_j (1 + r)^{t-j}$$

The volume of imports, M_t, required to sustain GNP in the year t is:

$$M_t = M_j + u' (Y_t - Y_j)$$

The rate of growth in exports, e, determines foreign exchange earnings as follows:

$$E_t = E_j (1 + e)^{t-j}$$

where E_t and E_j are exports of goods and services at years t and j respectively. Both u' and e are regarded as policy variables, with u' being determined in part by government measures affecting import substitution and e by measures affecting exports. The need for foreign assistance, F, to overcome the trade limit in year t is given by

$$F_t = M_t - E_t$$
$$= M_j + u' \, (Y_t - Y_j) - E_j \, (1 + e)^{\,t-j}$$

For the trade gap to be eliminated, either the export growth rate, e, must exceed the target growth rate, r, or the marginal import ratio, u', must be substantially below the initial average import ratio (Chenery and Strout, 1965, pp. 19-20 and p. 27). This condition establishes the trade criterion for progress toward a given rate of self-sustaining growth.

It may be noted that in Phase III potential savings are in excess of investment needs, and required savings, S_t, are equal to the difference betweeen investment I_t and F_t or

$$S_t = I_t - F_t = krY_t - F_t$$

In their analysis of empirical data pertaining to developing countries, the authors found that the rate of growth of exports plays a predominant role both in the case of the countries avoiding the trade gap limitation and in those that have not. Out of the 12 countries in their sample that satisfy the criteria for approaching or maintaining self-sufficiency, ten have an export growth rate of 6 per cent or more, while the most unsuccessful performers in their sample tend to be characterized by export stagnation. The authors (1966, p. 710) also point out that, "There is almost no example of a country which has for a long period sustained a growth rate substantially higher than its growth of exports through continuing import substitution." These findings would seem to support the contention that import substitution even for more industrially advanced countries such as Argentina and Brazil (both of which, according to Chenery and Strout, are meeting the savings criterion for eventual self-sustaining growth, but not the trade criterion) does not provide a means of avoiding an expansion of exports to a rate approximating the target growth rate. The authors also found no correlation between initial per capita income levels among developing countries and either marginal savings rates or balance of payments performance. Thus, performance in terms of the authors' savings and trade criteria for progress toward self-sustaining growth is not necessarily associated with a relatively high initial income level.

Before discussing the foreign assistance policy implications of the Chenery-Strout model, I want to examine briefly two other foreign assistance models which are in many respects similar to the Chenery-Strout model.

THE FEI AND PAAUW MODEL

I shall first deal with the foreign assistance model formulated by John C. H. Fei and Douglas Paauw (1965). Fei and Paauw are concerned with the implications of "self-help" in foreign assistance policy as they affect (a) the relationship between foreign aid and domestic austerity efforts; (b) the conditions for a reasonable termination date for the assistance program; and (c) the prospect that foreign aid will achieve its primary objectives in terms of an adequate rate of growth of per capita income. Their concept (1965, p. 251) of "self-help" is quite narrowly defined in terms of domestic austerity efforts or "the mobilization of domestic savings, which we take to be the essence of the self-help problem." Therefore they are concerned almost wholly with the savings limitation to the achievement of a reasonable rate of self-sustained growth.

Fei and Paauw believe that the relevant savings function is that which "postulates incremental per capita savings as a constant fraction, u, of increments in per capita income" which they refer to as the per capita marginal savings ratio (PMSR). In their open-economy model, they identify three categories of countries from the standpoint of the conditions favorable (or unfavorable) to the achievement of per capita growth rate objectives. The favorable case (1) is given by the condition

$$(1) \qquad h + r < \frac{s(O)}{k} = \eta_0$$

where h is the target rate of growth in per capita GNP, r is the rate of population growth, $s(O)$ is the initial *average* propensity to save, k is the capital-output ratio, and η_0 is the initial rate of growth of capital and GNP. For this case, no foreign aid is required, and in fact the country will export capital from the outset.

The intermediate case (2) is given by the condition

$$(2) \qquad \eta_0 < h + r < \frac{u}{k} = \eta_u$$

where u is the per capita marginal savings ratio (PMSR), and η_u is the long-run rate of growth of capital and GNP.

The unfavorable case (3) is given by the condition

$$(3) \qquad \eta_u < h + r$$

In the intermediate case (2) foreign assistance will be required, but aid will have a finite termination date. In this case, the per capita marginal savings ratio divided by the capital-output ratio (which defines the long-run growth rate of both GNP and capital) is greater than the target per capita growth rate, h, plus the rate of population growth, r. However, in the unfavorable case (3) where $h + r$ is greater than the long-run growth rate of GNP as determined by the per capita marginal savings ratio, u, and the incremental capital-output ratio, k, foreign aid will be required indefinitely with the aid-income ratio eventually approaching a constant value so that the absolute volume of foreign aid will grow at a constant rate equal to the rate of growth of GNP, $h + r$ (Fei and Paauw, 1965, p. 256).

The authors proceed to examine the conditions determining the aid termination date is governed by the growth target,[7] the rate of population growth and the other parameters in the intermediate case (2). Although in the normal case the aid termination date will vary directly with both the growth target and the population growth rate, in cases where population pressure is very heavy so that the rate of population growth exceeds the initial growth rate of capital, increases in the target growth rate will lower the termination date within a limited range. In fact only a large volume of assistance "enabling the country to maintain a rate of growth of per capita GNP high enough to mobilize savings through the effect of the PMSR" will enable the country to escape the trap of a falling per capita GNP (Fei and Paauw, p. 260). This means that "the target must be sufficiently high so that per capita GNP increases will yield adequate savings to minimize the termination date."

From the standpoint of foreign-aid policy, the intermediate case (2) is regarded by the authors as "gap-filling" in the sense that foreign aid complements the country's own self-help efforts, the success of which is indicated by the achievement of a critical level of PSMR. In this case "close administration of the assistance program is not needed to insure an adequate self-help response" (p. 261). The unfavorable case (3) is regarded as "gap-narrowing" but without greater self-help efforts (austerity measures) to raise PMSR, constant rate of growth with a terminal date for foreign aid cannot be achieved. In this case, foreign assistance must produce leverage effects on the growth of domestic savings capacity and technical assistance may be required for such measures.

The authors also distinguish between "glide path" and the "hump-scaling cases for external assistance. Under the former, required foreign assistance declines continuously, while in the latter case required assistance will increase for a number of years before reaching a peak from which it

7. The target rate of growth of per capita GNP reflects not only what is desired but what is regarded as feasible on the basis of past performance.

begins to decline. In the glide-path case, the growth of domestic savings operates continually to reduce foreign aid requirements; in the hump-scaling case, a number of years of increased aid will be required for domestic savings to grow to the point where it can begin to narrow the gap between savings and required investment.

In their statistical analysis of the data pertaining to a number of developing countries, the authors (1965, p. 262 [Table 2]) have estimated the values of the primary parameters of their model and from these together with initial population and GNP estimates have calculated the aid termination dates on the basis of their model. It is interesting to note that out of the 31 countries studied, 22 had aid termination dates of infinity and only 1 country, Yugoslavia, was in the favorable region of case (1) requiring no capital inflow. The 22 unfavorable case countries represented those to which a large proportion of U.S. aid has gone, including Brazil, India, and Turkey. Only 8 countries (Colombia, Greece, Mexico, Pakistan, the Philippines, Taiwan, Thailand, and Tunisia) were found to be in the intermediate region (2), with a finite termination date for aid. These results differ considerably from the calculations of Chenery and Strout on the basis of their model. For example, Chenery and Strout found that Colombia and Tunisia did not meet their savings criterion for a terminal aid date (that is, the marginal savings rate must be greater than the target investment rate), while the following countries which were in the Fei-Paauw unfavorable category (3) met the Chenery-Strout savings criterion: Israel, Panama, Peru, Honduras, Argentina, India, and Brazil with the first three countries meeting the trade criterion as well (Chenery and Strout, 1966, pp. 708-709).

MCKINNON'S FOREIGN EXCHANGE CONSTRAINT MODEL

Ronald I. McKinnon, in a 1964 article in the *Economic Journal,* analyzes the nature of the savings limit, the trade limit, and (briefly) the skilled limit on growth, but gives primary emphasis to the trade limitation. He begins by asserting that foreign aid can have a large favorable impact on the growth rate, even where the absolute amount of aid is small, when the aid is used to remove bottlenecks by providing strategic goods and services not produced in the developing economy (p. 388). In developing his model of the savings and trade limitations on growth, which is similar in many respects to the Chenery-Strout model, he points out that where the foreign exchange constraint is dominant, foreign aid will have a proportionately greater effect upon the growth rate than if the savings constraint holds. This is because expenditures for imported capital goods constitute only a fraction of domestic capital formation. Also, foreign aid will have a greater impact on growth, the smaller the import com-

ponent of investment expenditures. (This same point is made by Chenery
and Bruno, 1962.) McKinnon emphasizes the importance for aid allocation of choosing a growth rate which will minimize the amount of foreign
aid needed to achieve self-sustaining growth. Given a very high marginal
savings rate which permits domestic savings to rise very fast, a higher
target growth rate may actually require a smaller volume of total aid
than a lower one (McKinnon, 1964, p. 399). This point, which was
also made by Fei and Paauw (1965, p. 260), will be referred to later
on in my critical analysis of the general approach we are discussing.

In analyzing the foreign exchange constraint, McKinnon employs two
basic coefficients: e', "the net marginal propensity to export over and
above current account materials needs;" and β, a measure of the proportion of imported capital goods required for a unit of production capacity.
(The *higher* the value of β, the *smaller* the requirements for foreign
capital goods.) For any given value of β, the larger the net marginal
propensity to export, the smaller will be the amount of foreign aid and
the time during which aid will be required to maintain a given growth
rate (McKinnon, 1964, p. 402). The export capacity coefficient, e, measures the increase in exports (over and above current account materials
needs) as a function of output; the coefficient embodies the capacity of
a country both to export and to generate import substitutes for current
material needs, as output rises. In analyzing the nature of this variable,
McKinnon suggests that for developing countries whose exports consist
in large part of primary products, the sales of which are not readily
expandable, the amount of such exports might be regarded as a constant
and the export coefficient, e, would represent the ability of the economy
to earn or save foreign exchange as productive capacity increased.
McKinnon regards net import substitution in the field of capital goods as
being fairly limited, since investment in import substituting capital goods
will involve a high proportion of imported capital and intermediate goods.

The possibility of a terminal date for capital imports for eliminating
the foreign exchange constraint on self-sustaining growth depends upon
the existence of a net marginal propensity to export, e', higher than the
average propensity to export, e, by a critical amount. A somewhat oversimplified version of McKinnon's analysis is as follows:

$$w = q \cdot i$$

where w is the rate of growth, q, the output-capital coefficient, and i, the
investment ratio (equal to the savings ratio). $q/\beta =$ the proportion of
total investment that must go for capital goods so that

$$\frac{q \cdot i}{\beta} = \frac{w}{\beta} = e$$

where $1/\beta$ is a measure of the foreign capital goods requirement for a unit of productive capacity, and *e is* the average propensity to export. In order for self-sustained growth at rate *w* eventually to be achieved, the net marginal propensity to export, *e'*, must be larger than *e*, or $e' > w/\beta$. To take a numerical example, assume that the growth rate, *w*, is .06; the output-capital coefficient, *q*, is .3; and β is 1.2. Then $q/\beta = .25$, or 25 per cent of total investment must go for imported capital goods; and $w/\beta = .05$, so that *e'* must exceed .05 if the 6 per cent growth rate is eventually to be self-sustained.

The higher the amount that *e'* exceeds the critical ratio, .05, the smaller the total amount of aid and the shorter the time required for achieving self-sustained growth. Unless a developing country is able to increase its exports beyond the critical rate, capital imports for avoiding the foreign exchange constraint cannot be terminated without reducing the growth rate below the target level.

A CRITIQUE OF THE SAVINGS AND TRADE CONSTRAINT MODELS

Chenery and Strout have stressed that foreign assistance should make a contribution to the transformation of a poor, stagnate economy by raising the level of skills and improving economic organization through removing resource bottlenecks and encouraging self-help measures in the administration of foreign aid. This approach is in contrast to those which focus solely on the investment-savings or import requirements-foreign exchange earning gaps. However, in their model, Chenery and Strout have transformed Phase I, which is characterized as a period in which limitations on skills and organization prevent the attainment of a level of investment consistent with the target rate of growth, into a special savings-limit case. Foreign assistance in Phase I is needed to push the rate of growth of investment above the target investment rate so that the level of investment becomes high enough to support the target rate of growth. The potential rate of growth in investment is given by the highest compound rate of growth in investment in a recent five-year period. The authors find that the majority of developing countries in their 31-country sample have been able to achieve a compound rate of growth in gross investment of 12-15 per cent per year during a five-year period in the recent past, but that typically savings growth rates are only 6-8 per cent per year. It is postulated that this rate of increase in investment, which represents the skill limit or capital-absorptive capacity, could be restored or maintained if there were no savings limitation. Thus, if foreign aid were available to fill the gap between the increments in investment of which a country is potentially capable and the increments in savings, the level of investment could be raised to that consistent with the target growth rate.

It is by no means self-evident that the skill and organization capacity for *sustained* productive investment can properly be measured by the highest rate of increase in investment during a period in the recent past. Was this highest rate of increase in investment during a recent period made possible by increased capital imports, by higher export earnings, or even by a temporary rise in the savings ratio during the particular period when it occurred? Or was the period of rapid rise in the rate of growth in investment a consequence of other factors relating directly to investment demand, which may also have affected the volume of savings? The data supplied by Chenery and Strout do not provide an answer to these questions. However, until we know the factors conditioning this highest rate of growth in investment during a recent period, how can we postulate that it can be restored and maintained, or possibly even increased, by capital imports equal to the difference between increments in investment at this high rate and increments of savings? The highest rate of growth in investment in the recent past may be an indicator of the rate which the economy is capable of achieving. But the supply of savings is not necessarily the basic limitation on the ability of the country to maintain or even to increase this rate.

There are a variety of reasons why a rapid rate of increase in investment might occur over short periods of time but which is not sustained. For example, a rise in export prices may stimulate increased investment demand in the primary product industries and for a time in industries producing domestic goods as import substitutes. The failure of investment demand to be maintained at that level may have been a consequence of a shift in internal prices and income relationships. Alternatively, there may have been a failure of the economic organization to generate a sustained level of private and public investment, or the absence of labor and management skills for carrying out the kinds of investments required for sustained growth as the demand pattern changed. There is therefore no assurance that the earlier high rate of increase in investment demand will be restored by foreign assistance in the absence of the other conditions which gave rise to the temporary spurt in the investment rate.

I would prefer an approach to Phase I which gave greater emphasis to increasing skills and improving organization and to facilitating the adoption of policies which would enable the country to achieve self-sustained growth, including those policies which raise the savings level and expand exports. I do not believe a sharp distinction should be made between the skill and organization limit, on the one hand, and the savings and trade limit, on the other. All of the attributes of a viable and growing economy are interrelated. Improving the skill level probably requires a long period of technical and strategically designed financial assistance directed in large

measure to the improvement of human resources. Direct private investment provides a means of importing managerial skills for both direct operations and training; such investment also contributes to labor skills. However, there are limits to the importation of managerial and labor skills
through both direct investment and technical assistance. Much of the improvement in the skill level comes from within, with both domestic and
foreign resources directed to the improvement of human resources. This
requires a substantial degree of self-help in the area of institutional and
policy change. Rather than consider this process as a distinct phase, it
should be regarded as a continuous and integral part of the entire process
of economic and social development. Moreover, it cannot be reduced to a
"big push" effort involving a sudden increase in the rate of growth and
investment to a high level, financed by foreign assistance. The skill level
operates strongly at all stages of development by keeping productivity low,
holding down the level of productive investment, and preventing the optimum allocation of a country's human and material resources. This limitation is the essence of being underdeveloped. If this were not so, the miracle
of postwar Western Europe under the Marshall Plan could readily be repeated in the developing world.

In Phase II of the Chenery-Strout model, the primary limitation on
growth is savings, since it is assumed that skills and organization permit a
level of investment consistent with the target rate of growth. All of the
criticisms of the modified Harrod-Domar savings limitation model apply
to this approach. Is the ICOR independent of the rate of growth, or determined by it as Leibenstein has suggested? Is the savings function independent of the factors determining the level of investment? Are there not
forces determining both the level of investment and the output of the economy on the one hand, and the savings level on the other, which determine
the maximum productive capacity of the economy? To a considerable degree, these forces are determined by the governmental policies and the
administrative structure of the government of the developing country.

There are serious doubts underlying the basic assumptions of the savings function employed in the typical savings-constraint model. As has
already been noted, Chenery and Strout found little correlation between
initial income levels and either marginal savings rates or balance of payments performance, in their sample of 31 developing countries. As will be
noted below, there is inadequate statistical basis for the assumption that
because a country is poor in the sense of having a low per capita income
it necessarily has a low savings ratio which can only be raised over time as
its income increases. If, as Fei and Paauw suggest, the essence of self-help
is domestic austerity, should we not think in terms of major shifts in the
entire savings function as it relates to income? Economists have become
so wedded to growth models involving continuous functions that they are

unable to think in terms of structural changes which must occur in an economy if it is to develop. If there is a job for foreign aid in filling a savings gap, why not regard the function of aid as that of providing a temporary supplement to domestic savings during a period required for new tax systems to become effective and for programs to be introduced which will encourage and redirect savings for productive investment. Moreover, investment itself will involve structural changes which should provide a good portion of the savings required to finance these investments. Savings rates are also a function of institutional arrangements, such as the business structure, savings institutions and capital markets, together with environmental factors favoring savings, and government fiscal policies, including the policies of government enterprises. Surely these institutional factors should be regarded as an important part of what has been called the skill and organizational capacity for sustained growth and development.

Savings and investment are not independent functions. Savings are a function of investment in the sense that savings will be forthcoming for profitable domestic investment opportunities. Foreign capital may create such opportunities by providing complementary inputs, and a higher level of investment raises both overall demand and savings, which in turn create additional opportunities for investment.

THE STATISTICAL BASIS FOR THE SAVINGS FUNCTION

Statistics on rates of domestic savings display wide differences, both between countries and for individual countries during different time periods. A number of studies have sought to explain these differences (for a review of recent studies, see Morris, 1963). One approach seeks to relate the ratio of domestic savings to the national product and to per capita output. Simon Kuznets (1960), has calculated the ratios of gross and net savings to gross and net national product, respectively, for some 56 countries and these same ratios for 41 politically and financially independent countries. Kuznets' results, while indicating a tendency for high-income countries to have higher savings ratios, are far from being sufficiently convincing to warrant the formulation of a savings function related to per capita output as the single independent variable. Kuznets groups the 56 and the 41 countries each into 7 categories according to per capita product. In both cases, the 8 countries with the highest per capita product did not have the highest savings ratio; the highest savings ratio was to be found in the second category of countries based on per capita product. The group of countries with the lowest ratio of net domestic savings to net product was found in the third category of countries based on per capita product; the fifth per capita product category had a higher average savings ratio than the third and fourth categories (Kuznets, 1960, Tables I and IV).

Kuznets (1960, pp. 95-96) finds that the ratio of personal savings (households and unincorporated enterprises) to personal disposable income is positively correlated with per capita income and that personal savings are less important in overall net domestic savings in low per capita income countries as compared with high per capita income countries. However, Kuznets' results were not confirmed by H. S. Houthakker (1962), who found that per capita personal savings tend to be *proportional* to per capita disposable income. In part, the difference between the two studies lies in the fact that Houthakker weights his four groups of countries by population in calculating average savings rates for different per capita income groups. Houthakker does find that overall domestic savings rates tend to be higher in countries with higher per capita income. However, his studies also show that savings out of employment income tend to be zero for most countries and that per capita personal savings tend to be proportional to per capita income from property and entrepreneurship (income of unincorporated enterprises, dividends, rent, and interest). This would appear to indicate an important institutional factor in the determination of the overall savings ratio.

An alternative approach is to regard savings rates as a function of institutional arrangements: the business structure, savings institutions, capital markets, the environmental factors favoring savings, and government fiscal policies, including the policies of government enterprises. Thus, corporate savings of widely owned corporations are likely to be higher than those of unincorporated enterprises. Savings on optimum-size commercial farms are likely to be higher than those in traditional farming. Unfortunately, empirical studies of the savings ratios related to institutional factors present difficulties for statistical investigation. Nevertheless, in the light of the poor correlation between savings and per capita product or income, it seems likely that institutional factors, which are in part subject to government policy measures, are more important determinants of the savings ratio than per capita income. At least the results cast serious doubt on foreign aid models which are based on a continuously rising average savings ratio and a constant marginal savings ratio.

As has already been mentioned, Fei and Paauw found only 8 countries out of 30 aid-eligible countries for which the per capita marginal savings ratio was significantly above the average—so that in the absence of special self-help measures, no finite termination date for foreign aid was possible under the Fei-Paauw model. In fact, for 17 of the 22 countries, Fei and Paauw (1965, p. 252) found the marginal per capita savings ratio less than or equal to the average per capita savings ratio. Moreover, some of these same countries apparently have had much higher average per capita savings ratios in the past, which have been accompanied by (but not necessarily caused by) high rates of investment and growth.

It is my contention that the behavior of savings in developing countries has been far too erratic to provide a basis for a foreign-aid model in which the marginal savings ratio constitutes a critical variable. I suspect that the rate of productive investment as determined by investment opportunities, and the incentive for taking advantage of them, is the most important determinant of savings. When the rate of investment is high, the marginal savings ratio, if we must think in these terms, becomes exceedingly high over a relatively short period of time. Moreover, as both McKinnon (1964, p. 399) and Fei and Paauw have pointed out, for a very high marginal propensity to save, the amount of aid required to achieve self-sustaining growth will be smaller for a higher target growth rate than for a lower one.

THE FOREIGN EXCHANGE CONSTRAINT

Turning now to the trade limit or the foreign-exchange constraint on growth, I want first to return briefly to the consistency of the notion that there can be a foreign-exchange gap in the absence of a savings gap. In an *ex ante* sense, net capital imports are always a substitute for domestic savings, so that foreign aid employed for financing investment would appear to be creating excess savings at the level of income generated by total investment. Benjamin Cohen (1966), in a criticism of McKinnon's article on "Foreign Exchange Constraints in Economic Development," states that a difference between the excess of *ex ante* investment over savings and the excess of *ex ante* imports over exports is evidence of misallocation of domestic resources. Cohen suggests that foreign aid donors, therefore, should put pressure on recipients to eliminate the difference between the two gaps. McKinnon (1966), in his "Rejoinder," admits that the dual gap analysis implies a lack of flexibility and substitutability in resources, but believes that this is inherent in developing countries, a condition which must be accepted while efforts are made to improve resource distribution.

Aside from technical assistance and private foreign investment for increasing absorptive capacity, I believe that a removal of the foreign-exchange constraint is the most important function of foreign capital. While foreign aid at one and the same time also provides a temporary supplement to savings, the expanding level of investment, together with appropriate policy measures for increasing savings, should rapidly eliminate any short-term savings gap.

Should foreign aid be employed solely to finance capital goods or should it also be employed to finance deficits arising out of increased demands for materials and consumers goods? Without becoming involved in details of the foreign-aid programs at this point, I would suggest that aid be employed for both purposes. Given a realistic exchange rate and no quantitative restrictions on imports, an increase in investment demand will increase import demand for various types of goods, even though current savings are available for financing the direct domestic investment components such as local materials, labor, and intermediate goods. However, the rise of incomes will inevitably increase the demand for imports of consumers goods and materials as well as capital goods.

But does not this increase in import demand simply reflect a potential savings gap? Not necessarily, because even though increased savings are being generated by investment along with the operation of various policy measures, the rise of investment and incomes must have an effect upon import demand which cannot be wholly offset by increased savings. The production of import-substituting goods will offset some of this import demand, but total demand for imports must increase. This increase can only be financed by an expansion of exports. The export expansion, in turn, depends upon a proper allocation of investment to export goods.

I do not find the concepts of the long-run rate of growth in exports and of marginal propensity to export (as used by McKinnon) very useful in the estimation of foreign-exchange requirements for dealing with the trade gap. The amount of foreign assistance and the period of time during which it must be provided is better thought of in terms of a programming model for the country in the course of the fulfillment of which the output and demand structure of the country shifts toward external equilibrium at a given rate of investment. Where savings appear as a constraint beyond the capital supplied by foreign aid for meeting the temporary foreign-exchange constraint, it would be a signal for policy measures to induce austerity. During the period of transition to a high and sustained level of growth, the guiding principle for foreign aid would be the inducement of structural change and the mobilization of the indigenous human and material resources in the economy.

The philosophy here suggested is, I believe, at variance with that of supplementing resources over long periods of time during which functionally determined savings-investment and export-import gaps would be narrowed. Any gaps to be filled would arise from the time required for structural adjustment to take place, but the principal thrust of the foreign-aid programs would be the inducement of the structural adjustments themselves.

SOME PROJECTIONS OF GROWTH PATTERNS
AND AID REQUIREMENTS

Development planners and foreign-assistance agencies employ theoretical models of the type described in the preceding sections of this chapter as a means of projecting rates of growth under alternative assumptions with respect to the principal variables used in the models and for determining the required flow of aid for achieving target rates of growth. Projections of the growth patterns for 50 countries over the 1962-75 period were made by the AID staff on the basis of alternative values for the principal policy variables including the marginal savings ratio, the marginal capital-output ratio, the marginal ratio of imports to GNP, the rate of growth of exports, and the rate of growth of investment (Chenery and Strout, 1966, pp. 710-23). The alternative values chosen for these variables were (a) historical figures, (b) country-plan figures, and (c) an estimated upper-limit figure corresponding to the three levels of performance. In the case of exports, two alternative rates of growth were chosen, a low growth rate (1962-75) of 3.8 per cent per year, and a high growth rate of 5.2 per cent per year. For each set of variables corresponding to the three performance levels (and for the two export growth assumptions), external capital requirements were determined for each of three growth targets: (1) the historical target; (2) the country-plan target; and (3) the upper-limit target. The possible combinations of values for the parameters yielded 18 projections for each of the 50 countries. These alternative projections, plus certain modifications, were designed not only to estimate aid requirements but also to show the extent to which growth patterns (and aid requirements) might be modified by changes in policy variables assumed to be responsive to government policy. Thus, for the 50 countries studied, external requirements for the 1962-75 period for raising the average annual growth rate from 4.4 per cent (the average historical growth rate) in 1962 to 5.9 per cent (the upper-limit target rate) in 1975 differ substantially depending upon the level of performance—historical, planned, or best possible performance—and upon the export assumption. For example, at a 5.9 per cent growth rate and assuming a 5.2 per cent export growth, the upper-limit performance would reduce external capital requirements for the 50 countries by some 40 per cent as compared to requirements under the historical performance. In other terms, a somewhat larger capital inflow would be required to sustain a 4.4 per cent rate of growth with historical performance than would be required to sustain a 5.2 per cent rate of growth if all 50 countries were to achieve the upper-limit standard (Chenery and Strout, 1966, Table 8, pp. 715-16). An important purpose of the projections based on the growth model is to reveal the effects of varying performance ratios upon aid requirements for a given growth rate or upon the growth rate for a given level of aid. Since aid requirements are determined by the larger of the two gaps, the savings gap and the foreign-exchange gap, the projections are designed to indicate development policy changes for narrowing the dominant gap.

I have already questioned the usefulness of growth models for determining aid requirements based on projections of savings and foreign exchange gaps. On the other hand, I believe that quantitative models may be of value in pointing out the consequences for growth of a continuation of certain policies or certain performance ratios. This topic will be explored further in Chapter 5 when standards of performance in the administration of foreign-aid assistance programs are discussed.

CAPITAL ABSORPTIVE CAPACITY

Growth theorists have tended to devote far more attention to the relationship of the availability of savings and of foreign exchange to growth than they have to the factors determining the demand for productive investment. They have in most cases simply assumed a demand schedule for private investment based on the marginal returns to capital, and a demand for investment in the public sector based on social wants and the almost unlimited requirements of developing countries for economic and social overhead capital. Where the question of investment demand has been dealt with it has been conceived in rather vague terms such as the management and skill limitation or as a maximum rate of investment based on capital-absorptive capacity. For example, Roy Harrod (1948) in his *Towards a Dynamic Economics* distinguishes between the "natural rate of growth" as determined by population and skills, and the "warranted growth rate" as determined by the rate of savings. Chenery and Strout have identified Harrod's "natural rate of growth" with their "skill limit" or special concept of capital-absorptive capacity.

Development economists, on the other hand, are concerned more with the cultural and institutional factors in the growth process than with formulating formal growth models. They emphasize such factors as the lack of entrepreneurship, the social impediments to technological change and innovation, the low level of education, and the general immobility of productive factors as constituting the very essence of underdevelopment.

Specific attention has been focused on the ability of developing countries to employ or absorb productively additional amounts of capital as a consequence of operations of international development financing agencies. In the early history of the World Bank, its officials explained the

Bank's rather low rate of lending by the fact that there was a shortage of well-formulated projects presented to them for financing which made both engineering and economic sense. Although more recently there has been greater emphasis on low debt service capacity as a limitation on their loans, development lending agencies still regard capital-absorptive capacity as a serious limitation on their ability to make productive loans.

Recently, efforts have been made to define capital-absorptive capacity more precisely and to identify the factors contributing to this limitation on investment. Capital-absorptive capacity has sometimes been regarded as a more or less absolute limit to the amount of capital, foreign or domestic, that can be productively employed in the sense of yielding some net return over and above depreciation and obsolesence. Anything less than this would constitute either a subsidy to consumption or sheer waste. Many economists would not regard this as an adequate criterion for measuring the effective use of capital resources, since in developing countries capital resources should yield a rate of return in terms of increments to the social product well above the returns to capital in developed countries. It should be noted, however, that a high rate of return on capital in developing countries should not be postulated simply on the basis of factor proportions. As Theodore Schultz (1964, Chs. 6, 9, and 10) has shown, returns on capital in traditional agriculture tend to be low, and, unless capital investment is accompanied by modern technology and skills, capital investment in tradi- tional economies may not yield high returns. I believe the same conclusions can be applied to industry and other sectors of the economy—namely, that unless injections of capital are accompanied by new technology and mod- ern skills and methods plus the right mix of complementary investments in both physical and human capital, there is no reason to expect high returns on capital in developing countries simply because it is scarce. Scarce rela- tive to what? Capital certainly is not scarce relative to skills, management, and other productive factors as compared to the situation in developed countries. In this sense, immediately after World War II capital was very scarce in Western Europe, and I would say far more scarce than it has been in a country like Venezuela.

Edward S. Mason (1964) has defined capital-absorptive capacity in terms of the volume of investment on which the marginal rate of return is equal to the "socially acceptable discount rate." John Adler has proposed a sim- ilar definition of absorptive capacity as "that amount of investment, or that rate of gross domestic investment expressed as a proportion of GNP, that can be made at an acceptable rate of return, with the supply of cooperant factors considered as given." Adler (1965, pp. 1-5) presents a schedule of the expected rate of return on capital investment in which the rate of re- turn decreases with additional amounts of investment at the margin. Lim- ited absorptive capacity makes for a rather deeply sloped investment return curve as compared with that which would exist if there were no limitations on cooperant factors, that is, complementary factors such as skilled labor and competent management.

Adler's concept of absorptive capacity applies to the return on the marginal unit of total investment and not simply the return on a certain amount of capital supplied from abroad. The net yield on investments will vary between different uses of capital, but the net social return on capital in its least productive uses determines the marginal rate of return. But should not the marginal rate of return on each type of investment be equal to that for any other type when the rate of return is properly measured over time? This optimizing principle should certainly be employed in investment planning, but strict adherence may be impossible in particular investments which depend upon the availability of complementary factors and the preference of entrepreneurs for certain types of investments.

In determining absorptive capacity in terms of a minimum expected rate of return, the time period presents a difficult problem. In the short run, capital-absorptive capacity is limited both by the available cooperative factors and by a lack of complementary investments which may also compete for cooperant factors. Over time, however, it is possible to remove these limitations by investments in education and skills and through very carefully phased programs of complementary investments. Many investments in the public sector, such as highways which produce no direct revenue, will yield a net social return only if certain investments in agriculture, industry, and transportation take place as a consequence of the new highways. Moreover, such investments are lumpy or indivisible in the sense that highways and power plants cannot be built to supply the most important needs for one or two years, but must look forward to the requirements of ten or fifteen years hence. Thus, in determining capital-absorptive capacity, projects cannot be considered in isolation. There must be something of a programming approach to the determination of absorptive capacity. Even where countries have well-conceived development plans which provide a basis for judging an individual project at a particular point of time in relation to other projects to be undertaken over the planning period, uncertainties arise because of the possible failure of certain aspects of the plan to materialize.

An identification of the factors making for limited capital-absorptive capacity involves a listing of the characteristics and causes of underdevelopment itself. These include (a) a lack of knowledge of the natural resources in the country, of the appropriate technology (including the absence of research facilities), and of basic data on the economy; (b) a lack of skills; (c) a lack of managerial competence and experience in both the public and the private sectors; (d) institutional limitations which encompass all the attributes of good government from law and order to fiscal and monetary

CARL A. RUDISILL LIBRARY
LENOIR RHYNE COLLEGE

policies; and (e) cultural and social constraints which relate to education, worker incentives, and entrepreneurship (Adler, 1965, pp. 31-34). These limitations apply not only to the identification and formulation of specific projects suitable for financing from internal and external sources but also to the carrying out of the projects in proper phase with complementary projects and the utilization of the new capital facilities for efficient production (Gulhati, 1965). Common phenomena in developing countries are the existence of capital equipment rusting on the wharves, excess installed industrial capacity resulting from a lack of complementary inputs including imported items, and frequent machinery breakdowns and long periods of plant idleness as a consequence of the inability to make repairs or the unavailability of foreign exchange for spare parts. Expensive hydroelectric dams have been built, but the water in the reservoir has not been used to anything like its full potential for irrigating farms. Thus, absorptive capacity is not limited to the formulation of capital projects, but output is limited by constraints throughout the productive process.

One of the difficulties with employing the concept of absorptive capacity in foreign-aid administration is that foreign assistance involving capital outlays for imports of goods and services may be employed for overcoming limitations to absorptive capacity itself. There is a tendency to draw a sharp line between technical assistance, on the one hand, and the provision of financial resources, on the other. But not only is technical assistance itself a form of investment; it may also be packaged with the financing for capital projects. Many critics of development assistance programs have argued that sufficient advantage has not been taken of this possibility of combining a substantial amount of technical assistance with capital projects. (See, for example, Lewis, 1962, pp. 317-24.)

It must be recognized, however, that there are tolerance limits to the number of foreign personnel which can be put into a developing economy, and—since technical assistance programs involve careful planning and effective organization at the local government level—there is a kind of absorptive-capacity limit on technical assistance. This does not apply so much to large projects such as a steel mill or a hydroelectric dam, which in some cases are constructed on a turn-key basis; but in these cases the real problems may arise at the operating stage when the completed projects are turned over to the local officials by the foreign engineers.

Although the concept of capital-absorptive capacity has been employed as a means of determining the limits to the productive uses of foreign assistance in the case of both program loans, that is, those loans not tied to specific end uses, and project loans, its operational value would seem to be restricted mainly to foreign assistance for specific projects or for a number of interrelated projects. Even in the case of project loans, it would appear that the difficulties in determining the marginal returns to total investment for any given period of time are such as to make the concept impractical unless it is confined to a measurement of the direct and indirect returns to foreign investment. As has already been noted, there is no reason to expect the returns on invested capital to be high simply because a country is underdeveloped and therefore has a relatively small amount of capital per capita. Indeed, if the returns on capital invested in productive agriculture and industry in developing countries were exceedingly high, why do not domestic savers invest more capital in productive enterprise rather than in less socially productive forms in the domestic economy or in foreign securities? Capital flight is by no means fully explained by political risk factors; much of it arises from the lack of investment opportunities at home.

External capital in the form of foreign aid or direct foreign investment can yield quite high returns in terms of increments to the social product if employed in strategic ways which either remove bottlenecks to productive domestic investment or exploit opportunities not seen or seized upon by domestic capital. Thus it would appear that foreign-aid administrators should not be satisfied with financing projects which provide a rate of return no higher than the average return on total investment, but should rather seek out projects which will have important leverage effects by providing inducements to the mobilization of larger amounts of domestic capital, or by increasing productivity by introducing new techniques, new skills, and new methods of production and distribution. When foreign investors go into a developing country they do not simply buy out existing firms and go on producing and marketing in the traditional way. The high social productivity of foreign investment arises from the fact that the capital imports embody modern productive factors and methods. Much the same principle should guide foreign-aid administrators. They should not regard themselves simply as supplementing domestic savings for traditional investment. Thus, the principal function of foreign aid should be that of helping to change the structure of the economy by introducing new factor inputs. Since technological change must be embodied in capital instruments and in skills and managerial capacities generally not available in the developing economies, foreign aid is far more important than removing the foreign-exchange and savings constraints to growth.

I do not find the concept of capital-absorptive capacity especially useful, then, as a guide for foreign aid, either in terms of an absolute limit to the use of capital or in terms of a schedule of the marginal efficiency of capital with respect to which foreign-aid administrators establish a cutoff point based on a minimum rate of social returns on additional units of capital below which they will not go as a condition for providing additional aid. I would prefer that aid administrators look on their assistance, including capital for financing imports, technical assistance and advice and influence, as a means of shifting upward the whole schedule of the marginal efficiency of the capital. This calls for an investment or development strategy and the searching out of bottlenecks and leverage points for promoting growth. The factors which characterize absorptive capacity should be looked at not as a constraint on the introduction of inputs into the production function, but as an integral part of the production function itself, so that the problem becomes one of discovering the right inputs for inducing change. Admittedly, there are some limitations such as bad government or political turmoil about which little or nothing can be done from the outside. But from the standpoint of the foreign-aid administrator, absorptive capacity should be looked upon as the capacity for structural change which makes for higher levels of productivity from the indigenous human and material resources, and not simply the capacity for utilizing additional capital inputs on a declining schedule of marginal returns.

CHAPTER FOUR

The Microeconomics of Aid:
Debt Service and Loan Terms

IN THIS CHAPTER I shall discuss the implications of various patterns of capital inflow and debt service for net aid transfers, the measurement of debt-servicing capacity and its significance for foreign public lending, and the economic issues relating to the employment of soft loans.

CAPITAL INFLOW AND DEBT SERVICE MODELS

Since most foreign assistance takes the form of loans rather than grants, a consideration of the quantity of external aid as a net flow of resources over a given time period must take into account the terms of the loans. If it is assumed that loan recipients make repayments on their indebtedness, at some point in the future net resource transfers will decline as a consequence of debt repayments; at some future point the resource transfers will fall to zero or become negative unless gross lending always exceeds debt-service payments. Interest payments must also be considered in determining the pattern of net resource flow over time resulting from a given schedule of net capital inflow. Even if no net repayment of loans were required, interest payments on past borrowing may over time reach (and then exceed) the amount of current net borrowing so that net resource transfers would fall to zero (or become negative).

Projections of capital-import requirements based on quantitative growth models provide for a certain pattern of net resource inflow over a given time period, the net flow declining to zero with the attainment of self-sustaining growth. However this net capital-inflow pattern must be translated into development loan programs. Alternative loan programs which provide the required pattern of net resource flows may be determined by means of capital-inflow and debt-servicing models which reflect varying loan terms. Such models may also be used to determine the implications for net resource transfers of a given pattern of external financing and investment service. The longer the maturity of the loans and the lower the rate of interest on a series of annual loans of $1 million, the longer will be the period of net resource transfers and the larger their aggregative value. Alternatively, the present value over cost to the recipient country of a schedule of annual loans and debt service payments (which may be calculated by discounting the stream of annual net resource flows at the social rate of discount) will be larger, the more liberal the loan terms. (See Chapter 8.) Since resource inflows and debt service payments arising from foreign loans must always be accompanied by adjustments in the current account of the balance of payments, the savings and foreign exchange gaps are always identical in such models. However the net external capital requirements which may be translated into alternative capital inflow–debt service patterns may be derived from either savings gap or foreign-exchange gap models. Thus, a capital inflow–debt service model provides a convenient means of examining the balance of payments implications of the operation of a savings–investment gap model.

These relationships may be examined by a few hypothetical capital import–debt servicing models. Such models are frequently employed to analyze the implications for debt service of foreign loans designed to achieve a target rate of self-sustaining growth by filling a declining gap between investment and savings. (See, for example, Avramovic, 1964, Ch. IV.) Typically, there is a long period of net resource inflow as determined by the savings and investment functions; a somewhat longer period of net borrowing (since debt service is paid out of new borrowing); and a period of net resource outflow of longer duration than that of net resource inflow because of the interest on the debt. A model of this type is illustrated by Figure 1 (based on Table 1, pp. 74-75), the basic assumptions of which are as follows:

1) GNP grows at 5 per cent per annum.
2) The initial average savings rate is 10 per cent and the marginal savings rate is 20 per cent.
3) The incremental capital-output ratio is 3 to 1.
4) The initial investment coefficient is 15 per cent.
5) The interest rate on net debt is 5 per cent.
6) The amortization on net debt is 5 per cent.

In this model, net capital imports (net resource inflow) required to supplement savings in order to maintain the 5 per cent growth rate decline steadily after the initial year, shifting to net capital exports (net resource outflow) in the fifteenth year. However, net borrowing continues until the twenty-first year in order to cover interest charges on accumulated indebtedness. Debt repayments continue until all indebtedness is repaid by the thirty-third year. A lower rate of interest would have reduced the

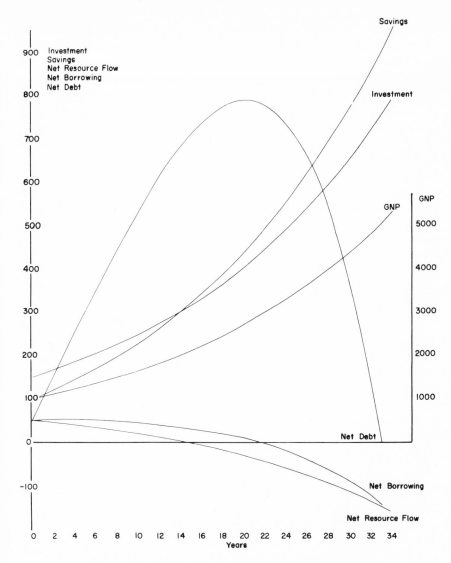

FIG. 1—REQUIRED CAPITAL INFLOW AND BORROWING
FOR 5 PER CENT PER ANNUM GNP GROWTH
Source: Table 1, pp. 74-75.

volume of net borrowing in the period required for repayment of the debt. A longer maturity for the debt, and hence lower amortization payments, would have reduced the annual amount of gross and net borrowing but extended the period of net indebtedness.

The effects of easier loan terms in the form of lower interest rates and longer loan maturities are illustrated by Figures 2 and 3. Figure 2 shows the decline in the net flow of resources to a borrowing country if gross lending is maintained at a fixed level of $100 per year. Figure 3 shows required gross lending per year in order to maintain an annual net flow of resources of $100 to the borrowing country, assuming various loan terms. Under International Development Association (IDA) loan terms of ¾ of 1 per cent interest and 50-year maturity (including a 10-year grace period), gross borrowing at a fixed level of $100 per year would provide a net flow of resources (after deducting interest and amortization) of about $90 per year in the tenth year after the initiation of lending and about $83 in the fifteenth year. Under hard-loan terms, such as those extended by the World Bank and the Export-Import Bank (5½ per cent interest and 13 years maturity, including a 3-year grace period), the net inflow of resources on gross loans of $100 per year would have fallen to zero by the ninth year and by the thirteenth year the borrower would be making net service payments (over and above an amount equal to the gross capital inflow) of $47 per year. Even under medium AID loan terms (3½ per cent interest and 20-year maturity, including a 3-year grace period), net inflow of resources from gross borrowings of $100 per year would fall to zero by the fourteenth year.

Looked at somewhat differently, in order to maintain an annual net inflow of resources of $100 a year, gross lending on hard terms would have to rise to about $430 a year at the end of 15 years. Under IDA terms, gross lending would need to rise only to about $120 per year to maintain an annual inflow of resources of $100 (Fig. 3).

Aid requirements for the achievement of self-sustaining growth at a particular target rate may involve varying patterns of net resource inflow. For example, instead of a steadily declining volume of net resource inflow (illustrated by Fig. 1), net aid may need to rise for a time until savings (assumed to grow as a proportion of GNP with the rise in GNP) have reached a level where net resource inflow plus domestic savings is equal to the amount of investment sufficient to support the target growth rate. Thus, if net aid increased at a rate of 5 per cent per annum, net aid in the tenth year would be 163 per cent of the amount of aid in the initial year. Under hard loan terms assumed in Figure 2, gross lending in the tenth year would be 370 per cent of the initial amount of aid, and in the fifteenth year gross lending on hard-loan terms, assuming a continual 5 per cent per annum increase in aid, would rise to 648 per cent of the initial annual resource inflow. In the case of loans made on AID's minimum terms (2.5 per cent, 40-year maturity including a 10-year grace period at 1 per cent per annum), gross lending at the end of 10 years would be 180 per cent of the initial volume of lending if net resource inflow were to rise at a rate of 5 per cent per annum. It is also worth noting that even in the case in

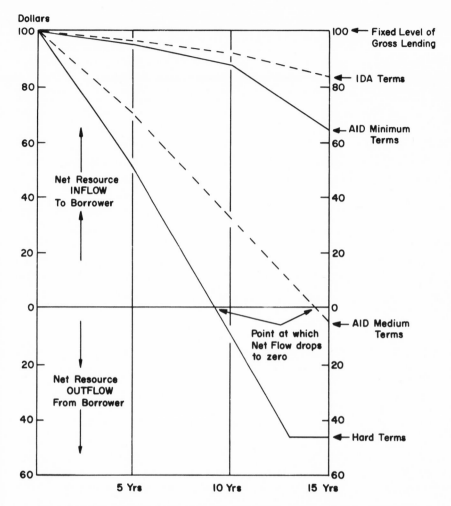

FIG. 2—DECLINE IN NET FLOW OF RESOURCES IF GROSS LENDING
IS MAINTAINED AT A FIXED LEVEL OF $100 PER YEAR
Source: *Loan Terms, Debt Burden and Development,* AID, April 1965.

which net resource inflow declined at a rate of 5 per cent per year, under
the hard-loan terms assumed above, gross borrowing would be equal to
209 per cent of the initial level of borrowing at the end of 10 years and
309 per cent of the initial level of borrowing at the end of 15 years. In
fact, even with a declining level of net resource inflow, gross debt may rise
so that borrowing for debt service payments would continue without limit
(AID, 1965).

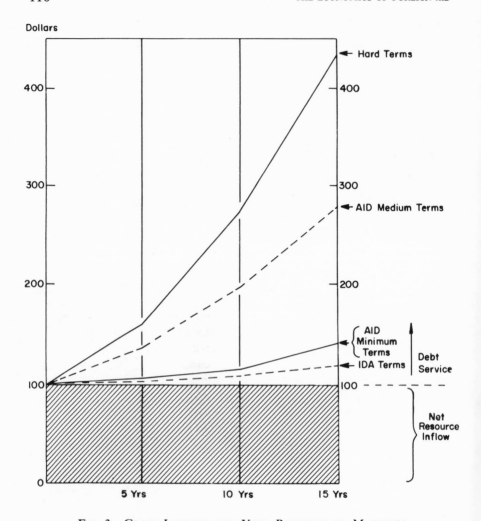

FIG. 3—GROSS LENDING PER YEAR REQUIRED TO MAINTAIN
AN ANNUAL NET FLOW OF $100
Source: *Loan Terms, Debt Burden and Development,* AID, April 1965.

IMPLICATIONS FOR FOREIGN TRADE

Turning to the foreign-trade implications of the models, note that in Figure 1 from (Table I), the borrowing country develops a trade surplus after the fourteenth year rising to 150 in the thirty-third year; this trade surplus is required to repay net indebtedness. Assuming that exports and imports are approximately balanced in the fourteenth year, and that imports equal 10 per cent of GNP, exports must rise over the 19-year period to the thirty-third year at a compound annual rate of nearly 7 per cent if the 10 per cent import ratio is maintained and the surplus generated in accordance with the model described in Figure 1. If the ratio of imports to GNP could be permitted to decline from 10 per cent to 8 per cent over the 19-year period, exports would need to grow by something over 5.5 per cent per annum (compound rate). If we assume that imports were 100 in the initial year (10 per cent of GNP) and that exports were 50 (since capital imports are 50 in the initial year), exports would need to rise at a compound annual rate of nearly 11 per cent for balance to be achieved in the fourteenth year.

Typically, debt-servicing models that illustrate borrowing and repayment for dealing with a foreign-exchange constraint assume certain growth paths for imports and exports, with capital imports filling a declining, or a rising and then declining, gap. The borrowing and debt-service pattern illustrated in Table 2 and Figure 4 is based on the following assumptions:

1) Imports in the initial year are $1000 and exports $750.

2) Imports grow at a compound rate of 4 per cent per annum and exports at a compound rate of 5 per cent per annum.

3) The borrowing country pays 5 per cent amortization each year on net indebtedness and 5 per cent interest on net indebtedness.

TABLE 2

ILLUSTRATION OF EXTERNAL CAPITAL REQUIREMENTS: FOREIGN-EXCHANGE GAP
(See text for assumptions)

Year	Imports	Exports	Net Resource Flow *	Debt Service	Net Borrowing (-Repayment)	Net Indebtedness
0	1000	750	+250	0	250	250
1	1040	788	+252	25	264.5	514.5
2	1082	827	+255	52	281.0	795.5
3	1125	868	+257	79	296.5	1,092
4	1170	911	+259	110	314	1,406
5	1217	957	+260	140	330	1,736
6	1266	1005	+261	174	348	2,084
7	1317	1055	+262	208	366	2,450
8	1370	1108	+262	246	385	2,835
9	1425	1163	+262	284	404	3,239
10	1482	1221	+261	324	423	3,662
11	1541	1282	+259	366	442	4,104
12	1603	1346	+257	412	463	4,567
13	1667	1413	+254	456	482	5,049
14	1734	1484	+250	504	502	5,551
15	1803	1558	+245	556	523	6,074
16	1875	1636	+239	606	542	6,616
17	1950	1718	+232	662	563	7,179
18	2028	1804	+224	718	583	7,762
19	2109	1894	+215	776	603	8,365

TABLE 2 (cont.)

Year	Imports	Exports	Net Resource Flow *	Debt Service	Net Borrowing (-Repayment)	Net Indebtedness
20	2193	1989	+204	836	622	8,987
21	2281	2088	+193	898	641	9,629
22	2372	2192	+180	962	661	10,290
23	2467	2302	+165	1016	673	10,963
24	2566	2417	+149	1096	697	11,660
25	2669	2538	+131	1166	714	12,374
26	2776	2665	+111	1236	729	13,103
27	2887	2798	+89	1312	745	13,848
28	3002	2938	+64	1386	757	14,605
29	3122	3085	+37	1460	767	15,372
30	3247	3239	+8	1536	776	16,148
31	3377	3401	−24	1614	783	16,931
32	3512	3571	−59	1693	787	17,718
33	3652	3750	−98	1772	788	18,506
34	3798	3938	−140	1850	785	19,291
35	3950	4135	−185	1929	780	20,071
36	4108	4342	−234	2007	770	20,841
37	4272	4559	−287	2084	755	21,596
38	4443	4787	−344	2160	736	22,332
39	4621	5026	−405	2233	712	23,044
40	4806	5277	−471	2304	681	23,725
41	4998	5488	−490	2372	666	24,421
42	5198	5762	−564	2442	657	25,078
43	5406	6050	−644	2508	610	25,688
44	5622	6353	−731	2568	553	26,241
45	5847	6671	−824	2624	488	26,729
46	6081	7005	−924	2672	412	27,141
47	6324	7355	−1031	2714	326	27,467
48	6577	7723	−1146	2746	217	27,684
49	6840	8109	−1269	2768	115	27,799
50	7114	8514	−1400	2780	−10	27,789
51	7399	8940	−1541	2779	−151	27,638
52	7695	9387	−1692	2763	−311	27,327
53	8003	9856	−1853	2733	−487	26,840
54	8323	10,349	−2026	2684	−684	26,156
55	8656	10,866	−2210	2616	−902	25,254
56	9002	11,409	−2407	2526	−1144	24,110
57	9362	11,979	−2617	2410	−1412	22,698
58	9736	12,578	−2842	2270	−1707	20,991
59	10,125	13,207	−3082	2100	−2032	18,959
60	10,530	13,867	−3337	1896	−2389	16,570
61	10,951	14,560	−3609	1658	−2783	13,787
62	11,389	15,288	−3899	1378	−3210	10,577
63	11,845	16,052	−4207	1058	−3678	6,899
64	12,319	16,855	−4536	690	−4191	2,708
65	12,812	17,698	−4886	0	−4886	−1,483

* Trade deficit represents net resource inflow; trade surplus is net resource outflow.

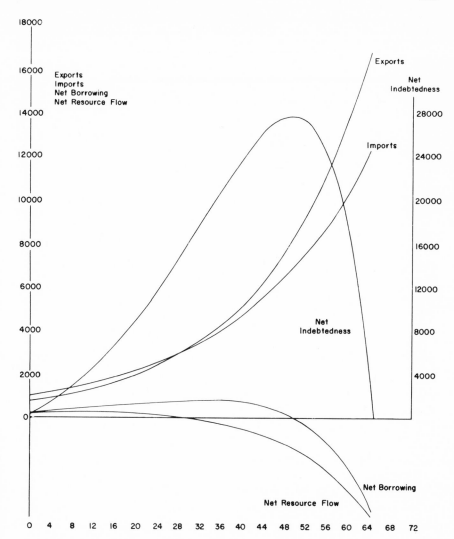

FIG. 4—REQUIRED CAPITAL INFLOW AND NET BORROWING FOR
FOREIGN-EXCHANGE GAP ASSUMING IMPORTS AND EXPORTS GROW AT
ANNUAL RATES OF 4 AND 5 PER CENT, RESPECTIVELY
Source: Table 2, pp. 111-12.

4) The country borrows each year an amount equal to its trade deficit
plus debt-service payments (interest and amortization) on net indebtedness
as of the end of the previous year.

As shown in Figure 4, the trade deficit shifts to a surplus during the
thirty-first year, but by this year net indebtedness has risen to nearly

17,000 and annual debt service is over 1,600 (Table 2). Net borrowing continues through the forty-ninth year when net indebtedness reaches a peak of nearly 28,000. However, the entire indebtedness is not discharged until the sixty-fifth year, by which time the trade surplus has risen to 4,886. Debt service reaches a peak of 2,780 in the fiftieth year, while annual net borrowing reaches a peak of 788 in the thirty-third year.

If exports do not grow at a rate higher than the rate of growth of imports for a number of years, as is the case for a number of developing countries apparently dependent upon capital imports at the present time, annual gross capital imports and debt service would soon reach huge proportions. For example, let us assume that commodity exports are $900 million the first year and commodity imports are $1,000 million and that exports grow at a rate of 2 per cent per annum and imports at a rate of 3 per cent per annum. The gap between exports and imports, which is $100 million in the first year, will rise to $470 million after 20 years. Assuming interest on capital imports at 5 per cent per annum, and amortization payments on net indebtedness is 5 per cent per annum, annual gross capital imports needed to fill the trade gap plus interest and amortization payments on all loans would rise to over $1.3 billion in the twenty-first year. Moreover, the ratio of export earnings to debt service after 20 years will have risen to about 66 per cent, assuming that the country had no external debt service to start with.

Certain observations may be made from the foregoing examples of typical borrowing and debt-service models. First, long periods of net resource inflows financed by loans on hard terms quickly build up a large volume of debt-service payments which could readily become unmanageable. The debt cycle pattern of 33 years from initial borrowing to final liquidation of total external indebtedness described by Figure 1 conceals the magnitude of the balance-of-payments adjustment which is required. A second observation is, therefore, that a debt cycle of reasonable length requires a high rate of increase in exports relative to the rise in import requirements. A third observation, based on typical models for financing development by means of external loans, is that the foreign-exchange constraint presents more difficulties for debt servicing than does the savings constraint. This is because the marginal propensity to save is assumed to be significantly higher than the average, thereby raising savings to the level required for self-sustaining growth over a period of about 15 years (Avramovic, 1964, pp. 50-54, 58). Such a pattern is feasible only where the rate of growth in exports is significantly higher than the rate of increase in imports associated with the target increase in GNP. This means, using McKinnon's terminology, a fairly high "net marginal propensity to export over and above current account materials needs." This condition exists in only a few developing countries.

An element of unreality in the typical debt-cycle models arises from the assumption that countries are net borrowers for 15 years or so and then begin net repayments. It is also unrealistic to assume they reduce the amount of their net resource inflow each year following the initial year of borrowing. Typically, countries turn over their debt as it becomes due and the only real resource drain is the interest payments to the extent that they do not borrow to make interest payments.

DEBT-SERVICING CAPACITY

It is customary to discuss debt-servicing capacity in terms of (a) the vulnerability of a country to balance-of-payments fluctuations over relatively short periods of time which would make it difficult or impossible to meet those payments, that is, the liquidity aspect; and (b) the long term aspect of debt-servicing capacity (Avramovic, 1964, Chs. III, IV, and V). However, as we shall see, this distinction is somewhat artificial in practice, especially since a country with a successful record of long-term growth in total output and in exports relative to import requirements is generally able to borrow for short periods to meet its debt-service payments or otherwise refinance its indebtedness.

THE LIQUIDITY ASPECT

For purposes of analyzing a country's vulnerability to default on debt service arising from short- and medium-term balance-of-payments fluctuations, we may divide the relevant factors into three categories:

1) *Disturbance variables,* including (a) reductions in the exports; (b) reductions in capital inflows; and (c) sharp increases in imports resulting from emergencies or inflation.

2) *Cushion variables,* including (a) foreign exchange reserves; (b) availability of short- and medium-term financing from the IMF and other sources; and (c) less essential imports which can be reduced or eliminated without impairing growth or minimum consumption standards.

3) *Rigid variables,* including (a) the minimum tolerable level of imports; and (b) debt service.

Fluctuating export proceeds constitute the most important factor which may threaten the capacity of a country to maintain debt service over the short- or medium-term. A sharp decline in export proceeds may also discourage capital imports in the form of direct investments or even inflows of public loan capital. Moreover, when the decline in exports is accompanied by import restrictions and there is no reduction in the total monetary demand, there is likely to be an increase in inflationary pressures which will both induce capital exports and render more difficult the holding down of commodity imports. The vulnerability of developing countries to export fluctuations is taken into consideration, along with the volume of reserves and access to compensatory financing, in assessing debt-service capacity. For many countries whose export industries are largely in the hands of foreign investors, the same factors that affect the world demand for their exports may also affect the direct capital imports and investment expenditures by foreign companies. Reduced earnings from exports by foreign investors will be accompanied by a decrease in the amount of reinvested profits in the developing country and, in some cases, foreign companies may repatriate all of their earnings plus depreciation reserves.

Reserves of most developing countries, including automatic drawing rights from the IMF, constitute less than half of their annual imports. Even when we add normal conditional drawing rights from the IMF, only about half of the developing countries for which data are available hold reserves and normal drawing rights from the Monetary Fund in excess of 50 per cent of their imports. Given annual fluctuations in export proceeds up to 25 per cent per year, the reserve and compensatory finance cushion is usually not sufficient for most countries to maintain normal import demand plus debt service in the face of a sharp decline in export proceeds. Moreover, for many developing countries, imports cannot be reduced substantially without affecting growth or internal stability. There is also a question of the extent to which a country is willing to compress imports in order to maintain investment service (which includes both interest and amortization payments on debt, as well as transfers of earnings on direct foreign investments).

If investment service obligations constitute a very small proportion of foreign exchange income, say less than 5 per cent, a country may prefer to deal with a balance-of-payments problem arising from a reduction in foreign-exchange income without disturbing investment service payments. Dividend transfers are of course the most vulnerable to restrictions, but such restrictions may greatly reduce or even terminate new investment inflow. Most of the debt service of developing countries represents obligations either to public international lending agencies or to foreign suppliers and financial agencies providing credits for imports. In both cases, defaults are likely to have quite serious consequences. Short- and medium-term supplier credits are normally turned over as they become due by obtaining new credits for additional imports from the same or other suppliers. Moreover, in many cases, foreign supplier credits are guaranteed by foreign governmental agencies. Thus, defaults on some supplier credits or on medium-term bank loans would impair the ability of the country to turn over its short- and medium-term foreign indebtedness. Defaults on obligations to public international agencies would impair the ability of the country to obtain a continual flow of development credits or emergency balance-of-payments credits. However, it should be said that in the past countries faced with a liquidity crisis have been able to renegotiate or refund their indebtedness with both public international agencies, foreign suppliers, and private financial institutions without the embarrassment of formal default. Frequently this is done with the assistance of the International Monetary Fund which may negotiate an agreement with the country whereby the country undertakes certain fiscal and monetary reforms.

THE DEBT SERVICE–EXCHANGE EARNINGS RATIO

A frequently employed indicator of debt-servicing capacity, or at least of vulnerability to default, is the debt service–exchange earnings ratio, or the ratio of annual debt service to the annual exchange earnings. The World Bank, for example, has reportedly employed the ratio of public debt service to current exchange earnings in appraising credit worthiness of prospective borrowers—on grounds that public debt has priority over private external debt in periods of exchange difficulties. However, for reasons indicated earlier, there seems little basis for distinguishing between government debt and private debt arising out of the financing of trade. Defaults on trade indebtedness occur not as a consequence of the inability of importers to make local currency payments, but rather because of the inability or unwillingness of the central bank to release foreign exchange for meeting external obligations. The fact that the government has granted import licenses to private importers implies an obligation on the part of the monetary authorities to permit foreign-exchange settlements for these imports. Moreover, as we have noted, many of the credits supplied by foreign exporters are guaranteed by their governments, and defaults on commercial debt would be regarded by the international financial community, both public and private, as perhaps even more serious than the failure to meet an installment of scheduled debt service to the World Bank or the Export-Import Bank.

Another variant of the ratio is the investment service–exchange earnings ratio, which includes—in addition to debt service—dividend remittances by foreign investors. However, in the case of foreign investments in the export industries, earnings remittances tend to reflect the movement of export earnings; they also reflect investment-expenditure patterns by the foreign investors. Thus it is difficult to assign a representative value to this variable for any particular year. Also, governments are far more inclined to restrict remittances of direct investment income in periods of balance-of-payments difficulties than they are to default on public and private indebtedness.

Although the debt service–exchange earnings ratio is relatively easy to calculate, and provides a straightforward relationship between the most important variables, its significance as a measure of either vulnerability to default or of the debt burden is open to question (Avramovic, 1964, Ch. IV; Finch, 1951; Mikesell, 1962). To begin with, the history of defaults on loans provides little basis for determining the maximum ratio countries can sustain without default or interference with the transfer of private investment and debt service. For example, Australia managed to avoid defaults on public and private debts with an investment service–exchange earnings ratio ranging from 34 per cent to 44 per cent during the period 1930-34. Canada avoided defaults and the imposition of exchange restrictions on current transactions with an investment service ratio of 32 to 37 per cent over the 1931-33 period. On the other hand, certain Latin American countries, including Bolivia, Brazil, Colombia, Cuba, Peru, and Uruguay, defaulted on their public debt service during the period 1931-33 in a year when the ratios of their scheduled public debt service to exports alone were substantially smaller than the investment service–exchange income ratios for Australia and Canada (Finch, 1951, pp. 60-85; Avramovic, 1958, p. 194). In 1889, Argentina's investment service–exchange earnings ratio rose to 66 per cent, the highest ratio in recorded history, but she was forced to renegotiate her debts in 1891.

We are not dealing here with a question of the maximum ratio a country can tolerate: over a period of time, a country's balance of payments can adjust to a fairly high debt service–exchange earnings ratio. Rather, the ratio is regarded as a measure of vulnerability to default. A high volume of debt service may simply mean that a country's debt structure is relatively short-term and that it normally turns over its indebtedness every few years, while interest payments may constitute a relatively small proportion of total debt service. Thus, for example, if a country purchases all of its imports on the basis of one-year credits, it will be making debt payments equal to the total value of its imports every year. The net burden of debt-service payments as a charge against its foreign-exchange income available for imports would be the interest paid on its import credits, say 5 to 6 per cent of the total value of its imports each year. On the other hand, if a country were paying off a total indebtedness equal to the total volume of its exports at a rate of 10 per cent a year plus interest, and were not reconstituting any of this debt, its debt service–exchange earnings ratio would be much lower but the net charge against its foreign-exchange income would be considerably higher—that is, 10 per cent of its indebtedness plus the interest on the debt. It is true that in the former case in which a country revolves its debt every year, there is greater vulnerability in the event of a sharp reduction in its export receipts. If the country were to refinance its entire indebtedness so that the debt was amortized over a

10-year period, only one-tenth of the debt would come due each year, which amounts could be paid by borrowing again on the basis of 10-year loans.

LONG-TERM ASPECT OF DEBT-SERVICING CAPACITY

The long-term aspect of debt-servicing capacity should be considered from the standpoint of the contribution of capital imports to the economic growth of the country and to long-run balance-of-payments equilibrium. Looked at in terms of a successful growth pattern, the interests of the borrowing country and its creditors are identical. The conditions for successful growth with the aid of capital imports are fairly clear. The additional capital resources should make possible an expansion of net domestic output corresponding to a net return on the investment well above the rate of interest in the international capital markets. In fact, the external capital, by removing bottlenecks arising from the foreign exchange constraint and by making possible strategic investments which might not otherwise be made, should promote the mobilization of additional amounts of domestic savings which would not otherwise be directed to productive investment.

Increased investment and output growth, if it is to be maintained, must provide for a proper allocation of investment to import-substituting and export industries. By and large, import substitution changes the pattern of imports but does not reduce the total volume of imports either in absolute amount or in proportion to GNP. Studies made of the relationship between output growth and the volume of imports reveal substantial variations from country to country depending upon size, character of natural resources, and rate of growth. A United Nations study of the relationship between capital goods imports and gross domestic capital formation over the period 1950-58 reveals that out of a total of 25 countries, 4 showed a rising import content; in 15 the ratio of capital goods imports to gross domestic capital formation was stable; and in 6 there was a decline in the ratio (UN, 1960, Ch. 2; Avramovic, 1964, pp. 137-39). Although there is a somewhat greater tendency for the ratio of imports of consumption goods to gross domestic product to decline with the rise in domestic output, for a number of important countries—including Chile, Mexico, and Peru—the import content of domestic consumption actually rose between 1950-51 and 1957-58 (Avramovic, 1964, p. 139). In a study of the growth patterns of 63 countries, Hollis Chenery (1960, p. 634, Table 4) found that the growth elasticity of imports with respect to per capita GNP was approximately unity for the 1952-54 period, although the elasticities varied for different categories of commodities (Avramovic, 1964, pp. 137 ff.). A World Bank study of the ratios of percentage growth of imports to percentage growth of total production for 23 developing countries found the median value of the ratio to be about 1.0, indicating an equal rate of growth for production and imports. However, the pattern differs considerably from country to country and, even ignoring the extremes, there is a range in the ratio of 0.5 to 1.8 for the countries in the sample (Avramovic, 1964, pp. 134-35).

The results of these studies would seem to indicate that for most developing countries imports must grow at a rate which is not substantially below the rate of increase in domestic output and investment, although these rates may differ considerably from year to year. This means that over time exports must grow at a rate approximating the rate of growth in output, although the pattern of growth will depend upon the pattern of capital imports and debt-servicing obligations. I have already noted that if the rate of growth in exports lags behind the rate of growth of imports for long periods of time, the volume of indebtedness and of debt service under hard-loan terms will grow to huge proportions. This is not to suggest that there is anything wrong with a continual expansion of total external indebtedness for a country whose per capita output is growing at a satisfactory rate and whose exports are rising so that the ratio of import requirements financed by capital imports does not continue to rise indefinitely. The situation under which the ratio of imports financed by capital imports continues to rise for long periods of time would indicate an improper allocation of investment as between domestic and export industries. Where such capital imports are financed under hard terms there would soon result a very large volume of indebtedness, and interest payments alone would absorb the bulk of a country's export earnings.

I am not suggesting that there is any rigid limit to be assigned to either debt service or total indebtedness. Even though total indebtedness may continue to expand, the ratio of capital imports both to domestic savings and to imports should show a declining trend over time. This in fact has been the situation in countries such as Canada and Australia which, although growing at satisfactory rates, continue to be net capital importers.

Debt-servicing capacity, then, should be considered mainly in terms of the successful performance of an economy as determined by its per capita rate of growth and the expansion of its export capacity, on the one hand, and the contribution of further borrowing to the enhancement of this performance, on the other. If further capital imports are not expected to yield a net return in terms of additional gross domestic product well in excess of the cost of borrowing capital, and if total investment is not allocated in a manner which will increase exports relative to imports associated with growth by an amount at least sufficient to cover the interest payments on the additional borrowing, lending becomes both risky for the foreign lender and undesirable for the borrowing country as well. The level of the debt service–exchange earnings ratio has no particular relevance in this type of assessment, although it does have importance along with other liquidity factors in determining vulnerability of default in the event of unexpected fluctuations in exports or import requirements. In the words of Avramovic (1964, p. 42), "the debt service ratio is a cash flow concept rather than a profitability or productivity concept. Because it is a cash flow concept, it includes amortization as a charge. But debt, whether of a corporation or of a country, is normally rolled over; and whenever it is repaid, it cannot be expected that a very large part of the total debt be repaid out of a year's income." If the long-run prospects are good, countries are almost inevitably able to obtain resources for meeting short-run balance-of-payments crises. But if the long-run prospects are poor, even a relatively favorable liquidity position will not make a country a good credit risk.

THE CRITICAL RATE OF INTEREST

It has been suggested that over the long run the extreme limit on a country's capacity to increase its external debt is determined by the rate of increase in its domestic product in relation to the rate of increase in interest charges. Although a country might continue to increase its net indebtedness indefinitely, it would eventually run into difficulties if it had to borrow additional sums in order to meet its interest obligations rather than have the additional net borrowing supplement capital formation. J. P. Hayes (1964) has formulated a concept of "the critical rate of interest" which he defines as that rate which, given the ratio of external debt to gross domestic product (GDP), will result in an increase in debt at the same rate of increase as GDP. In other words, the critical rate of interest is the highest rate that the country can afford to pay on external borrowing to cover its investment-savings gap, without letting the interest charges rise faster than its national product. A simplified version of the formula for determining the critical rate of interest may be stated as follows (assuming no external debt at the beginning of the initial year):

$$i = \frac{r \ (s_o - s')}{s_o - kr}$$

where i is the critical rate of interest; r, the rate of growth in GDP; s_o, the initial savings ratio; s', the marginal savings ratio; k, the incremental capital-output ratio.

Thus, if GDP rises at a rate of 5 per cent per annum, the capital-output ratio is 3:1, the initial savings ratio is 10 per cent, and the marginal savings ratio is 15 per cent, the critical rate of interest would be 5 per cent. Alternatively, if the marginal savings rate were 20 per cent, the critical rate of interest would be 10 per cent. And if the marginal savings ratio were only 12 per cent, the critical rate of interest would be 2 per cent.

The critical rate of interest is of particular interest in view of the distinction between soft loans and borrowing on conventional hard terms. For a given target rate of growth, a country can achieve a steady growth with the assistance of conventional loans without increasing its interest-service burden, that is, letting interest charges rise faster than GDP, provided the critical interest rate is equal to or higher than, rates on conventional loans. When the critical interest rate is lower than that on conventional loans, the implication is that soft loans will be required.

DEBT-SERVICING CAPACITY AND LOAN TERMS

The terms on loans from development finance agencies vary substantially from hard loans with maturities of 10-20 years at rates of interest reflecting the cost of borrowing in private international money markets, to soft loans at no interest other than a ¾ per cent per annum service charge with 50-year maturity, such as those made available by the International Development Association. Both hard- and soft-loan development financing agencies are concerned with debt-servicing capacity of borrowers and the burden of debt payments. Hard-loan agencies (or the hard-loan windows of agencies which make both hard and soft loans) are concerned with the security of their loan assets, especially since most of them are required to raise the bulk of their loan funds by selling their securities in private international money markets. A wave of defaults would both impair the ability of these institutions to sell their own securities on world markets and, in addition, reduce the willingness of developed-country members to increase their capital subscriptions to the institutions from time to time, most of which tend to take the form of subscriptions subject to call only in the event of the inability of the lending institutions to meet obligations to its creditors. Soft-loan agencies such as AID and IDA, while perhaps not primarily concerned with the security of their loan investments, take careful account of the debt-servicing capacity of a prospective borrower for two reasons. First, loans on concessionary (soft) terms are generally limited to countries whose debt-servicing capacity is such that they cannot afford to obtain all of their development loan capital on conventional (hard) terms even if it were available. Thus, for example, AID is not supposed to make loans on concessionary terms where the same loan would have been available from a hard-loan agency such as the World Bank. Second, soft-loan agencies are concerned with debt-servicing capacity as it relates to the principle that developing countries should not be dependent upon concessionary aid for an indefinite period of the future. In fact, the philosophy of self-sustaining growth which underlies development assistance requires that at some finite point in the future developing countries will achieve a basic growth target without further injections of aid. Hence, an expansion of exports in line with import requirements is an essential condition for self-sustaining growth.

THE ARGUMENT FOR SOFT-LOAN TERMS

In recent years, officials of development assistance agencies and of developing countries have expressed considerable alarm at the rapid growth of external indebtedness of developing countries and, more particularly, at the increase in the annual volume of debt-service liabilities on external indebtedness. Thus, between 1955 and 1963 public and publicly guaranteed external debt of 37 less-developed countries increased from $7 billion to $21.5 billion, while service liabilities (interest plus amortization) on this same debt rose from $0.7 billion in 1956 to about $2.7 billion in 1964. However, some two-thirds of the total debt-service payments in any one year on official and officially guaranteed loans are accounted for by guaranteed private export credits, most of which are relatively short-term (OECD, 1965a). One consequence of this continuing rise in debt-service liabilities is that a considerable portion of new gross lending is offset by interest and amortization charges arising from lending in the past. Thus, estimates of India's needs for foreign exchange in her fourth Five-Year Plan indicate that about one-third is needed for interest and amortization payments, and for Latin America about two-thirds of the foreign-exchange deficit is accounted for by debt-service obligations. The tendency for debt-service obligations to increase much more rapidly than export earnings of developing countries is cited as an important argument for the softening of loan terms, both by extending loan maturities and reducing interest rates.

It is important to distinguish between the liquidity problem which may arise from a high ratio of debt-service payments to export earnings and possible difficulties in turning over debt during certain periods, on the one hand, and the long-term burden of the gradual rise in interest payments on net indebtedness, on the other. One obvious improvement in the debt pattern would be for countries to substitute long-term development loans for the high level of short- and medium-term indebtedness arising out of export credits. The problem of debt maturities concerns both the officials of the developing countries and those of international financing agencies. However, in the past it has proved difficult to get countries to avoid accepting export credits which are offered to them so generously by developed countries anxious to promote the sale of their exports. Hence, a refinancing of a country's short- and medium-term indebtedness by long-term credits is likely to result in a rapid reconstitution of the short-term indebtedness, perhaps to an even higher level than before.

If borrowing countries can make amortization payments on old loans out of the proceeds of new loans, the real burden of the indebtedness is confined to the interest charges on net indebtedness. The usual argument for soft loans is based on a model of borrowing and repayment which reflects the well-known characteristics of a geometric progression. A decade or so of net borrowing according to a pattern in which new capital imports cover both amortization on old loans and current interest payments inevitably results in a huge volume of indebtedness and a continual gross capital inflow long after net resource inflow falls to zero. It is the interest payments on accumulated indebtedness assumed in debt models which make for a pattern in which net indebtedness continues to rise long after net resource inflow has ceased or has shifted to a substantial resource outflow; such a pattern presents an almost hopeless picture for a country borrowing for a relatively long period of time on hard terms.

The fundamental case for soft loans is that low-income countries with large populations, low productivity as a consequence of low levels of education and skills, and perhaps relatively poor natural resources as well, require a relatively long period of net resource inflow in order to assist them in making structural changes which are essential to sustained growth. This is particularly true of investments in human resources and certain types of economic and social overhead capital. However, the fact that investments have long gestation periods (or high capital-output ratios) does not mean that over the long run their impact on output constitutes a return less than the rate of interest in international capital markets. It may simply mean that the direct and indirect impact on output, while quite large, is delayed. The impact of investment on savings may also be delayed as a consequence of the time taken for structural changes. But if proper policies are followed, there ought to be a sharp rise in the savings ratio and not simply a long period during which a higher than average marginal savings ratio gradually increases the average. Similarly, the structural changes required for an expansion of exports will take time as a larger volume of investment resources are directed to export industries with the help of foreign aid, but, again, export performance should not be looked upon in terms of long-run constant, or gradually rising rates of growth.

A given annual flow of soft loans constitutes a much larger amount of real resources than the same nominal flow of hard loans. As indicated in Figure 2, the annual net resource transfer embodied in a series of 5½ per cent loans repayable in 13 years declines to zero in less than 10 years, while the annual net resource transfers embodied in a series of loans on IDA terms continues close to the nominal amount of the loans for a period of 15 years more. In order to maintain the same level of resource transfers with hard loans, the total level of borrowing would need to expand very rapidly over a 10- or 15-year period, by the end of which time the borrower is saddled with a very large volume of debt service payments.

The importance of a grace period during which no debt service is required may be illustrated by making certain alternative assumptions in the model illustrated by Table 2. Let us assume that the country with initial imports of 1,000 and exports of 750 borrows 250 per year for 10 years, but that by the eleventh year it has achieved a balance of exports and imports at roughly 1500. Assuming a continuation of the 4 per cent per annum growth in imports, its import requirements in the twentieth year would have risen to approximately 2200. Now let us assume that during the initial 10-year period no interest is paid on any of the annual loans for a period of 10 years, after which 5 per cent per annum is charged on each of the ten annual loans as it reaches a maturity of 10 years. Assuming no capital repayments, both import requirements and interest payments on the series of annual loans could be covered if, after the initial 10-year period, exports were to grow at approximately 4½ per cent per annum. If exports were to grow at 5 per cent per annum after the first 10 years, interest charges on additional loans of 250 per year could be met for the next 10 years, assuming that interest payments on these loans would begin immediately, that is, that there would be no grace period. Loans at this level could be continued indefinitely or even increased gradually after the twentieth year, assuming that the 5 per cent export growth rate was maintained.

This pattern presents an entirely different picture from that flowing from the initial assumptions for the model illustrated by Table 2, under which net borrowing continued until the fiftieth year and net resource inflow began to drop off sharply after the fifteenth year and terminated in the thirtieth year. In contrast, under our second set of assumptions involving the same rate of growth in exports after the tenth year as in the initial assumptions (5 per cent per annum), net resource inflow is actually higher during the first 20 years than it is under the initial assumptions, and could continue with a gradual rise in annual inflow for an indefinite period. Under our first set of assumptions, indebtedness reached nearly 9,000 by the twentieth year, as against 5,000 under our second set of assumptions. Moreover, if under the second set of assumptions net borrowing or net resource inflow continued at the level of 250 for 30 years, total indebtedness would reach 7500, as against over 16,000 under our initial assumptions (Table 2). Meanwhile, aggregate net resource inflow after 30 years under our first assumptions would have been about 6,100 as against 7,500 under the alternative assumptions.

Table 3 provides an illustration of the operation of the model under the second set of assumptions in which there is continuous borrowing at an annual rate of 250 from year 0 to the twentieth year, except for year 10, when imports and exports are balanced. After year 10, exports are assumed to rise at an annual rate of 5 per cent, imports at 4 per cent per annum, plus a constant capital inflow of 250 per year. It may be noted that the compound annual rate of increase in exports over the first 10 years is approximately 7.2 per cent, thereafter declining to 5 per cent per year. However, there need not be a steady rate of export growth during the first 10 years. Given the net resource inflow averaging 250 per year, most of the rise in exports might well occur in the later years with the gap being filled by larger capital imports during the earlier years.

TABLE 3

ILLUSTRATION OF EXTERNAL CAPITAL REQUIREMENTS: ALTERNATIVE MODEL
(See text for assumptions)

Year	Imports	Exports	Net Resource Flow *	Debt Service	Net Borrowing	Net Indebtedness
0	1000	750	250	0	250	250
10	1500	1500	0	0	0	2500
11	1810	1572.5	250	12.5	250	2750
20	2450	2450	250	250	250	5000

* Trade deficit.

The grace period on interest payments in the model illustrated by Table 3 should correspond to the estimated time required to achieve the structural adjustments necessary for sustained growth. Once this adjustment is achieved, net borrowing can continue as a supplement to domestic resources for an indefinite period and at a maximum level governed by the export growth rate, the rate of growth of import requirements, and the rate of interest. It is assumed that gross borrowing would be high enough both to make amortization payments on old loans and to permit the net annual capital inflow indicated by the conditions stated. The policy implications of this approach are considered further in the concluding chapter of this book.

CHAPTER FIVE

The Microeconomics of Aid: Foreign-Aid Strategies

HOWEVER WE MAY REGARD the models employed in the macroeconomics of foreign aid in determining aid requirements for achieving target growth goals, the major day-to-day concern of the aid practitioner is with the assessment of aid for particular projects and programs in relation to specific objectives, and of alternative forms of aid available for achieving these objectives. I shall refer to this general area of concern as the microeconomics of aid, although the macroeconomic models discussed in Chapters 3 and 4 are employed as tools for dealing with specific aid strategies. Aggregative aid analysis of the kind explored in the previous chapters involves certain assumptions regarding the impact of aid and the economic performance of aid recipients, such as a rising savings ratio and critical rates of growth in investment and export earnings. However, except for certain spokesmen for the recipient countries, few people would advocate a policy of transferring unconditional external purchasing power to developing countries simply on the basis of estimated requirements for achieving aggregative growth goals. Foreign-aid administrators and policy makers must be concerned with all of the complex problems relating to social and economic progress in developing countries. Aid, by its very nature, involves strategies and priorities on the part of the donor.

Foreign-aid policies and strategies for achieving economic objectives in developing countries are formulated on the basis of development theories such as those reviewed in Chapters 2 and 3. Since resources provided by all foreign-assistance agencies constitute at most no more than 20 per cent of the investment in developing countries, and an individual assistance agency may provide only a fraction of the total external capital flow, foreign-aid agencies devise strategies for maximizing the impact of their assistance on growth and development. In doing so they may give varying weight to different development objectives. Thus, a particular agency may be concerned mainly with promoting a high rate of growth in output, while another agency may emphasize social development. In seeking to achieve maximum returns from a given amount of assistance, foreign-aid agencies usually follow some combination of two broad strategies. One has to do with the end use of the resources transferred, making sure that the resources are employed efficiently and have a maximum impact on the economy of the recipient for realizing the development objective to be served. The other strategy relates to the influence of the aid on policies and economic performance of the recipient. Different forms of aid and aid-negotiating procedures give varying emphasis to each of these strategies, but as a rule both are present in the aid-giving process. Thus, aid for individual projects tends to emphasize the end use of the assistance, while program aid, balance of payments, and governmental budget support emphasize leverage effects on the policies of the recipient.

In providing aid, whether for specific projects or for balance-of-payments or budget support, donors are concerned with the relationship of the aid to the economy as a whole, and frequently to political and social developments as well. The evaluation of applications for project assistance must be concerned with the relationship of the project to the various sectors of the economy with which the project will interact, and with the requirements for achieving certain development goals. As a rule, foreign-assistance agencies prefer to make loans or grants for "high priority" projects, although they sometimes make available assistance to lower-priority but nevertheless strategic projects which they may feel would otherwise be neglected by private or public investors. Thus, if the government is allocating substantial resources to arterial highways but little to feeder roads, the foreign-assistance agency may seek to encourage investment in feeder roads. Likewise, when AID makes a program loan it expects the government to allocate all the investment funds over which it has control in a manner designed to promote certain agreed-on development goals, and in accordance with the principles of maximum efficiency.

The determination of investment priorities is a difficult problem because of economic interdependence and the dynamics of growth. For this reason, developing countries have employed development plans, and foreign-assistance agencies have been insisting upon well-formulated plans as a basis for aid decisions. Foreign-assistance agencies may also prepare their own quantitative economic models for projecting aggregates—such as GNP, investment, savings, and exports and imports—on the basis of varying assumptions, in order to determine the policies and standards of performance and the amount of external capital which may be required to achieve certain objectives. The general nature of these models was discussed in Chapter 3, but their employment in AID decisions and strategies will be dealt with briefly later in this chapter.

The success of aid programs depends mainly on the performance of the recipients. Foreign-assistance agencies are concerned with performance both in using aid as a means of influencing policies and actions which will lead to good performance, and as a condition for providing aid. I shall discuss the various measures of performance in the context of the aid-dispensing process.

I. ECONOMIC PROBLEMS IN FOREIGN ASSISTANCE DESIGNED FOR FINANCING SPECIFIC ACTIVITIES

Most foreign assistance is intended to finance one or more capital assets and/or commodities and services designed to carry out a particular economic or social activity or category of activities. Such assistance is usually designated as "project assistance," although the terms "project" and "program" aid are loosely defined. Thus, a loan for an irrigation dam is called a "project" loan. However, a loan for agricultural development which specifies the use of the loan proceeds for imports of fertilizer and machinery, production credits to farmers, and the hiring of technical advisers, is—in effect—aid for a broad program involving a number of projects designed to promote economic activity in a sector. Such a loan might be designated either as a "project" loan or as a sectoral "program" loan, depending upon the terminology employed by the agency.

I shall discuss the economic considerations involved in foreign aid designed primarily to finance specific activities, as against general aid for economic development in the form of program loans or budgetary or balance-of-payments support. I shall begin with certain approaches and techniques associated with project analysis, and then turn to a discussion of particular categories of projects or activities.

ECONOMIC CRITERIA FOR PROJECT ASSISTANCE

The more narrowly the project or activity financed under an aid agreement is defined, the greater is the degree to which certain well-established principles of project analysis can be applied. Analysis at the project level includes engineering studies, estimation of the cost of the project and operating costs, estimation of the market for the commodity or service produced and its market price or social value, and the application of the techniques of benefit-cost analysis. The techniques of project appraisal are well developed for projects such as power plants, multipurpose dams, industrial plants, railroads and highways, but social projects such as urban renewal, health and education present difficult and largely unsolved problems.

BENEFIT-COST ANALYSIS

Benefit-cost analysis is concerned with a comparison of the present value of the expected benefits of a project with the present value of the costs, including both the capital cost of the project itself and the operating costs associated with the output of the good or service. The various techniques employed for calculating the present values of benefits and costs need not concern us. (See, for example, AID, Office of Engineering, 1963). There are, however, a number of important issues in the identification and valuation of the direct and indirect benefits and costs which are of significance for implementing foreign aid policy (for a review of the literature see Prest and Turvey, 1965, pp. 683-735).

Benefit-cost analysis is important (a) for determining whether the discounted value of the benefits exceeds that of the cost; (b) for comparing the relative advantages of alternative methods of supplying the good or service; and (c) for assigning priorities to various projects under consideration. There are, however, severe limitations on the use of benefit-cost analysis as a means of establishing the priority order of proposed projects, say, by giving preference to those projects where the ratio of present value of benefits to present value of cost is highest. Projects that are mutually interdependent give rise to difficult problems of assessing joint costs and benefits. Also, the analysis of costs and benefits expressed in terms of monetary values, whether actual or imputed, is more applicable to industrial, agricultural, and economic overhead projects such as power and transportation than to projects in the field of health or education. This is not to say that rigorous analysis should not be undertaken with regard to social impact projects. Nevertheless, an ordering of projects which cuts across widely differing sectors such as power and education or health is probably not warranted by the accuracy or even comparability of the estimates. Priorities must often be determined more on the basis of investment strategies involving the relative importance to be given to particular sectors of the economy, with due regard for the long-run development goals. Nevertheless, all projects should be put to the test of determining whether the present value of benefits exceeds the present value of costs, even where informed judgments of magnitude must be substituted for reliable data.

Bureaus of public works concerned with projects in the fields of water and land use, electric power, and transportation have for many years been engaged in the process of formulating and applying benefit-cost techniques for determining the feasibility and economic and technical soundness of proposed projects. The Office of Engineering of AID has issued a manual [1] for guidance of AID officials in the evaluation of projects, but the application of the AID guidelines presents a host of conceptual and technical problems, even where estimates are available based on direct monetary costs and benefits. However, most projects in the public sector yield outputs that are either not sold, or are sold at prices which do not provide a proper measure of the benefits. Where market prices are not available or are inappropriate, prices must be computed in a way which will properly reflect the social value of the output. Thus, the price charged farmers for irrigation water may cover little more than the direct costs of making available water from a multiple-purpose dam. The social value of the water may be calculated by estimating the excess of the value of the increased output which the water makes possible over the increased costs of all other inputs by the farmers. If the output of the project has a market value, it may be desirable to take account of the consumer surplus as a social benefit arising from the availability of larger output at a lower price.

Monetary costs involved in the project may also need to be adjusted so as to reflect social costs. For example, there is a divergence of social and private costs when the project involves the use of unemployed labor. Thus, it has been argued that the market price of labor under conditions of unemployment may overvalue labor used in constructing a project (Prest and Turvey, 1965, pp. 694-95).

There are various externalities and secondary benefits which need to be considered in benefit-cost analysis. There may be benefits arising from new industries induced by the construction of a road or the provision of additional power. Thus, in an example given in an AID manual (1963, p. 22), the value of secondary benefits from a hydroelectric power project includes estimates of the annual anticipated investment in expanded and new industries and in the general increase in related business and industry. While such secondary benefits certainly ought to be taken into account in the consideration of investment strategies, it would not be proper to relate them to the cost of the project. Inducement effects must be considered not simply in terms of the total value of the induced investment, but in terms of the social benefits and costs of such investment. There are also external costs associated with certain projects such as those arising from increased population in the area where the projects are located and additional drains on skilled labor from industries in regions where such skills are in short supply.

Another important secondary benefit relates to the impact of a project on the balance of payments of the country, an impact which may be

1. *Benefit-Cost Evaluations as Applied to AID-Financed Water or Related Land Use Projects* (Washington, D.C.: U.S. Dept. of State, May 31, 1963).

favorable or unfavorable. If the exchange rate is an equilibrium rate, presumably the market prices and costs do not need to be adjusted for the foreign-exchange effect. However, if as is so often the case, the exchange rate is overvalued, it may be desirable to adopt a shadow price of foreign exchange and adjust imports and exports associated with the costs and benefits of the projects by the shadow rate. In the case of industrial projects, a comparison of production costs with world prices provides an important test of the efficiency of the project at the current exchange rate, and a basis for determining its efficiency at a devalued rate if the exchange rate appears to be overvalued. Where products are subject to tariffs or import restrictions, market values ought to be corrected to reflect the international value of the product. Alternatively, a subsidy represented by the tariff or import restriction might be regarded as a part of the social cost. Other subsidies such as those reflected in subsidized power or transportation might also be included in the social costs of production.

As we move away from water, land, industrial, and transport projects to the areas of education and health, where one is faced with such problems as the economic value of a partially employed agricultural worker or the marginal social product of an additional year of schooling for a million children, calculations of social benefits as well as costs become more and more nebulous. Certainly the important work currently being undertaken in the economics of education and the economics of health will provide both a better conceptual framework, and—it is to be hoped— some statistical benchmarks for project evaluation in these fields. Moreover, even where benefit-cost analysis cannot provide reliable quantitative answers, it forces those who evaluate projects to ask the right questions, the results of which may exercise a negative role in screening out certain projects and in illuminating the advantages of some projects over others.

It is well simply to recognize the limitations of benefit-cost analysis and not try to define and estimate benefits and costs in a way which would involve an excursion into general equilibrium analysis. Benefit-cost analysis provides at least a first step in the judging of projects within a given framework of prices and costs. It is of course possible to use accounting or shadow prices for purposes of benefit and cost estimates, but such accounting prices would need to be supplied by others engaged in a programming analysis for the economy as a whole. A benefit-cost analysis exercise is useful as a study in depth of the operation of the project within a well-defined framework. Development strategy which is concerned with inducement effects, external economies, and various longer-run inter-sectoral relationships, movements of productive factors, balance of payments, and the general pattern of growth may in some instances give a higher priority to a project with a lower ratio of present value of benefits to costs than to one with a higher ratio. But at least the strategists will know what the ratios are within the framework of the benefit-cost analysis. Thus, a project for expanding exports or for import substitution or for increasing food output, while desirable from the standpoint of development strategy, may prove to be much too costly in terms of benefit-cost analysis—but only penetrating analysis of the project would reveal this fact. Also, there is no substitute for benefit-cost analysis in judging between alternative ways of providing a good or service once it is decided that a particular economic sector should be expanded.

ESTIMATING THE COST OF CAPITAL

A vital element in all benefit-cost analysis is the choice of the rate of discount for determining present values of benefits and cost. This rate of discount should reflect the relative scarcity of capital in the country, or the marginal rate of return on investment plus the risk premium. The use of varying risk premiums as the basis for the comparison of projects introduces a number of difficult problems relating to social and private costs with which I will not now attempt to deal. If the rate of discount chosen is too low, the value of the benefits in relation to the costs of the project will be overstated. In practice there has been a tendency to undervalue the rate of discount in relation to one which properly reflects the marginal productivity of capital. However, there is usually little agreement regarding what the proper rate should be. Capital markets in developing countries are notoriously imperfect, and maximum long-term interest rates are frequently fixed by government decrees and capital is rationed in various ways. Market rates may also reflect various risk premiums including default risk and inflation risk premiums. The existence of various distortions within developing economies has led to the suggestion that an accounting price for the use of capital be determined which would reflect the marginal productivity of capital in an optimum situation after taking account of all alternative uses. Such accounting prices must be determined by means of comprehensive growth models such as those formulated by Chenery (1959), Solow (1963), and others (Schmedjte, 1965; Qayum, 1960; Chakravarty, 1964). However, since the variables and parameters of the models cannot in most cases be empirically measured, and, in addition, they involve rather restrictive assumptions with respect to economic growth, they are of little value in practice. Perhaps more useful is the return-on-all-real-assets approach employed by Arnold C. Harberger (1962) in seeking to estimate the economic cost of capital in India. This approach involves estimates of rates of return on net fixed assets and inventories for over a thousand Indian joint companies. Its weakness lies in the fact that the real assets have to be measured in terms of book values which often bear little relation to their economic values. While there is no easy answer to the problem of establishing appropriate rates of discount, judgments based on empirical studies of rates of return on capital, with appropriate adjustments for various risk elements, seem to offer the most fruitful approach. Mention should also be made of the fact that simply because capital is scarce does not mean it will earn a high return in a developing country. Distortions of factor prices and the general low level of productivity result in yields lower than they would be under ideal circumstances.

SECTORAL ANALYSIS

Most projects concern activities which are a part of an identifiable economic sector of a country such as agriculture, transportation, power, housing, education, or industry. It is often difficult to appraise a project out of context from an economic sector. For example, a proposal for modernizing a railroad line must be judged in terms of the total demand for transportation in the area and alternative means of transportation such as highways and water. Also, transportation requirements in any one region are closely related to those in other regions, and judgments regarding priorities in the field of transportation must be made on the basis of a knowledge of that sector—including projections of requirements for and of impacts on other sectors. Likewise, a project for the colonization of a particular agricultural area must be appraised on the basis of a knowledge of the entire agricultural sector and some idea of its potentialities. For example, more intensive utilization of areas already under cultivation might constitute a more productive use of human and capital resources than colonization of new areas. Likewise, analysis of power projects involves consideration of alternative ways of providing the power and alternative locations, since power can be transported over long distances.

Sectoral analysis provides a link between projects and overall development plans and also provides insights into dynamic intersectoral demand and supply relationships which are often missed in comprehensive planning based on input-output matrices. Some countries, like Mexico (which has had a relatively successful development experience), have emphasized sectoral planning as opposed to sophisticated comprehensive planning. And foreign-assistance agencies such as the World Bank group and the Inter-American Development Bank (IDB) have been helping to finance and execute a number of sectoral studies. For example, in 1965 a World Bank team was engaged in a study of the development potential of the water and power resources of West Pakistan. The World Bank also acts as the executing agency for several sectoral studies financed by the United Nations Special Fund, for example, the development of the irrigation and power facilities in two river basins in the Dominican Republic, a transport survey in Surinam, and a study of telecommunication needs in Pakistan. The Inter-American Development Bank has recently made several loans for preinvestment studies usually carried out by development planning agencies in the recipient countries. Some of the preinvestment studies relate to individual projects, but in many cases they are designed to analyze and formulate sectoral programs. For example, the IDB made a loan in December, 1965, to the government of Argentina to conduct studies and formulate programs for several sectors of the economy. In many cases, foreign lending agencies (such as the World Bank) have made a series of project loans in a particular sector over a period of time, following a detailed study of the sector.

DEVELOPMENT PLANS AND THE FOREIGN-ASSISTANCE AGENCIES

Development plans became popular among the underdeveloped countries in the early postwar period, while they were still being viewed with some suspicion as an instrument of socialism in the donor countries. Although planning and development plans are now almost universally recognized as essential in promoting growth and the efficient allocation of resources, there is considerable debate regarding the value of certain types of plans and great skepticism regarding the value of many of the plans that have been formulated (Waterston, 1965). Nevertheless, international assistance agencies and the governments of donor countries (such as the United States) have in recent years not only encouraged development planning but have tended to make planning a condition for external assistance. This has sometimes led to the hasty drawing up of plans as a condition of eligibility for aid.[2]

There are several reasons why foreign-assistance agencies began to encourage planning. First, projects cannot be properly appraised on the basis of engineering standards and partial equilibrium benefit-cost analysis alone; their priority and contribution to the economy as a whole must be determined in relation to a dynamic analysis of the growth pattern or alternative growth patterns. Project and sector analysis must be dynamic in the sense that the demand for the output and the supplies of inputs depend upon the rate of growth of other sectors and the growth of national output and demand. There must also be a concern for the external sector both as a source of demand for the products and as a source of foreign

2. For example, Brazil's *Plano Trienal* was produced in ten weeks, mainly for the purpose of obtaining external assistance. Several other Latin American countries were spurred to formulation of plans of varying quality by the Punto del Este Charter which stressed development plans as a basis for external assistance (Waterston, 1965, p. 103).

exchange for imported inputs and debt-service payments on loans. Only a comprehensive picture of the entire economy, and the rate and pattern of change in its major elements, can provide the information necessary for an adequate appraisal of a project.

The second reason for the interest of foreign-assistance agencies in development plans relates to the goals of the economy and overall progress toward these goals. In the early 1950's the World Bank was satisfied to make project loans which met the Bank's engineering and accounting standards, provided the country was following economic policies consistent with reasonable price stability and external balance. The World Bank did, however, stress the need for comprehensive economic surveys which would provide the basis for the determination of investment priorities. But priorities cannot be determined without an economic framework which links the various sectors together—which is of course the basis of a development plan. During the early postwar period, the U.S. government was not committed to the promotion of development on a broad scale; most of our bilateral foreign assistance took the form of defense support to countries with which we had military alliances, and of Export-Import Bank loans. It was not until the late 1950's with America's involvement in the Indian and Pakistani Five-Year Plans, and more particularly with the inauguration of the Alliance for Progress in 1961 (which set forth quantitative growth goals as well as a variety of social goals), that U.S. bilateral assistance programs became oriented to the achievement of specific development goals. While their techniques are different, the World Bank Group, both unilaterally and as a member of aid consortia, has stressed specific development goals and is seeking to relate its project aid to the implementation of overall development and sectoral plans. Thus, most foreign-assistance agencies, both national and multinational, at least profess to relate their aid to development plans and goals. However, these agencies have not been satisfied with a single goal such as a minimum rate of growth in per capita GNP. There has been a tendency on the part of foreign assistance agencies to emphasize sectoral goals in such fields as education or agricultural output and to influence development plans with respect to the priority to be given to these sectors. An example has been the emphasis given by foreign-assistance agencies to the private industrial sector by providing loans and technical assistance to industrial development banks and by making program loans to finance imports of capital goods and other imported inputs required by private industry. Another example has been the recent emphasis given to agriculture and the criticism of a number of development plans for not paying sufficient attention to agriculture.

A third reason for emphasizing development plans relates to the increasing involvement of foreign-assistance agencies in overall development policies. Throughout the postwar period, foreign-assistance agencies—in cooperation with the International Monetary Fund—have been concerned with monetary and financial policies, and indeed a considerable portion of U.S. foreign aid has taken the form of stabilization loans usually in conjunction with IMF standby agreements in which the recipient promises to undertake fiscal, monetary, and exchange reforms. In many, if not most, cases, such assistance failed in its primary objective since the underlying structural conditions leading to the balance-of-payments crises were not altered. But in the early 1960's AID began to employ program loans to a limited number of countries, partly as a device for influencing a broader range of policies designed to achieve development targets. Foremost among these targets was the achievement of a minimum rate of increase in output per capita within a given period of time, following which this rate of growth could be expected to continue without further external assistance, at least that provided on concessionary terms.

The goal of a terminal date for aid has by and large not been built into the multiyear development plans of the aid recipients; it has not been regarded as an attractive goal by the developing countries themselves. But for political as well as economic reasons it has constituted an important policy of the United States government. The principle of a terminal date for external assistance, or at least a date beyond which net external capital inflow declines rather sharply, is also based on balance of payments and debt-service capacity considerations, since—as we have seen—debt service tends to rise very sharply with a continual inflow of conventional loans. This aspect has been stressed in a number of studies by the World Bank. As will be discussed later, the objective of influencing development policies and of assigning a terminal date for aid required to achieve development goals have led the AID and, to a lesser extent, the World Bank staffs to formulate their own growth models for aid recipients.

Unfortunately, the methodological weaknesses and superficial nature of most national development plans greatly limit their usefulness to foreign-assistance agencies as a basis for specific project evaluation, or for the formulation of aid strategies. They are often deficient in basic statistics and lack analysis in depth at the sectoral level. Frequently they involve little more than statements of growth and employment targets and projections of such aggregates as consumption, employment, private and public investment, savings, taxation, imports, and gap-filling external capital requirements on the basis of models employing parameters having little basis in either historical performance or what might be expected from changes in economic policies. In fact, the failure to relate plans to policy instruments constitutes one of the most important shortcomings of national plans. This shortcoming has been stressed in recent evaluations of Latin American planning. (Economic Commission for Latin America,

1963). In reviewing planning experience in Pakistan, Albert Waterston (1963) notes that:

One of the key lessons revealed by Pakistan's experience is the importance of relating plans to basic economic, financial and fiscal policies. Until recently various government bodies adopted policies without any consistent attempt to relate them to the objectives of the plans prepared by the Central Planning Agency. Consequently, economic policy has often conflicted with plan objectives. Thus, agricultural price policy has hampered the achievement of targets; agricultural programs and controls have often impeded the development of industry along lines laid down in development plans (pp. 57-69).

There has been a tendency to substitute comprehensive model-building employing highly sophisticated techniques for basic information involving not only data-gathering but knowledge of potential markets, production costs, business decision-making and obstacles to private investment decisions, and social and economic barriers to expanding agricultural output (Vernon, 1966, pp. 57-69). I shall discuss the role of quantitative growth models in foreign-aid policy later, but whatever their value to the national planning authorities, they are not likely to be accepted, or their calculated gaps underwritten, by foreign-aid authorities who prefer to construct their own models based on their own judgments with respect to the relevant parameters. What the aid authorities need are solid data, intensive sectoral analyses, and studies which illuminate the probable relationships between policy instruments and performance in both the public and the private sectors.

PROJECT ASSISTANCE IN THE PRINCIPAL ECONOMIC SECTORS: SOME MAJOR ISSUES

Taking a broad look at the overall distribution of external aid resources by the major external development agencies, we find that about half of the development assistance (excluding defense support assistance by AID) has gone for power, transportation, and other economic overhead projects, mainly in the public sector; about a third has gone for program loans and loans to industrial development banks; the remainder, for a variety of agricultural programs, including large irrigation and land reclamation projects, and to education, health, sanitation, and other so-called social impact programs. The distribution of aid among these various categories differs considerably between development agencies, with the World Bank and IDA committing two-thirds or more of its resources to power and transportation, AID making heavy commitments in the form of program loans, and the Inter-American Development Bank providing a relatively large proportion of its resources for industry, agriculture, and social impact programs, with a much smaller proportion going for power and transportation. Agencies tend to specialize in certain types of assistance partly as a consequence of the limitations of their charters or legislative history, and partly for other reasons. Development-assistance agencies operating with relatively small staffs and concerned with the development problems of a large number of countries are under certain obvious constraints with respect to the types of assistance provided. With respect to financial resources, they are essentially wholesalers of aid—in the sense that they have neither the staff nor the knowledge of economic conditions and problems within each individual country to make thousands of loans, but must operate mainly through governments and financial intermediaries. Similarly in the field of technical assistance, external development-assistance agencies cannot send thousands of technicians to individual countries, but must utilize their technical personnel for broad surveys, the training of foreign technicians for work in industry and agriculture, assistance in the establishment of productivity centers, the provision of advisors to central government agencies, and demonstration projects in various fields. Keeping in mind these institutional constraints, we shall discuss briefly some of the problems relating to resource allocation and priorities which are faced by external assistance agencies in the major sectors of developing economies.

ECONOMIC OVERHEAD PROJECTS [3]

The traditional preference on the part of external development agencies for financing economic overhead projects such as transportation and power is quite understandable. They require large amounts of capital, in most cases have a heavy import content, and the projects are readily susceptible to analysis in terms of engineering feasibility and benefit-cost studies. Developing countries characteristically lack these facilities, and they can never become modern productive societies without a substantial investment in economic infrastructure. While governments of developing countries are especially anxious to have large economic overhead facilities, they usually cannot be financed on what is regarded as an adequate scale from domestic sources. The tendency toward urbanization, industrialization, and the

3. The term "economic overhead capital" is used to denote investments in the fields of electric power, transportation, communication, large-scale irrigation, and land reclamation, and the like, which provide services directly in support of industry and agriculture. I have used the term "social overhead" or "social impact" projects to cover the fields of education, health, sanitation, housing, urban and rural water supply, and the like, aimed primarily at the improvement of human resources.

creation of modern centers characterized by a high proportion of automobile ownership and the use of modern electrical appliances, even in countries where the mass of the population lives outside of the urbanized market economy, has created a huge and growing demand for these facilities. The source of this demand differs from that arising from the need for railroads and other transport required to bring export commodities to the ports for shipment to world markets. This was the major stimulus for the construction of railroads in the developing countries during the nineteenth and early twentieth centuries. Much of this export-oriented transportation was financed privately by, or with the help of, foreign and domestic business interests engaged in the production and marketing of primary products. In fact, mineral and petroleum companies still supply much of their own requirements of transportation and other economic overhead facilities.

Economists have raised a number of questions regarding the heavy allocation of scarce capital resources to power and transportation in developing countries. First, there is the question of the degree to which these facilities induce development, particularly the right *kind* of development. There are the obvious cases of modern highways stretching across hundreds of miles of underdeveloped rural areas, while feeder roads do not extend even to the villages that can be seen from the highway. There is likewise the almost insatiable demand for subsidized power in the metropolitan centers of poor countries which, except for the ring of slum dwellings on the edges, are scarcely distinguishable from the cities of North America and Western Europe—while, at the same time, thousands of poor villages in the same country do not boast a single street light or an electric pump for their water supply. It is perhaps not so much a question of whether the modern urban centers should have these facilities as it is whether individually and collectively they should pay their full costs, including power rates and taxes high enough to finance them, rather than have them provided by low-cost external loans and governmental subsidies. What I am suggesting is that in the allocation of external capital for economic overhead projects, more attention should be paid to influencing changes in the existing pattern of development, rather than looking solely to effective demand arising from the existing pattern. Thus, if feeder roads will enable remote rural areas to get their produce to market and open up new lands for commercial cultivation, funds for this type of transport might be given a higher priority than those for 70-mph arterial highways which are often underutilized except by passenger cars on holidays. Moreover, since the highways are demanded by people who can well afford to pay for them, they will be constructed and maintained in any case. Similarly a larger proportion of the external aid for power might go for small generators to provide power for essential services in the villages of rural areas. It is true, of course, that a considerable portion of the power in the urban centers is required for industry; but if power shortages exist, will not this be overcome by the demand of the users for greater supply and their willingness to pay rates and taxes sufficiently high to provide the necessary facilities? On the other hand, industrial decentralization, which is considered desirable in most developing countries, might be induced by providing power for industry, together with transportation facilities, outside of the large urban centers.

A second question has to do with the high capital intensity of foreign-financed overhead projects. External financing of economic overhead capital involves decisions regarding capital intensity, just as in industry and agriculture. Undoubtedly, road building and the construction of dams and irrigation works could be made much more labor-intensive, and if the relative prices of labor and capital properly reflected their relative scarcities, more labor-intensive methods might be employed. It has often been suggested that because external assistance agencies provide only the import components of projects under financing terms well below the cost of capital within the country, production methods tend to be capital-intensive and involve a high foreign-exchange component. It is recognized of course that labor-intensive methods do not always provide the highest output per unit of capital employment, and this should be an important factor in the decision.

A third question is whether foreign-assistance agencies, in their preference for financing import and capital-intensive infrastructure, have contributed to a misallocation of scarce resources in developing countries, particularly at the expense of private industry and agriculture. National development plans tend to emphasize projects in the public sector requiring both domestic and external capital; this allocation of resources tends to be reinforced by the preference of foreign-assistance agencies for such projects. It might be objected that external financing of economic overhead projects releases domestic capital and foreign exchange for other uses such as industry and agriculture. But we are not dealing with equilibrium economies with flexible prices and high factor mobility. Foreign-assistance agencies have a responsibility for employing development strategies which promote a proper allocation of investment. This does not necessarily mean that external assistance agencies should direct their project aid solely on the basis of overcoming misallocations of capital in the developing countries. But they can influence domestic policies and provide the kinds of capital and technical assistance that will help countries to improve the pattern of investment. This calls not only for greater flexibility in the forms of aid and in the types of activities financed by external assistance agencies, but for a continual assessment of overall development requirements and of the policies for achieving them.

A development strategies approach to project aid allocation is subject to two important conditions of feasibility. First, governmental authorities of the recipient countries—either at the federal or at the local level—must cooperate to the extent of formulating and implementing projects suitable for external assistance to which the external agency has assigned high priority. It may very well be that the government authorities are not sufficiently interested in such projects to take the initiative in formulating them, and that there is no group, governmental or private, at lower levels capable of taking action required for the formulation and implementation of the projects. The second condition is that the projects considered to be strategically important by the external assistance agency should not be so much at variance with the development plan and the allocation of internal resources as to make them impractical or relatively valueless as a contribution to economic progress. An external agency may favor feeder roads over the improvement of arterial highways or assistance to power and transportation facilities in cities and villages outside of the principal urban center, but these facilities must complement other activities, both public and private, if they are going to be of value. Thus, to a considerable degree, decisions by aid authorities with respect to economic overhead projects must complement activities and policies of the government itself. In practice, however, most development plans, including proposals for external assistance, provide for a certain amount of flexibility, especially in the phasing over time of the projects and activities. While local representatives of external agencies may give informal advice regarding planning and the formulation of proposals for external assistance, they rarely initiate proposals. External agencies usually have an opportunity to choose from among a number of project aid proposals, and often this is done through informal contacts by country representatives before formal aid applications are actually made by the developing country. In this way, project assistance can influence the emphasis given in the implementation of a development plan, both as regards the projects directly financed by the external agency and, also, complementary activities and policies. Unfortunately, however, the dearth of sound projects has led some development assistance agencies to finance whatever good projects come their way. Thus, availability of projects rather than development strategy becomes the determining factor in aid allocation.

EXTERNAL AID TO INDUSTRY

Development theories present a confusing array of guidelines for industrialization in respect to (a) the allocation of total investment resources to industry, (b) the industrial categories to be emphasized, (c) the criteria for determining comparative advantage, and (d) the choice of techniques in particular industries. We have seen good reason to doubt the thesis that industrialization should be maximized in order to absorb workers from the rural areas. In many developing countries, industrialization has been deliberately subsidized, usually at the expense of agriculture, by means of indiscriminate protection, low-cost loans, the holding down of agricultural prices, or the taxation of agricultural exports. Thus, investment in industry and complementary economic overhead services must be balanced against agricultural development, and where agricultural output is stagnating or lagging in relation to both domestic requirements and agriculture's potential contribution to foreign exchange earnings, a heavy emphasis on industry would appear to constitute a misallocation of resources. As has already been pointed out, except for large industrial projects such as steel, pulp and paper, basic chemicals and the like, external assistance agencies do not as a rule provide significant amounts of direct assistance to industry; most of the assistance to industry has been provided through program loans, balance-of-payments assistance, and industrial development banks.

In the case of large industrial projects in basic industries, there are certain obvious criteria which have not always been followed by external agencies. The justification for a steel industry in India, which has both a large internal market and the basic materials for steelmaking, or of a steel industry in Chile which has an excellent resource base and the ability to compete in a regional market, is far different from that of Colombia, the ability of whose steel industry to supply its internal market depends upon a high level of protection. Another seemingly obvious criterion would be that a proper proportion of a country's industry should be directed toward the export market. A third criterion would be to discourage any industry which could only be maintained by an indefinite high level of protection. This principle is especially important in the light of attempts to encourage the expansion of intraregional trade among developing countries. Thus, for example, the development of the high-cost Argentine steel industry in the face of a low-cost source of steel from Chile makes little sense either nationally or regionally. The same can be said of the development of a very inefficient automobile industry in Arica, Chile, some 1,000 miles north of Santiago (L. L. Johnson, 1965).

Industrialization is frequently slanted in the direction of production of upper- and middle-class consumer goods, particularly consumer durable goods, as against production of mass consumption items such as shoes, low-cost clothing, farm implements, non-mechanical tools, and a variety of cheap household goods. This distribution of industrial effort is due in part to the fact that a large portion of the populations lacks the purchasing power to acquire almost any industrial goods, and in part to the fact that the protective duties or absolute prohibitions on imports of middle-

and upper-class goods, particularly automobiles and consumers' durables, makes their domestic production and sale exceedingly profitable. If import duties on these goods were accompanied by an equivalent excise tax on domestically produced counterparts or substitutes, a somewhat different distribution of industrial investment might be achieved. Middle- and upper-class consumers' goods have a high import content, but the duties on equipment, materials, and the components required to produce them are often relatively low. Thus, import policies have an important influence on the pattern of industrial investment.

In the absence of higher effective demand for mass consumption goods, more investment will not be directed toward these commodities. The expansion of effective demand for these commodities requires a general increase in productivity, especially in the agricultural sector, a change in the distribution of income, and in some cases improved transportation and marketing (including lower markups) so as to make industrial commodities available to a larger proportion of the population. In many countries a change in market structure is required. Industry tends to be dominated by oligopolies that follow a policy of high prices with little concern for cost-reducing investment. Competition and entry of new firms are often hampered by collusion between business and government to keep out foreign firms and to prevent potential domestic competitors from obtaining capital or import allocations. As the Japanese have shown, mass, low-cost production of import substitutes paves the way for competitive marketing in world markets. In the field of manufacturing, the ability to compete in world markets usually does not arise from deliberately establishing industries designed for the world market. Manufacturers must first be produced efficiently on a mass scale for the domestic market.

Capital intensity, in manufacturing as well as in other fields, is governed by a variety of conditions and policies peculiar to each country and industry, over which external assistance agencies ordinarily have little direct control. Much of the borrowed technology employed in industry in developing countries is designed for developed countries with far different ratios of the productive factors. On the other hand, factor price ratios in developing countries frequently undervalue capital and overvalue labor; in addition, capital-intensive methods may be a means of economizing on scarce skills and supervisory and managerial experience. The use of capital-intensive and labor-saving techniques in developing countries with surplus labor is unfortunate not only because such techniques do not economize on the scarce factor, capital, but, perhaps more significantly, because they do not provide for a larger amount of on-the-job training and experience, which is of the greatest importance for human resource development. In the short run, owing to the shortage of skills and experience, capital-intensive techniques may yield a higher output per unit of capital. In the longer run, this tendency may be offset by an expansion of the trained labor force. Technical assistance agencies and productivity centers established with the help of external assistance might well devote their efforts to the development of technologies, together with on-the-job training programs, which are best suited to the factor endowment and human resource development requirements of developing countries. There ought to be options between cottage industries and two- or three-man handicraft shops, on the one hand, and the highly automated factories typical of U.S. production, on the other.

Turning briefly to the role of foreign aid in industrial development, development-assistance agencies, and particularly multilateral agencies, do not provide substantial amounts of direct aid for industrial projects. Much of the direct loan assistance to industry by the Export-Import Bank and the external lending agencies of other governments is influenced more by the desire to promote commercial exports than by a concern for the development of the recipient country by the application of appropriate development strategies. Some external financial assistance is being made available to industry indirectly through industrial development banks. The advantages and potentialities of this technique for extending aid are considerable, and should be given greater emphasis in aid programs (Adler and Mikesell, 1966; Mikesell, 1966a). However, under this technique, there are severe limitations on the employment of investment criteria from the standpoint of the economy as a whole. Certain guidelines relating to project evaluation can be required of industrial development banks, especially since their loans out of external aid capital are subject to review. But these guidelines necessarily apply to the soundness of projects within the existing framework of prices, costs, and supply and demand as determined by governmental foreign trade and exchange policies and internal tax policies. Thus, for example, an industrial development bank could not properly be requested by an external assistance agency to deny credits to a relatively high-cost import-substituting industry if government policies have made such an operation profitable. The external assistance agency might, however, suggest that the government adopt trade policies consistent with an efficient use of resources as an important self-help measure and make the adoption of these policies a condition for receiving aid.

AGRICULTURAL PROGRAMS

The recent rediscovery of agriculture by development economists has been echoed by an increased interest in aid to agriculture by external assistance agencies. Important contributions have been made by foreign technical missions to agriculture in developing countries. However, improvements in agricultural productivity do not as a rule call for substantial amounts of external aid in the form of direct commodity imports. Even large irrigation projects which may involve considerable capital investment can often be undertaken with highly labor-intensive production techniques requiring modest amounts of imported equipment and materials. Nevertheless, imported items may be strategic, and a contribution to the local currency costs of agricultural programs (which inevitably have some indirect balance-of-payments impact) may be necessary for the improvement of agriculture. Far more important, of course, is the change in agricultural organization and methods, which requires action not only on the part of governmental authorities but a change in social attitudes and motivation. Frequently, a good deal of technical research is needed in order to determine the types of crops, fertilizer, and production techniques that are required for increasing agricultural productivity. This research, followed by the organization of training programs, and making available necessary materials and tools, requires financing far in excess of the limited resources of technical assistance agencies such as the U.N. Food and Agricultural Organization (FAO). In October, 1964, the World Bank and the FAO entered into an agreement whereby the two agencies would cooperate in the identification and preparation of projects to the point where they can be considered for financing by the Bank or by IDA.

External financing agencies, in cooperation with technical assistance agencies, need to formulate strategies for dealing with dozens of problems in the field of agricultural productivity. In most cases, these strategies should favor labor-intensive techniques that will both expand employment in agriculture, and increase output per worker. Higher incomes for agricultural workers and small farmers will increase their demand for industrial products, both consumer goods and producer goods, and will reduce the movement to the large urban centers. Greater prosperity for rural areas far from the overcrowded metropolitan centers will contribute to the growth of industries in the smaller cities and towns near these areas, and to the movement of capital and industry away from the metropolitan centers. Decentralization of productive activity at all levels is extremely important for the social and political progress of developing countries, and external assistance agencies can contribute to this process in the choice of projects or broad agricultural programs which they are willing to assist. Some loss may be involved in not exploiting more fully the external economies present in the burgeoning metropolitan centers, but in the longer run the creation of new areas with external economies will offset the diseconomies and the social and political disadvantages of the further concentration of capital and population in the large urban communities.

Foreign assistance to agriculture requires support of comprehensive programs that depart from the traditional project approach to foreign assistance. Not only do the programs involve a large number of interrelated activities (for example, production credits to farmers, fertilizer, seed, implements, technical training, assistance to marketing cooperatives, irrigation, land tenure reform, etc.), but the direct import content is likely to be small compared with the total outlays. They also require a number of legislative and administrative measures and cannot be successful in the absence of vigorous self-help activities on the part of local and federal governments and of the members of the rural communities. In addition to requiring a considerable amount of external technical assistance, especially in the program or project preparation stage, they require flexible forms of financing in which foreign assistance is closely coordinated with domestic financing, often from several sources. In view of the necessity of close policy and financial coordination, aid for comprehensive agricultural programs would appear to represent good candidates for sectoral program loans of the type discussed in Chapter 6. The commitment of assistance could be based on a detailed, mutually agreed-upon program, but the disbursements would be made as required by the several activities, which could only go forward as the agreed-upon self-help measures were implemented and the matching funds from domestic sources were made available.

HUMAN RESOURCE DEVELOPMENT AND SOCIAL IMPACT PROJECTS

The growing importance attached to education, health, and other factors in human resource development, together with the concept of investment in human capital as a major factor in the growth process, has led external financing agencies such as the World Bank to revise their policies regarding the proper role of external aid in these areas. This is not to say that external financing and technical assistance agencies have been oblivious to the importance of education and human resource development in economic growth. In fact, much of the technical assistance during the postwar period has been directed toward formal education, technical training programs, health, sanitation, etc. But these activities were thought of more in terms of improving the environment or promoting productivity rather than in terms of capital investment. Moreover, expenditures on education, health, low-cost housing, improved water supply for urban and rural communities, etc., were thought of more in terms of a direct contribution to social welfare than as an expansion of the capital stock of the country which could yield returns in terms of measurable output. It is true, of course, that investments of the social impact variety affect consumption and welfare, as well as productivity and output. But this is also true of investments in power and transportation—the services are employed both for directly increasing consumption and for increasing productivity and output in industry and agriculture. Nevertheless, there has been a substantial bias on the part of external financing agencies in favor of physical capital assets which turn out final products for sale in the market, or provide tangible inputs in the production process. Moreover, capital formation in economic overhead projects and in so-called directly productive activities in industry, mining, and agriculture were traditionally financed by international capital flows and were associated with "sound" investment, while investments in social projects were a matter for local governments to the extent that the communities could afford them out of the production of measurable outputs of goods and services generated by inputs of labor, land, and "productive" capital. In addition to the traditional prejudice against social impact projects as being somehow unsound or less sound activities for international finance, such projects are difficult to evaluate in terms of the usual banking standards, and there was no way to measure their contribution to the output of goods and services. Social impact projects also involve a heavy component of local currency expenditures which are difficult to supervise and control and violate the general preference of external agencies for financing only imports. Their evaluation and implementation require specialized personnel, and a heavy packaging of technical assistance with the external financing, which is ordinarily not available in the external financial institutions.

Although AID and its predecessor agencies have made a number of grants for so-called social impact projects such as education, hospitals, etc., and a considerable amount of technical assistance has been provided by both national and multinational agencies, development loans for these purposes are of rather recent origin. Since 1961, with the establishment of the Social Progress Trust Fund administered by the Inter-American Development Bank, loans in such social project categories as education, water, sewage systems and low- and medium-cost housing (particularly the financing of home loan institutions) have been gaining in importance in the loan activities of the IDB, AID, and, more recently, the World Bank Group. Frequently these activities are packaged with technical assistance provided in the form of either grants or loans, often in cooperation with specialized agencies such as UNESCO or the World Health Organization. It might also be said that the idea of loans for technical assistance in a variety of areas is relatively new; such loans are being provided frequently in combination with, or included as a part of, the loan for the project.

The problems involved in providing assistance to education are exceedingly complex if the external assistance agency is properly to evaluate programs and to influence the allocation of total expenditures in this field. The allocation of a given volume of expenditures for education among the various educational levels, in order to make the maximum contribution to development in the particular country, differs considerably with the stage and general direction of development and with the educational progress that has already been made. Social objectives established by governments must also be considered. For example, the achievement of six years of primary education for all Latin Americans was established as one of the goals of the Punta del Este Charter. However, in terms of maximizing output, such a goal may not constitute the best allocation of available resources for some Latin American countries. In fact, it may be nearly impossible to meet this goal within a ten-year period without a heavy allocation of resources to secondary education for the training of teachers. As has frequently been pointed out, there is considerable misallocation of resources devoted to higher education. Training people for skills and occupations for which there does not exist a sufficient demand is not only a waste of scarce resources, but it also leads to individual frustrations and social and political instability.

What does development research have to offer assistance agencies in establishing criteria and guidelines for the allocation of financial and technical resources to human resource development? The efforts of development economists to calculate the proportion of the "residual" in the Cobb-Douglas production function which should be attributed to the improvement in the quality of labor, the attempt to calculate the rate of return from expenditures on education, and correlations between the expenditures on education and various indicators of growth are of little value in providing criteria applicable to specific projects or programs. Theodore Schultz' findings (1961, Tables 5 and 6, p. 580; 1962, pp. 1-8) that resources allocated to education in the United States for the period 1900-56 grew about three-and-one half times faster than gross formation of physical capital, and that the ratio of the stock of educational capital to the stock of reproducible physical capital rose from 22 per cent in 1900 to 42 per cent in 1957, scarcely provides a guide for the allocation of resources to education in Nigeria or Pakistan. Such analysis may, however, provide some idea of the proportion of a nation's assets that ought to be devoted to education at various stages of its development as a necessary but not a sufficient condition for growth.

Harbison and Myers (1964) have prepared quantititive indicators of human resource development from which they have constructed composite indexes for individual countries grouped in terms of four categories of human resource development: (1) underdeveloped; (2) partially developed; (3) semi-advanced; and (4) advanced. Their composite index is based on (a) enrollment at the second level of education and (b) enrollment at the third level of education, as a percentage of the appropriate age group, with (b) given a weight of 5. They compared their composite index of 75 countries with available indicators of economic development and found significant correlation coefficients between the composite indexes and GNP per capita. The authors readily admit, however, that quantitative relationships do not establish causal relationships. Also, their composite index, whatever its shortcomings, gave some peculiar results in individual situations. For example, India's educational index appeared to be quite high relative to that country's per capita GNP.

Harbison and Myers (1964, Chs. 4-7) proceed to analyze the experience of countries at each of the four levels of human resource development in an effort to suggest an appropriate strategy for the typical country at each level. They point out (Ch. 10) that it is quite possible for a country to invest inefficiently in human resource development, to emphasize the wrong kinds of formal education, or fail to give proper weight to in-service training, and that education and other aspects of human resource development should be an integral part of development planning. They admit, however, that it is not possible to equate the marginal efficiency of capital invested in education, say, with that invested in industry, agriculture, and road building, but that total allocations for general education must inevitably be based in large measure on judgments of public officials, social values, and political pressure. About all that can be said is that for most countries in the modern world there will be a tendency to increase the proportion of resources allocated to human resource development, and that development plans should allow for an increased proportion of expenditures in this field.

Perhaps the most significant contribution of Harbison and Myers lies in their suggestions for planning strategies in the field of education as they relate to the level of development and the goals of a development plan. These strategies should provide a guide to external assistance agencies in determining obvious weaknesses and bottlenecks in educational and training programs. For example, developing countries in the semi-advanced stage are notoriously weak in secondary education and in the training of workers in certain skills, either in technical schools or by means of on-the-job training. Similarly, institutions of higher learning tend to overemphasize law and the humanities as against high-quality training in engineering, economics, business and public administration, and agriculture. There is also a failure to combine research oriented to the technical problems of the developing countries with higher education in these countries. Thus, U.S. foundations, such as the Ford and Rockefeller foundations, along with AID and other development agencies, have sought to strengthen education in developing countries by assisting them in filling obvious gaps in their programs, frequently with the aid of U.S. educational institutions.

Other areas of human resource development, such as health, sanitation, water supply, low-cost housing and community development, present even more difficult problems for a rational allocation of resources. Few would deny that social investment of this kind has a certain payoff in terms of measurable GNP, but the goal of the development plan should not be simply the production of marketable goods and services, but social welfare broadly conceived. The achievement of a relatively high level of per capita income in Venezuela has not eliminated the slums surrounding Caracas or the miserable living conditions in a large part of the rural area. Nor would a doubling or tripling of Venezuela's per capita income over the next generation guarantee a substantial improvement in these conditions.

Human resource development is not something which can be dealt with by massive injections of capital; it is largely a matter of teaching and inducing people to help themselves. What is involved is the whole social and political fabric of the country, particularly at the community level. Although the central government can provide a certain amount of credit and technicians, there is perhaps altogether too much of an attitude of dependence upon the central government for improvement in this area. What is required is the willingness and ability of communities to organize programs, tax themselves to finance them, and mobilize the human and material resources to carry them out efficiently and without corruption and political bickering. But the failure to do these things is in large measure the essence of being underdeveloped.

One of the most effective programs in the low-cost housing field has been the organization and provision of seed capital for home-loan institutions: IDB and AID have made a number of loans to Latin American countries for low-cost housing. Investment and entrepreneurial activities in home construction, operating under certain standards and profit margins established by the home-loan systems, have been stimulated, and the larger volume of construction of essentially the same type of housing tends to lower costs. In December, 1961, the IDB made two loans of $10 million each to the Venezuelan government in support of a national rural water-supply program designed to help build water-supply systems in 338 communities with a combined population of about 300,000. In 1964, a third loan of $10 million was made available by the IDB to build water systems in some 300 additional communities. Venezuela now has a goal of supplying water-supply systems to all towns with populations of 500-5,000 by 1967. These two loans were made by the Social Progress Trust Fund on concessionary terms with the loans repayable in local currency. The question might well be raised as to why loans on such generous terms were made to Venezuela, a country which, compared with other developing countries, has ample foreign exchange and could undoubtedly well afford to finance such important projects on its own. The answer undoubtedly lies in the fact that the willingness of the IDB to finance such important projects stimulated the Venezuelan government and the local communities benefiting from the projects to provide capital and other resources for their undertaking.

The inducement effects of assistance in the social project field can be enormous. They provide a way of overcoming administrative inertia in inaugurating programs involving various levels of government and the activities of private groups for mobilizing domestic resources. Development assistance agencies should certainly give a high priority to social impact projects where there exists an opportunity through the use of seed capital and technical assistance to stimulate investment and cooperative social activity which would not otherwise take place. They should not do the entire job, since this would defeat an important purpose of this type of assistance, namely, that of encouraging people to help themselves. In terms of the financial contribution, the ratio of external assistance to domestic resources should be no higher than, say, 1 to 3. Moreover, such activities should carry with them a demonstration effect which will induce other communities, perhaps with some assistance from the central or state government, to undertake similar activities without help from foreign assistance agencies.

II. FOREIGN ASSISTANCE AS A MEANS OF INFLUENCING DEVELOPMENT POLICIES OF RECIPIENTS

Virtually all foreign assistance has some influence on development programs and policies of recipients. This influence tends to be minimal where aid is provided by several donors, each financing single projects in various sectors of an economy, without any effort to coordinate their activities. Much of the development assistance during the postwar period has been made available in this way. Maximum influence on development policies by aid donors as a group would require (a) coordination of assistance programs at the country level, and (b) formulation of joint aid programs designed to achieve development objectives agreed between donors and the recipient with the performance of the recipient subject to periodic review by donors with a view to assessing self-help efforts as conditions for continued assistance. The prerequisites for maximum influence have never been approached, although a certain amount of donor coordination does exist with respect to some countries. Particular agencies, especially AID, have devised aid-negotiating and implementing techniques for achieving a substantial degree of influence over the economic policies of recipients.

In the theoretical literature on foreign aid, there is a tendency to identify self-help with actual performance in terms of certain quantitative indicators. Thus, an increase in the savings ratio constitutes an important indicator of self-help on the assumption that if a government adopts the correct policies (for example, fiscal reforms and measures to encourage private savings), the savings ratio will rise. Similarly, an increase in the rate of growth in exports and in investment are regarded as indicators of self-help. Chenery and Strout (1965, p. 9) include the marginal capital-output ratio among their principal policy variables, but the factors determining this ratio are quite complex and certainly not readily amenable to government policies in a mixed economy. It is well known, of course, that under certain circumstances these self-help indicators may not respond to governmental measures, or that governments with the best of intentions may adopt the wrong policies for improving the indicators of self-help. Self-help is often identified with success, so that the whole complex relationship between governmental policies and measures, on the one hand, and indicators of performance, on the other, tends to be ignored.

In the following discussion I shall use "self-help" to mean the adoption of policies by aid recipients designed to improve actual economic performance, while performance itself can be measured by various objective indicators. Thus the passage of tax-reform legislation together with efficient administration constitute self-help measures which, it is hoped, will result in a higher ratio of government revenues to national income, an important indicator of economic performance. Similarly, price stabilization measures and measures to promote savings are self-help measures designed to achieve stability and raise the savings ratio. Thus, development aid policies seek to promote self-help measures which are expected to result in improved economic performance.

THE ROLE OF QUANTITATIVE GROWTH MODELS

The desire to influence development programs and policies of aid recipients has been intensified with the adoption of specific development goals and targets by the foreign-assistance agencies. The identification of the external assistance agencies with specific development goals as a measure of success of their aid programs means that they become rather deeply involved in the process by which these goals are to be accomplished. The assistance agency seeks to project the relationship of an annual volume of aid to the realization of quantitative development targets under a number of assumptions regarding the internal performance indicators in the developing countries. This has led to the formulation of growth models by the assistance agencies themselves designed to determine the conditions under which alternative targets could be realized, including both the amounts of external aid and the self-help measures undertaken by the recipient countries. The models are also employed to test the consistency of national development programs and to indicate how they might be improved. In some cases, the national-development plans provide both the data and the functional relationships needed for these projections, while in other cases existing plans are inadequate for this purpose.

The elements of the quantitative growth model which has been employed by the AID staff for determining external requirements for target rates of growth with varying assumptions with respect to economic performance were described in Chapter 3. How useful is this technique as a means of identifying desirable self-help measures and development strategies, on the one hand, and of providing a framework for influencing development policies and programs of recipient countries, on the other? A major question has to do with the reliability of the judgments with respect to the fundamental coefficients—savings ratio, rate of investment, capital-output ratio, and export growth rate—which are regarded as policy variables subject in large degree to the measures adopted by the recipient countries. Not only do these assumptions prejudge performance, but they also assume that recipient countries know, and are capable of implementing, the policies and programs that will result in the performance indicators behaving in a certain fashion. Moreover, the performance indicators reflect basic structural changes in the economies which constitute the very essence of development. Without a deeper knowledge of how these structural changes take place, changes which involve social processes not directly amenable to traditional policy instruments, it is difficult to have much confidence in the assumed behavior of the performance indicators. The only guide is history, and I fail to find an orderly movement of these basic variables in the past experience of most developing countries which would provide a basis for projection over a decade or two.

Leaving aside the difficulties in relating actual government policies to performance, and the wide margin of error arising from estimates of capital-output ratios, import ratios, rates of export growth, etc., based on historical data, the hypothetical growth models are of value in revealing the longer-run implications of either continuing current patterns of economic behavior or of assumed alterations in such patterns. They can be useful in assessing economic performance in terms of the basic indicators and in identifying elements of performance crucial for development, even though the links between governmental measures and the basic performance indicators are not well established or even fully understood. The usefulness of quantitative country models in foreign assistance may be illustrated by the following suggested procedure:

1) Using historical data for GNP, savings, investment, imports, exports, population, and other relevant variables, estimate the coefficients and parameters linking the variables employed in the model, for example, capital-output ratio, the investment ratio, the savings ratio, the rate of export growth, and the import ratio.

2) Keeping the coefficients constant, project the magnitude of the basic variables, for example, per capita GNP, investment, savings, imports, and

exports, assuming no change in net capital inflow. To the extent permitted by the data, check the realism of the model by projecting from an earlier base period to a recent period and compare with actual experience.

3) Assume a target rate of growth in per capita GNP and identify the changes in the magnitudes of the other basic variables (and in the parameters linking the variables) which would be required *assuming no change in capital inflow.* Identify those variables (and parameters) most subject to manipulation through changes in national policies, and those which tend to reflect the basic economic and social structure, the stage of economic development, the pattern of private and social demand, etc.

4) Determine the rate of growth in per capita GNP under varying assumptions with respect to those parameters subject to change as a consequence of alteration of internal policies.

5) Estimate the probable effects of current or intended policies on the parameters subject to policy alteration and the potential effects of alternative policies on these parameters. Then estimate the effects of these changes in the parameters on the growth rate over a period of time.

6) Consider how varying amounts and types of external assistance might be employed to facilitate the changes in the parameters through policy alteration or to induce a desirable change in the social structure, for example, education and technical assistance of various types.

It should be noted that in the approach suggested above, foreign aid is not automatically calculated from the model as the amount required to fill either an investment-savings gap or an import-exchange earnings gap. Rather, the model would serve to indicate the changes in the basic economic relationships required for various target growth rates and provide a basis for policy determination. In the context of a given economic, social, and political structure, governmental measures may have limited effectiveness in shifting the parameters employed in the growth model. The probable effects of governmental self-help measures must be estimated and the estimates continually adjusted on the basis of experience. Under this approach, the role of foreign aid is to facilitate policy change and an improvement in skills and organization by eliminating temporary shortages and providing a margin of resources during the period of structural change. The required amount of aid cannot be calculated from the model but can only be determined by experience involving the relationship between policy measures and the shifts in the performance indicators, on the one hand, and the volume and nature of the resource gaps created during the adjustment process, on the other. The amount and nature of the aid would be determined by the progress of the complex process of adjustment toward sustained development progress and would be conditioned by such factors as business attitudes toward investment, the character of public administration, social attitudes toward work, consumer preferences and savings, the level of education, etc. Certain types of aid can help to induce policy and structural change. It follows also that external assistance should be regarded in disaggregated terms, since it serves as a cooperative and often as a catalytic agent in the complex process of development.

Models should be capable of revealing the interdependence among the parameters and performance indicators. For example, a country may not be able to increase its rate of savings and investment without an increase in the export growth rate, and the savings rate may be shown to be dependent in part upon the volume and direction of investment. Even the ICOR is not independent of the growth rate and the complex factors that determine growth (Leibenstein, 1966, pp. 20-27). These interdependencies are important in analyzing performance and in explaining why certain policy measures may prove ineffective in the absence of other policy measures or in the absence of certain structural changes.

Quantitative models of the type described may be used to analyze development plans prepared by aid recipients, to check on the realism of the plan, given the parameters explicitly or implicitly assumed by the plan, and to evaluate the parameters themselves. The models may also be employed to point up the need for improved performance (for example, rate of export growth or ratio of fiscal revenues to GDP) for embodiment in the plan as a condition for its success. Development plans usually postulate a single set of amounts and types of external requirements for achieving a planned target. The amounts of assistance postulated in the development plan may either be unrealistic in terms of foreign capital availabilities, or may be at variance with the aid criteria established by the providers of foreign assistance. It would be desirable for the representatives of the principal donors or of a consortium of donors, to discuss these questions with the planning authorities before a plan is completed and made public. Planning models prepared by donors would be useful as a framework for such discussions.

FOREIGN AID AND ECONOMIC PERFORMANCE

Foreign aid is closely associated with economic performance in two basic ways. First, various types of aid may provide a means of *inducing* policies and programs which lead to improved performance. Second, aid may *facilitate* the implementation of policy measures for promoting improved performance necessary to achieve development goals. The goal of concessionary aid is to help countries achieve a level of performance which will enable them to develop at a satisfactory pace through the efficient use of their own resources. Thus, the function of *concessionary* aid is not *pri-*

marily to *supplement* the resources of the recipient, but rather to help the recipient mobilize its own resources and perhaps to attract private and public nonconcessionary external capital for achieving its development goals.[4]

PERFORMANCE VS. SELF-HELP

As already noted, a certain amount of confusion exists in the literature with respect to the terms, "self-help" and "performance." Performance as measured by such indicators as savings and investment ratios, the export growth rate, or the rate of growth in GNP, is always objective. Over certain time periods, the performance indicators may reflect fortuitous or adverse forces in international markets for a country's principal exports. Countries have been known to experience a relatively high growth rate and satisfactory performance as measured by the indicators for considerable periods of time without having a broadly based development, either in the sense of social development or in the sense of mobilizing and increasing the potential of their national resources for sustained growth without heavy dependence on one or two rapidly growing exports. Self-help, on the other hand, has to do with governmental policies and activities, plus those of private business firms and of social or community organizations, directed toward an improvement of both economic performance and the structural conditions required for broadly based development. Thus, self-help measures would encompass: (a) financial policies and programs designed to encourage private savings and productive investment, including both fiscal and monetary policies and the creation of development banks and technical assistance agencies for serving private industry and agriculture; (b) land-reform measures designed to increase agricultural output; (c) good planning and budgetary management; (d) foreign-exchange and trade policies designed to promote exports and avoid uneconomic import substitution; (e) the preparation of good investment projects for implementing the economic plans; and (f) the formulation of social programs and projects at all levels of government and by nongovernmental groups.

Should aid be related to the taking of self-help measures or to the performance indicators? Conditioning aid on performance, with the sanction that aid will be withdrawn if performance is unsatisfactory, assumes that performance is fully within the control of the policy makers in the aid re-

4. Many nations, including Australia, Austria, Italy, and Japan, which have achieved a satisfactory rate of growth and a broadly based development, continue to borrow from the World Bank on terms which reflect the cost of capital in private international markets, primarily as a means of supplementing their domestic resources.

cipients. An alternative is to condition aid on the willingness of the recipient to undertake certain self-help measures mutually agreed upon with the foreign-assistance agency or aid consortium. The measures would need to be adjusted on the basis of experience, with a view to promoting a level of performance consistent with a satisfactory rate of growth and development without further concessionary aid. The implications of these two approaches for various types of aid will be discussed later.

We simply do not know enough about the relationship between governmental policy measures and programs and the magnitude and timing of their impact on economic performance to identify self-help measures with performance. Self-help is sometimes judged in terms of the marginal savings ratio or of the per capita marginal savings ratio (Fei and Paauw, 1965, p. 251). Thus, a marginal savings ratio which is higher than the average ratio indicates that the country is moving toward an average savings ratio consistent with self-sustaining growth. However, it is my view that such simple indicators do not reveal the complex factors in the development process, and even where they can be determined on the basis of reliable statistics they are likely to be quite misleading. For example, they may simply reflect an improvement in the country's terms of trade.

It may be objected that relating assistance to self-help measures as I have defined them, does not constitute a satisfactory standard for use in foreign-aid policy. Nothing succeeds like success, and rewarding effort is not good enough. Aid recipients have an obligation to identify and adopt those self-help measures which will result in satisfactory performance. Moreover, there is a large element of self-help, involving the entire community and not just the government, in the carrying out of certain policies and measures in a manner which will in fact lead to satisfactory performance. For example, it is not enough to legislate new tax laws; there must be an increase in the ratio of government revenues to domestic product. It is not enough to promulgate stabilization measures; reasonable price stability must be achieved. It is not enough to adopt policies for encouraging private domestic and foreign investment; such investment must grow at a satisfactory rate. And so on with measures for increasing exports, raising agricultural production, achieving balance-of-payments equilibrium, reducing inequality of income, expanding social services including education, improving public administration, and raising the growth rate. But the attainment of these goals constitutes the process of development itself, a process which is far more complex than the most sophisticated growth models that could possibly be devised. In practice, therefore, the adequacy of self-help measures must be continually checked against performance and continually altered and improved in order to realize good performance.

My own view of the relationship between foreign assistance, on the one hand, and self-help measures and performance, on the other, is predicated on the following view of the primary function of foreign aid. Maximum self-help efforts properly coordinated within the framework of an overall development plan should, over time and in the absence of internal catastrophes or a sudden slump in world demand, lead to a level of performance which would make possible the realization of development goals consistent with the efficient employment of a nation's resources. But developing countries need help in implementing policies and programs, and the expectation of external aid is often required to induce them to initiate policies and programs for the mobilization of their resources. External assistance is required because it takes time to mobilize a country's resources for maximum results and consistency in the growth pattern. Meanwhile, critical shortages and bottlenecks will appear and their removal will require outside help. Also, the adoption of policy measures for achieving good performance is a trial-and-error process, and the self-help policies, in line with Western standards of political and social progress, should be adopted within the framework of democratic governments and a substantial degree of economic freedom. I therefore view the need for foreign aid not in terms of an aggregate supplement to the total resources of a country, but as disaggregated assistance for overcoming strategic shortages which appear in the process of domestic resource mobilization and redirection. It is for this reason that I have rejected the aggregate-gap approaches to foreign aid. Moreover, I see no way of predetermining the volume of aid required for this purpose over a period of several years. After a country has achieved a state of satisfactory progress based on a reasonably efficient employment of its own resources, it may want to supplement these resources with additional private foreign capital and public loans at conventional rates. But this does not require a special aid program based on development strategies and the provision of concessionary financial assistance. However, the international financial structure should always be such as to provide opportunities for a flow of capital on conventional (hard) terms from the relatively capital-rich to the relatively capital-poor countries.

Although I prefer to regard foreign assistance as a means of helping countries achieve good economic performance through appropriate self-help measures (and not as a reward for good performance), performance criteria are important in the aid process in order to judge the effectiveness of self-help measures and the success of the aid program in inducing and facilitating such measures. Measures of performance also enter into decisions regarding the need for aid, especially concessionary aid. I shall summarize briefly a few of the measures of performance that have been suggested.

SELF-SUSTAINING GROWTH CRITERIA

In Chapter 3, I discussed several aid-growth models, including the Chenery–Strout and Fei and Paauw models, which establish performance criteria in terms of certain parameters which determine the conditions for self-sustaining growth and a terminal date for aid. These parameters include the marginal savings ratio (or the per capita marginal savings ratio), the rate of growth of investment or capital, and the rate of growth of exports. In the operation of the models, these parameters must have certain critical values in relation to other variables or coefficients, if the investment-savings gap or the import-exchange earnings gap is eventually to close so that aid can have a terminal date.

In line with the self-sustaining growth thesis, Arthur Lewis (1964) has suggested as a measure of performance the ratio of the sum of public expenditures (excluding transfer payments and military outlays) and gross capital formation to gross domestic product. He has stated that this ratio should not be less than 30 per cent if foreign aid is to be effective in assisting countries to achieve self-sustaining growth.

Without denying the value of growth models for certain purposes, many economists regard measures of performance based on parameters indicating self-sustaining growth criteria as both inadequate and unreliable guides in the aid-dispensing process. The hypothetical models constitute a gross oversimplification of the development process. The unreliability of the data and our lack of understanding of complex factors determining the parameters provide little basis for confidence in projections which are dependent upon the stability of, or orderly change in, the parameters over a period of years. In addition the parameters reveal the conditions for only one aspect of development. Thus, many economists prefer a more disaggregated approach to performance, one which includes not only the parameters embodied in growth models, but also indicators which reveal basic structural changes in the direction and character of investment and output, and progress in various areas of social development.

DISAGGREGATED INDICATORS OF PERFORMANCE

There are many dimensions of development, some of which are not even reflected in national accounts estimates, and some of which cannot be measured statistically. A disaggregated picture of performance is important for foreign-aid practitioners since most aid is directed toward specific sectors and for the achievement of limited goals. Much of foreign aid, for example, is provided for infrastructure or for inducing social change, which constitute preconditions for the creation of a modern economy capable of rapid development. Poor performance in certain sectors (such as agriculture) may be regarded as a strategic bottleneck in growth. For some purposes, the level of employment may be regarded as a more significant indicator than the rate of growth in per capita GNP. Finally, there may be a desire to construct a composite index of performance made up of strategic elements not reflected or given proper weight in GNP.

Paul G. Clark (1962) has identified seven indicators of development performance (which he refers to as self-help indicators) as follows:

1) increase in GNP in constant prices;
2) increase in agricultural production;
3) increase in electricity production in response both to rising incomes and to extending urbanization and industrialization;
4) share of gross investment in GNP (which Clark regards as the least reliable statistical measure of the group);
5) domestic tax revenue as a share of total government expenditure;
6) increase in the quantity of exports;
7) number of post-primary students per thousand population.

Although Clark defends these indicators as reflecting the primary elements of progress, he has been influenced in his choice of statistical indicators in part by the availability of comparable data and admits that the list might be expanded. For example he might have included an index of the increase in employment. Clark has assembled data for calculating the indicators for 21 Latin American countries, the indicators of *increase* being stated over a period of 3 years and the indicators of *shares* as an average over a 3-year period. Each indicator was converted to a ranking from 1 to 21 and the sum of the 7 ranks taken as the joint measure of economic progress or self-help. Clark then correlates each of the 7 indicators with the composite ranking for each of the 21 countries and finds that, except for electricity, all of the coefficients of rank correlation are significantly different from zero at the 5 per cent level of statistical significance.

A major weakness of Clark's rank-sum index of performance is that it gives equal weight to all performance indicators in arriving at a composite index. More sophisticated statistical techniques could be employed in which the weights would be varied according to judgment or in accordance with certain statistical principles designed to isolate the most important common element in the indicators.[5] The rank-order method of measuring performance would be useful in selecting those countries with relatively good per-

5. R. M. Sundrum, in a paper prepared for internal circulation in the World Bank, has formulated several alternative statistical methods for ranking countries according to performance.

formance for purposes of allocating aid, or in helping to identify areas of poor performance on a comparative basis. Clark (1962, p. 7) also suggests that measures of economic performance should be supplemented by "political and social evidences of a government's commitment to progress, which are not readily measured statistically." Among these, he mentions:

1) democratic processes respecting individual freedoms;

2) adoption of a well–conceived long-run development plan;

3) high standards of efficiency and honesty in government administration;

4) private and public commitments to national decision-making;

5) effective programs to improve land tenure systems;

6) tax systems which are equitable while raising adequate revenues;

7) trade and exchange policies which promote balance-of-payments equilibrium.

The above items would be included in what I would regard as self-help measures designed to achieve development progress.

EXTERNAL CAPITAL-ABSORPTIVE CAPACITY AS A
MEASURE OF PERFORMANCE

As a condition for receiving aid, the most important single measure of performance in the past has undoubtedly been the capacity of a country to formulate a stream of development projects regarded as "aid worthy" by foreign-assistance agencies. Since foreign-assistance agencies have tended to finance only foreign-exchange costs of projects, or no more than a fraction of the local currency costs or indirect foreign-exchange costs, performance in this sense also includes the ability of the recipients to provide financing for a portion of the projects assisted and, perhaps also, to provide all of the financing of complementary investments required for the efficient utilization of the aid-financed project. For a project or a package of projects to be aid worthy, certain standards of project evaluation must be met, including engineering, managerial, accounting, and economic standards such as benefit-cost comparisons. Such project appraisal must extend beyond the project itself, since the efficiency of its operation, its priority, and its contribution to output will depend upon a wide range of economic activities and, to a degree, the successful operation of the entire economy. One aspect of aid worthiness, the ability to service external loans, obviously applies to the economy as a whole.

When a foreign-assistance agency finances a series of projects or group of projects covering a significant segment of a country's total investment, determination of aid worthiness must involve an evaluation of performance at the macroeconomic level. If foreign-assistance agencies finance only a portion of the total local currency and foreign-exchange costs of projects, and if a large amount of other private and governmental investment and current expenditure is required for the successful operation of the projects, the volume of aid-worthy projects becomes a function of the aggregate level of domestic investment, and indeed of the rate of growth of the economy itself. Since the implementation of some projects will require higher levels of government expenditure, there must be a satisfactory increase in governmental revenues. Good performance requires a reasonable degree of price stability, and a growing level of domestic investment requires a rate of growth of exports commensurate with expanding imports. Thus, the volume of project assistance made available becomes directly related to performance at the macroeconomic level.

The World Bank, in its published reports and internal operational memoranda, has set forth a number of conditions pertaining to macroeconomic performance which are supposed to be taken into account in its lending operations. These include performance relating to (a) the volume of domestic savings; (b) the volume and effectiveness of total investment; (c) internal price stability; (d) balance-of-payments equilibrium as determined by foreign-exchange and trade policies; (e) the volume of private investment and the productivity of the private sector; (f) the capacity to service debts; and (g) the formulation and the implementation of good development plans.

It may be objected that a listing of general indicators of good performance is not a sufficient guide for aid policy. First, the criteria are not sufficiently objective or precise for use by loan officers in making decisions on particular loans or even for determining the level of lending over a given period. By the same token, they are not taken seriously or regarded as credible by the aid recipients. Second, if macroeconomic performance criteria are to be made conditions for project lending for a specific volume of project loans over a given period, quantitative estimates of performance should be related to the projects financed by foreign aid and to the activities flowing from these projects. For example, what increase in the level of domestic savings and investment should accompany a proposed annual package of foreign-financed projects in order for the projects to be implemented and make an appropriate contribution to growth and development? What increase in governmental revenues should accompany an annual package of foreign-financed projects in order both to avoid inflation and to implement the projects? What increase in the rate of export growth is required as a consequence of both the higher volume of investment and output resulting from the foreign-financed projects and the increase in debt service? Answers to these and similar questions obviously require macro-analysis. But such analysis ought to be conducted on a continuous basis and not in terms of long-run projections on the basis of assumed

parameters. Only in this way can the volume and nature of project assistance be continuously adjusted in accordance with macro-performance
criteria.

An objection to the capital-absorptive capacity approach to aid, even
where macroeconomic performance criteria are employed along the lines
outlined above, is that the volume and character of assistance are not
determined in relation to a development goal or goals to be achieved
within a specific time period. This objection is especially important in the
case of concessionary aid, which most donors believe should be limited in
amount and duration and directed toward realizing a specific goal, such as
a target rate of growth which can be maintained without further external
assistance. It is possible to establish an upper limit to the amount of aid
which would be made available to a particular country whatever its capital-
absorptive capacity, this limit being determined by the requirements of a
development plan or for the achievement of self-sustained growth. But
capital-absorptive capacity does not in itself provide a rationale for any
particular volume of aid or a set of objectives to be promoted through aid
strategies. Assisting a country in the realization of its national development
plan is not a sufficient rationale for the provision of concessionary aid. It
neither justifies concessionary aid as against external capital on conventional terms, nor does it provide goals and performance standards generally applicable to all aid recipients. The attractiveness of the approach to
aid based on an investment-savings gap model for achieving a self-sustained
growth target is that it provides the goals, performance standards, and the
means of calculating the amount and duration of aid. On the other hand,
the theoretical basis for this approach has serious weaknesses and has
been rejected by many economists. In the concluding chapter of this book,
I suggest an alternative approach to foreign aid which provides a rationale
and goals for both concessionary and conventional external capital
assistance.

PERFORMANCE INDICATORS RELATED TO BALANCE-OF-
PAYMENTS ASSISTANCE

A substantial volume of public foreign loans has been made to developing countries to assist them in dealing with balance-of-payments difficulties.
Sometimes these difficulties are a consequence of unforeseen forces not
easily amenable to corrective actions by governments, such as a crop failure, a sudden decline in export prices, or a natural catastrophe. Frequently,
however, they are the result of long-term factors affecting the demand and
supply of foreign exchange but which suddenly appear as crises when

countries are no longer able to increase or roll over their short- and medium-term indebtedness. In still other cases, developing countries with chronic balance-of-payments disequilibria, coupled with severe trade and exchange controls, have secured balance-of-payments support loans from foreign-assistance agencies as a part of a comprehensive development assistance program to enable them to finance a larger volume of imports required for their investment programs. It has been customary to condition the volume of balance-of-payments assistance, especially in cases where countries are in structural disequilibrium, on the taking of measures designed to correct or mitigate the disequilibrium.

The most familiar examples of performance criteria related to balance-of-payments assistance are those found in the standby agreements of the International Monetary Fund, by which the Fund assures member countries of a certain amount of assistance, if and when needed, on condition that specific financial policies, often involving quantitative guidelines, are followed. The conditions include undertakings by the country relating to fiscal policy, central bank and commercial bank policies and operations, interest rate policy, exchange rate policy, external debt and reserve policies, import policies, and other policies and measures affecting internal price stability and the balance of payments. Countries entering into standby agreements with the IMF have sometimes borrowed at the same time from other public and private sources, with the loan agreements tied in effect to the standby agreement with the IMF. Thus, for example, in April, 1959, the government of Chile received credits totaling $119 million, largely for the purpose of stabilization. The IMF provided only $8 million of this amount under a standby agreement; the bulk of the credits was provided by the Export-Import Bank, the International Cooperation Administration (predecessor to AID), the U.S. Treasury Exchange Stabilization Fund, the German Reconstruction Loan Corporation, and private U.S. banks. All of these credits were tied to negotiations culminating in a letter of intent of March, 1959,, by the Chilean Finance Minister and the President of the Central Bank of Chile to the Managing Director of the IMF. This letter set forth specific undertakings relating to the budgetary deficit, the total loans and investments of the Central Bank, and the rediscount rate, together with budget estimates and undertakings relating to fiscal expenditures and tax measures. The final paragraph of the Chilean letter of intent reads:

If at any time during the period of the standby agreement, 1) central bank loans exceed the limits specified in the above paragraphs, or 2) central bank credits to the government exceed the limits set forth above, or 3) the total volume of credit exceeds the limits discussed in previous paragraphs, the government will consult with the Fund before drawing any credits and shall agree with the Fund regarding the purposes for any additional drawings.[6]

Similar IMF package loan agreements have been made with Brazil, Colombia, and other Latin American countries.[7] The IMF standby agreements and the package credit arrangements involving other creditors have been criticized on the grounds that the commitments fail to deal with the more fundamental factors in price stability and external equilibrium, at least in a manner consistent with development progress. It is not enough to trim government expenditures; governments must expand revenues through tax legislation and improved administration. Balance-of-payments loans combined with measures for holding down imports, including devaluation, may simply set the stage for more serious crises later on. Steps must be taken to change the structure of the economy through a better allocation of investment, agricultural reform, and the establishment of a competitive economy with free entry, including encouragement to private foreign investment.

In recent years AID has made program loans to several countries, with the recipient country agreeing to a number of self-help or performance conditions. Releases of funds under the program loans are conditioned upon a review of country performance and the determination that these loan conditions have been satisfactorily met. In the case of program loans to Latin American countries, the conditions are sometimes stated in the form of letters of intent addressed by the government to the Inter-American Committee on the Alliance for Progress (CIAP). Although these letters of intent or other agreements outlining conditions under program loans cover a much broader range of self-help and performance undertakings, most of the specific quantitative commitments have to do with financial measures such as the level of the central bank's domestic assets, fiscal expenditures and deficits, and limitations on the volume of short- and medium-term supplier credits. I shall consider these agreements further in the discussion of program loans in Chapter 6.

6. For a text of the letter, see *Public International Development Financing in Chile*, (a report prepared by the Columbia University School of Law in cooperation with the Institute of International Studies and Overseas Administration, University of Oregon [New York: Columbia University, March 1964]), Appendix A, pp. 105-107. (Mimeo.)

7. See, for example, "Balance of Payments Loans to Colombia, 1954-1963," in *Public International Development Financing in Colombia* (a report prepared by the Columbia University School of Law in cooperation with the Institute of International Studies and Overseas Administration, University of Oregon [New York: Columbia University, June 1963]), pp. 106-129.

CHAPTER SIX

Economic Issues Relating to the Major Types of Aid for Development

THERE ARE MANY TYPES OF AID, and it is not my purpose to review the taxonomy of aid. (For a discussion of the forms of aid, see Little and Clifford, 1966, Ch. VII; Mikesell, 1966b, Ch. II.) In this chapter I am concerned mainly with certain economic issues relating to the principal forms of aid for promoting development. The form which aid takes (as distinguished from the terms on which aid is provided) involves both the nature of the resources transferred and the conditions established by the donor with respect to its end use. Thus, aid transfers may take the form of currency balances or general lines of credit which may or may not be tied to purchases in the country of the donor; of specific commodities and services such as agricultural commodities or technical assistance; or of a broad shopping list of commodities and services, the composition of which is related to the purpose or end use. Conditions with respect to the end use of aid, regardless of the form of transfer, range from general balance-of-payments or internal budget support to aid for specific identifiable projects such as a highway or power plant. Sometimes projects are broadly defined or involve a number of related projects not specifically identified. In other cases, end use may not be related to projects at all, but rather to broad purposes such as liberalizing imports by the private sector of the economy or financing a portion of the government budget devoted to agricultural programs, or simply general development.

Table 4 provides a breakdown of aid commitments by OECD members and multilateral agencies by purpose or end use (average 1962 and 1963). It will be noted that "non-project" assistance constituted less than 40 per cent of all commitments, and that the bulk of this aid was for the purpose of financing current imports. However, not all non-project assistance constituted aid with no end use specification (other than the promotion of general development), since some of the U.S. non-project assistance was designed to liberalize certain categories of imports such as capital goods and industrial raw materials required for use by the private sector of the recipient country. Also, a substantial portion of U.S. non-project assistance consisted of surplus agricultural commodities. However, as we shall discuss later on, surplus agricultural commodities are frequently employed as a means of contributing to general development or even to specific projects, and not simply for expanding consumption of agricultural products. About 42 per cent of the total aid as summarized in Table 4 was desig-

TABLE 4

OFFICIAL BILATERAL COMMITMENTS BY OECD MEMBERS AND COMMITMENTS BY MULTILATERAL AGENCIES, BY PURPOSE, 1962 AND 1963 AVERAGE
(In millions of dollars)

	Total, OECD and multi- lateral agencies	Total, multi- lateral agencies	U.S.	Other OECD members
I. Capital project financing:	$3,438.0	$1,069.7	$1,136.0	$1,224.6
1) Agriculture, forestry and fishing	392.3	146.2	114.0	132.1
2) Transport and communications	874.1	370.4	244.0	259.7
3) Development of energy resources	791.1	303.2	273.0	214.9
4) Indus. Basin Fund	48.1	......	30.0	18.1
5) Industry	781.1	184.2	259.0	337.9
6) Social infrastructure	508.1	51.2	216.0	240.9
7) Still unspecified, or multipurpose	43.3	15.7	......	27.6
II. Contributions for clearly specified current expenditures	205.0	......	20.0	185.0
III. Non-project assistance	3,176.9	......	2,696.0	480.9
1) Not directly linked with imports	394.6	......	138.0	256.6
2) To finance current imports	2,782.3	......	2,561.0	221.3
IV. Technical assistance	965.8	69.7	406.0	490.1
V. Consolidation and refinancing credits	90.1	......	10.1	80.1
VI. Other	351.8	62.0	78.0	211.8
VII. Total	8,227.5	1,201.4	4,344.0	2,674.5

Source: *The Flow of Financial Resources to Less Developed Countries, 1956-1963* (Paris: OECD, 1965b), pp. 160-63; and Little and Clifford, *International Aid* (Chicago: Aldine Publishing Company, 1966), p. 69.

nated for capital project financing, and nearly 90 per cent of the commitments of multilateral agencies was for this purpose. However, in the case of the United States, only 26 per cent went for capital project financing, 62 per cent for non-project financing. It should be noted, however, that a portion of U.S. non-project financing took the form of so-called "supporting assistance" to countries such as Vietnam and Korea, where a combination of political, economic, and military objectives was to be served, rather than normal development goals.

As to the nature of the resource transfers, the vast bulk of the assistance summarized in Table 4 consisted either of specific commodity or service transfers or was directly linked to current imports. Thus, most project aid was provided in the form of financing for import components of the projects, and most non-project aid did not consist of cash transfers which the recipient could employ as he pleased, but rather of credits tied to imports, mainly from the country of the donor. A relatively small portion of the project aid, however, was provided in the form of free cash balances for conversion into local currency to be used for local expenditures related to the projects. Most of the aid provided by multilateral development agencies, while tied to imports, is not tied to imports from a specific country (IMF assistance is not included in Table 4; IMF credits are not tied to imports.)

THE ISSUE OF PROJECT VS. PROGRAM ASSISTANCE

Several years ago AID began designating certain non-project assistance as program aid. Program aid has been made available to a limited number of countries comprising those which have received the bulk of development loan assistance from the United States, including Brazil, Colombia, Chile, Greece, India, Israel, Pakistan, Taiwan, Tunisia, Turkey, and Vietnam. According to AID (1963, pp. 34-37), program assistance is linked to an assessment of the overall requirements and resource availabilities of the country, and finances imports in support of development programs without tying the aid to specific projects. The use of program assistance has stirred up a considerable amount of controversy, since the traditional approach to development assistance (as opposed to defense support, emergency balance-of-payments aid, or subsidization of fiscal budgets of the colonial or former colonial territories) has been the financing of identifiable projects. The project approach is reflected in the charters of the World Bank, IDA, and the IDB, and the United States has generally tended to oppose proposals by the developing countries for loans or grants in support of general development or the underwriting of development programs. In discussing the merits of program vs. project assistance, I shall distinguish among three types of considerations: (1) the determination of the total amount of assistance to be made available for accomplishing certain economic objectives; (2) the use of aid as an incentive or a means of influencing self-help measures; and (3) the determination of the best techniques for providing aid as a means of achieving development objectives.

The argument for program assistance as providing a better means of adjusting the volume of aid to the realization of development goals is closely related to the use of quantitative growth models for aid-level determination. Once a level of external capital flow required for achieving a target rate of growth (which, under certain performance assumptions, will eventually become self-sustaining) is determined, it is argued that this level can best be assured through program assistance. Project assistance may be irregular because of the timing required to facilitate, approve, and make disbursements on project loans. However, this is a matter of aid technique which might be dealt with by an improvement in the project-financing process. Much more fundamental is the principle that the *level* of aid should be determined by gap calculations based on growth models, rather than directly related to the ability of a country to formulate a stream of aid-worthy projects, that is, the absorptive-capacity approach.

It may be argued that in the case of countries which have little diffi-culty in preparing a stream of projects for external financing, and where the general standards of development performance for the efficient utiliza-tion of aid are amply met, project formulation for aid-worthy projects may not provide an acceptable criterion for determining the maximum overall level of aid. For example, a country may be able to present a volume of aid-worthy projects greatly in excess of the total volume of external assist-ance regarded as appropriate in the light of competing demands for a lim-ited volume of aid availabilities. In such cases, growth models may be of some assistance, depending upon how much confidence one can have in the parameters. However, aid authorities may reject the self–sustaining growth hypothesis and base their overall aid level judgments on other tests. These might include capital requirements for absorbing unemployment or for completing a number of infrastructure projects believed necessary for long-run progress but requiring extraordinary assistance over a relatively short time span, or for fulfilling a well-conceived development plan. In other words, the total volume of assistance to be provided over a period of several years might simply be determined on the basis of the sum total of aid required to fulfill certain sectoral or other objectives not based on the self-sustaining growth hypothesis.

A poor country might be able to achieve a sustained rate of growth at a low level, but truly rapid development progress might require sizable outlays for infrastructure and social programs. I have never felt that quantitative growth models dealt with this type of situation adequately, particularly because the capital-output coefficient is either regarded as stable or as subject to slow decline as a reflection of efficiency. But at a certain stage of development, large amounts of capital with a high capital-output coefficient may be required over a period of several years in order to provide the basis for structural change. Judgments regarding assistance programs for this purpose cannot depend wholly or even largely on growth models. Moreover, the project approach has definite advantages in the de-termination of aid levels in such cases.

Turning now to the relationship between incentives and aid, one of the arguments for program as against project assistance is that program aid provides a more effective means of influencing broad governmental policies. Since program loans finance import requirements for the economy as a whole, aid-recipient countries will be more willing to accept conditions relating to these overall economic policies than they would in negotiations on external financing of specific projects. Program loan negotiations provide an opportunity not only to review the overall development performance and self-help policies of the recipient, but to influence decisions on self-help measures for improving performance. Because developing countries are usually in more urgent need of general balance-of-payments support than for specific capital projects which may require years to complete, program loans have a greater influence potential than specific project financing. This is true in considerable measure because many, if not most, developing countries are faced with continual foreign-exchange shortages. Also, most developing countries have relatively little difficulty in securing financing for good projects, either from multilateral institutions or through bilateral public loans or by means of government guaranteed supplier credits. On the other hand, general import assistance is available mainly from AID, thereby giving AID a unique asset which is eagerly sought after. Finally, unlike project commitments which must be implemented over a period of years, program aid can be adjusted from quarter to quarter, depending upon the degree to which the recipient is fulfilling his self-help commitments.

The validity of the above arguments for program aid as having a superior influence potential arises from the structure of the world aid machinery, including uncoordinated sources of project assistance, often actually in competition for good projects. A different structuring of project assistance might well improve its leverage effects on broad economic policies.

Project assistance has certain types of incentive and leverage effects which cannot be achieved through program loans. There is of course the incentive to prepare good projects, preferably a series of them which can be presented in order to receive a steady inflow of capital. Project evaluation affords an opportunity to exert greater influence over the nature of the projects and can affect the scale of priorities in development at both the project and the sectoral level. Some economists, including Hans Singer (1965), have argued that since the volume of aid constitutes only a fraction of total investment requirements, the external financing of those projects selected by the donors simply releases resources for the financing of what may be lower-priority projects by the recipients. However, we must compare the case of program aid as against an equivalent amount of project aid, and not project aid as against no aid. If total resources, including aid, are insufficient for all of a group of possible projects, the choice of projects implemented with a given amount of program aid is likely to differ from that under the same volume of project assistance in which the donor determines the choice of the projects.[1]

The third type of consideration has to do with whether program or project aid constitutes the best technique for achieving a specific development objective, quite apart from either the total level of assistance or the leverage or incentive aspects. It is argued that developing countries need resources for purposes which do not readily lend themselves to project treatment. Countries require a substantial volume of imports of industrial raw materials, spare parts, and replacement equipment in both the private and the public sectors for current operations. Local expenditures associated with capital projects give rise to indirect foreign-exchange drains. Reliance on project aid which tends to be limited to direct import components may lead to an overemphasis on large import-intensive projects, while the major bottleneck on development may be a shortage of exchange for general imports associated with a wide range of investment activities. Frequently, investment in the private sector is hampered by import and exchange controls employed to conserve foreign exchange, or agricultural programs may be impeded by the inability to obtain exchange for fertilizer, livestock for breeding, or agricultural equipment. Thus, program aid may induce a balanced set of development activities, especially those in the private sector. Finally, program aid is more flexible and permits a quick flow of resources to bottleneck areas. The argument that since resources are fungible the form of aid makes little difference in the long run, overlooks the fact that developing countries lack the flexibility to mobilize resources for meeting the most urgent requirements if all of their external assistance is tied to the import requirements of projects.

The aid technique argument probably constitutes the strongest case for having at least a portion of total aid provided in program form. The case would be somewhat weaker, however, if project assistance covered all or a part of the local currency expenditures associated with projects, and if project assistance could be organized in a manner which would result in a reasonably steady flow of aid disbursements, including that portion used to cover local expenditures. The flexibility argument for program as against project aid also raises the question of how narrowly or broadly projects are to be defined. The terminology has not been standardized, as so-called project assistance has sometimes been made available for a wide

1. Assume a total of 20 possible projects and internal and external resources available for only 15. Also assume a different rank order of priorities for all 20 projects as between the aid donor and the recipient. If the donor provides project aid for 5 of the projects, he will presumably select the 5 with the highest priority according to his scale. If one or more of these projects is in the lowest 5 in the priority scale of the recipient, the composition of the projects will differ in the case of project aid as compared with their composition under program aid.

range of activities relating to the development of a sector or subsector of an economy. For example, a loan for agricultural development may finance a package of interrelated activities covering specialized credits to farmers for productive activities, imports of machinery, fertilizer, and seed, and irrigation and infrastructure projects such as feeder roads. Credits to industrial development banks enable them to make loans to private firms for a broad range of productive purposes. In some cases, loans to liberalize a broad list of imports required by the agricultural or the industrial sector have been designated as project loans, even though such loans are not related to identifiable projects. Thus, the more flexible the project loans, the less persuasive are the arguments for the superiority of program loans. This is more than a matter of definition, since the unique element in project lending is end-use designation and supervision.

PROGRAM LOANS IN OPERATION

The pure program loan establishes no conditions with respect to the nature of the imports to be financed or to the use of the local currency counterpart of the foreign exchange which may be sold by the recipient government to the central bank for local currency. In practice, however, AID not only ties the program credits to procurement in the United States (with certain minor exceptions), but frequently limits the use of funds to a shopping list of imported commodities. If a program loan is to assist a particular sector, such as private industry, the credit must be used for imports by private industry and limited to a list of capital goods, spare parts, and industrial raw materials. Under a recent program loan to Brazil for liberalizing imports required by private industry, it was found that private import demand was not sufficient for the utilization of the proceeds of the loan, so that the initial shopping list was broadened.

In some cases, the loan agreement provides that the local currency counterpart of the loan must be used for designated purposes, either for projects approved by the donor, for expansion of credit to the private sector, or for broad development programs. The leverage achieved by control over the use of counterpart, whether derived from program loans, from sales of agricultural commodities under PL 480, or from grants, is debatable, however. The local currency generated does not constitute additional resources and governments may therefore be slow in utilizing funds for agreed-upon purposes since they can readily generate funds for other purposes without additional inflationary effects so long as the counterpart funds remain unutilized.

To the extent that a country would need to import agricultural commodities in the absence of PL 480 shipments, surplus agricultural sales for local currency may serve much the same purpose as program loans available for a broad list of imports, since the agricultural imports release foreign exchange for other purposes. I shall discuss the contribution of direct commodity aid to development in a later section. Whatever such aid may be called, it is in fact non-project aid unless the end use of the commodities is designated and controlled in a special way.

As has already been noted, self-help agreements accompanying program loans, whether bilateral or multilateral, as in the case of the CIAP letters, cover a wide range of commitments on the part of the recipient. Some are stated in quantitative terms, as is frequently the case with internal financial commitments, while others are stated in terms of broad policy intentions which provide little basis for objective evaluation of performance. Early in 1966 the Chilean Minister of Finance delivered a letter to CIAP outlining his government's policy and program undertakings, including legislative proposals; this letter constituted the basis for AID's program loan and other assistance commitments to Chile for the fiscal year 1965-66.[2] Some of the important elements of this letter are:

1) *Agricultural Development—*
    a) The letter notes that the Chilean administration has submitted additional land legislation to the Congress, that about 8,000 farm families will be settled in 1966, and that credit and technical assistance will be provided to about 60,000 farm families.
    b) The governmnt has prepared a multiyear plan for increased agricultural production with targets for increased output of items currently being imported (for example, wheat and beef), and for export items such as fruit and wine. To this end, the government will permit agricultural prices to rise by more than the overall price index by adjustments in farm price controls, including floor prices. It also intends to provide large amounts of credit for agriculture, to improve public administration in agriculture, and to improve agricultural marketing.

2) *Industrial Development—*
    a) The Chilean government intends to complete the preparation of a multiyear industrial sector plan, setting forth specific targets, policies, and programs for the attainment of the objectives.

2. So far as I am aware, the text of this letter has never been published, although it was the subject of considerable discussion in the Chilean press. This discussion is based on a copy of this letter. (Chile's letter of intent to CIAP of November 22, 1964, setting forth its programs and policies for 1965, covers many of the same subjects but is less detailed. For the text of this letter, see *United States Foreign Aid in Action: A Case Study,* a report of the Subcommittee on Foreign Aid Expenditures of the Committee on Government Operations, U.S. Senate, 89th Congress, Second Session, USGPO, Washington, D.C., Appendix VII.)

b) During 1966 the government will promote substantial new investments in the following fields: petrochemicals, cellulose and paper, fertilizers, electronics, chemicals, textiles, and sulphuric acid production.

c) The government will review and prepare a report on existing legislation and administrative regulations that place special restrictions on private economic activities. It intends to eliminate those restrictions that tend to stifle competition, raise prices, and limit the opportunities for economic expansion, and to introduce necessary legislation for this purpose.

d) The government intends to expand industrial credits to the private sector by 30 per cent over 1965 in real terms, with special emphasis to export industries, industries providing inputs for agricultural and industrial production, and industries producing wage goods for a popular market. In this connection, it is expected that a private development bank will be created in 1966.

3) *Financial Stabilization—*

a) The government intends to reduce the rate of inflation during 1966 to no more than 15 per cent (as against a 25 per cent rise in the official cost of living index during 1965). To this end, the government has agreed with the IMF on a monetary program including a ceiling on total domestic assets held by the Central Bank.

b) The government will introduce legislation to establish maximum legal or contractual adjustments in wages and salaries for the entire economy. This maximum adjustment will be no more than 100 per cent of the increase in the cost of living for wages and salaries up to three times the minimum wage; for those earning more than three times the minimum wage, the adjustment will be 60 per cent of the rise in the cost of living.

c) The government intends to continue a flexible exchange rate policy and other policies designed to encourage investment in production for exports.

d) The government intends to reduce existing obstacles to the importation of goods essential to development, especially capital goods, or the importation of agricultural products which are temporarily in short supply. The government also intends to complete a review of existing import and export regulations in order to bring these policies more in line with economic development needs.

e) The letter outlines the government's fiscal expenditure intentions in some detail, including public sector investments and transfers to state enterprises. Plans are to be prepared for reducing subsidies to decentralized agencies, such as transportation enterprises.

f) The government intends to introduce legislation and take administrative steps to expand tax revenues, including administrative reforms.

g) In 1966, an increasing share of total investment expenditures will be in agriculture, industry, and mining, and transfers to the private sector to finance these investments will expand at least as much as the overall expansion of the public sector investment program.

In addition to the undertakings summarized above, the letter sets forth certain legislative and administrative plans with respect to education, and announced intentions relating to improved development planning and project preparation.

It will be observed that the CIAP letter of intent summarized above combines general policies and proposals to secure legislation and prepare sectoral plans with specific commitments, mainly in the monetary field. Similar letters of intent have been prepared by other CIAP members receiving AID program loans. Each year there is a review of the performance of each Latin American member by CIAP, attended by representatives of the principal assistance agencies and by representatives of the member country. The review is based on an annual report prepared by the staff of the Organization of American States.

More significant have been the quarterly reviews by AID, on the basis of which a decision is made regarding the release of an additional tranche of the program loan to those countries to which program loans have been made. On a few occasions, program loans have been suspended as a consequence of the failure of governments to implement agreed-upon self-help measures, mainly in the areas of budgetary and monetary controls and foreign-exchange policies. For example, U.S. disbursements under a 1963 program loan to Brazil (Bell-Dantas Agreement) were suspended in 1964, but a new program loan was negotiated with the Branco government in December, 1964 (for examples of experience with program loans, see Gulick and Nelson, 1965). Likewise, disbursements under the 1964 AID program loan to Colombia were suspended in 1965, pending a change in Colombia's financial policies, including a devaluation of the peso (AID, 1966, p. 53).

Program loans have sometimes been employed as a means of inducing countries to liberalize imports needed by the private sector of the economy. Thus, AID assured the government of Pakistan of up to $140 million of non-project aid for fiscal year 1965 to help meet the foreign-exchange requirements from a liberalization of imports of raw materials and spare parts. In June, 1964, IDA made a loan of $90 million to India to enable that country to liberalize imports of components of materials required by three major industries—commercial vehicles, industrial machinery, and construction equipment. In August, 1966, IDA made a loan of $150 million to India for liberalization of imports required by a broader list of industries, including those producing inputs for agriculture.[3] Such credits remove bottlenecks on production in important areas. However, unless the economic structure, including internal price relationships and the exchange rate, is changed so that exports are expanded and import substitution of an uneconomic nature is avoided, the foreign-exchange shortage will continue. Program loans specifically designed for liberalizing imports by the private sector are in part required because governments absorb too large a share of available foreign exchange for the public sector, whether from export earnings or from foreign aid. The desirability of sectoralizing a program loan in this way, as opposed to general program loans for allocation by the government, points up a weakness of general program loans. Theoretically, the conditions stated in the program loan agreement should assure a proper allocation of the program loan, but in practice this cannot be counted on.

The experience of AID under its program loans does not warrant unqualified judgment of either success or failure. Political factors often limit the ability of governments to carry out their commitments since they frequently depend upon legislation or full agreement and cooperation among elements within the administration in power. The latter, for example, has been a factor in the delay in the Chilean government's establishing an adequate system of industrial development banks for private industry. Even in the area of economic stabilization—where the agreements are often initially negotiated with the IMF and tend to be stated in quantitative terms —performance has often been weak. Not only have price stabilization efforts proved to be disappointing, as in the case of Brazil and Chile in the past few years, but the measures employed to slow down the rate of inflation have conflicted with other objectives. In the period 1964-66, Chile, while adopting a flexible exchange-rate system, did not permit the escudo to depreciate in line with domestic price increases, and agricultural prices have been held down in relation to nonfarm goods and farm wages. Thus, price stabilization efforts have actually contributed to price distortions which tend to impede agricultural output and exports. Monetary controls have often had their greatest restrictive effect on private investment in productive industry and agriculture, while government expenditures in real

3. These loans constitute rare examples of program loans by the World Bank Group; IBRD and IDA normally make only project loans, although some projects cover a fairly wide range of investment activities.

terms continue to rise. Program loans usually have not been successful in achieving a shift in the pattern of investment from the public sector to one which favors private industry, agricultural, and production for exports. The treatment of government policies and of budget allocations affecting the sectoral distribution of investment tends to be vague in program loan agreements.

While the quantitative performance criteria in the monetary and fiscal areas are usually met, inflation has continued, first because the basic structural factors necessary for both stability and growth are not affected, and second, because the performance criteria are not sufficiently comprehensive to avoid inflation. For example, the government or governmental agencies can avoid additional borrowing from the central bank by not paying their bills. Government ministries have been known to let contracts for public works in amounts well above budgetary limits, with credits being allotted to the contractors through the banking system, often at negative real rates of interest. Thus, despite formal compliance by Chile with IMF standby agreements (to which the AID program loans were related during 1963 and 1964), inflation continued at an annual rate of about 40 per cent.

Critics of AID program loans point to the unwillingness of the United States to exercise its power to reduce or suspend disbursement on the basis of poor performance and to the consequent lack of "credibility" of the sanctions involved in program lending. Despite a few examples of suspension of aid in cases of gross failure in performance, the U.S. government is understandably reluctant to risk the political consequences of embarrassing the government of the aid recipient by reducing or terminating program aid. This criticism is well stated in the following paragraphs from a U.S. Senate subcommittee report entitled *United States Foreign Aid in Action: A Case Study* (Committee on Government Operations, 1966):

But shortcomings in the [program loan] technique far outweigh these advantages. The long and diverse list of commitments assumed by the recipient vitiates the "carrot and stick" concept upon which program lending is based. Since it is unlikely that any government can perform in a satisfactory manner simultaneously on the diverse commitments enumerated, from the outset both recipient and donor know that something less than perfect performance is anticipated. But what? How is overall performance to be evaluated, and by whose yardstick? Thus, both participants know that overall performance is subject to elastic interpretation, but neither knows at what point AID would be justified in exercising its option to reduce or eliminate assistance. This ambiguity undermines the credibility of the implied threat of sanctions for unsatisfactory performance.

Program lending also, ironically, provides the recipient nation the leverage with which to neutralize AID's "stick." Program loans are announced with great fanfare. The general public in the host nation, of course, is not apprised of the little detail which links disbursements to country performance. . . . Imagine the uproar, hostility, and friction that could be generated by a U.S. decision to apply sanctions? The truth about the fine print would never catch up with the howls of "imperialism" and "intervention." At the same time, all the blame for the country's ills (caused by its own government's mismanagement which led to the sanctions) would be heaped upon "rich, heartless" United States. In short, the political fiasco which could result from a U.S. decision to terminate aid acts as an effective brake upon the United States taking that step. This fact can hardly have escaped the attention of shrewd officials in the recipient nations.

While the "stick" is a paper tiger, the "carrot" is a dubious incentive. The commitments undertaken as conditions for assistance cannot be carried out under the controlled conditions of a scientific laboratory. Many factors having nothing to do with the availability of U.S. assistance influence the recipient's performance. Public opinion, the pressures of special interest groups, and the composition and temper of the Congress are among the many variables with which the recipient administration must cope.

The plain fact is that the desirable economic measures set forth as conditions for continued U.S. assistance involve political determinations, and nothing in our experience gives us superior knowledge of the best political strategy to pursue in an alien environment. . . . In these circumstances, the prospect of U.S. assistance is a very minor factor, if any, in a government's decision to meet or not to meet the commitments upon which program loans are conditioned (pp. 110-11).

The Senate subcommittee report also criticizes program loans on the grounds that they "erode the recipient's incentive to formulate its investment programs in terms of sound projects" (pp. 111-13). In addition, the report alleges that program lending circumvents Section 611(a) of the Foreign Assistance Act which provides that no agreement constituting an obligation of the U.S. government in excess of $100,000 may be entered into if it requires "substantive technical or financial planning," until "engineering, financial, and other plans necessary to carry out such assistance" and "a reasonably firm estimate of the cost to the U.S. government have been completed."

The necessity of complying with the Section 611(a) has been given by AID authorities as an argument for program as against project assistance. It is certainly true that assistance to a sectoral program involving many projects would be hampered by a strict application of Section 611(a), as would also loans to development banks for relending to private firms. The degree of U.S. evaluation and supervision over all expenditures of aid funds is a complicated administrative issue. However, it would appear that the application of Section 611(a) to all such expenditures would place an almost impossible burden on our aid administrators. It is far more im-

portant that they give greater emphasis to economic evaluation at the sectoral and national level, and to employing aid programs for influencing
development policies and the mobilization and overall allocation of the
total resources of the aid recipients. Given the limited personnel of U.S.
AID missions, it is my view that too much effort is being devoted to accounting for specific expenditures in order to comply with the large number of legislative and administrative regulations. The real need of our
AID missions is for more development specialists capable of analyzing and
making recommendations with respect to the major sectors of the economy
—agriculture, industry, foreign trade, education, etc.

PROPOSALS FOR DEALING WITH THE PROJECT VS. PROGRAM
ASSISTANCE DILEMMA

There is a growing recognition of the need to devise aid techniques
that combine the advantages of project and program assistance, while
avoiding the limitations of too great a reliance on either. Few would deny
that project loans should have an important role in supporting sizable development projects. Moreover, assistance is being made available to programs involving a number of interrelated projects under the name of project assistance. Certainly the advantages of project aid, both in providing an
incentive to the formulation of sound projects and in influencing the character of the projects through involvement at the technical level should
be preserved. This applies not only to economic overhead projects such as
roads and power plants, but to comprehensive agricultural programs, educational programs, and various other social projects or programs. Financial
and technical assistance to specialized credit institutions for agriculture, industry, and housing, under certain guidelines, also constitutes an important
aid technique which combines certain advantages of both project and program assistance.

If we want to provide a substantial flow of resources to a country over
a period of time, and exact maximum influence over its overall policies and
the pattern of total resource allocation, we must go beyond the traditional
project approach. I shall outline briefly several approaches which have
been suggested.

One proposal is that foreign assistance agencies such as AID (or a
well-coordinated consortium of agencies supplying aid to a particular
country) make an advance commitment to finance $100 million worth of
projects over a specified period of years, but the projects themselves would
not be identified until properly formulated and approved. This advance
commitment would follow negotiations on broad economic policies leading
to an agreement similar to agreements accompanying program loans. In
addition, the agreement might include the willingness of the government

to accept a consulting team to make feasibility studies or to assist in project preparation in various sectors of the economy.

The fact that the initial commitment would be relatively large would increase its desirability to the recipient, and the foreign-assistance agency might be able to exert much the same degree of influence on macro-economic policies as it does under the program loans. In addition, the combination of advance commitment and technical assistance to develop projects would deal directly with one of the major problems of project assistance, namely the dearth of good projects.

On the other hand, a steady flow of good projects could not be assured, and the lumpiness of the capital inflow would make overall development planning and implementation difficult. Much would depend on whether a portion of the local currency expenditures on the projects would be financed by the external loan and the timing of such financing. Because of the urgent need of governments from time to time for untied foreign exchange in financing their development programs, program loans would continue to have far greater leverage potential than would advance commitments on projects in which all aid would be tied to project disbursements. There would frequently be pressure brought on the aid authorities to release a portion of the advance commitment in the form of program loans. Indeed, this has happened before in the case of advance commitments for project financing, such as the $100 million allocated for earthquake reconstruction in Chile of 1961. In this case, the pressure on the part of the Chilean government for the release of the dollar funds to meet its foreign-exchange obligations led to the approval of a number of hastily and ill-conceived projects. Disbursements under this loan were not specifically related to foreign-exchange expenditures associated with agreed-upon projects but rather to escudo expenditures for mutually agreed-upon reconstruction projects (Committee on Government Operations, 1966, pp. 16-23). Thus, the advance-commitment-for-projects approach raises two credibility problems. First, there is the willingness on the part of the U.S. aid authorities either to convert a portion of the advance commitment into general program assistance or to release substantial amounts of the dollar aid for general balance-of-payments purposes equal to the local currency equivalent of a number of hastily devised projects. And second, there is the familiar credibility question regarding the determination of the United States to cut off aid as a consequence of poor performance in the area of broad economic policies.

A variation of the advance-commitment-for-projects proposal is to segregate that portion of the project loan commitment designed to cover a portion of local currency expenditures associated with the projects into an accompanying program loan. Disbursement under the program loan would be related to the progress of project implementation, but a certain amount of flexibility in the program loan disbursements would be permitted in response to both the needs of the country and to its performance. While there are certain advantages in this approach in relating aid to the indirect foreign-exchange drain arising from development projects—by timing the disbursements more in relation to foreign exchange need than to the timing of the actual local currency expenditures—most of the disadvantages of the advance project commitment proposal, including the credibility problem, would remain. In fact, there would be substantial pressure on aid authorities to disburse the program loan portion of the commitment well in advance of the formulation and implementation of the projects.

A third approach, which I shall call a combination of program and project assistance at the sectoral level, constitutes a summary of my own conclusions based on unpublished memoranda and discussions with officials in several foreign-assistance agencies, including those in AID missions. One of the major weaknesses of program lending has been the failure to influence the allocation of total investment resources in a manner which would contribute both to long-run internal and external stability and to broad development progress. Under this proposal, both project and program assistance would be related to sectoral plans. Project assistance would be based on the principle of advance commitments and extensive technical assistance for feasibility studies and broadly conceived project preparation within individual sectors, for example, agriculture, private industry, power, transportation, education, housing, community development, etc. Emphasis would also be given to specialized credit institutions as channels for technical and financial assistance to private industry, agriculture, and housing; such financing institutions might also be employed as channels for loans and technical assistance to municipalities and semi-independent regional development authorities. In addition, sectoral program assistance would be made available to governments on the following basis.

Advance agreements would be reached with the government with respect to the allocation of fiscal revenues to various ministries and agencies concerned with particular sectors of the economy. Sectoral program loans would be made covering a certain percentage of the budgetary allocations to these ministries or agencies, but program loan releases would only be made *pari passu,* with actual expenditures on sectoral programs in accordance with the agreed-upon sectoral plans. Sectoral program loans would not be tied to imports required by the sectoral programs, and thus the foreign exchange would be available for general balance-of-payments purposes. The entire package of assistance, including both project and program aid, would also be conditioned on self-help criteria in the areas of fiscal, monetary, and foreign-trade and foreign-exchange policies.

This proposal would appear to have several advantages. First, it provides virtually all the flexibility as an aid technique as does general program assistance. Its influence potential would be greater, since the Minister of Finance would know that supplements to his fiscal budget and foreign-exchange availabilities would depend upon investment activities at the sectoral level in accordance with sectoral plans. Credibility would be increased, since releases of program loans could be determined directly by expenditures at the sectoral level on the basis of a matching formula. If programs were delayed, program loan disbursements would be retarded simply because larger disbursements were not needed. If ministries and agencies were deterred in carrying out programs because of a delay in budgetary allocations, the reason for the reduction in program loan disbursements in accordance with the agreed-upon matching formula would be clear. Quarterly reviews in anticipation of program aid releases would be focused on performance in relation to the sectoral plans, and not simply on overall performance. If government revenues were not sufficient to cover sectoral budgetary commitments without violating the monetary and fiscal guidelines set forth in the overall aid agreement, both budgetary expenditures and aid would be cut back until fiscal revenues were expanded.

It is well to keep in mind the social and political limitations on self-help measures and performance in the development field. Practitioners in the art or diplomacy of foreign aid are dealing with societies that in large measure are poor because they lack the social and political as well as the economic prerequisites for economic growth; they are not manipulating hypothetical growth models. Basing aid on broad commitments to self–help involving highly sensitive political decisions presents difficult problems for relations between sovereign states. Correct policies can be influenced by patient diplomacy, but I doubt if they can really be forced upon countries by pounding the conference table and threats of aid denial or withdrawal. It is for this reason that I believe that aid should be tied as closely as possible to specific activities as a means of facilitating these activities rather than providing general aid on the basis either of promises of performances or an *ex post* review of performance. Project aid, of course, is ideally suited to this principle, but we must recognize the limitations of project aid as a technique for providing sizable amounts of the appropriate types of assistance for assuring development progress. Sectoral program loans related to activities within the framework of an agreed-upon sectoral plan appear to me to provide a workable compromise.

DEVELOPMENT AID IN THE FORM OF
AGRICULTURAL COMMODITIES

In this section I am concerned with the contribution of foreign aid in the form of agricultural commodities to economic development. I shall not deal here with the real costs of this type of assistance to the donor country or with the justification for this form of aid from the standpoint of the donor. Nor will I be concerned with the use of commodity aid for dealing with famines or other disasters or for purposes other than making a contribution to economic development.

Aid to developing countries in the form of agricultural commodities constitutes a substantial proportion of total bilateral and multilateral aid, 15 to 20 per cent, depending upon how aid is measured. During fiscal year 1965, Food for Peace program (PL 480) commitments in the form of sales of agricultural commodities for local currencies, commodity grants, and dollar credit sales amounted to about $1.5 billion, as against total U.S. economic assistance commitments of $4.9 billion, or some 30 per cent of U.S. economic aid commitments. The vast bulk of the agricultural commodity aid comes from the United States, but Canada and Australia have contributed food aid in the form of grants, and there is a small multilateral food aid program, the World Food Program, directed by the FAO. Not all of the shipments under PL 480 have been made for the purpose of promoting economic development; a substantial volume has gone for emergency relief. This is particularly true of shipments under Titles II and III of PL 480 and even a portion of the sales of agricultural commodities for local currencies under Title I have been motivated more by other considerations such as emergency relief and contributions to defense.[4]

Over the period since July, 1954, when PL 480 was enacted, planned uses of foreign currencies under Title I Agreement have provided for some 60 per cent of the local currency receipts to be made available for economic development loans and grants to the recipient governments.

4. Title II of PL 480 authorizes the use of surplus agricultural commodities held by the Commodity Credit Corporation for grant assistance for emergency relief and economic and community development. Under Title III, agricultural commodities are made available to voluntary agencies such as CARE for foreign donations. Title IV provides for the sale of commodities under long-term dollar credits. The bulk of the PL 480 shipments are under Title I, which provides for the sale of the commodities for local currencies. A portion of these receipts are reserved for U.S. government uses such as embassy expenditures; another portion is reserved for loans to American or foreign private industry; the bulk of the proceeds are used for grants or loans to the government of the recipient country.

About 23 per cent of the local currencies were reserved for the use of the U.S. government, a considerable portion of which represented expenditures which would otherwise have been made in dollars. During the period from mid-1954 to mid-1965, commodities having an export value of nearly $13 billion have been made available under PL 480 Title I agreements. The major commodities in order of their export value are wheat and wheat flour, cotton, fats and oil, rice, feed grains, tobacco, and dairy products, with the wheat and wheat flour constituting over half of the total in terms of value (Food for Peace Director, 1965; data supplemented from other sources). The principal recipients of PL 480 Title I shipments in order of export value have been India, Pakistan, the United Arab Republic, Yugoslavia, Turkey, Spain, Brazil, and Korea, with India and Pakistan accounting for nearly one-third of the total. Other recipients of substantial amounts of PL 480 Title I commodities include Tunisia, Indonesia, Israel, Taiwan, Chile, Colombia, and the Philippines.

The nature and magnitude of the impact of direct agricultural commodity assistance on economic development has been a subject of a substantial amount of inquiry and debate. I shall deal with the following questions relating to this impact:

1) Does agricultural commodity aid simply provide a temporary supplement to consumption or does it make possible increased investment? If there is increased investment, how is it generated?

2) Do increased imports of agricultural commodities result in a misdirection of investment by reducing the incentive to expand agricultural production?

3) Does control over the uses of local currency proceeds provide a means of influencing development policies, including investment in agriculture, by the donor agencies?

CONTRIBUTION TO INVESTMENT

Under ideal conditions with respect to governmental planning and policies, the introduction of any resource through capital imports should enable a country not only to increase investment, but if it knew how long and in what quantity the resource would continue to be made available, investment expenditures should be distributed in an optimum manner for achieving the real output goals of the country. The simplest case would be one in which a country plans to spend foreign exchange for an equivalent amount of the agricultural commodities imported under PL 480. It could then use the exchange to import additional investment goods and services. However, the intent of PL 480 was to provide surplus agricultural commodities over and above the amounts which the recipient country expected to import and could afford. In practice, however, PL 480 imports have constituted a substitute for commercial imports in many countries, notably in the case of Israel and Pakistan (Kahn, 1962; Witt and Eicher, 1964, pp. 24-25). Of course, the availability of additional foreign exchange does not guarantee an increase in investment; it may simply result in increased imports for consumption. But for the moment we are assuming a governmental policy directed toward utilizing the increased resources for an expansion of investment.

Let us assume the PL 480 imports are, in fact, in addition to planned imports of these commodities and that they are not competitive with domestic production, for example, cotton, in the case of a country whose climate and soil are not suited for cotton production. Let us assume that cotton has not been rationed as a consequence of import controls, but that increased supplies of cotton will reduce prices and enable producers to expand output of cotton textiles for the domestic market (and possibly for export), by lowering the price of textiles. Assuming no decrease in savings, consumer demand for other goods would have been shifted to cotton textiles, thereby releasing capacity and productive factors for increased investment expenditures (and increased consumption generated by the investment) financed by the local currency proceeds from the sale of the cotton. Alternatively, if inflationary pressures already exist as a consequence of the total level of investment and consumer demand in relation to output, increased supplies of cotton would tend to reduce these pressures, with a consequent encouragement to real savings and investment.

Since much of the PL 480 sales constitutes food and feed grains for livestock, the argument that increased food supplies will finance an equivalent increase in investment is frequently stated in terms of enabling unemployed workers to be put to work on capital projects. Ignoring for the moment any adverse effects of the increased food supplies on domestic production, it is argued that the funds derived from the sale of food can be used to employ additional workers without increasing the pressure of demand on food prices. However, not only does man not live by bread alone, but most investment products require additional capital instruments and raw materials. Hence, it has been argued by some that to be effective in expanding investment, agricultural commodity imports would have to be accompanied by other types of assistance. While this may be true for some countries, this argument assumes complete rigidity of demand and supply for nonfood goods by the rest of the economy. The agricultural commodities constitute additional resources provided to the economy without generating money incomes. These resources are equivalent to additional savings which can be used to purchase goods and services required for the development program like any other resources; the only difference is that some relative price changes may occur. The newly employed workers may be deployed to produce both consumer goods and investment goods as required by the new pattern of demand. Moreover, some of the investments should be in the export industries, so as to provide additional foreign exchange required for the expanding level of investment. All of this does not mean that there would not be a period of structural adjustment which would require increased nonfood imports which might have to be supplied by other kinds of aid. But certainly the additional food supplies should make a major contribution to the expansion of investment, given appropriate economic policies and a reasonably flexible economy.

Imports of agricultural commodities under the aid program may also increase investment by releasing resources devoted to the production of those same commodities. Thus, if it is true that workers cannot be drawn from the farms without a reduction in farm output or, at least, a reduction in farm output available for the market economy, increased food imports could more than make up for the reduction of food output involved in a release of workers from the farms. Conceivably, the reduction in farm output would be a temporary one if the movement of workers out of farming were accompanied by changes in land tenure and farming methods and techniques, including the application of fertilizers, insecticides, and machinery which would become available as a consequence of new investment in the industrial sector. Thus, the food imports could tide the country over a period of adjustment in which both the number of farm workers would be reduced and farm output substantially expanded. I do not mean to suggest, however, that a reduction in the number of farm workers is a necessary prerequisite to a change in farming methods which would lead to an increase in productivity and output. It is quite possible that the increased investment in industries producing industrial farm inputs, such as fertilizers, or capital investments serving farming directly, such as irrigation dams, will absorb unemployed workers whose demand for food would increase; commodity aid could supply this increased demand pending the rise in agricultural production.

EFFECTS ON AGRICULTURAL OUTPUT

The question of whether agricultural commodity aid will reduce agricultural output in the recipient countries, either in the short-run or over the longer period, as a consequence of reduced investment in agriculture, obviously turns on the nature of the policies in developing countries. If the recipient countries use the imported commodities simply to depress food prices relative to other prices and relative to costs in farming (other than perhaps in periods of crop failures), and do nothing to provide com-

pensatory incentives for expanding farm output and investment in farming, agriculture commodity aid may lead to a misdirection of investment.
In fact, such policies may simply increase food consumption of city
workers with no increase in investment. On the other hand, increased
agricultural imports can promote an increase in agricultural investment
and productivity, but—in the process—compensatory price or income
policies must be adopted which will maintain or expand incentives for investment in modern agriculture. In some countries, comparative advantage dictates a shift in agricultural output away from wheat or rice, to the
production of fibers and livestock. Imports of feed grains under aid programs may contribute to an expansion of the livestock industry, while
imports of food grains may enable a country to expand production of
cotton by reducing acreage devoted to wheat. There are certainly countries
where long-run comparative advantage would dictate that they be continuous importers of certain agricultural products. But where this is true,
long-range development plans must provide for an expansion of exports
to cover foreign-exchange costs. There is certainly no reason why every
developing country should strive to be self-sufficient in food, but virtually
every developing country needs to put a very high priority on a rapid increase in agricultural productivity and a shift from traditional to modern
agricultural methods.

TECHNIQUES FOR INFLUENCING INVESTMENT

Turning now to the question of the use of commodity aid for influencing investment programs and policies in developing countries, there are
three means by which such influence may be exercised. First, conditions
may be attached to PL 480 Title I sales agreements whereby the recipient
countries are committed to certain policies and investment programs. Thus,
in the course of negotiations on a new long-term wheat agreement with
India under PL 480 in late 1965, AID authorities were reportedly insisting that India undertake certain programs for improving agriculture,
including the production and distribution of fertilizer and the introduction
of better seeds (*New York Times,* Nov. 8, 1965). Sales of agricultural
commodities under long-term dollar credits (PL 480, Title IV) may also
provide that the recipient employ the local currency proceeds from the
sale of the commodities for certain types of investment projects. For
example, under a PL 480 agreement with the Algerian government in
February, 1966, providing for $12.6 million worth of surplus foodstuffs
along with substantial technical assistance, it was stipulated that a substantial portion of the local currency proceeds would be used to finance
a series of crop improvements and irrigation projects. This program also

included the provision of a number of U.S. agricultural specialists (*New York Times,* Jan. 4, 1966; U.S. Dept. of Agriculture, 1966).

A second method of influencing investment programs is through the use of agricultural commodities directly for the payment of wages or of a portion of the wages associated with specific investment projects. Thus, in 1958, a Title II grant of wheat was made to Tunisia for carrying out work-relief projects mainly in the agricultural field. Initially, the daily wage consisted of 4 kilos of American hard red winter wheat which amounted to two-thirds of the daily wage, plus one-third paid in Tunisian currency. Most of the nearly 200 projects were related to water conservation in rural areas. However, since the principal diet of the Tunisians consists of semolina produced from local durum wheat, permission was secured for the exchange of the American wheat for semolina. Later, the ratio of semolina to cash wages was changed so that the workers received two-thirds of their wages in cash and one-third in semolina (Witt, 1964, pp. 352-53). Since 1958, food grants for use in projects involving partial payment of wages in food have been made to a number of countries—including Algeria and India for rural rehabilitation projects, to Peru for road construction, and to Turkey for minerals and water resource development. A food grant was made to Bolivia for partial payment of teachers' salaries, and food grants were made available to Brazil for loans in kind to settlers in new colonies.

The tying of specific agricultural commodities to wage payments in kind for agreed-upon projects is admittedly a clumsy device, although a number of the projects have been regarded as quite successful. The number of food items suitable for immediate use by the workers and the necessity of establishing a special distribution system cannot be regarded as an efficient means of providing foreign assistance. It can only be justified in cases where governmental authorities are incapable of carrying out projects financed by normal means through the monetary system. Presumably the "food for wages" system would have important publicity effects for the donor country, since the workers as well as the beneficiaries of the projects would know who was paying their wages.

Thus far most of the PL 480 aid which has been designed in part as a means of contributing to and influencing development has been made available under Title I of the Act, with the proceeds from the sales allocated to loans or grants for specified development purposes. Under this third method, title to the local currency proceeds from the sale of the commodities remains with the U.S. government until they are made available as a loan or grant to the recipient country for specified purposes, mutually agreed upon by the two parties. However, the existence of accumulated local currency proceeds does not put pressure on the governments to utilize the funds. So long as the funds are held in the form of idle balances they serve the purpose of reducing the volume of purchasing power in the country, thereby opening the way for central bank-financed development expenditures in any area that the government considers desirable. The employment of these local currency proceeds does not provide real resources to the country; real resources have already been transferred by the sale of agricultural commodities.

The effectiveness of PL 480 local currency loans and grants has been the subject of considerable debate. In practice, there has been a tendency for the aid recipient either to delay the use of counterpart funds for long periods, or for the U.S. government to approve uses of local currencies for whatever projects appear to be reasonable, or to turn over the funds as local-currency program loans or grants, without their being identified with specific projects. Thus, on December 31, 1964, of the total accumulated local currencies earmarked for loans or grants to the recipients under PL 480 commodity sales agreements, nearly $1.6 billion had not been disbursed, of which $623 million equivalent represented Indian rupees (Committee on Foreign Affairs, 1965). Although a substantial portion of PL 480 sales proceeds have been loaned for specific projects, it is difficult to determine the degree to which the direction of investment has been influenced by U.S. foreign-assistance authorities or even the extent to which the commodity aid had resulted in a net increase in investment as against consumption. Undoubtedly some investments have been made with PL 480 proceeds that would not otherwise have been made from other sources. For example, PL 480 proceeds have provided an important source of financing for industrial development banks, and a number of agricultural projects might not have been undertaken in the absence of such financing. But the degree to which the overall volume and broad direction of investment can be influenced by the donor probably depends more on the negotiation of agreements relating to the development policies of the recipients. PL 480 assistance may also be tied to comprehensive agreements covering the development policies and programs of the recipients similar to agreements negotiated under program loans. In fact, some program loan agreements include the provision of both agricultural commodities and foreign exchange for industrial products. Much the same arguments with respect to foreign exchange program loans apply equally to commodity program loans or grants. However, the weaknesses of the general program approach are perhaps even greater in the case of food aid than in the case of dollar program assistance. Would the United States cut off food shipments to hungry people because of a failure of the recipient country's government to achieve good development performance?

It is suggested that agricultural commodities provided under aid programs should not be sold by the U.S. government for local currencies, as is provided under PL 480 Title I sales agreements. Rather, they should be treated in the same way as other dollar aid and financed in the form of long-term, low-cost dollar credits. (This is provided for as a long-run goal under the 1966 Food for Peace Act.) Commodity aid could be provided to finance sectoral programs along the same lines as the sectoral-program dollar loans suggested in the previous section. The domestic sales of the agricultural commodities by the recipient government would generate local currencies for employment in the sectoral programs, much in the same way as sectoral dollar loans would generate local currency. The deliveries of the commodities would be related to actual expenditures of the local currencies on projects encompassed by the mutually agreed-upon sectoral programs. Any delay in the implementation of the agreed sectoral programs would automatically reduce the financing requirements, and hence the flow of commodities. In most cases, the agricultural commodity aid should finance projects and programs in the agricultural sector. In addition, the overall aid agreement would need to stipulate as precisely as possible certain agricultural policies affecting incentives, such as agricultural price policies.

THE EMPIRICAL EVIDENCE

Empirical studies of the effects of PL 480 programs have been made for a few recipient countries (College of Agriculture, Univ. of Arizona, 1962; Witt, 1964, pp. 339-59; Witt and Eicher, 1964; Goering and Witt, 1963; Dept. of Agricultural Economics, MSU, 1964). Experience under the programs has differed greatly from country to country, and the studies are by no means conclusive with respect to the questions raised above. Israel has been one of the largest recipients of PL 480 Title I commodities on a per capita basis and her experience appears to have been quite favorable, both from the standpoint of contribution to general development and to agricultural expansion in particular. Because of Israel's limited arable land and the need for a large amount of irrigation, grain production is high-cost and larger returns are available from other types of agriculture, such as meat and poultry production, dairy products, and fruits and vegetables. Public Law 480 programs made a direct contribution to Israel's foreign exchange by reducing her need for commercial imports of wheat and feed grains. In addition, the feed-grain imports helped to promote Israel's livestock industry. Imports of wheat and other foods enabled Israel to relax rationing and to decontrol many food prices, with the result that the prices at which most farm output was sold rose while black market prices fell, with the resultant encouragement to agriculture. (By and large, dealers rather than producers received the benefits from the black market prices.)

Israel's almost wholly favorable experience was not duplicated in Colombia where, partly as a consequence of PL 480 imports, wheat prices lagged behind other prices, and production failed to rise, although some farmers shifted to dairy production and other crops. On the other hand, PL 480 imports of cotton were accompanied by an expansion of cotton production, partly as a consequence of price guarantees to producers, and partly through technical assistance. Pakistan, like Israel, was able to sub- stitute PL 480 food grant imports for commercial imports and thereby save foreign exchange. It is not possible to determine the extent to which Pakistan would have made greater efforts to expand her domestic agricul- ture in the absence of PL 480 food imports. There is some evidence, however, that wheat imports have had an adverse effect on agricultural prices and income. India's experience has been complicated by the exist- ence of periods of favorable and unfavorable harvests due to weather con- ditions during the period of PL 480 food imports. Although analysts dis- agree regarding the effects of food imports on India's agricultural output and prices, it seems probable that the existence of PL 480 and the large proportion of India's total aid which has taken the form of wheat imports, have prevented India's development planners from giving a higher priority to investment in agriculture.

SOME CONCLUSIONS ON AGRICULTURAL COMMODITY AID

We may conclude that as a technique for promoting economic devel- opment in accordance with appropriate investment policies, direct com- modity assistance has severe limitations. One of the major weaknesses of the PL 480 program from the standpoint of policy formation in both the donor and the recipient countries is that the program was based in con- siderable measure on a desire to get rid of U.S. agricultural surpluses generated by domestic agricultural policies. This led to a tendency on the part of both donor and recipient to regard the commodities supplied under PL 480 as resources having less value than resources provided under other aid programs. Public Law 480 programs were regarded as something over and above what might be expected under regular aid programs from various sources, including the United States. Uncertainty as to the time period during which U.S. agricultural surpluses would be available also affected the development policies of the recipient. There has been a failure on the part of the donors to integrate PL 480 programs with other de- velopment aid. The 1966 Food for Peace Act,[5] which was proposed by the Johnson Administration as a successor to PL 480, is designed to elim- inate these weaknesses by:

5. The Johnson Administration has called the new program under the 1966 Food for Peace Act (PL 89-808, 89th Congress), "Food for Freedom."

1) making self-help an integral part of the U.S. food aid program;

2) eliminating the "surplus" requirement for food aid, in favor of deliberate production of food for foreign aid programs;

3) shifting the financing of food aid from sales for foreign currencies to long-term dollar credits within a period of five years;

4) achieving better coordination of food aid with other economic programs (AID, 1966, pp. 29-30).

The Johnson Administration also looks forward to the implementation of a domestic agricultural program which will eliminate unwanted surpluses. (Indeed, surpluses of most agricultural commodities, with the notable exception of cotton, have already been substantially reduced or eliminated.) It seems clear that a substantial proportion of the world's increasing food needs cannot be met by the U.S. farmer, and it is therefore urgent that our foreign-aid authorities make sure that food aid is not reducing the incentive of developing countries to expand and modernize their agriculture.

The substantial comparative advantage of the United States in the production of food grains should be reflected in a continued, and perhaps growing, volume of U.S. exports, much of which may go to developing countries. But their development programs should allow for foreign-exchange earnings sufficient to import agricultural products on a commercial basis. Countries need not plan to be self-sufficient in all foods or in all agricultural commodities, any more than they should be self-sufficient in all industrial commodities. Indeed, the optimum pattern of world production and trade may be one in which many densely populated developing countries would become important exporters of industrial products while importing grains from the United States and Canada. These conditions are not going to be achieved without careful planning and the adoption of appropriate policies and incentives.

CHAPTER SEVEN

Foreign Aid by Any Other Name

THUS FAR I have not defined foreign aid, but the subject matter of this and the following chapter forces me to do so. I shall define official foreign aid as a transfer of real resources or immediate claims on resources (for example, foreign exchange) from one country to another, which would not have taken place as a consequence of the operation of market forces or in the absence of specific official action designed to promote the transfer by the donor country. Like all definitions this one is designed for a special purpose, namely, to include certain transactions not normally included in most definitions of foreign aid. Thus this definition includes both direct government transfers and those promoted by special official action such as government guarantees. It avoids the motivation of the donor as a criterion for aid; the donor may be motivated entirely by the desire for economic gain. Motivations of donors differ widely and do not in themselves determine the nature and the extent of the benefits to the recipients.

Nor does this definition seek to isolate the "aid" element in a transaction in a sense of the net cost (over benefits) to the donor or the net benefit (over cost) to the recipient. I shall deal with the "aid" element in transactions in the following chapter. In spite of the importance of private aid, I have not included it in this definition since I am concerned only with aid transfers involving governmental policy. Finally, the above definition is not well designed for the purpose of measuring official foreign aid statistically. It would scarcely be proper to aggregate such transfers as development grants, government-guaranteed commercial credits, and private investments with expropriation guarantees. For this purpose we need a definition which provides a standard unit for measuring aid transactions of differing quality. But to measure the "aid" element in various resource transfers requires a normative definition of aid based on "costs" or "benefits."

In the following paragraphs I have listed several types of official aid transactions which conform to my definition, some of which are not ordinarily considered as aid:

1) Bilateral loans and grants of commodities, services, and foreign exchange, by governments to foreign countries.

2) Loans and grants of commodities, services, and foreign exchange, by multilateral agencies out of funds supplied directly by governments or from funds borrowed in private international capital markets, guaranteed by member governments.

3) Assistance to compensate countries for balance-of-payments deficits arising from unforeseen or temporary causes or for short-term fluctuations in prices of exported commodities or in export earnings.

4) Government sales of commodities to foreign countries for local currencies which are subject to restriction as to use by the recipient.

5) Importation of commodities by governments at prices higher than free international market prices (or by private entities required by their government to pay higher than international market prices), including participation and cooperation by governments of importing countries in international commodity arrangements designed to raise or maintain prices of commodities at levels higher than would prevail in the absence of such arrangements.

6) Private loans, credits, or direct investments, guaranteed by the government of the capital exporter against loss from all or specific risks.

Types (1) and (2) transactions would appear to be fairly straightforward; yet they do raise difficulties. One has to do with the maturity of the loans by governments or government agencies. Prior to 1966, the Development Assistance Committee of the OECD excluded from its definition of official bilateral aid, loans of less than five years maturity.[1] The purpose of this limitation is to exclude government commercial credits, but the period is obviously arbitrary since commercial credits extended or guaranteed by governments may run to 10 or even 15 years. There are also non-commercial loans by government agencies of less than 5 years. International Monetary Fund transactions are also excluded by DAC, although some of the IMF credits are not repaid within 5 years. I have included drawings from the IMF together with other balance-of-payments credits and credits to cover shortfalls in export earnings under the category of compensatory aid (3). Compensatory transactions involve special conceptual problems which will be discussed later on in this chapter.

Loans and credits provide resources to the recipient countries regardless of the purpose of the lender. Nevertheless, to include on a gross basis

1. Beginning in 1966, DAC data on official aid included loans with a maturity of over one year. Apparently this change was motivated by a desire to bring DAC's long-term financial flow data into line with standard balance-of-payments practice, rather than constituting a change in the concept of aid (*Development Assistance Efforts and Policies, 1966 Review*, Chapter III).

all short-term credits—whether made by governments or guaranteed by them—as a part of aid is scarcely warranted, since credit transactions are involved in virtually all trade. On the other hand, an increase in the volume of net credits to a country relative to its total trade certainly must be regarded as a transfer of resources. A related question has to do with whether all loan assistance should be calculated on a *gross* or a *net* basis. From the standpoint of aid as a transfer of resources, loans should be calculated on a net basis, subtracting new loans from capital repayments. Moreover, a gross concept would give a heavy weight to a series of short-term loans as compared with longer-term loans. Thus, DAC calculates official bilateral aid on a net basis. Interest payments, of course, should not be included in calculating net lending, since they belong in the current account. Yet interest payments on old loans reduce the net flow of resources from donors to aid recipients. Some of these questions will be considered further in the following chapter (which deals with the impact of aid on donor countries).

Type (4) transactions, involving sales of commodities for inconvertible local currencies, have already been discussed as a form of aid which, as in the case of PL 480 Title I programs, may involve credits or grants, depending upon the conditions set forth in the sales agreement with respect to use of local currency proceeds by the seller. Bilateral payments and clearing agreements also involve acceptance of inconvertible currencies or credits in a clearing account, the uses of which are restricted. In the early postwar period, a substantial portion of the world's trade was conducted under reciprocal trade and payments agreements, but in recent years such arrangements have been confined almost entirely either to trade among Communist-bloc countries or trade between Communist-bloc and certain developing countries. The primary purpose of these arrangements has been to finance bilateral trade without the use of convertible foreign exchange. However, where one country under the agreement runs a substantial deficit which is not liquidated for several years, there is in fact a transfer of resources which may or may not have been originally intended. In the case of a number of the Communist-country agreements with developing countries, it was expected that the developing country would run a deficit under the agreement as a consequence of large initial shipments to the developing country; this credit would be subsequently repaid by shipments of raw materials and foodstuffs from the developing country to the Communist-bloc country (Mikesell and Behrman, 1958). This has been the standard method by which Communist-bloc countries have extended foreign aid. In some cases, however, delays in deliveries of Communist-country goods relative to purchases of primary products from the developing-country trading partner resulted in a clearing-account balance in favor of the developing country, so that the latter ended up giving rather than receiving credit.

Type (5) transactions represent aid arising out of governmental arrangements whereby prices paid for imports are higher than free international market prices. For example, U.S. sugar imports from certain countries have been purchased at controlled U.S. domestic prices which are substantially higher than free international market prices. The willingness of importing countries to enter into international commodity agreements which establish prices to exporting members at levels higher than free international market prices also constitutes a form of aid. I shall discuss aid transfers through trade arrangements in the following section.

Type (6) transactions, having to do with government guarantees of credits or loans and direct investments, raise a number of problems in considering them as aid transactions; these problems will be dealt with briefly later on in this chapter.

In addition to the categories of official aid outlined above, there is private foreign aid which amounts to several hundred million dollars each year. Just what private remittances should be regarded as being in the aid category presents some difficult conceptual problems. Clearly, the important foreign-assistance activities of such institutions as the Ford and Rockefeller foundations must be regarded as foreign aid, while remittances to families and friends abroad should not be so regarded. CARE operations are in effect a combination of private and government assistance, since CARE operations are heavily subsidized under Title III of PL 480. It would certainly not be appropriate to regard all remittances of institutions as falling in the category of aid. For example, worldwide religious and other private organizations (for example, the Vatican) transfer funds among themselves for purposes of covering operating expenses of organizational headquarters, or for spreading religious or political beliefs, which have nothing to do with aid. On the other hand, churches and other private organizations do carry on genuine educational, medical and other assistance programs in the developing countries, and these should be regarded as private aid.

While the principal focus of this book is on economic aid for development, it is not possible fully to separate the contribution of the transfer of resources to development from the contribution to consumption, or stabilization, or even defense, solely on the basis of the purpose for which aid is intended. Thus the IMF has certainly made a contribution to development by preventing fluctuations in the balance-of-payments from interfering with investment; PL 480 commodity transfers have both promoted investment and subsidized consumption; and a portion of U.S. wheat shipments to India has released exchange for the purchase of arms.

A recent PL 480 agreement with Egypt has been criticized as an indirect contribution to that country's military outlays; it has been suggested that a similar agreement with Israel is required to redress the military balance (*New York Times,* Jan. 5, 1966, p. 8)! Whether or not there is a contribution to development depends more on the policies of the recipient than the intentions of the donor.

Aid transactions are not always easy to identify and, as we shall see in the following chapter, the attempt to determine statistically the amount of aid provided by a country directly, or indirectly through international organizations, is beset by almost insuperable conceptual and statistical difficulties. In identifying transactions that involve an element of aid, the greatest amount of confusion and misunderstanding arises out of three types of transactions: (1) purchases of commodities at prices higher than those which prevail (or which would prevail in the absence of market interference) in free international markets; (2) government guarantees of private loans and direct investments; and (3) compensatory assistance of various types.

AID THROUGH TRADE

It has been generally recognized that aid and opportunities for trade are not only complementary, but that they may be substitutes for one another. But the popular slogan, "trade, not aid," has often been misused. No amount of trade, as such, constitutes a net transfer of resources in the sense that we have defined aid. However, opportunities for increased exports can raise real incomes by making possible a fuller utilization of domestic resources and a realization of the gains from specialization and trade. The removal of restrictions on imports of commodities from developing countries, including the elimination of excise taxes, may also improve the terms of trade of developing countries. Freer world trade does not constitute foreign aid, since it contributes to the real income and welfare of exporting and importing countries alike. (This is not to say, of course, that one country cannot improve its terms of trade and economic welfare by imposing tariffs.) On the other hand, arrangements entered into by developed countries which artificially raise the prices of exports of developing countries above their long-run equilibrium levels may result in a transfer of resources to the developing countries, which transfer may be regarded as a form of aid.[2] It is desirable to distinguish between arrange-

2. Import and excise taxes in developed countries levied on primary commodities such as coffee, cocoa, etc., which tend to depress prices received by the exporting countries, may constitute a transfer of resources from the poor to the rich countries.

ments which seek to iron out price fluctuations above and below long-term trends, and those which establish prices above long-term equilibrium levels. The former might properly be regarded as involving a type of compensatory aid, the nature of which is discussed in another section of this chapter.

Although I shall not discuss the details of the various forms of commodity arrangements which may raise export prices of developing countries above long-run equilibrium levels, it is well to distinguish between several major categories in these arrangements. First, there is the international commodity agreement under which exporting and importing countries agree upon a total amount of the commodity to be marketed by the exporting countries, and establish both export and import quotas for the exporting and importing countries respectively. The import quotas are generally necessary in order to enforce the export quotas and to limit or eliminate imports from non-member countries. International commodity agreements may also employ a buffer stock for controlling market prices, as in the case of the International Tin Agreement, or they may rely on export and import quotas, as in the case of the International Coffee Agreement.

Another type of arrangement—sometimes employed with respect to temperate zone primary commodities produced by both developing countries and developed countries which are also net importers—is the establishment of import quotas by a developed country, permitting a certain amount of imports from selected countries at the domestic support price. Thus, under the U.S. Sugar Act of 1948, as amended, a number of sugar-producing countries (mainly Latin American countries and the Philippines) have been able to export limited amounts of sugar to the United States at prices significantly above the world market price. A variant of this arrangement suggested by the French delegation at the United Nations Conference on Trade and Development in 1964 would be for the importing country to establish import fees equal to the difference between the world market price and the internal support price and then remit these fees to the governments of the developing countries (whose products were imported) for financing development projects.[3] Such arrangements in effect give to developing countries, or to specified developing countries, a portion of the subsidy granted to domestic producers in the developed country by reason of the production and import restrictions in the developed country. It might be argued that this payment is simply

3. See "Memorandum Concerning Certain Items on the Agenda of the U.N. Conference on Trade and Development," submitted by France, U.N. Conference on Trade and Development (E/CONF/46/74, Geneva, February 26, 1964). Other aspects of the position of the French delegation at the U.N. Trade and Development Conference discussed here are based on this memorandum.

returning to the developing country's exporters what they have lost as a consequence of the decline in the world price caused by the restrictions. However, in order to determine whether the developing country exporters were better off under this system as compared with a regime of complete freedom of trade, one would have to know a good deal about world supply elasticities in various producer countries.

A number of proposals for raising prices of primary commodity products exported by developing countries were discussed at the U. N. Conference on Trade and Development held in Geneva, March-June, 1964. Although some of the arrangements discussed were put forth as mechanisms for price stabilization, many were frankly designed to maintain the terms of trade of developing countries, or to restore terms of trade to a level corresponding to those existing in earlier periods regarded as "normal." It is argued that the operation of free competitive markets for primary commodities almost invariably means a decline in the terms of trade of primary commodity exporting countries because of the differences in price and income elasticities which characterize primary commodities as compared with manufactures.[4] Thus the position of many developing countries has been that the administration of primary commodity prices through international arrangements is not so much aid, but rather a means of assuring them what they regard as a fair or just price which developed countries are morally obligated to pay.

I do not regard the argument that developing countries have a moral right to receive a just price, or to maintain their terms of trade at some historical level, as either convincing or relevant. Programs for administering the prices of exports of primary producing countries above their long-run equilibrium levels constitute a form of aid or transfer of resources and, as such, the effects of this assistance on economic development and other objectives should be evaluated much as any form of aid. Provided such assistance is properly directed toward a structural adjustment of production in developing countries, aid in this form may make a contribution to development. Unfortunately, however, this is rarely the case.

4. This is the well-known doctrine popularized by Raul Prebisch that the terms of trade inevitably move against the primary commodities. Prebisch argues that because world price and income demand elasticities for primary commodities are low while supply elasticities of the commodities are also low, increased output resulting from improvements in productivity and increased inputs of labor and other factors tends to lower prices and total receipts. On the other hand, the high income and price elasticities for manufactured goods, together with rising factor prices and the ability to control output of manufactures in the developed countries, keeps export prices and manufacturers stable or rising, even with increased productivity. For a statement of this argument see Raul Prebisch, "Commercial Policy in the Underdeveloped Countries," *American Economic Review, Papers and Proceedings*, May, 1959.

Aid in the form of international price-support programs for the products of developing countries is, in effect, financed by a tax on consumers in the importing countries. Where the demand for the product is highly inelastic there is little impact on the demand for the imported products. However, over the long run, higher prices are almost certain to encourage the development of substitutes in the form of synthetics or in the utilization of other natural commodities which can be used as substitutes (such as the substitution of aluminum for copper). There is a tendency on the part of producers to understate the elasticity of demand for their products and to overlook the fact that products which may appear to be quite inelastic in the short run are fairly elastic over the longer run. The more elastic the demand for the product, the smaller the rise in total revenues and the smaller the amount of the aid transfer. The amount of the aid transfer may be regarded as equal to the increase in total revenues arising from the increase in the administered price over the price which would have prevailed in the absence of administrative controls. The reduction in demand which occurs whenever the demand is not completely inelastic involves some decrease in costs to the producing country. But in the short run, and in the absence of adjustments in production, the opportunity cost of the inputs saved from the reduction in output or sales is likely to be quite low. In fact, there may be no reduction in output but simply increased stockpiling of the surplus in the producer countries. The cost of such arrangements to the donor as compared with an equivalent amount of direct aid transfer will be examined in Chapter 8.

DISCRIMINATION AS A FORM OF AID

The U.N. Conference on Trade and Development in 1964 and subsequent meetings of the Trade and Development Board have been marked by a demand on the part of the developing countries for a favorable discriminatory treatment of their exports of manufactured goods to developed countries as a means of promoting their industrial exports. The African countries associated with the European Economic Community, as well as Associate Members of the EEC, have received favorable tariff treatment on their exports to the EEC, which discriminates against both primary commodity and manufactured exports from the rest of the world. Many developed countries, including Britain which already discriminates in favor of Commonwealth countries, favor an arrangement by which all developed countries would provide discriminatory tariff treatment for certain industrial products coming from all developing countries. This might mean complete elimination of tariffs on goods originating in developing countries, or it might mean a substantial reduction in the tariffs on such goods not granted to goods from developed countries. France, on the other hand, has favored special agreements between individual developed countries or economic communities such as the EEC with individual developing countries, whereby the manufactured exports of the latter would receive favorable tariff treatment, discriminating against imports from all other sources, including other developing countries.[5] The rationale for this proposal, which has been called the Brasseur Plan, after the Belgian official who first formulated it, is that special tariff advantages would be given on specific products only to certain countries that could hope to produce these commodities on a competitive basis in world markets. By limiting the special tariff treatment to one or a few developing countries producing a particular commodity, the advantage would be far more significant than if all developing countries were afforded the same advantage. It should be said that most developing countries, as well as developed countries, have rejected the Brasseur Plan, partly on the grounds that it would set up a system of bilateral preference arrangements which would tend to destroy whatever remained of the most-favored-nation principle established by the General Agreement on Tariffs and Trade. Many developing countries outside the Associated African Countries are already the victims of EEC discrimination against their exports; in fact some of the Latin American countries are demanding that the United States discriminate in favor of Latin American exports to offset the discriminatory tariff given by the EEC countries to the Associated African Countries.

The merits of discriminatory tariff treatment of imports from developing countries have been the subject of considerable debate both on economic grounds and from the standpoint of political and administrative feasibility. The U.S. government has taken a position against such discrimination partly on the grounds that the arrangements violate the most-favored-nation principle of the GATT and would not be permitted under U.S. trade legislation.[6] The U.S. government has bolstered its position with the argument that preferences would mean very little in promoting the industrial exports of developing countries. The latter argument has been developed by Gardner Patterson (1965, pp. 18-30; 1966, pp. 343 ff.) who has sought to show that tariff duties on most industrial products in developed countries are (or will be after the Kennedy Round of negotiations) too low to provide a margin of preference which would be a

5. For a discussion of various types of preferences see *Preferences: Review of Discussions,* Report by the Secretary-General of the Conference, U.N. Trade and Development Board, Special Committee on Preferences (TD/AC.1/1, March 25, 1965).

6. The U.S. softened its position on preferences at the OAS Conference of Heads of State at Punta del Este, Uruguay in April, 1967. At that Conference it agreed to consider preferences on imports from all developing countries in cooperation with other developed countries. Such preferences would require U.S. congressional action (*New York Times,* April 13, 1967, pp. 13-14).

decisive factor in expanding exports of the less-developed countries to the developed nations. Assuming a 50 per cent reduction in tariff rates in favor of imports from the developing countries, Patterson believes that the price advantage arising from preferences would be of the order of 5 to 7 per cent. Harry G. Johnson rejects Patterson's *de minimus* argument mainly on grounds that Patterson relies on nominal tariff rates rather than on an analysis of the tariff structure in terms of "effective" rates.[7]

My principal concern here is not so much with the merits of discriminatory tariff treatment as a means of promoting developing-country exports as it is with whether such arrangements can properly be regarded as a form of aid as I have defined it. Assuming that the supply capacity of the preference-receiving country is small relative to the import demand of the preference-giving country, the granting of duty-free status to imports from the preference-receiving country would enable that country to supply a larger proportion of the market in the preference-giving country and receive a higher price for its product. The net transfer received by the preference-receiving country would be the excess of price paid for the imports less the additional unit cost of the additional production stimulated by the preference. On the other hand, if the total output of the preference-receiving country is large relative to the import demand of the preference-giving country, so that the price in the preference-giving country declines to the world market price, there is no net transfer of resources. It is also conceivable that other world exporters would seek to maintain their market share of the imports of the preference-giving country and lower their price in order to offset the tariff advantage of the preference-receiving country.

Thus, the proper calculation of the amount of the aid transfer might be the difference between what the developing country received for its exports under a discriminatory tariff arrangement and the world market price for the commodity in the absence of all tariffs. Conceivably for some commodities, developing countries might gain as much by selling in a world completely free of tariffs on their exports as they would if all developed countries admitted these exports free of duty from developing countries, while maintaining tariffs on these same commodities coming from developed countries. One would have to know a great deal about the cost structure of the industry and the relevant supply elasticities to know whether developing countries would gain significantly more from

7. Effective tariff rates represent the duties levied as a percentage, not of the total value of the imported commodity, but of the value added by the industries protected. Assuming that value added by manufacturing is 50 per cent of the total value of the product and the raw material inputs are free of duty, a nominal tariff of 10 per cent provides an effective rate of protection of 20 per cent. See Harry G. Johnson, *Economic Policies Toward Less-Developed Countries* (Washington, D.C.: The Brookings Institution, 1967), Chapter VI.

a discriminatory tariff than from a general elimination of all tariffs on
the commodity in question. It would not be appropriate to regard measures tending to free international trade from non-discriminatory restrictions as a form of aid. Aid transfers arise from discriminatory treatment
only in cases where the preference-receiving country receives a price for
its product higher than the free-market world price that would exist in the
absence of all restrictions on the part of the preference-giving country.

GOVERNMENT GUARANTEES OF LOANS AND
DIRECT INVESTMENTS

A substantial proportion of total aid transfers as we have defined them
takes the form of government-guaranteed private loans, export credits, and
direct investments (for a description of these programs see Whitman,
1965). Some idea of the magnitude of these transactions is indicated by
the following figures. In 1964, AID negotiated over $700 million in
specific risk guarantees on U.S. direct private investment in the developing
countries, plus smaller amounts of Latin American housing guarantees
and extended risk guarantees.[8] During the fiscal year ended June 30,
1965, the Export-Import Bank issued guarantees on export credits
(mainly medium-term) totaling $283 million.[9] The governments of other
developed countries reportedly extended or guaranteed export credits with
maturities in excess of one year, totaling over $700 million in 1964
(OECD, 1965a, p. 125). In addition to guarantees of bilateral credits,
the funds for the bulk of the loans made by the World Bank and the
Inter-American Development Bank (from Ordinary Capital Resources)
are derived from the sale of bonds in private international capital markets,
the bonds being guaranteed against loss by the uncalled subscriptions of

8. Specific risk guarantees include those against expropriation, inability to convert local currency earnings, and war damage. Extended risk guarantees cover both
political and normal business risks on direct investments and long-term loan financing
in developing countries. Latin American housing guarantees provide for 100 per
cent coverage on loans and direct investments in support of the construction of
new housing in Latin America. The investors pay certain fees to the government
for these guarantees. For a description of these programs see *Proposed Mutual
Defense and Development Programs, Fiscal Year 1966,* Summary Presentation to
Congress, Agency for International Development, March, 1965, pp. 153-56; see also
Staff Memorandum on International Lending and Guarantee Programs, House Committee on Foreign Affairs, 88th Congress, Second Session, Washington, D.C.,
December 1964, pp. 61-68.

9. The Export-Import Bank during the fiscal year 1965 participated with the
Foreign Credit Insurance Association in guaranteeing $272 million in short-term
export credits. However, as indicated earlier, there are good reasons for excluding
short-term export credits from the aid category.

the member governments of these institutions. In 1964, loans of the World Bank and the IDB (Ordinary Capital Resources) totalled about $1 billion.

On what basis are we to regard government-guaranteed private loans and investments as aid? Should we not limit the aid element to the losses or the estimated risk exposure by the government not compensated by fees charged to the investors? So far as losses to the U.S. government on these operations are concerned, there had been no net losses as of the end of 1964 on either the investment guarantee program or the export credit guarantee programs. Although one claim had been paid on a specific risk guarantee, and several claims paid on export credit guarantees, these payments had been recovered by the sale of the assets taken over from the private investors and by other means (Foreign Relations Committee, 1965, pp. 504-529; Whitman, 1965, pp. 323-25). Cumulative fees collected by the U.S. government under the specific risk guarantee program totaled $22 million as of December 31, 1964, while administrative costs are estimated at about $400,000 annually. Not only have the guarantee programs not resulted in a net loss to the U.S. government—in fact they have been profitable—but there is no actuarial basis for determining likely losses on the $1.7 billion in specific risk guarantees outstanding on December 31, 1964, or on the $1 billion in contingent liabilities arising out of guarantees and insurance issued by the Export-Import Bank. Moreover, barring a worldwide catastrophe, there seems little likelihood that the unpaid callable subscriptions of the U.S. government to the World Bank and the Inter-American Development Bank will be called to meet losses of these institutions. The fact that the U.S. government (along with other developed countries in the case of subscriptions to the World Bank) has directly or indirectly guaranteed these investments, and is therefore a contingent creditor, makes a significant amount of loss rather unlikely except in the event of another world war.

The real basis for regarding government-guaranteed private loans and investments as aid arises from the fact that a large proportion of the private transfers of resources would not have been made in the absence of the government-guarantee programs. In terms of cost to the donor nation, it makes little difference whether resources are transferred abroad by means of a direct government loan or by a private loan or investment guaranteed by the U.S. government. The relevant question in determining the amount of official foreign aid is what portion of these resources transferred was induced by the guarantee program, whether they were 100 per cent guaranteed or guaranteed against specific types of risks. The actual burden of the transfers on the donor differs with the terms and conditions of the transfer, but this is true whether the transfers are made on direct government account or privately with the inducement of guarantees. Some

types of investment, such as direct investments in foreign resource industries, may result in substantial economic benefits to the investor. Likewise,
medium- and long-term export credit guarantees are made available almost solely for the purpose of expanding the exports of the credit-extend-
ing country. But they are nevertheless transfers of resources which take
place as a consequence of government action involving the assumption
or sharing of the credit risk. They certainly provide resources for the recipient country which would not otherwise have been made available in
the absence of government action. Whether, and to what extent, they make
a contribution to economic development or welfare of the recipient
country is another question. But, again, it makes little difference whether
the Export-Import Bank makes a direct loan to the foreign government,
say to purchase aircraft on 7-year credit terms, or whether the Bank guarantees a 7-year supplier credit. The motive for making available the
credit may be entirely commercial or may be a mixture of commercial
interest and a desire to assist the foreign economy. The transaction may
involve a net benefit for the U.S. economy or a net social cost, but in
either case the transaction constitutes aid as I have defined it.

COMPENSATORY ARRANGEMENTS

Temporary assistance made available to individual countries or groups
of countries for ironing out fluctuations in the world market prices of
their exports above and below long-term trends, or to meet unexpected
fluctuations in exports receipts, import requirements, or drains on reserves resulting from capital movements, constitute a special form of aid
which we shall call compensatory aid. Compensatory aid as defined here
must be for relatively short periods, as against, say, assistance for long-
term development programs, and the need for such assistance must be
unplanned. Compensatory aid also presumes that the need for such assistance will be terminated within a relatively short period of time, either
as a consequence of the reversal of the forces giving rise to the need for
such assistance, or by replacing compensatory aid with long-term assistance required for structural adjustments. The rationale for considering
compensatory aid under a separate category arises from three important
characteristics. First, it is unplanned, as defined above. Second, the arrangements usually involve mutual benefits. For example, under the IMF
arrangement it is impossible to forecast over a period of time which
countries will be recipients of compensatory aid and which will be con-
tributors; thus, the arrangements are frequently analagous to an insurance
fund. Third, compensatory aid arrangements are often tied to the creation
of international reserves. For example, an expansion of the credit trans-

actions of the IMF provides foreign exchange to the borrower while increasing the international reserves of the country whose currency has been lent by the Fund. Under such arrangements, the pattern of real resource transfers becomes complicated and cannot be determined in advance of the provision of compensatory aid.

INTERNATIONAL COMMODITY AGREEMENTS

We may begin with international commodity arrangements participated in by both producing and importing countries, the avowed purpose of which is to iron out fluctuations in prices above and below long-term equilibrium levels without seeking to maintain prices above long-term trends. A number of schemes requiring cooperation between exporting and importing countries are possible, including (1) international buffer stock arrangements designed to maintain prices within a given range by means of purchases and sales from the buffer stock; (2) multilateral long-term contracts involving an agreement among exporting and importing countries to sell or purchase minimum amounts within a certain price range; and (3) export quota agreements (supplemented by import quotas imposed by importing members of the agreement) designed to maintain prices at or near the calculated equilibrium levels by means of temporarily limiting market supply. Whether or not direct financial assistance may be provided by the importing countries, such as for example in the case of financial contributions to a buffer stock scheme, international commodity agreements will result in commodity prices being at times above free market levels and, presumably, at times below free market levels. When the agreement prices are above free market levels (which would have prevailed in the absence of the agreement), there is a transfer of resources from the importing to the exporting countries. On the other hand, the mutuality of the arrangement arises from the possibility that at times agreement prices will be below prices that otherwise would have been paid by importing members of the agreement. There are also mutual advantages arising from the more economical use of resources, and lower costs induced by the avoidance of uneconomic short-run price fluctuations (for a discussion of international commodity agreements see Swerling, 1962; Mikesell, 1963a, pp. 294-312).

COMPENSATION FOR EXPORT SHORTFALLS

The limited number of commodities for which international commodity agreements are feasible, together with some disillusionment regarding the effectiveness of such arrangements, has led in recent years to an interest in schemes designed to compensate developing countries for unex-

208 THE ECONOMICS OF FOREIGN AID

pected reductions in export receipts. Fluctuating export receipts have undoubtedly constituted a serious problem for developing countries during the postwar period, and although such fluctuations have been equally if not more severe in earlier periods, they have attracted special attention during the past decade when developing countries have been seeking to carry out development programs. A number of plans for compensating countries for shortfalls in export receipts have been formulated over the past decade, but the first one to receive prominent attention was that put forward by the U.N. Committee of Experts entitled *International Compensation for Fluctuations in Commodity Trade* (1961). The U.N. experts' scheme provided for a development insurance fund to which both developed and underdeveloped countries would contribute, and compensations would be made to both low-income and high-income producing countries for shortfalls in export proceeds in accordance with an automatic formula. The compensations would take the form of either grants or contingent loans. The development insurance fund would be financed by an initial subscribed capital fund and annual contributions, plus repayments of contingent loans, the repayment obligations being related to any increases in export proceeds over a three-year moving average. Shortfalls to be compensated would be measured from a moving average of the three preceding years, with the amount of compensation established as some percentage of the shortfall. While this proposal was described as a kind of mutual insurance program, capital subscriptions and contributions to the insurance fund would be established in a manner which would assure that the benefits would substantially exceed contributions and repayments for the low-income countries, while just the opposite would be true for the high-income countries. Thus, in operation there would be a net flow of resources from high-income to low-income countries, although under one form of the proposal countries would be under obligation to repay the fund as their commodity export proceeds rose.

In recognition of the problem of fluctuating export proceeds of developing countries, the IMF in 1963 established a new compensatory drawing facility equal to an additional 25 per cent of each developing member country's quota over and above its normal credit tranche.[10] However, such additional drawings would have to be repaid within a five-year period. The problem of fluctuating export proceeds was a major issue at the 1964 United Nations Conference on Trade and Development (UNCTAD), and a large number of proposals were put forward and debated. Some of the schemes advocated by certain of the developing countries sought to compensate primary commodity-producing countries for reductions in their terms of trade and were based on appeals of "jus-

10. The IMF liberalized this arrangement in 1966 by permitting supplemental drawings up to 50 per cent of the quota of an eligible developing country.

tice" or "need," as opposed to the principle of compensation for unexpected and reversible decreases in receipts from exports. Such schemes were generally rejected by the developed-country participants at the Conference, but there was considerable sympathy expressed by the representatives of the industrialized countries for the position that existing facilities, including those provided by the IMF, were inadequate for dealing with interruptions to development programs arising from unexpected shortfalls in export proceeds. After considerable debate, the Conference adopted a recommendation without dissent, but with ten abstentions (all Soviet-bloc countries), to the effect that the World Bank should be invited to study and make a report on a plan for the establishment of supplementary financial machinery to be administered by the International Development Association for dealing with unexpected shortfalls in export earnings of a nature or duration which could not adequately be dealt with by existing facilities. The purpose of such machinery would be to prevent the disruption of sound development programs (IBRD, 1965, pp. 73-75). This recommendation was originally sponsored by the United Kingdom and Sweden but was formulated in close cooperation with the United States and other developed countries.

In response to the UNCTAD resolution, the World Bank prepared a study entitled *Supplementary Financial Measures,* which was submitted to the Secretary General of the United Nations in December, 1965. This study found that special financial facilities for dealing with the problem as stated in the UNCTAD resolution were both desirable and feasible, and set forth a concrete proposal to be administered by a separate agency without specific recommendation as to whether the agency should be IDA, as proposed by the UNCTAD resolution, or some other agency. I shall not be concerned with the details of the World Bank proposal, but certain fundamental principles of the plan may be noted:

1) Assistance would be provided for dealing with unexpected reductions in export earnings of developing countries which will have an adverse effect on their development programs. The proposed scheme is not designed to deal with a foreseeable deterioration in export receipts or stagnating export earnings, the solution for which may involve long-term foreign capital for financing a development program designed to achieve structural adjustments in the economy.

2) The scheme recommended would provide financing in cases where drawing facilities from the IMF were either not sufficient or were inappropriate because of the balance-of-payments position of the country or the expected duration of the shortfall.

3) Financing would not be automatic but would be closely integrated with the country's development program. Its purpose would be to avoid

disruption of a country's development program as a consequence of its inability to carry out planned programs and projects. While financing would not necessarily be tied to specific projects,

access to the Scheme would depend on the implementation of development programs and related policies previously agreed with the Agency. In this exacting sense, the satisfactory performance of members would be a pre-requisite for assistance. There need be no prior international agreement on the issue of how supplementary finance is to be conveyed quickly enough under the Scheme to prospective recipients. It could be left to the discretion of the Agency to work out an agreement with the member country as to how the finance would be applied to ensure that the development program could go forward (IBRD, 1965, pp. 58-59).

4) The terms of the financing would be "geared to the servicing capacity of the member country as well as other relevant factors." In general it is expected that the terms would provide for low rates of interest and long maturities.

5) While the IBRD report finds it difficult to determine on the basis of past experience just what amount of resources the agency would need, it suggests that it should have total resources of $1.5-$2 billion for an initial experimental period of five years (IBRD, 1965, p. 71). Presumably all or the vast bulk of the resources would have to be supplied by subscriptions from the developed country members of the agency.

6) Availability of benefits under the scheme would depend on the willingness of the developing country member governments to enter into agreements with the agency concerning (a) its expectations; (b) its development programs and policies; and (c) feasible adjustments to unexpected shortfalls without disrupting the agreed-upon development program. Export forecasts would be related to the planning period of the member country—normally a range of four to six years—and the member would have assurance of assistance in case of an export shortfall during the plan period (IBRD, pp. 8-9).

The essential merits of the IBRD scheme over other proposed compensatory arrangements are that it does not involve automatic compensation for reductions in exports whatever the cause, and that it provides for assistance closely integrated with a country's development program. It seeks to fill a gap in the arsenal of aid instruments for developing countries which is something between the short- and medium-term compensatory financing facilities provided by the IMF, and long-term development aid programs. The World Bank scheme contains some of the elements of compensatory aid, but since financing is to be provided by long-term loans, the assistance should properly be regarded as being in the same category as other long-term development aid.

SHORT-TERM BALANCE-OF-PAYMENTS ASSISTANCE

Compensatory aid in the form of balance-of-payments or stabilization credits has been provided by the United States in the form of loans, or under an exchange agreement with the U.S. Exchange Stabilization Fund whereby the aid recipient is entitled to "purchase" dollars from the Fund with its own currency over a given period, but must "repurchase" its currency with gold or dollars within a stipulated time period and pay interest on the net amount of dollars held during the period. Balance-of-payments credits may also be obtained from the IMF when a country draws foreign currencies in an amount beyond its gold tranche.[11] A true stabilization or balance-of-payments credit is one designed to finance unplanned and temporary or reversible deficits in a country's balance of payments. Very often conditions are placed on such credits, such as an agreement on the part of the borrowing country to take policy measures designed to restore balance-of-payments equilibrium. However, not all so-called balance-of-payments or stabilization credits meet the criteria of being unplanned and temporary or reversible in character. Countries may deliberately pursue policies which result in continuing deficits which could readily be anticipated and are neither temporary nor reversible within a reasonable period of time, say three to five years. Correction of a balance-of-payments deficit may require major shifts in monetary and fiscal policies, a devaluation of the currency, or policies designed to shift the pattern of investment and production, which may require a substantial period of time, perhaps with the aid of long-term external assistance. Thus, some so-called balance-of-payments assistance is in reality a form of long-term aid.

Compensatory aid made available to developing countries is usually designed to meet a current account deficit and hence involves a net transfer of resources. There are cases, however, in which balance-of-payments assistance is required to meet deficits arising largely or wholly from capital outflows. Financial assistance to cover capital outflow does not involve a net transfer of real resources, since such transfers can only take place through the current account. Frequently, developing countries obtain assistance from foreign assistance agencies in order to meet maturing indebtedness, in which case the assistance enables the country to meet its

11. A country's gold tranche is usually equal to 25 per cent of its IMF quota (provided the country has subscribed 25 per cent of its quota in gold or convertible currencies), and such drawings are permitted to be made automatically by the IMF. Also, the gold tranche is regarded as part of the official reserves of a member of the IMF. Drawings beyond the gold tranche into the country's credit tranche (usually 100 per cent of a country's quota) require special approval of the IMF Executive Board.

debt obligations without a reduction in imports. Whether or not this situation is temporary depends upon the future pattern of debt payments and, perhaps, upon the ability of the country to refinance shorter-term obligations by a long-term loan. Sometimes a developing country which is normally a long-term borrower will find that its long-term capital imports are interrupted, and it incurs a credit squeeze arising in part from payments on past indebtedness. Under such conditions, compensatory aid may tide a country over a period of temporary interruption of long-term capital inflow.

Although developing countries sometimes experience deficits as a consequence of capital flight (usually arising from capital exports of their own citizens), foreign-aid agencies, including the IMF, generally do not provide credits to developing countries to meet deficits arising from speculative capital flight. On the other hand, compensatory assistance to developed countries for meeting speculative capital outflow is quite common, and has at times reached substantial proportions. Compensatory aid to developed countries raises special conceptual and analytical problems, particularly in the case of reserve currency countries such as the United States and the United Kingdom.

BALANCE-OF-PAYMENTS CREDITS TO DEVELOPED COUNTRIES AND
INTERNATIONAL LIQUIDITY

Balance-of-payments deficits of developed countries may arise from current account deficits, from capital flight initiated by their own residents, or from capital withdrawals by foreigners. The latter type of capital movement is particularly important in the case of reserve currency countries such as the United States and the United Kingdom. For non-reserve currency countries, temporary deficits arising from deficits in the current account involve problems similar to those of developing countries. Moreover, speculative capital outflow initiated by residents of such countries is usually followed by the establishment of capital controls when the outflow reaches proportions that threaten international reserves. Deficits of reserve currency countries affect the volume of international reserves, either by increasing them or causing them to decline, depending upon how the deficits are financed. Drawings from the Monetary Fund also affect the volume of international reserves. Finally, compensatory balance-of-payments assistance arising out of "swap" transactions between major developed countries, particularly where one of the countries is a reserve currency country, affect the volume of international reserves. Many of these compensatory aid transactions involve complex problems with respect to the transfer of real resources, which need to be examined.

The complex relationships between balance-of-payments deficits, compensatory aid transactions, and the creation of international liquidity may be illustrated by the following example, which reflects the recent experience of the United States. The U.S. balance-of-payments deficit has been financed for more than a decade in considerable part by an increase in liquid dollar liabilities to foreigners.[12] So long as foreigners are willing to hold liquid dollar liabilities, the U.S. deficit is financed by an increase in international reserves. However, when foreign holders of dollars sell them in the foreign-exchange markets, the U.S. monetary authorities must either use some of their gold or convertible currency holdings to support the value of the dollar (or, alternatively, convert dollars presented by foreigners into gold when the dollar reaches the gold export point), or arrange to borrow foreign currencies from foreign governments, or draw foreign currencies from the IMF.

One of the methods used by the U.S. government for obtaining foreign currencies to support the dollar in the exchange markets has been to enter into "swap" agreements with a foreign monetary authority whereby each country agrees to exchange, say, $100 million (or equivalent) of its currency for that of the other country for a certain period of time. Each country counts the holdings of the other country's currency as a part of its reserves, so that total reserves are increased by the swap agreement. If the U.S. government uses $50 million of the foreign currency acquired under the swap arrangement to support the value of the dollar in the foreign-exchange market, is this an aid transfer, or simply the use of U.S. reserves? The partner has not, in the first instance, at least, lost any reserves since it continues to count the dollars it holds under the swap agreement as a part of its reserves, and the liability in terms of its own currency has been shifted from the United States to other holders, perhaps even its own citizens. If the U.S. deficit arises entirely as a consequence of capital transactions, no real resource transfer to the United States takes place. Conceivably, however, a capital export from the United States to a

12. According to the official U.S. Department of Commerce concept, a deficit occurs when there is a net reduction of official holdings of gold and convertible currencies, plus an increase in liquid dollar liabilities to foreigners. (Liquid dollar liabilities consist of short-term dollar assets of foreigners plus long-term marketable U.S. government securities.) See *Balance of Payments Statistics of the United States, A Review and Appraisal* (USGPO, April, 1965). In its presentation of the balance of payments, beginning with 1965, the Department of Commerce employs both the Department of Commerce concept of deficit or surplus, and the official settlements concept as recommended by the Bureau of the Budget (Bernstein) Committee. Under the official settlements concept, a deficit or surplus is measured by the change in U.S. official gold and convertible currency holdings, plus the change of liquid dollar liabilities to foreign monetary authorities. See *Survey of Current Business,* December, 1965, p. 19.

third country might result in a real resource transfer from the swap agreement country to the third country.

Alternatively, the United States might draw the $50 million in a foreign currency from the IMF in order to support the exchange value of the dollar. In this case, the reserves of the country whose currency is drawn rise by an equivalent amount, since that country's gold tranche position in the IMF is increased by the drawing. If the U.S. drawing does not exhaust the U.S. gold tranche in the IMF, it is simply using a portion of its official monetary reserves. If total drawings were to exceed 25 per cent of the U.S. quota, the United States draws a part of its credit tranche. Such a drawing is generally regarded as aid, although the reserves of the country whose currency is drawn are increased by the amount of the drawing. However, by a simple policy determination, the IMF could decide that the first 25 per cent of each member's credit tranche could be drawn automatically, thereby increasing the reserves of all members by this amount. In this event, the United States would again be drawing on its own reserves, in the process of which the reserve position of the IMF member whose currency was drawn would have been increased by an equivalent amount (for discussion of IMF drawing mechanism, see Group of Ten, 1965).

Deficits of reserve currency countries and increased drawings on credit tranches in the IMF (drawings beyond initial gold subscription) result in the creation of international reserves which constitute a claim on goods and services as well as representing a liquid asset. The net resource transfer, or "aid" aspect, involved in reserve creation through compensatory financing of balance-of-payments deficits has been an important topic in the recent discussions on international monetary reform (Roosa, 1965; Group of Ten, 1965). In this discussion I shall not attempt to explore the complex issues relating to international monetary reform, but rather concentrate on the question of the aid element in reserve asset creation.

Let us begin with the familiar case in which a non-reserve currency country experiencing a current account deficit draws a portion of its credit tranche from the IMF in the form of, say, French francs, and uses half of the drawing, say $10 million, for the purchase of goods from France, the other half for the purchase of goods from Germany by first converting the francs into deutschmarks. Initially, as a consequence of the drawing, French reserves rise by $20 million as a result of the increase in France's automatic drawing rights. However, as a result of the conversion of francs into deutschmarks, France loses $10 million in reserves, and Germany has gained $10 million in reserves. Thus, France and Germany have each given up $10 million worth of goods and services but each has acquired $10 million in reserves. If their preference for additional reserves is higher than that for domestically produced goods and services, they have gained from the transaction; if it is not, they can restore their earlier position by policy actions which will either reduce their exports or increase their imports so that their reserves decline to the original positions. However, it is argued that such policy action may either be politically difficult (for example, placing a tax on exports), or may interfere with domestic price stability (for example, expanding credit and monetary income so as to increase the demand for imports). But there is a further argument analagous to the argument against increasing purchasing power in a domestic economy which has reached full employment. An increase in the demand for world goods and services as a result of the increased monetary assets made available to deficit countries may raise world prices by stimulating inflationary pressures in a number of countries of the world. Hence, the question of the real cost of creating additional reserves for providing a net increase in compensatory assistance to countries experiencing current account deficits hinges on the demand for liquidity and the pattern of that demand as the liquidity positions of individual countries are affected.

The current account deficits of the countries drawing from the IMF might have been met by France and Germany by the extension of export credits to these countries, in which case no international reserve creation would have taken place. If the export credits do not constitute any expansion of total credit facilities in the exporting country, they must be provided at the expense of domestic credits; alternatively, if they constitute a net addition to the total volume of credit in the country, they are just as inflationary as if the exports had been financed by the acquisition of an additional reserve asset. In both cases, however, there is a transfer of resources from the exporting to the importing country without the acquisition of a reserve asset. It is interesting to note that some of the countries that seem most reluctant to see an expansion of international reserve assets are quite willing to compete for exports by extending short- and medium-term export credits.

In the examples just given, it is clear that the deficit country has received aid, whether through the creation of reserve assets or an expansion of export credit, regardless of the burden, if any, on the exporting country. Somewhat less clear is the case in which there is a general increase in international reserves, say by a mechanism under which the first 25 per cent of every member country's credit tranche in the IMF is converted into an automatic tranche. Alternatively, there could be an increase in the price of gold which would increase the foreign currency value of all gold holdings. Under such circumstances, would the decision on the part of a country to cover a deficit with the increase in the monetary value of its gold or the increase in its IMF gold tranche represent aid? This is not a wholly academic question since some members of the Group of Ten [13] have argued that the distribution of any general increase in international monetary reserves should be limited to the developed countries on the grounds that they are less likely to use them for financing current deficits.

The issue of whether an increase in international reserves—whether brought about through an increase in the price of gold, an increase of automatic drawing rights in the IMF, or through one of several proposals for expanding total reserve assets—constitutes a form of aid raises the question of whether any distinction should be made between using reserves (assets) and using borrowed funds (liabilities) to finance a deficit in defining an aid transaction.[14] In a sense, any current account deficit involves drawing resources from other countries, whether it is financed by reserve assets or by borrowed funds. However, most countries place a high value on the accumulation of reserve assets, whether in the form of gold, reserve currencies, or automatic claims on the IMF. They would regard it as strange, indeed, if they were told that a sudden expansion of their exports to the United States, which enabled them to add to their dollar reserves, constituted in effect an aid transfer to this country. In any case, transfers of real resources in exchange for reserve assets arising from commercial transactions are excluded in my definition of aid.

When foreign aid is provided by a reserve currency country in the form of its own currency balances, and when in addition the reserve currency country is running a current account deficit, the question arises as to whether that country or other countries are the actual donors. Harry G. Johnson (1962, p. 4) has argued that a substantial portion of the $60 billion of U.S. foreign aid extended during the period 1950-60 was indirectly provided by other countries through U.S. deficits financed by the accumulation of dollars by foreigners and by gold exports. The almost continual deficits of the United States since 1950, which have been financed in considerable part by an expansion of liquid dollar liabilities, have arisen not from a current account deficit in which there has been a flow of real resources to the United States, but rather from an increase in long-term capital outflow in the form of direct investments, private loans and portfolio investments, and foreign aid. Charles Kindleberger argues that the U.S. deficits have not only performed an important service in supplementing the world's monetary reserves, but that they have also equalized the demand for, and supply of, liquidity arising out of international differ-

13. The Group of Ten refers to a group of Finance Ministers and heads of Central Banks appointed by the governments of ten countries, including the United States, Canada, Japan, and seven Western European countries, to study and prepare recommendations for international monetary reform, including proposals for the creation of reserve assets.

14. This point was raised in a note to the author by Harry G. Johnson.

ences in liquidity preferences. Thus, according to Kindleberger (1965) Europeans have a higher liquidity preference than Americans, so that Americans have acquired long-term assets in Europe in exchange for short-term liabilities, to the mutual benefit of both areas. In fact, Kindleberger suggests a method of calculating balance-of-payments equilibrium in which short-term U.S. liquid dollar liabilities acquired as a consequence of differences in liquidity preferences (and matched by the acquisition of long-term foreign assets) would be placed "above the line" in the balance-of-payments accounts and, therefore, not shown as a deficit. It has also been argued by some economists that under the present system the costs borne by a reserve currency country in supplying increments to world reserves exceed any benefits arising from the ability to pay for goods and capital assets with short-term reserve liabilities.[15]

The current discussions on international monetary reform by the Group of Ten concern both the burdens involved in supplying an adequate volume of reserves, on the one hand, and the distribution of the benefits, on the other. Apparently, the official position of virtually all members of the Group of Ten is that the world's supply of liquidity should not depend on chronic U.S. deficits, although many U.S. and British economists take issue with this position in terms of the usual definition of deficits. It is also generally agreed that the volume of world reserves should not be subjected to erratic changes arising from shifts on the part of the reserve asset holders from currency reserves into gold, and that there should be a mechanism for an orderly expansion of reserves to meet increasing world liquidity needs. But the question of how reserves should be expanded, and in what form, and what countries should be the initial beneficiaries of the increased reserves constitutes the basic issues in the current controversy. Nevertheless, any expansion of international reserves means those acquiring reserves will obtain a claim on international resources; their use, except for the acquisition of foreign capital assets, must inevitably involve a net transfer of real resources, even though the country or countries providing the resources will acquire an addition to their reserve assets. Whether and under what conditions such net resource transfers should be regarded as aid is mainly a matter of definition.

As a final complication, the IMF system, as well as a number of the

15. The alleged costs to a reserve currency country arise from the necessity of adopting domestic monetary and fiscal policies required to maintain a reserve currency status, which are incompatible with full employment and maximum growth. See for example Herbert G. Gruble, "The Benefits and Costs of Being a World Banker," *The National Banking Review*, 2 (December, 1964), 189-212; see also Alan P. Kirman and Wilson E. Schmidt, "Key Currency Burdens: The U. K. Case," *The National Banking Review*, 3, September, 1965), 101-102. For my own views on this question see Raymond F. Mikesell, "United States as World Banker," *The National Banking Review*, 4 (December, 1966), 145-50.

currently discussed proposals for international monetary reform and reserve asset creation, has the character of a mutual insurance scheme in which the distribution of future benefits and costs in terms of resource transfers cannot be determined in advance, nor can a country's preference as between real goods and services and reserve assets be anticipated in the future. Balance-of-payments deficits are expected to be reversed so that the aid transfers involved in financing them are shifted in the opposite direction later on. Moreover, all countries stand to gain from a smoothly working reserve and compensatory finance system to the extent that it permits a freer flow of trade and international financial transactions which promote the economic employment of world resources.

CHAPTER EIGHT

Foreign Aid Donors
and the Burden of Aid

I HAVE DEFINED AID in a manner that avoids any relationship to the economic burden on the donor; in fact, certain aid transactions may confer net economic benefits on the donor. In the following discussion I shall limit my concern to the direct economic costs and offsetting economic benefits; I shall assume that the hoped-for political, security, or humanitarian rewards justify the net costs. In choosing the topics for discussion, I have emphasized those which have a bearing on major policy issues relating to the burden of aid on the donor: (1) To what degree does foreign aid provide compensating benefits to the donors? (2) What should be the basis for an equitable distribution of aid to developing countries among the donor countries? (3) To what degree does aid tying reduce the real value of aid? (4) How far does aid tying reduce the balance-of-payments burden of aid on the donors? (5) What is the real burden of commodity agreements on importing countries? (6) How would a shift from bilateral to multilateral aid affect the distribution of the aid burden?

CAPITAL EXPORTS AND NATIONAL ECONOMIC ADVANTAGE

What are the factors that determine whether capital exports result in a gain or loss in terms of the social product to the capital exporting country? The theoretical literature on this subject is surprisingly slender, although much has been written on issues which have an important bearing on this problem (Simpson, 1962; Murphy, 1960; Jasay, 1960; MacDougall, 1960). The fact that returns to the owners of capital may be higher abroad than at home does not in itself mean that there is a net benefit to the social product in a capital-exporting country. Under full employment conditions, the loss of output in the capital-exporting country will depend upon the nature of the production function. For example, if there are no diminishing returns to capital, the loss of output would be substantially greater than in the case of strong diminishing returns. The existence of unemployment in the capital-exporting country may also mean a reduction of employment if capital is invested abroad rather than at home. On the other hand, foreign investment may not be at the expense of domestic investment if savings are larger than domestic investment opportunities. It has also been argued that additional foreign investment reduces the rate of return from abroad on all *past* foreign investment. But this view of diminishing returns to capital abroad over-looks the fact that direct foreign investment embodies management and technical skills which promote productivity abroad.

Capital exports affect the volume and composition of trade and the terms of trade. Factor movements may, under certain conditions, decrease trade and tend to equalize factor returns. The literature on the tendency of trade to equalize factor prices is perhaps relevant here, but the assumptions are too restrictive to be of much value in a world of rapid technical and structural change. Capital movements have both trade-creating and trade-substituting effects, but static models are likely to miss the trade-creating tendencies. There is little doubt that capital movements affect the composition of trade between developed and less-developed countries. But the effects of these shifts in trade composition on the welfare of the capital-exporting countries are difficult to predict. There is an extensive literature on the effects of capital exports on the terms of trade, but the neoclassical view that the terms of trade will necessarily move against the capital-exporting countries has been subject to serious question. The following quotation from Paul Samuelson (1952) is worth noting:

> If we rigidly adhere to the assumption of literally zero transport costs and admit no impediments to trade or imperfections of competition into our analysis, then the orthodox presumption that the terms of trade in the paying country will tend to deteriorate turns out to fall completely to the side (p. 298).

More recently, Kindleberger (1958, p. 360) has stated, "It seems probable that the literature overemphasizes the importance of the terms of trade for normal international lending, and the presumption that the terms of trade favor the borrower is positive, but small." Hans Singer (1950) has taken the opposite position—that the terms of trade of capital-importing countries whose major exports are primary products tend to deteriorate *vis-à-vis* the industrial capital exporting countries. Singer's argument is similar to that of Raul Prebisch regarding the long-run terms of trade of primary commodity-exporting countries, discussed in Chapter 7.

Foreign investment, and particularly direct investment, involves not only capital movements but the export of entrepreneurship, management, and technical knowledge and experience, which constitute the assets of the investing firms. The social costs of exporting personnel of investing firms may be as important as the capital itself, depending upon their alternative uses in the absence of foreign investment. It should be noted however that there is a close relationship between modern trade and foreign investment in the form of capital and skills. Foreign trade is not simply a matter of executing orders from foreign dealers contacted by salesmen. It involves the establishment of distribution facilities including warehouses, assembly plants, and even the production abroad of certain components, as determined by cost and competitive conditions. Thus, foreign investment may constitute in part the price paid for reaping the gains from international trade. Another factor in direct foreign investment which is sometimes overlooked is the loss of tax revenue to the government of the capital-exporting country on earnings from foreign investment as compared with earnings on the same amount of capital invested domestically. Thus, if a U.S. firm pays a 50 per cent tax on earnings abroad, that tax is deducted from its U.S. tax liabilities. To the extent that the foreign investment constitutes an alternative to domestic investment, and assuming the same rate of return on the investment in both cases, half of the before-tax earnings are lost to the U.S. government and hence constitute a direct social cost.

The conclusions of Paul Simpson (1962) based on a critical survey of both the theoretical and the empirical literature on the benefits and costs to capital exporting countries probably constitutes the best assessment of the general case:

The following conditions are highly beneficial to the capital exporting nation: (1) High capital returns abroad; (2) expanded output of goods needed by the capital exporting nation produced abroad as a result of the capital export; and (3) increased employment of labor or natural resources abroad, or exceptional external economies abroad. If, however, the capital earnings differential is small, or if competitive goods are developed through diversion of natural and human resources to the competitive outputs, the gains from capital export may be sharply adverse. Terms of trade losses will exceed the gains from the earnings differential. It appears from this analysis that investments which are profitable from the productivity point of view will be largely limited to those in primary commodities imported by the capital exporting country. General development of industrial competition abroad will probably be harmful to the capital exporting nation (p. 504).

RATES OF RETURN ON CAPITAL AT HOME AND ABROAD

Attempts to determine the net cost or benefits of capital exports on the basis of a comparison between the rate of return on capital in the capital exporting country and the rate of return on investment abroad, constitutes an inadequate approach to the problem. Yet this approach is widely used in determining the burden of foreign aid on the donor country. It also seems evident that the level of long-term interest rates in the capital-exporting country does not provide an adequate guide to the social productivity of capital. The attempts to allocate historical increases in output in terms of the contributions of labor, capital, natural resources, and productivity by means of aggregate production functions and other types of analysis provide varying answers to the question of the marginal productivity of capital. Also, one can never be sure of the alternative uses of capital involved in any particular investment decision.

There is good reason to believe that the social rate of return on capital in the United States is well above the yields on long-term government and other high-grade securities (Cooper, 1965, p. 21; Tobin, 1964, p. 15). For example, Robert Solow (1963b) suggests a rate of return of between 15 and 20 percent for the United States and West Germany. E. S. Phelps (1962) calculates the overall rate of return on tangible investment in the U.S. at about 14 per cent in 1954. Thus, social rates of return on capital would appear to be well above interest rates in the capital markets.

From a world point of view, capital should go where the world social rate of return is highest. But maximizing the world social return on capital by means of capital exports will not necessarily maximize the social return from the standpoint of the capital-exporting country. In this section we are concerned with a comparison of the social rate of return to the capital-exporting country on capital exported abroad with the social opportunity cost of foregoing the employment of the capital at home. From the standpoint of the capital-exporting country, the major sources of gains (or losses) from exporting capital arise from (1) the rate of return on the capital invested abroad, (2) the effect of production abroad on the terms of trade, and (3) the gains from expanded trade which may be stimulated by the direct and indirect impact of foreign investment on output abroad. I shall consider these gains quite apart from the balance-of-payments impact, which will be considered in a separate section.

So far as the direct rate of return on capital invested abroad is concerned, the margins between the returns to U.S. investors on capital invested abroad and in the United States after an allowance for risk are not significantly large and, in most cases, the returns on foreign investment are less than the marginal social returns on the same capital invested in the United States. Interest rate differentials between long-term rates in the United States and those on high-grade foreign securities and public and private loans rarely exceed 1.5 per cent. Differences in interest rates on domestic and foreign loans are mainly accounted for by risk differentials. In the case of U.S. direct foreign investment, net earnings as a percentage of invested capital abroad in most industries have been no higher, and in some cases lower, than after-taxes earnings in the same industries in the United States. Earnings on foreign investments in petroleum and mining have tended to be somewhat higher than after-tax earnings in the same industries in the United States. However, the ratio of net earnings to book value on U.S. direct foreign investments in manufacturing was 10.8 per cent and 10.5 per cent in 1964 and 1965, respectively (calculated from data in *Survey of Current Business,* Sept., 1965, and Sept., 1966, issues), as compared with a ratio of net income after taxes to net worth for leading domestic manufacturing corporations of 12.7 per cent and 13.9 per cent in 1964 and 1965, respectively (First National City Bank of New York, 1967). It may also be noted that earnings ratios on U.S. manufacturing investments abroad were somewhat higher in Western Europe than in Latin America.[1] A comparison between rates of return on British foreign investments and those on investments in the United Kingdom showed similar results.[2]

Since U.S. firms are permitted to deduct income taxes paid abroad from their U.S. tax liability on income earned abroad, taxes paid to the U.S. government on direct foreign investment earnings are only a small fraction of those paid on the same earnings from domestic investment. Thus, a U.S. foreign investor may be receiving a somewhat higher rate of return on his investment abroad than he receives on similar investments in this country, but the social rate of return for the U.S. economy may be considerably less because the taxes are paid to the foreign government rather than to the U.S. government. If we are to discover any net social

1. Net earnings on direct foreign investment are *after* foreign taxes but *before* U.S. taxes. Although not strictly comparable with net income after taxes on domestic investments, earnings on U.S. direct investments abroad pay little U.S. taxes, since the U.S. liability is largely offset by credits for income taxes paid abroad.

2. J. H. Dunning finds that over the 1958-64 period the average rate of return (net of tax) on British foreign investments was significantly less than the average rate of return (gross of taxes) on investments in the United Kingdom. However, Professor Dunning does not regard the relative rate of return on overseas investments as a reliable guide to the value of such investment from the point of view of the investing country. See J. H. Dunning, "Further Thoughts on Foreign Investment," *Moorgate and Wall Street: A Review* (London: Hill, Samuel and Co., Autumn, 1966), pp. 5-37.

gain over cost from foreign investment, we will have to look to sources of gain other than that arising from a differential between rates of return on domestic and foreign investment.

TERMS OF TRADE EFFECTS

There are undoubtedly important gains arising from improved terms of trade accompanying U.S. investments in foreign-resource industries, although these gains are shared with other countries of the world which are consumers of the products of these industries, just as the United States gains from investments by foreigners in resource industries. It might be possible to calculate the real value of these gains to the American consumer. However, it would be unrealistic to assume that if U.S. firms had not made the foreign investments, other countries would not have done so. Foreign investments in manufacturing industries whose products compete with our exports may tend to reduce U.S. terms of trade, but failure of the United States to undertake such investments does not necessarily mean that they would not have been made in any case. Moreover, foreign investments in manufactures increase the demand for a variety of U.S. products, including both capital equipment and components. Thus, the net effect of U.S. investments in foreign manufacturing on the terms of trade cannot readily be determined.

THE GAINS FROM TRADE

We now come to the third possible source of gain from aid, that related to the gains from trade which may arise from an increase in output abroad. This is a frequently expressed argument in favor of foreign aid of all kinds, but it is almost never couched in terms of a rigorous analysis of social costs and gains. There are certainly many cases where foreign investment or foreign aid has been a major factor in inducing a rapid increase in economic growth in the host country. The Marshall Plan aid program together with U.S. private investment in Western Europe after World War II is certainly a good example of this. Europe's rapid recovery was accompanied by a very substantial expansion in commercial trade between the United States and Europe and also stimulated the general increase in world trade. While the rapid rate of growth in postwar trade has undoubtedly been accompanied by significant gains from trade to the United States, there is a tendency to overestimate these gains in relation to the costs of foreign assistance. For example, the increase in the annual volume of total trade between the United States and the Organization for European Economic Cooperation (OEEC) countries between 1949 and 1960 was less than half the amount of the grants and low-interest loans made available to these countries during the Marshall Plan period, 1949-52. The gain from increased trade is likely to be only a small fraction of any increase in trade volume. I would be surprised if the discounted value of the annual gains from the increased trade with Europe would constitute more than a small fraction of the net cost to the United States of the Marshall Plan aid.

Except for foreign investments in export industries, capital exports to most developing countries have probably yielded little if anything in the way of gains from increased trade to the capital-exporting countries. It would be difficult to show that direct investment in import-substituting industries in developing countries would achieve anything for the investor country in the way of gains from international specialization. Nevertheless, there may be gains from a shift in trade from exports of finished goods to capital goods made possible by foreign investment and the expansion of markets in the developing countries.

The relationship between trade and direct capital investment abroad is complicated by the fact that so much of modern trade is facilitated by, and directly related to, foreign investment. For example, in 1964 25 per cent of all U.S. exports went to foreign affiliates of U.S. firms. In the case of investment in manufactures this ratio was over 35 per cent (Pizer and Cutler, 1965, pp. 12-16). The bulk of these exports are for further processing or assembly abroad, or for resale without further manufacture, but a portion represents capital equipment for use abroad. Although production by U.S. firms operating abroad is competitive with direct U.S. exports, it cannot be assumed that U.S. exports would have been higher in the absence of these foreign-investment facilities. The reason is twofold. First, U.S. exports could not in many instances compete with production abroad because of high tariff barriers or lower production and transportation costs; second, U.S. investments abroad have created additional markets for U.S. products which are processed, assembled, packaged, or marketed without alteration through distribution facilities established by U.S. firms operating abroad. Thus, much direct foreign investment in manufacturing, trade, and resource exploitation may be regarded as a necessary complement to, and not a substitute for, trade. Except in the case of the output of resource industries, only a small amount of the production of U.S. firms operating abroad is shipped to the United States. However, increased income generated by U.S. foreign investment and the contribution to technical knowledge and productivity abroad has certainly been an important factor in the rapid growth in trade among the industrial countries. Increased income from the sales on world markets of resources produced by American and European firms in developing countries stimulates their imports from the rest of the world. The value of the gains from increased trade that accrues to American consumers in the form of lower prices, better quality, and a wider range of products from which to choose is virtually impossible to estimate. It is clear, however, that U.S. demand for imports of goods and services, together with U.S. government expenditures abroad, is large and growing. Exports, often necessarily accompanied by an outflow of capital and skills, must also expand in order to match receipts against outpayments. Failure to achieve current account balance over the long run would necessitate devaluation and a consequent increase in the relative costs of imports of goods and services and a loss of real income arising from a deterioration of the terms of trade. The contribution of direct foreign investment to trade must therefore be taken into account in assessing the social returns of such investment to the capital-exporting economy.

Capital exports in the form of tied loans and export credits present difficult problems of analysis in terms of benefits and costs. Export credits and loans, however closely tied to individual transactions, may not result in an equivalent net increase in exports; some of the exports financed by credits would have occurred without credits. If capital exports exceed the net increase in exports, there may be a loss of gold, or foreigners may simply hold additional dollars so that the foreign loans are matched by short-term capital imports. Leaving aside the possible balance-of-payments burden, and assuming that export credits or loans actually finance U.S. exports, we must weigh the social-opportunity cost of employing the capital domestically against the possible gains from its use in financing exports. It seems clear that the social-opportunity cost of the capital is well above the relatively low rates of interest received on export credits. To this extent, the export of the goods is being subsidized. Normal commercial credits of, say, from three months to a year are given and received by all countries in trade so they may tend to cancel out. However, important industrial goods exporters like the United States provide far larger credits and under longer terms than they receive. While exports financed by long-term credits may stimulate some trade that otherwise would not have taken place—by promoting economic growth and export capacities abroad—the net contribution to the national welfare of the capital exporter is doubtful. Government-supported credits on an increasingly generous scale have become an important part of competition for foreign markets and thus constitute a part of the social costs of exporting. I suspect that if suddenly all countries were to agree not to extend more than normal commercial credit facilities, and not to compete for export markets with long-term government-financed and guaranteed private export credits, industrial countries would realize substantial net social gains. On the other hand, this option may not be available to an individual exporting country that decides not to extend further long-term export credits since, over the long run, the receipts from exports might fall substantially below import requirements.

MEASURING THE REAL BURDEN OF AID

Economic analysis of the real burden of aid on the donor countries has been stimulated mainly by policy considerations relating to the distribution of the aid burden among the major donors (Pincus, 1963; Kravis and Davenport, 1963). Such analysis has sought to provide a means of measuring the relative costs of differing aid terms to the donor (Schmidt, 1964). A popular method of calculating the burden of aid on the donor is to subtract from the amount of aid extended at one point in time, the discounted present value of the interest and amortization payments (if any), the rate of discount reflecting the social rate of return on capital in alternative employments in the donor country. One problem raised by this approach is the choice of the social rate of return. The "aid" element in the transaction may differ substantially depending upon whether the rate on long-term government securities is employed, or a higher rate which takes into account the loss of the increments to the social product which would have accrued had the capital been invested at home.

Employing the method described above, the present value of the returns from a $50 million loan which is repayable in installments of $1 million per annum without interest and discounted at 8 per cent is $12.2 million or 24.4 per cent of the initial amount of the loan. In this case, nearly 76 per cent of the loan may be regarded as the subsidy element or the aid burden, assuming that 8 per cent represents the social rate of return on capital in the donor country. Now assume a five-year Export-Import Bank loan of $50 million repayable in five annual installments at 6 per cent on the unpaid balance. The present value of the total payments discounted at 8 per cent is $47.6 million, so that the subsidy element or aid burden constitutes only 4.8 per cent of the loan.

The above method constitutes a rather simple approach to the problem of comparing aid burdens arising from grants and from loans with different maturities and rates of interest, and, in addition, provides a basis for making inter-country comparisons of aid burdens which would be more realistic than comparing aggregate amounts of aid transfers by individual donors. Unfortunately, however, the problem is far more complex, first because the market value of aid given in kind (or in some cases credits tied to specific commodity exports from the donor country) may not be readily determined in terms of world market prices, and second because there may be benefits to the donor country arising from the transaction which are not included in amortization payments on the loan. The latter problem is especially important in the case of governmental credits or credit guarantees made available in whole or in part for the purpose of promoting exports. Many long-term credits made available by the Export-Import Bank, as well as by official agencies of other governments, serve a dual purpose. Conceivably, they would not have been made available in the absence of a desire to promote economic development abroad. On the other hand, a decisive factor in their being made available may be their contribution to export promotion, or possibly to the development of a foreign resource required by the capital-exporting country. While balance-of-payments considerations (which will be discussed in the following section) may be responsible for much of the tying of aid to the exports of the donor country, the Export-Import Bank was making development loans tied to U.S. exports (and justified in part by the Bank's statutory obligation to promote U.S. exports) long before the United States had a balance-of-payments problem. The vast bulk of the bilateral assistance made available by France and certain other European powers has gone to countries with which the donors maintain close commercial and financial relations. Even grants are not unrelated to broad commercial interests. Moreover, French grants for subsidizing the budgets of her former colonies which are now in the franc area are used to generate local currency backed by increased reserves in the form of deposits in French banks. In this way, a portion of the French grants for budget support is matched by short-term capital imports represented by the increased franc holdings, so that a real transfer of resources does not occur.

THE VALUE OF PL 480 AID

One of the problems in determining the burden of U.S. aid arises from the calculation of the value of surplus agricultural commodities provided under PL 480, which in some years has constituted one-third of the total U.S. bilateral economic assistance. The United States values PL 480 Title I sales of agricultural commodities at world market prices, while Titles II and III shipments are valued at the cost of the commodities to the Commodity Credit Corporation (above world market prices). However, as John Pincus has pointed out, if the commodities shipped under PL 480 had been sold on the world market, prices would have been lower. Thus, on the basis of assumed world demand elasticities for the commodities involved, Pincus (1963, Tables 1 and 6) calculates that the true value of PL 480 exports might be as much as $583 million less than the value of PL 480 aid commitments for 1961 ($1,491 million) reported in the OECD (DAC) estimates of U.S. assistance to developing countries. Public Law 480 Title I commodities are sold to the recipient countries for local currencies; a portion of the proceeds are reserved for U.S. uses and the remainder for loans and grants to the recipient countries. There is a problem of how to treat the loans repayable in local currency, some of which will become available for U.S. government uses but the bulk of which, including interest, will undoubtedly be reloaned to the recipient countries themselves, and hence must be regarded as aid. Pincus assumes that in 1961, 80 per cent of PL 480 Title I sales should be regarded as grants, the remaining 20 per cent as loans.

THE VALUE OF TIED AID

There is also a question as to whether a given amount of aid (other than surplus agricultural commodities) tied to purchases of commodities and services in the donor country has the same value as aid in the form of free foreign exchange. The value of tied aid as against untied aid gives rise to several kinds of problems. First, where prices are not competitive within the donor country, tying permits the charging of monopolistic prices. Second, even if prices are competitive within the donor country or if aid authorities enforce a system of *bona fide* competitive bidding for contracts to supply commodities and services under aid programs, competitive prices in the donor country may be above world competitive prices. In fact, prices determined by world competitive bidding may prove to be lower than domestic prices in any of the donor countries because of the existence of oligopolistic markets for many commodities within donor countries generally. The third problem has to do with whether the aid is tied both to the financing of the specific commodities (such as electric generators and diesel locomotives) and to the purchase of these commodities in the donor country. If the recipient country normally purchases a substantial proportion of its imports from the donor country, tied aid which can be used for purchasing a broad list of commodities and services enables the recipient to substitute aid financing for purchases which would have been made in the donor country in any case. Thus, tied aid given by the United States to a Latin American country which is permitted to employ the dollars for purchasing a very broad list of commodities and services in the United States may represent much the same real value as completely untied aid.

To take the other extreme, if a country whose products are not very competitive in world markets provides a certain amount of aid in the form of a contract to build a cement factory with all purchases made in the donor country, the cost of the factory may be well above what it might have been if the recipient country were free to build the factory on the basis of worldwide competitive bids for the various commodities and services acquired. Although the prices paid for U.S. equipment under Export-

Import Bank and AID loan contracts are supposed to be determined by competitive bidding among U.S. suppliers, this does not guarantee a truly competitive price. In the case of U.S. loans to finance specific types of equipment which must be purchased in the United States, the cost of such equipment may in some cases be 10 to 20 per cent above that for the same equipment acquired from, say, Britain or Germany. If the U.S. suppliers were competing with Japanese or German suppliers the bids might well be considerably lower.

THE BURDEN OF PRIVATE INVESTMENT PROMOTED BY
GOVERNMENTAL INCENTIVES

Another problem in trying to measure the real burden of aid as I have defined it is that many types of aid do not readily lend themselves to a determination based on the market value of the aid less the discounted present value of the investment service payments. As I have already noted, a government investment guarantee or credit program may actually prove profitable to the government agency in the sense that the fees charged will exceed the cost, although of course there is no actuarial basis for measuring the risk exposure of the government insuring agency. Moreover, an investment guarantee by AID may serve to promote an investment which is profitable both to the private investors and to the U.S. economy in terms of the social opportunity costs of employing U.S. capital.

In addition to investment guarantees, tax incentives have been used for promoting direct private investment in developing countries. Currently, for example, the U.S. government does not tax reinvested profits of U.S. affiliates operating in developing countries, but it does tax the undistributed profits of affiliates in developed countries. Unlike the guarantee program—which has not resulted in any direct loss to the U.S. Treasury Department—tax discrimination in favor of developing countries does reduce Treasury revenues, or postpones them until earnings are remitted. In 1964 the U.S. administration proposed an overseas investment tax credit providing for a tax credit which could be applied against U.S. investors' total tax liability equal to 30 per cent of the value of new investment in certain businesses in eligible less-developed countries. For purposes of calculating the credit, reinvested earnings in excess of 50 per cent of total earnings would also be considered new investment. A less-developed country investment credit bill was introduced in Congress in July, 1964, but no action had been taken on this bill at the time of this writing.

Tax incentives for promoting private investment in developing countries constitute a subsidy to foreign investment arising from the loss or postponement of tax revenues. To the extent that tax incentives promote resource transfers by governmental action, they constitute a form of aid, but the direct cost involves a transfer from the Treasury to the private investor and not to the aid recipient. The net social cost, if any, arises from the difference between the social-opportunity cost of employing the capital at home and the social return on the foreign investment.

THE BURDEN OF AID NOT INVOLVING A TRANSFER OF REAL RESOURCES
FROM THE DONOR

Not all aid involves a direct transfer of resources between the donor and the aid recipient. An untied U.S. loan to a developing country may be spent entirely in Europe or Canada. If U.S. exports to the rest of the world rise as a consequence of the loan, the real burden will be much the same as if the funds were spent directly in the United States by the recipient. But what is the real burden on the United States of a loan to a developing country, the entire amount of which is spent in Canada or Japan and added to the reserves of these countries in the form of low interest investments such as U.S. Treasury Bills, or of deposits at the Federal Reserve Bank of New York? Unpaid subscriptions to international agencies (callable only in the event of the inability of the agency to meet its obligations) which borrow on the basis of these subscriptions in the international financial markets also raise complex problems for the determination of the aid burden. An increase in the U.S. subscription to the World Bank may increase the Bank's effective borrowing power, but—because of the U.S. balance-of-payments deficit—much of the borrowing may be done in Europe. The United States along with other World Bank members has guaranteed the repayment of the funds borrowed for increasing the Bank's loans. However, the countries whose funds are borrowed may not experience a commensurate increase in their exports; they may simply lose gold or foreign exchange to those countries in which the actual purchases of goods and services are made as a consequence of the increased loans made by the World Bank.

The illustrations given above raise some problems with respect to the definition of aid in terms of transfers of real resources to aid recipients. In my definition of aid, however, the transfer of resources need not come from the aid donors but may arise from an increase of net imports from third countries. Aid is provided by a donor if an official grant or loan or an official guarantee of loans or direct investments is involved, regardless of where the funds may come from or where they are spent. Thus, loans financed by the issuance of World Bank bonds in Europe under a guarantee represented by the U.S. uncalled subscription to the World Bank constitutes a form of U.S. aid. It also represents aid provided by other members of the World Bank to the extent that their uncalled subscriptions to the Bank constitute a credible portion of the total member guarantees of World Bank securities. Obviously, Brazil's uncalled subscription to the World Bank does not have the same weight (indeed, if it has any) as a contribution to the security of World Bank bonds as do the subscriptions of the United States and Germany. Where the aid burden lies in all of this is difficult to determine. Sales of World Bank bonds in private European markets do not constitute aid as I have defined it. There well may be a burden arising from private capital exports which has nothing to do with aid. Moreover, there may be little or no direct burden on the donor country as defined, but there may be an indirect burden on other countries arising out of either increased exports of goods and services not offset by increased imports, or as a result of a foreign-exchange drain from private capital exports as a consequence of the purchase of the obligations of international agencies.

The definition of aid in terms of the transfer of real resources to the recipients raises a problem in the case of aid for refinancing debt. This problem could be avoided if aid were measured as the face value of the resources transferred less the discounted value of the service payments, since a stretching out of the payment period with no increase in the interest charge obviously raises the net value of the aid. The *value* of the aid to the recipient (if any) and the *burden* on the donor (if any) depends upon the terms on which the aid is provided and the social rates of discount which are assumed. In order to avoid these complications, I prefer a definition of aid in terms of a net resource transfer requiring governmental action on the part of the donor. In the case of a loan for refinancing debt, a transfer of real resources may be involved in the sense that the borrower's level of imports may be maintained as a consequence of lower debt service, or as a consequence of the ability of the recipient to obtain additional loans and credits. Very often the refinancing loan is made by a government agency to refinance private debts, for example, export credits, that had nothing to do with aid transfers, as defined, to begin with.

In some cases, loans have been made in order to supplement a country's foreign-exchange reserves. Here again no real transfers take place directly or indirectly, and there is no net capital movement either. However, a loan to build up reserves transfers command over real resources. Such assistance constitutes a form of what I have called "compensatory aid" which, presumably, at some time in the future will enable the recipient to maintain its imports or possibly expand them in event of a balance-of-payments contingency.

AID TERMS AND BENEFIT-COST ANALYSIS

It has been noted that the aid burden (if any) on the donor may not be commensurate with the benefits from aid to the recipient. Building on this principle, Wilson Schmidt (1964) has applied a kind of benefit-cost analysis to the problem of choosing aid terms. Schmidt regards the logical approach to aid as one in which the benefactor provides the largest amount of present value benefits to the recipient per dollar of present cost to the benefactor; alternatively, the benefactor should select the terms which involve the lowest present cost for any given level of present value of benefit to the recipient. The present cost to the benefactor is the amount of the loan (or grant) less the discounted value of interest and amortization payments on the loan, the rate of discount reflecting the yield on capital in the benefactor nation. On the other hand, the present value of benefit to a recipient is the value of the loan (or grant) less the present discounted value of the amortization and interest payments, the rate of discount being that which represents the yield on capital in the recipient nation. In his model, Schmidt shows that where the yield on capital is higher in the benefactor nation than in the recipient nation, the present cost to the benefactor in providing a given present value of benefit to the recipient will be lower in the case of a grant than in the case of a loan. Just the opposite is true if the yield on capital is higher in the recipient nation than in the benefactor country. Thus, for example, Schmidt (1964, p. 389) shows that where the yield on capital in the benefactor nation is 8 per cent and in the recipient nation is 7 per cent, an annual grant of $1.00 provides the same present value to the recipient as a loan of $100 at 6 per cent, but the present cost to the benefactor of the annual grant is about half the present cost of the $100 loan at 6 per cent. On the other hand, assuming the yield on capital to be 8 per cent in the recipient country and 6 per cent in the benefactor nation, the present cost to the benefactor of an annual grant of $1.00 is $15.76, while the present cost to the benefactor on a $50 loan at 6 per cent is zero. Both provide the same present value of benefits to the recipient. Schmidt argues that the possibility of a return on capital being higher in the benefactor nation than in the recipient nation is not unrealistic. In terms of existing real rates of return on capital in many backward societies, Schmidt's view is undoubtedly correct. On the other hand, foreign aid should be made available in a manner which will change methods of production to achieve a more economical allocation of resources, increase the productivity of capital and labor, and promote savings and investment, so that the direct and indirect effects on the social product are considerably higher than the current yields on capital in the recipient country, at least over the longer run.

The cost of aid to the benefactor as we have seen is also quite complex and cannot readily be determined by current yields on capital. Although Schmidt's analysis is exceedingly interesting, I do not believe it provides a significant guide to determining either the amount of aid or the terms on which aid should be made available. The amount of aid must be determined by capital-absorptive capacity and a consideration of development strategies. The terms cannot be separated from the amounts and duration of the net resource transfers required to achieve the goals of the development program which the aid is designed to promote. However, Schmidt's analysis does provide an illustration of the fact that the benefits of aid to the recipient may bear little relationship to the cost of aid to the benefactor—though the determination of these costs and benefits is far more complex than that suggested by Schmidt's model.

THE BURDEN ARISING FROM COMMODITY AGREEMENTS

Commodity agreements which raise prices above their long-term equilibrium levels (as opposed to compensatory arrangements), and which are participated in and depend for their success upon cooperation from the importing countries, constitute a form of aid transfer as I have defined it. Higher prices are paid by consumers in the developed countries as a consequence of actions taken by their own governments, the benefits of which go to the primary commodity-exporting countries. While such aid does not take the form of public expenditures, there is clearly a burden on consumers in the developed countries. Although the burden in welfare terms might be measured in various ways, the most objective measure of the burden or tax on the consumer is the product of the increase in price over the equilibrium price and the quantity consumed, plus the "excess burden" from the reduction in consumption. (The price to the consumer is usually increased by more than the import price by reason of a percentage markup, but this generally stays in the importing country.) However, this is not necessarily the best measure of the net resource contribution to the exporting countries. Where exporting countries have a very inelastic supply function, and can only reduce exports by stockpiling or destroying crops, their marginal costs may be virtually zero. The main objective is to increase revenue by raising the price where the demand is inelastic. Thus, the aid element might be regarded as the difference between the revenue at the higher administered price and the revenue at the equilibrium price. In Fig. 5 the export earnings resulting from a commodity agreement which fixes the price at OP' minus the revenue that would have been received at the equilibrium price, OP, is $OP'AQ' - OPEQ$. The burden on the importing country, as defined, is equal to $PP'AF + AFE$ (the "excess burden on consumers"). Now it can be shown

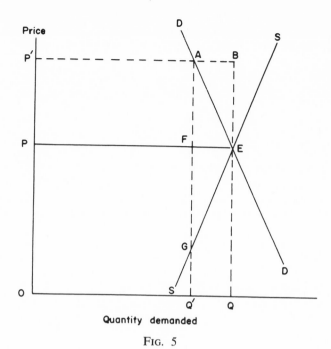

FIG. 5

that the aid burden is larger than the amount of aid as defined, since

$$OP'AQ' - OPEQ = P'PAF - FEQQ'$$

It has been pointed out that a direct subsidy payment to the exporting countries equal to the amount of the increase in their export revenue resulting from the establishment of an administered price under a commodity agreement as compared with export earnings at the equilibrium price would be less costly to the consumers in the importing countries than an administered price. Thus, a direct subsidy payment equal to $OP'AQ' - OPEQ$ would be less than the additional foreign-exchange expenditure under the administered price, equal to $PP'AF$, and would, in addition, avoid the excess burden on consumers, AFE. Where the exporting country is able to reduce production under an administered price scheme and not simply destroy excess output, foreign-exchange earnings are not the proper measure of benefit. With a reduction in output, $Q'Q$, the resource saving to suppliers would be $EQQ'G$. The net benefit of an administered price arrangement would be

$$OP'AQ' - OPEQ + EQQ'G = P'PAF - FEG$$

In this case, a direct subsidy equivalent to $P'PAF - FEG$, would be less than $PP'AF + AFE$, the burden on the importing country arising from the administered price.[3]

In addition to reducing the aid burden, there are longer-term advantages to the exporting countries in keeping the price at the equilibrium level for a time and receiving a direct subsidy for the purpose of helping countries reallocate resources. Eventually, as productive capacity becomes adjusted to long-run demand, and as factor prices rise as a consequence of increased productivity in the economy, the long-run equilibrium price of the commodity may rise. Meanwhile, maintaining an equilibrium price tends to maintain demand and to discourage the use of synthetics. There is a tendency to underestimate demand elasticities of primary commodities over the longer run. Maintaining lower prices also discourages the opening up of new areas of production which may be induced by artificially maintained prices and encourages the withdrawal of production on marginal lands.

While recognizing the advantages of direct subsidy payments to developing countries over price supports, John Pincus tends to favor administered prices achieved by commodity agreements on the grounds of expediency. He notes for example (1965, p. 165) that "direct subsidies paid by industrialized countries to developing countries would logically be considered an extension of economic aid programs." Since he believes that the governments of developed countries tend to be somewhat niggardly in their aid programs, he regards price supports as a means of expanding the amount of effective aid. Although I believe that subsidy payments should be regarded as a part of aid programs, I seriously doubt if subsidies made available at a much higher cost to the donor countries in the form of administered prices for imports will contribute very much to long-run economic development. Direct subsidy payments can be geared to adjustments in production which will make a long run contribution to development through a more economical allocation of resources, such as for example the transfer of coffee plantations to food production. Simply increasing coffee prices by means of export and import quotas may contribute little or nothing to productive investment and raise the incomes of only a small proportion of the population in the developing countries.

3. The author benefited greatly from Harry G. Johnson's suggestions in this analysis. For background, see Pincus, 1965, pp. 147-50; also, Howell, 1954; H. G. Johnson, 1967, pp. 159-62.

INTERNATIONAL BURDEN SHARING

A major concern of aid donors and of the Development Assistance Committee of the OECD has been the measurement of the relative aid burden and the determination of a formula for the equitable sharing of the aid burden among the major donors. DAC has been presented with a formidable problem even in determining which transactions should be regarded as aid. DAC prepares annual statistics on "the flow of financial resources to less-developed countries and multilateral agencies," broken down by "official" and "private" flows from DAC members (see Table 5). The financial flow data are on a net disbursement basis, so that amortization on past loans is subtracted from gross disbursements. For example, on a gross basis, official bilateral flow in 1965 was $6,540 million as against $5,773 million on a net basis. Long-term financial flows exclude official and private credits with a maturity of one year or less. Disbursements of multilateral agencies are not included but are accounted for indirectly by official grants and loans to these agencies plus private purchases of the obligations of multilateral agencies. Under long-term official flows (official aid) DAC recognizes the following types of transactions: (1) bilateral grants; (2) bilateral loans repayable in the recipients' currencies; (3) transfer of resources through sales for recipients' currencies (consisting almost entirely of U.S. surplus agricultural commodity sales under PL 480) [4]; (4) bilateral loans with a maturity of more than one year; (5) grants and capital subscription payments to international agencies for development purposes; and (6) official net purchases of the obligations (with maturity of more than one year) of international institutions (principally the World Bank and the Inter-American Development Bank [OECD, 1965a, Ch. III and Appendix, Table 7]).

The DAC definition of official aid omits loans and credits with maturities of one year or less, government-guaranteed private export credits, insured private direct investment, and all private and international institutional assistance. Subscriptions to the International Monetary Fund are omitted from DAC figures on official aid, mainly because of the special financial arrangements under which the Fund operates. As DAC readily recognizes in its reports, however, the Fund is certainly an important source of compensatory assistance to developing countries (OECD, 1965b, p. 43). Official aid resulting from contributions or subscriptions to multi-

---

4. In estimating this item, DAC deducts the amount of the recipient's currency made available for use by the donor country, for example, U.S. Embassy expenditures out of PL 480 proceeds.

TABLE 5

FLOW OF LONG-TERM FINANCIAL RESOURCES FROM DAC COUNTRIES TO LESS-DEVELOPED COUNTRIES AND MULTILATERAL AGENCIES, 1965

(Disbursements)

(In millions of dollars)

	France	Germany	United Kingdom	United States	Other DAC Countries	Total
Total official and private, net (I-IV)	$1,319	$705	$923	$5,478	$1,724	$10,149
Total official, net (I-II)	757	427	480	3,730	877	6,271
Total Private, net (III-IV)	562	278	443	1,749	847	3,879
I. Total Official Bilateral, net	780	432	428	3,463	670	5,773
Grants and grant-like contributions	623	176	261	2,300	438	3,798
of which: Technical Assistance	344	94	89	424	97	1,048
Reparation and indemnification payments	.....	75	.....	.....	66	141
Loans repayable in recipients' currencies	.....	.....	.....	130	0	130
Transfer of resources through sales for recipients' currencies	.....	.....	.....	810	0	810
Government long-term capital, net	107	256	168	1,163	281	1,975
Loans, net	107	256	146	1,163	282	1,954
Loans extended	170	421	207	1,458	457	2,713
Amortization received	63	165	61	295	175	759

Other, incl. central monetary institutions, net			21			21
II. Total official multilateral, net	27	−5	52	268	156	498
Grants and capital subscriptions	27	37	52	268	145	529
Bonds, loans and participations, net		−42			9	−31
III. Private investment and lending, net	395	220	(336)	1,735	452	3,138
Direct investment	394	104		1,155	554	2,207
New direct investment	199	70		855	247	(1,371)
Reinvested earnings	(195)	34		(300)	307	(836)
Bilateral portfolio investment and other				436	208	(641)
Multilateral portfolio investment, net	1	119		144	26	(290)
IV. Private export credits, net	167	58	107	13	396	741
Over 1, to and including 5 years	44	9		24	235	285
Guaranteed	40	7		24	199	244
Non-guaranteed	(4)	2			47	40
Over 5 years	123	50	134		149	456
Guaranteed	111	40	128		135	402
Non-guaranteed	(12)	10	(7)		26	55

DAC countries include Australia, Austria, Belgium, Canada, Denmark, France, Germany, Italy, Japan, Netherlands, Norway, Portugal, Sweden, United Kingdom, United States.

Figures in ( ) are provisional.

Source: *Development Assistance Efforts and Policies, 1966 Review* (Paris: OECD, 1966), Appendix Table 7, pp. 156-57.

lateral organizations includes only actual payments available for use by the organizations and not unpaid but callable subscriptions. The bulk of the World Bank's funds are raised by sale of bonds in the private financial markets, sales which are made possible by the guarantee of the Bank's obligations represented by the unpaid capital subscriptions of its strong industrial country members; much of the IDB's loan funds are raised in the same manner. Thus, loans made by the World Bank and certain other institutions out of funds raised in the private capital market on the basis of governmental guarantees are not reflected in official aid; they are rather included in private capital flows in the form of private portfolio investments in the securities of multilateral agencies. Such private capital flows, as well as official contributions, do not become disbursements to less-developed countries until they are utilized by multilateral agencies such as the World Bank in loan disbursements to developing countries. In my own definition of aid, I have included private loans guaranteed by governments, whether guaranteed directly or indirectly through the guarantee of the obligations of international agencies.

THE ONE PER CENT FORMULA

In 1965, following the recommendations made by the United Nations Conference on Trade and Development in 1964 (Recommendation A IV 2), DAC endorsed the principle that each member should provide a volume of aid to developing countries in an amount equal to, or in excess of, one per cent of its national income. The UNCTAD conference recommendation (OECD, 1965a, pp. 52-55), which was approved by all DAC members, reads as follows:

> Each economically advanced country should endeavor to supply . . . financial resources to the less developed countries of a minimum net amount approaching as nearly as possible to one per cent of its national income, having regard, however, to the special position of certain countries which are net importers of capital.

The one per cent formula, which includes both official aid and private capital flow, leaves a number of unanswered questions, and without special refinement and interpretation does not provide an adequate basis for comparison of the aid burden among donor countries. Different types of net capital flows to developing countries provide varying benefits to recipients and involve differing burdens on donors, there of course being no necessary correspondence between the benefit and burden for any particular type of capital flow. The UNCTAD one per cent formula makes no distinction between private capital flow and official aid, nor does the formula

TABLE 6

FLOW OF FINANCIAL RESOURCES TO DEVELOPING COUNTRIES AND MULTILATERAL AGENCIES AS A PERCENTAGE OF NATIONAL INCOME, 1962-65

(Percentages)

	Total Official Flow				Total Private Flow				Total Official and Private Flow			
	1962	1963	1964	1965	1962	1963	1964	1965	1962	1963	1964	1965
Australia	(0.59)	(0.60)	(0.61)	0.64			0.11	0.12	(0.59)*	(0.60)*	(0.72)	0.76
Austria	0.25	0.04	0.22	0.49	0.31	0.06	0.10	0.19	0.56	0.10	0.33	0.68
Belgium	0.77	0.83	0.68	0.92	0.47	0.86	0.76	0.91	1.24	1.69	1.44	1.82
Canada	0.19	0.32	0.39	0.34	0.19	0.11	0.09	0.09	0.38	0.43	0.48	0.43
Denmark	0.12	0.15	0.15	0.17	0.12	(0.01)	0.30	(0.03)	0.25	(0.17)	0.45	(0.21)
France	1.76	1.39	1.25	1.08	0.77	0.68	0.83	0.80	2.53	2.07	2.08	1.88
Germany	0.66	0.59	0.53	0.50	0.27	0.23	0.34	0.33	0.93	0.82	0.87	0.83
Italy	0.35	0.31	0.14	0.16	0.96	0.65	0.48	0.43	1.32	0.96	0.62	0.59
Japan	0.19	0.26	0.19	0.37	0.44	0.26	0.31	0.37	0.63	0.52	0.50	0.74
Netherlands	0.83	0.32	0.35	0.41	0.48	0.92	0.58	1.12	1.30	1.24	0.93	1.53
Norway	0.17	0.48	0.35	0.22	0.10	0.19	0.20	0.49	0.27	0.66	0.55	0.71
Portugal	1.69	1.98	2.29	0.75				0.33	1.69	1.98	2.29	0.75
Sweden	0.16	0.18	0.24	0.25	0.16	0.24	0.25	0.20	0.32	0.42	0.48	0.45
United Kingdom	0.64	0.60	0.67	0.61	0.47	0.40	0.56	0.56	1.11	1.00	1.22	1.17
United States	0.80	0.78	0.67	0.68	0.18	0.18	0.25	0.31	0.97	0.96	0.92	0.99
Total DAC Countries	0.74	0.70	0.62	0.62	0.30	0.27	0.34	0.38	1.04	0.97	0.96	1.00

* Official flows only.

Figures in ( ) are provisional or incomplete.

Source: *Development Assistance Efforts and Policies, 1966 Review* (Paris: OECD, 1966), Table VI, p. 51.

distinguish between long- and short-term capital flows. Table 6, prepared by the DAC Secretariat, shows the total official and private flow of long-term financial resources to developing countries and multilateral agencies as a percentage of the national income of the donor, excluding loans and credits of one year maturity or less. For the DAC countries as a group, the total official and private flow has averaged about one per cent of total national incomes over the 1962-65 period, although for individual countries this percentage has varied from well under .5 per cent in the case of Canada and Denmark, to more than 2 per cent for France, with the U.S. percentage falling slightly below one per cent. The share of official capital flow has ranged from .62 per cent of national incomes in 1964 and 1965 to .74 per cent in 1962 for DAC countries as a group, the remainder being represented by private capital flow.

The problem of comparability within this hodgepodge of capital flows from the standpoint of benefits to recipients is virtually insurmountable. For example, the benefits received from certain types of direct investments accompanied by technical and managerial skills may be several times that of an equivalent amount of public grants or loans. While recognizing the benefits of private capital investment in developing countries and the desirability of encouraging private capital flows, the major problem faced by DAC has been that of developing some formula for comparability of official aid flows on the basis of the burden on the donor. The DAC Secretariat has experimented with various approaches to this problem, but has not at the time of this writing endorsed any particular formula for determining comparability of the aid burden. While complete comparability would not be possible, given the fact that a substantial portion of the loans and credits to developing countries is designed in part to promote exports, it is possible to apply a formula for comparing official grant and loan transactions involving differing terms for the loans without regard to benefits other than interest and amortization receipts.

One approach which has already been discussed is to determine the "aid" or "grant" element in a transaction by subtracting from the face value of a loan the discounted present value of interest and amortization payments. This approach not only raises the question of the proper rate of discount, which should reflect the opportunity cost or yield on capital invested in the donor country, but also whether the rate of discount should vary as between donor countries. For example, should the same rate of discount be applied to loans made by Japan or Italy as is applied to those made by the United States or Germany? Internal money market rates provide little guide to the social productivity of capital in a given country, since market rates are largely determined by the mix of monetary and fiscal policies employed by the government in regulating the economy. As we have seen, there is no ready formula for determining the social pro-

ductivity of capital within any country. However, some differential in
the rate of discount might be justified as between net capital-importing
countries, such as Japan and Canada, and net capital-exporting countries,
such as the United States.

Once the amount of official net capital flow or aid provided by each
donor is estimated on a comparable basis, there remains the problem of
establishing a criterion for equitable burden sharing, or for determining the
degree to which individual countries are providing their proper share, in
accordance with some target such as the one per cent formula. While the
usual approach is to compare net aid flows with the national product,
whether or not adjusted for differences in per capita incomes, there is a
question as to whether a comparison should be made with national income
or gross national product. In a recent report of a United Nations Experts'
Group, a preference was expressed for gross national product at market
prices over national income on the ground that the measurement of depreciation in the calculation of national income is to a large extent arbitrary and strongly influenced in practice by differences in systems of taxation and corporate accounting practices (OECD, 1966, pp. 50-51). The
DAC Secretariat has used national income as the denominator in its calculations of capital flows as a percentage of national product, but points out
that had gross national product at market prices been used, there would
have been little change in the relative position of countries although the
percentages would in general have been reduced about 18 per cent if GNP
were used as the denominator.

Once the problem of the denominator has been resolved, two further
problems arise: (1) How shall we compare national income or GNP
among the principal donor countries, since it is well known that official
exchange rates do not provide a proper comparison of real purchasing
power? (2) Is equity in burden-sharing properly determined by aid as a
percentage of national income or GNP, or should we seek to apply the
principles of progressive taxation in equalizing the burden among aid
donors?

Considerable work has been done on adjusting national incomes for
purposes of real income comparisons.[5] Official national incomes of Western European countries are believed to understate real income as compared with the United States when official exchange rates are used to
convert them into U.S. dollars (Pincus, 1965, Appdx., Ch. III). Since

5. One approach to making national incomes comparable is to compute the
output of goods and services of one country in terms of the prices of a second, and
then compute the national income of the second country in terms of the prices of
the first country, all expressed in terms of a common currency unit, and then
take the geometric mean of the resulting income computations. (See Gilbert, 1957;
Kravis, 1957).

the understatement of real income by national income statistics appears to increase with the degree of disparity between per capita income in the United States and per capita income in other countries, a burden-sharing formula which provides for aid from each donor in an amount which represents the same percentage of its national income (without adjustment of exchange rates to purchasing power comparisons) will tend to introduce a degree of progressivity in terms of real per capita income (Kravis and Davenport, 1963, p. 318; Neale, 1961).

If aid contributions are strictly proportionate to real national income adjusted for comparability in terms of real purchasing power, the principle of proportionality would be applied to both nations and to individuals (except for the fact that nations have tax systems with varying degrees of proportionality or progressivity). When we attempt to apply the principle of progressive taxation to international burden-sharing, a number of difficult conceptual and statistical difficulties are met with. Are we, for example, concerned with applying a progressive tax formula to individual nations on the basis of average real per capita income, or are we concerned with applying a progressive tax on incomes of individuals for a group of countries as a whole? (For an analysis of this problem, see Kravis and Davenport, 1963, pp. 320-22.) In the latter case, international taxation would need to be based on a worldwide distribution of real income among individuals, with each country paying a portion of the total tax equal to the proportion that its citizens would pay under a given progressive personal tax system. It would not be proper to determine the distribution of world income on the basis of the number of individuals in each income class without regard for nationality, since a relatively high-income class, say in Japan, would have the same income range as a medium-income class in the United States. Data on income distribution differ substantially between countries in terms of the definition of the income class, the definition of income, and the concept of the income-receiving unit. Thus, Kravis and Davenport have devised a method of constructing national and worldwide distributions of per capita incomes for 1960 on the basis of the U.S. income distribution that could be most appropriately compared with each foreign country. This information was used to construct a single world distribution by utilizing the lognormal form of national income distributions to fit national populations into income classes.

Although Kravis and Davenport have developed an imaginative approach to the application of the principle of progressive taxation to individuals in a number of countries so that individuals in the same income category, appropriately determined, would be subject to the same amount of taxation for the support of aid programs, the method has a number of drawbacks, which make its usefulness somewhat doubtful. First, one must accept the principle that equity in taxation requires progressive as against proportional tax rates, since proportional tax rates based on real per capita income could be achieved by applying a uniform percentage of real national income to all donor countries. The theoretical basis in welfare economics for progressive taxation of individuals within particular countries is weak enough, and there is certainly little basis for applying the principle to countries. Moreover, the actual amount of foreign aid supplied by any individual in a country will depend not simply on his country's share in the total aid contribution, but upon the tax structure of his own country. Although most developed countries have a progressive tax system, at least at the national level, the systems differ widely and their complexity makes comparison as to progressivity extremely complex, if not impossible. Finally, even if a satisfactory world income distribution can be calculated, there remains the problem of determining the appropriate international tax system to be applied. For example, the Germans might prefer a mildly progressive tax system as against the more progressive U.S. and British income taxes. (For a criticism of the Kravis and Davenport method of progressive taxation, see Pincus, 1963, pp. 64-65.) Kravis and Davenport have compared the national cost shares of aid as a percentage of total aid for ten developed countries using various methods of assessment. Using the method of a proportional tax on money income, the U.S. would pay 61.4 per cent of the total cost, while this percentage would be reduced to 55 per cent in the case of a proportional tax on real national income (adjusted for comparability of purchasing power). The method of progressive taxation of real incomes applied to individuals (based on a "world" income distribution) at U.S. income tax rates would mean that the United States would pay 66.7 per cent of the total aid bill, while if German or British income tax rates were applied, the percentage U.S. share would be 59.6 and 69.2 per cent respectively (Kravis and Davenport, 1963, p. 323, Table I). It is also possible to apply progressive taxation to nations, rather than to individuals, by basing the rate on per capita national average incomes. This method would be much simpler to apply and more readily understood. If U.S. income tax rates are applied to nations on the basis of per capita real incomes, the percentage share of the total aid burden for the United States among the ten countries comes out to 64.5, as against 66.7 per cent when applied to individuals under the complicated formula for determining a "world" income distribution developed by Kravis and Davenport.

If progressivity is desired based on per capita national incomes, an alternative approach would be to establish an exemption level, say equal to $250 per person. Each country would then have an exemption equal to $250 times its population and its aid target would be equal to a given percentage of its national income (real or money) minus the exemption. Under this system, it would only be necessary to determine the amount of income per person to be exempted (OECD, 1966, p. 47).

It is frequently suggested that account be taken of the balance-of-payments position of aid donors in determining their proper share, and balance-of-payments considerations have undoubtedly influenced U.S. aid contributions in recent years. For example, the World Bank and IDB have been requested to limit their sales of bonds in U.S. markets to avoid additional drains on the U.S. balance of payments, and in some cases issues have been placed directly with European central banks. While there may be some justification for relating the form of aid to a country's balance-of-payments position, the distribution of the aid burden should, I believe, be based on contributions which reflect either a proportional or a progressive tax on real per capita income. Balance-of-payments deficits, especially for reserve currency countries like the United States, may arise from forces which have nothing at all to do with the ability to contribute real resources. In recent years the balance-of-payments difficulties of the U.S. have arisen in large measure from the fact that financial capital outflows have not been matched by real transfers of commodities and services. The reasons for the U.S. balance-of-payments deficits are complex, but they do not arise from the inability of the United States to supply additional real resources to other countries.

AID TYING AS A MEANS OF REDUCING THE AID BURDEN

It is estimated (OECD, 1965a, p. 90) that about two-thirds of gross bilateral assistance was contractually tied or otherwise limited in 1964; most multilateral assistance was untied, however.[6] The principal reasons for aid tying may be listed as follows:

1) *The promotion of exports.* As has already been noted, a considerable proportion of loan assistance to developing countries is motivated largely (if not wholly) by the desire to promote exports. For most donor countries, large-scale bilateral aid for development grew out of the activities of agencies initially established to provide credits and credit guaran-

---

6. All aid made available by the World Bank and its affiliates, IDA and IFC (International Finance Corporation), is untied, as are also loans made with dollars by the Inter-American Development Bank out of its Ordinary Capital Resources. However, loans made by the IDB out of its Fund for Special Operations are tied to purchases in the United States or other western hemisphere countries. In addition, the IDB has made tied loans from funds provided by nonmembers including Canada. With certain exceptions, aid made available by the European Development Fund is tied to the exports of EEC member and associated countries.

tees for exports. This was true, for example, in the case of the Export-Import Bank of Washington, whose development assistance antedated the postwar development aid institutions such as the Agency for International Development and its predecessors.

2) *Limiting the impact of aid on the balance of payments.* This has become a major reason for aid tying by the United States in recent years. Prior to 1961, most U.S. bilateral aid (other than the Export-Import Bank loans and surplus agricultural commodity assistance) was untied.

3) *Utilizing excess productive capacity.* Countries such as Italy, with substantial unemployment, have given this as an argument for tying aid.

4) *Disposing of surplus agricultural commodities.* Aid has played an important role in the United States in supporting a domestic agricultural policy designed to produce surpluses. Hopefully, this country may now be moving toward a policy in which deliberately determined foreign requirements for agricultural commodities will govern agricultural production programs. Such an approach on the part of a country with a tremendous comparative advantage in the production of grains and fibers may not be an uneconomic one. We must assume however that aid authorities will allocate a given dollar value of U.S. economic assistance between agricultural commodities and other types of aid on the basis of maximizing the contribution of the aid to well-defined development goals.

5) *Identifying aid with the donor.* There is frequently a desire to identify aid as coming from the donor country by an appropriate mark on the commodity or by identification with a particular project, such as a hydroelectric dam or factory.

6) *Gaining domestic public support for aid programs.* Aid in most countries is more popular if it can be shown that the commodities and services made available directly provide jobs and markets. "Give them our goods, not money," is a popular slogan in unsophisticated discussions of foreign-aid policy.

I shall not attempt to explore in detail all of the above reasons for tying aid; some of them are not unique economic arguments, and some are frankly political in character. I believe that they can all be reduced either to a balance-of-payments argument, or to one which employs a form of foreign aid as a means of supporting a domestic economic policy determined mainly by domestic political considerations. For example, the domestic unemployed resources argument for tying aid seems to imply that the making available of untied aid would either not result in an expansion of exports commensurate with the amount of the aid (balance-of-payments argument), or that the increased export demand would not be directed toward particular industries or geographical areas in the donor country where there is unemployment and excess capacity. Yet the more

rational approach would appear to lie in the adoption of domestic measures designed to achieve a reallocation of unemployed resources, or to increase productivity in certain industries which will enable them to compete
in export markets. Except for short periods of unexpected agricultural
commodity surpluses, the same analysis can be applied to the commodity-
surplus argument for tying aid.

The export-promotion argument for tying aid is related to the balance-
of-payments, but is complicated by the fact that since the 1930's there
has been a growing competition in government-assisted export credit,
somewhat analogous to the growth of consumer credit competition in domestic markets. From the standpoint of an individual country, it can be
argued that unless that country is competitive in credit terms, it may not
be able to sell goods in world markets in which it is competitive in terms
of price and quality. In selling to developing countries which are short of
foreign exchange, more liberal credit terms may have an appeal to prospective purchasers which is out of proportion to its value or cost in terms
of price equivalent. Thus, for example, a country willing to offer ten-year
credit terms may be able to charge 20 or 30 per cent more on the same
items than a country which offers only one-year terms. Now if we could
completely separate credit competition from aid, we could relegate loans
and credits for export promotion to commercial transactions and not consider them as aid, at least from the standpoint of donor countries. However, many loans and credits which are tied to commodities have a dual
purpose in the sense that governments might not have been willing to make
available credits on generous terms, in the absence of motivations more
relevant to aid. On the other hand, such credits are regarded as part of
the entire export promotion programs of the government. DAC's limitation of official aid to loans and credits in excess of one year (and its omission of all government-guaranteed private export credits from long-term
financial flow estimates) constitutes a recognition of the difference between export promotion *per se* and aid, but the one-year limitation is
obviously an artificial one which does not even eliminate cases where the
motivation may be entirely that of promoting exports, to say nothing of
those where motivation may be mixed.

THE BALANCE-OF-PAYMENTS ARGUMENT FOR AID TYING

In an equilibrium world where the current account adjusts readily to
movements of long-term capital, there can be no justification for aid tying
on balance-of-payments grounds. In the normal course of trade as determined by comparative advantage, there is no reason to expect a shift in
the bilateral current account position between aid donor and recipient
equal to the net aid flow; the adjustment of the donor's current account

should result from shifts in the multilateral pattern of trade. In fact, aid tying is almost certain to involve some trade diversion even though total trade is expanded, and this trade diversion will involve a shift from lower-cost to higher-cost sources of imports for the aid-receiving countries. It should also be said that aid tying will only provide balance-of-payments benefits for the donor country when it is operating at less than full capacity, since any transfer of resources from an economy operating at full capacity will result in an expansion of import demand from other countries unless total expenditure is limited in some way to available output.

Obviously we do not live in an equilibrium world, and adjustments of the current account to capital flows arising from aid transactions are often only partial. For two reasons the problem has become especially acute in the case of the United States. First, there is the chronic U.S. balance-of-payments deficit which has been especially severe and the subject of official concern since 1958. Second, U.S. aid contributions, which have constituted well over 60 per cent of the official bilateral aid of the developed countries, is well out of proportion to the share of U.S. exports in total industrial-country exports to developing countries. In 1964, U.S. exports to developing countries totalled about $8 billion, as against $15 billion for the other industrialized countries. Thus, even if all aid to the developing countries was untied, the United States would have to increase its share of the total exports to developing countries by a substantial margin (or, alternatively, increase its share of total world exports) if it were to avoid a further balance-of-payments drain by a general untying of aid. Much of the aid of the continental European countries goes to Africa and other areas, the bulk of whose imports normally come from Europe. Thus, if the aid transfers of each donor country were approximately proportional to that country's exports to each of the developing regions of the world, a general untying of aid should have no adverse affects on the balance of payments of any donor as long as it maintained its share of the total exports to the developing regions. It should be noted, however, that the balance-of-payments drain from aid experienced by the United States is a reflection of the larger problem of imbalance resulting from the tendency of a few continental European countries to accumulate surpluses which they are unwilling or unable to employ in expanding their imports or capital exports, or are unwilling to hold in the form of increased dollar reserves. A discussion of the solution to this larger problem is beyond the scope of this study. However, it is my view that a general untying of aid would add little to the severity of the broader problem; that must be dealt with by means of a major reform of the international monetary and balance-of-payments adjustment mechanisms. The advantage of having the United States take the lead in eliminating the practice of aid tying would appear to outweigh any disadvantage of adding to the severity of the U.S.

balance-of-payments problem. Surely the correct approach to the world's monetary ills is not an increase in bilateralism and trade diversion which increase the real costs of aid.

There are various forms of tied aid with varying effects on the balance of payments. Completely untied aid will not have a 100 per cent adverse effect on the balance of payments (unless the aid donor is a small country with no trade relations with the recipient). Assuming no change in trade patterns resulting from the aid itself or from other causes, it is possible to estimate the foreign-exchange drain from untied aid to various areas of the world by constructing a matrix of trade relationships among the regions of the world for a given year, showing the ratio of imports for each region or major country from each of the other regions or major countries, and the total imports of each importing region or major country (Hicks, 1963). Such a matrix can provide the basis for estimating "feedback ratios," or the proportions of the untied aid to each region which eventually returns to the donor, which we will assume is the United States. Thus if 56 cents out of every dollar paid to Northern Latin America is spent in the United States, 28 cents is spent in Western Europe, and 16 cents in the rest of the world, and it is further assumed that the 28 cents spent in Western Europe produces no feedback to the United States, but that the 16 cents spent in the rest of the world will be used in part for imports from the United States, depending upon the relevant import ratios, it is possible to calculate what the total feedback to the United States will be after several spending periods. After four successive rounds of spending, the accumulative returns of $1 of untied U.S. aid to Northern Latin America has been estimated at 63 cents on the basis of 1960 Free World import shares (Hicks, 1963; Salant, 1963, p. 276). On the basis of the method developed by Whitney Hicks, the Brookings Institution's report on *The U.S. Balance of Payments in 1968* (Salant, p. 171) estimates the percentage of untied aid to each region which would be eventually respent in the United States as follows: Latin America, 55 per cent; Far East (excluding Japan), 47 per cent; Near East and South Asia, 31 per cent; and Africa, 15 per cent.[7]

I shall consider briefly the way in which the various forms of aid tying affects the U.S. balance of payments within the context of the present international trade and financial system. To begin with, no system of aid tying will avoid all of the balance-of-payments drain indicated by a system of completely untied aid. Even aid in the form of surplus commodities which are designed to constitute an addition to normal commercial purchases, or in the form of commodities designated for specific projects, will most likely displace some normal imports from the United States or per-

7. Estimates are based on 1960 import data.

haps imports from third countries whose purchases from the United States would thereby be adversely affected. For example, the Brookings report suggests that in the case of Latin America, 40 per cent of aid expenditures for commodities delivered to that region are substitutes for normal imports from the United States and thus free an equivalent amount of foreign exchange for other uses. This percentage tends to be lower for regions whose commercial imports from the United States normally constitute a smaller proportion of their total imports. A substantial proportion of U.S. aid takes the form of program loans which are available for a broad shopping list of imports from the United States, the end uses of which are not tied to specific projects. Dollar aid is made available in the form of irrevocable letters of credit which can be used to finance almost any imports from the United States, barring certain luxury items. The Brookings report (Salant, p. 172) suggests that 90 per cent of the commodities imported from the United States by Latin American countries under aid made available in this way would represent substitutes for normal imports of the region from the United States, while in the case of Africa, 70 per cent of U.S. aid in this form would constitute substitutes for normal imports from the United States by that region. However, in the case of commodities and services provided for specific projects, substitution for normal imports will be considerably less, depending upon the nature of the project and the region receiving the aid. Direct agricultural commodity aid under PL 480 is supposed to constitute an addition to normal commercial exports from the United States, but there have been important exceptions. For example, PL 480 assistance to Israel was known to constitute a substitute for normal commercial imports from the United States. Very often, however, direct commodity aid constitutes a diversion of imports from third-country sources such as, for example, wheat exports to Pakistan which took the place of commercial imports from Australia. Such transactions of course have an effect on Australia's imports from the United States.

THE COSTS OF AID TYING

The objections to aid tying are well known. It constitutes a form of bilateralism that diverts trade from normal patterns, and even though total trade is almost always increased, third countries may be the victims of net trade diversion. Aid tying in the form of government-sponsored or assisted export credits (which often provide repayment terms in excess of ten years) constitutes government subsidized exporting—the modern form of competitive currency depreciation—which may harm the national welfare of the donors while in many cases not contributing to the long-run economic and social goals of the recipient. Finally, aid tying, quite apart

from export credit competition, is an expensive way of providing development assistance and reduces international price and quality competition.

A considerable portion of the debt burden of developing countries has
been accumulated not as a consequence of loans by development assistance
agencies carefully tailored to finance projects and programs essential to
the development progress of the recipients, but as a consequence of exporter credits for financing a wide variety of imports, including luxury
commodities, which bear little relationship to rational development plans.
In fact, in some countries, governments have not been able to obtain control of, or to regulate in a rational manner, the contraction of debts by
their own importers, debts which constitute a charge against future foreign-exchange earnings of the nation. The accumulation of these debts reduces the borrowing power of the government for financing imports under
long-term development credits from the World Bank and other hard-loan
institutions and forces them to turn to soft-loan agencies to the extent that
funds are available from these sources. Many countries have experienced
periodic balance-of-payments crises with a consequent interruption of the
flow of essential imports or imports required by important development
projects. The creditor countries must then, either singly or in concert, arrange a refinancing of unplanned credits, often on concessionary terms. All
this increases the cost of foreign aid and shifts the burden of development
financing to concessionary aid institutions such as IDA and AID, while
other imports, often of an unessential nature, continue to be financed by
export credits and are acquired not from sources which offer the lowest
prices and the best quality, but from those which provide the most attractive credit terms (for a discussion of the effects of aid tying on developing countries, see Bandera, 1965).

There is overwhelming evidence that aid tying increases the cost of
procurement and thereby reduces the effectiveness of a given nominal
value of aid (Wilson, 1963). Several years ago the World Bank made a
study of competitive bids on some 40 contracts for the procurement of
equipment totaling over $190 million. It was found that in more than half
the cases the lowest bid was at least 35 per cent cheaper than the highest
bid and more than 20 per cent below the average. Even though national
development-assistance agencies may insist on competitive bidding on
contracts for equipment which they are financing—they may even insist
on international competitive bidding even though they will only finance
exports of their own nationals—it is well known that collusive arrangements among producers in individual countries frequently result in identical bids, or there is a prior agreement as to which firm will submit the
lowest bid within the industry. On the other hand, international markets
are more competitive. There is, for example, considerable evidence that
European firms quote substantially lower prices for exports, particularly

outside of Europe, than they do for domestic or European sales. But where loans are tied to goods sold by nationals, there is no reason to quote prices which will be competitive with firms located in other countries.

In addition to the price factor, there are other dimensions of procurement which are affected by aid tying. There are substantial differences in delivery time as between firms in different countries. The type of equipment available in the aid donor may differ from that which the industry in the aid-recipient country may have obtained in the past and this equipment may not gear well into established systems or it may be of a type which is unfamiliar to engineers in the recipient country. Long-established relationships between foreign suppliers and importers may be disrupted and thus may result in delays and losses due to unfamiliarity of suppliers with the requirements of the importers. Aid tying may also increase transportation costs. For example, some aid donors, including the United States, insist that aid materials be carried on ships registered in the donor country. It has also been suggested that aid tying discourages procurement in neighboring developing countries, thereby interfering with the process of regional economic integration.

Some efforts have been made by either the donor country or the recipient to avoid these disadvantages of aid tying by insisting that contracts for equipment and other commodities be negotiated only on the basis of international competitive bidding, and that in cases where the firms of the donor country are underbid, financing would not be provided for those items. Where aid recipients receive loans permitting the financing of a broad shopping list of imports, they may be able to utilize all of the aid for purchases from the donor on competitive terms and employ their free exchange for purchases of other goods in countries offering lower prices. But where the aid is tied both to the import components of a particular project and to the source of procurement, this approach may not work. On the one hand, foreign firms will not be eager to go to the expense of submitting bids on equipment unless they feel they have a fair chance of obtaining an order, while on the other hand the country needing the aid will be under pressure to accept it on whatever price terms are offered, rather than purchase the equipment at competitive world prices on normal commercial terms.

Considering the additional costs involved in aid tying, and the limitations on the ability of donor countries to achieve net foreign exchange savings from this practice, serious consideration might be given by the United States to eliminating aid tying entirely. This should be done in concert with other major donors. A practical difficulty exists in the fact that there is a rather close relationship between certain forms of aid and export promotion, but it makes little economic sense for a country to employ aid on very generous terms as a means of export promotion. Prob-

ably the most feasible way of reducing aid tying is to shift a large proportion of bilateral aid to multilateral assistance; indeed, this is a major
argument in my own mind for multilateral assistance.

MULTILATERAL VS. BILATERAL AID

The arguments favoring multilateral over bilateral aid, or vice versa,
are perhaps more political and administrative in nature than economic.
Foreign aid has become an important instrument of foreign policy and this
instrument is being employed not only in the Cold War between the larger
Western powers and the Soviet bloc but is used by individual members of
the Western bloc for promoting their special foreign-policy interests, by
developing countries such as Egypt (for political influence in the Middle
East and Africa), and by protagonists in the political-ideological war between the Soviet bloc and Communist China. It is unlikely, therefore, that
nations will renounce all bilateral aid in favor of multilateral assistance. It
may be argued that the elimination of bilateral aid would result in a substantial reduction of total aid to developing countries, since multilateral
assistance would not command the public support based on both economic
and national interests that bilateral aid engenders. Nevertheless, the countries of the Free World have a broad area of collective interest in promoting economic progress in the developing countries, and a considerable
portion of the existing bilateral aid effort is not uniquely associated with
a special national interest of the donor but supports a collective interest
which could readily be served by multilateral agencies. This is especially
the case with development aid made available either in the form of grants
or loans on such generous terms as to rule out any net economic benefit
from export promotion and where no special political or military objectives are involved. A substantial portion of the aid to India and Pakistan,
organized by consortia of nations under the chairmanship of the World
Bank, would appear to meet these conditions for multilateral aid.

By its very nature multilateral aid should be untied, although the
United States has tied a portion of its assistance made available through
the Inter-American Development Bank, just as the EEC countries tie their
aid through the European Development Fund to procurement in member
and Associated EEC countries. The tying of contributions to a multilateral
assistance agency to the purchase of goods and services in the contributing
countries leads either to the disproportionate use of the contributions of
those countries whose goods tend to be preferred by the aid recipients, or
to pressure by the multilateral agency on prospective aid recipients to
balance their aid-financed imports as between preferred and nonpreferred
sources. During the 1950's most European members of the World Bank

would agree to release their paid-in subscriptions to the Bank only on condition that these subscriptions be employed for purchases in the subscribing country. Although there was a disproportionate use of the U.S. paid-in subscription, there were cases in which countries were urged to employ European currencies in utilizing their loan funds.

In practice, the paid-in domestic currency subscriptions of only a few of the Bank's members, mainly the large industrial countries, have been employed by the Bank to any significant extent. A small portion, 2 per cent, of the original subscriptions to the Bank's capital were payable in gold or dollars available for use by the bank without restriction. In the case of subscriptions to IDA, however, all subscriptions by developed country members are made in convertible currencies and unrestricted as to use by IDA.

To what extent should purchases of the World Bank and other multilateral agency securities by private residents of a country be regarded as a burden? This is a difficult question because the answer depends in part upon the extent to which, say, World Bank bonds sold in Germany represent a substitute for purchases of domestic securities, and to what extent they may represent a substitute for purchases of U.S., British, or Swiss securities. Assuming that the rate of return on multilateral agency securities is less than the marginal social productivity of capital in the country of the purchaser, there will be a burden to the extent that there is a net capital outflow. On the other hand, to the extent that the purchases of World Bank securities by Germans constitute a substitute for purchases of U.S. securities, there is a net burden on the United States. Because of the interrelations between financial markets in the developed countries, sales of World Bank bonds to a considerable degree tap a pool of international financial capital and hence constitute a collective burden on all of the developed countries. Certainly, an inequitable burden exists when developed country members either do not permit multilateral agencies to sell their securities in their markets or prevent their own citizens from buying multilateral agency securities issued in other markets. Hence, until there exists a completely unified international financial market, at least among the developed countries, the Bank should seek to achieve an equitable sharing of the burden by borrowing in the national markets of its industrial members in accordance with some agreed-upon quota.[8]

8. The Articles of Agreement of the World Bank provide that members must give their permission for the Bank to sell securities in their national markets. The vast bulk of the Bank's bonds have been sold in the United States. It is worth noting, however, that a considerable portion of the sales of the Bank's bonds in the U.S. market have been made to the nationals of other countries, but such transactions depend upon the exchange control regulations of the foreign countries, most of which exercise capital controls.

CHAPTER NINE

Conclusions for Aid Policy

THE SUBJECT OF FOREIGN AID is much broader than the topics dealt with in the preceding chapters. My principle concern has been with the relationship of aid to economic and social progress and, to a lesser extent, with the economic costs of aid to the donors. Aid involves much more than economics, since it is an important instrument of foreign policy. This does not mean that aid cannot be governed by rational principles in terms of relating costs and benefits; it simply means that the benefits are more difficult to quantify. However my concern is the more modest one of analyzing the contribution of various forms of aid to economic development, on the assumption that the benefits of successful development by poor countries are worth the cost to the donors—at least up to one per cent of their national income!

Foreign aid is in trouble in the United States and in other donor countries as well. The flow of official aid from DAC countries in 1965 was no higher in real terms than in 1961, and substantially lower as a percentage of the aggregate real GNP of donor countries. The U.S. congressional aid appropriation for the fiscal year 1966-67 was the smallest since 1957, and multilateral agencies are finding it increasingly difficult to obtain funds to sustain their lending operations. But the relative decline in the flow of aid does not reveal the extent of the difficulty. Foreign aid is not in trouble because there is opposition to aid in the United States or because there is less than enthusiastic support for aid in Europe; there is perhaps less opposition to the principle of foreign aid than there was a decade or so ago. The most vocal and disturbing criticism of aid is coming from internationally minded leaders in the U.S. Congress and elsewhere who are fundamentally in favor of the basic objectives of aid. The following statement from a subcommittee of the Joint Economic Committee of the Congress (1966) reflects the current status of aid:

The will of the industrial countries to help the less developed seems to be fading even though material advance in our own domestic economies is creating an increasing capacity to give such help. In the United States, the architects and champions of foreign aid in Congress, as elsewhere, are withdrawing their advocacy of long commitments, if not indeed of any commitments at all. Our European partners seem to deny the obligation to participate in such efforts except on a strictly commercial basis. The proposal to increase the flow of aid through the International Development Association and thereby to internationalize it has been shrugged off. The prosperous Common Market turns increasingly inward, and the other industrialized countries therefore begin to look to their separate interests (p. 2).

Lack of support for aid arises from a disillusionment over aid programs and skepticism regarding the ability of these programs to achieve announced objectives. It also arises from a feeling that aid programs are closely tied to political and military objectives with which many liberals are not in sympathy. It is partly for this reason that many U.S. senators and congressmen favor multilateral as against bilateral aid. Much of the recent congressional criticism of aid is sophisticated, searching, and informed—perhaps more so than the answers given by foreign aid officials (Legislative Reference Service, 1966; Committee on Government Operations, 1966). This questioning of aid covers a broad range of issues—national security, political impact on recipients, cooperation from European allies in foreign aid, and the contribution of aid to economic and social progress—all of which demand cogent answers. What is most urgently required, at least from the economists, is a more credible economic rationale for aid designed to promote economic development in the broadest sense of the term, a goal which is widely accepted by the American public.

A satisfactory economic rationale for development aid must deal with the following questions:

1) To what extent is successful development dependent upon external assistance?

2) If the factors determining economic development are in large measure social and political, why is so much emphasis given to aid?

3) What form should aid take, and upon what conditions should it be made available?

4) What is the relationship between trade and aid, and why have aid recipients made so little progress towards external balance?

5) What is the role of foreign private investment in development?

6) What should be the terms of aid, and are hard-loan terms for aid incompatible with the achievement of viable economies?

7) What countries should be assisted, and how should a limited amount of aid be allocated?

8) How is it possible for aid from a multiplicity of sources to make

a significant contribution to development progress in individual countries? Why not have all aid funds administered by a multilateral agency such as the World Bank?

9) How much aid is needed for the developing countries and how should the aid burden be shared?

Some of these questions have political, administrative, and other implications that go beyond economic analysis. For example, the question of whether aid should be provided mainly by multilateral agencies instead of bilaterally must be dealt with almost entirely in political and administrative terms. I shall limit my discussion of the above questions to policy implications arising out of the analysis of the economic factors dealt with in the preceding chapters.

THE CONTRIBUTION OF AID TO DEVELOPMENT

Development economists frequently begin with the caveat that no amount of external capital will guarantee successful development, and then proceed to construct growth models in which the amount of capital inflow is the principal independent variable. Conclusions with respect to aid policy are then based entirely upon the models. Alternatively, it may be alleged that development *requires* a certain volume of capital inflow without any rational determination of the specific level. Historically, some countries have developed without significant capital imports and, in some cases, the achievement of sustained growth preceded a substantial capital inflow. On the other hand, large capital inflows have frequently made little contributions to development. As a general proposition, external capital or aid is neither a necessary nor a sufficient condition for development.

In the preceding chapters I have recognized two basic contributions of aid in the development process: (1) to assist countries in implementing private and public measures which will mobilize and reallocate their human and material resources for maximum social and economic progress; and (2) to supplement a country's domestic resources for higher rates of growth and social progress. By and large, countries that are not making satisfactory progress, regardless of their per capita income, have failed to realize the potential returns from their own resources. What is required are policies and programs for mobilizing, adapting, and reallocating these resources, including the training of human resources for the operations of a modern economy.

The first function of aid indicated above is to facilitate economic and social transformation by overcoming temporary shortages in specific human and material resources, by promoting strategic activities, by inducing and facilitating critical governmental policies, and by providing a certain amount of working capital or margin of resources for carrying out programs involving a shift in the structure of the economy. The amounts and kinds of external assistance that can usefully be employed in facilitating this transformation depend upon the response and the degree of dedication to development in the developing country. This approach does not regard foreign aid as fundamentally an aggregate supplement to domestic resources but, rather, as disaggregated assistance for overcoming strategic shortages which arise in the process of domestic resource mobilization and redirection. Moreover, since I do not regard the savings ratio as a critical independent variable in development, this approach is not consistent with one which views aid in terms of filling a gap between savings and investment. This first function of aid is sometimes regarded as necessary to remove the "skill" limitation on growth, or to increase capital-absorptive capacity. These terms are not precisely defined, but my own concept of the organization of indigenous resources for growth encompasses far more than the lack of skills or the ability to put together projects suitable for investment. Whatever this function may be called, it is not sufficiently differentiated in most models from the function of aid as a supplement to investment resources. Moreover, my approach is based on the assumption that most, if not all, developing countries are potentially capable of sustained development progress with some positive rate of per capita growth, on the basis of their own resources.

The second function of aid noted above—the employment of external capital for supplementing domestic resources for achieving a higher level of investment and rate of growth in output—is logically distinct from the first. Such aid is not primarily for the purpose of facilitating a basic transformation from a nonviable or nongrowing economy to one which is able to mobilize its resources for development. It is true of course that external capital will increase the productivity of existing resources. However, in the case of a country not making reasonably productive use of its resources, its primary need is not supplemental resources from the outside but, rather, the organization and reallocation of its internal resources for productive employment. These two processes may of course go on simultaneously and may reinforce one another. But for purposes of aid policy and strategy they ought to be kept distinct. Thus, from the standpoint of aid strategy, in countries that are not developing successfully because of a gross failure to employ their resources productively, the primary emphasis should be on promoting and facilitating self-help measures and in overcoming strategic bottlenecks. To put it differently, a country should not aim primarily at supplementing its resources until it is making reasonably adequate use of what it has.

For a variety of reasons, most developing countries today are in urgent need of external assistance related to the first function of aid described above. Whether such assistance will be accompanied by development progress depends upon the efforts made by the country and the skill with which the aid is administered. The amount of aid required cannot readily be projected very far in advance, since the amounts which can be appropriately utilized are determined by the response of the country itself, including the efforts of various levels of government and of private firms and organizations, in formulating, financing, and administering a variety of self-help measures in agriculture, industry, economic overhead, and human resource development. The terminal date for aid in performing this catalyzing function will also depend on the response of the country and the stage of its development. In countries like Brazil and Chile, which are relatively well endowed with natural resources and possess a large corps of trained and experienced personnel, the period during which aid may be needed for this first function should be relatively short, certainly less than a decade. For emerging African countries, a longer period will be needed for establishing modern economies capable of sustained social and economic progress. In the case of India, the sheer magnitude of the problem in terms of the large and growing population in the face of a paucity of resources, will require an extended period for modernizing the economy, since only the widespread application of modern technology at a level comparable to that of, say, Japan, will enable India to achieve the basis for sustained progress.

Once countries have reached a stage of sustained growth through the efficient mobilization of their resources, external supplements for maintaining a higher rate of investment may be provided either continuously or intermittently. Such supplements are being provided from both public and private sources to relatively poor countries, such as Mexico, and to relatively well-off countries, such as Australia. In my own view, this aid function involves a different category of aid policy decisions, and different administrative arrangements from those appropriate to the first function. I do not think this second function should be based on minimum target rates of growth, since in large measure the rate of growth a country seeks to attain, once it has achieved a condition of sustained progress, will depend upon decisions relating to its internal policies. A country should not, for example, adopt policies consistent with a 3 or 4 per cent growth rate and depend upon external resources to fill an indefinite gap for sustaining a 5 or 6 per cent growth rate. It might, however, adopt policies designed to achieve a 6 per cent growth rate, within say four or five years, and borrow abroad for several years in order to make certain changes in its economic structure, including its export capacity, required for the higher growth rate. Although growth models may be of some value in planning for a higher rate of growth with the aid of external capital in such cases,

I have rejected the validity of models employing an assumed or historically determined marginal savings ratio. However, shifts in the investment and savings ratios (which are highly interdependent) can be achieved over time by means of governmental policy measures.

THE FORMS AND CONDITIONS OF AID: THE CHOICE OF AID STRATEGIES

Having in mind the two functions of aid outlined above, aid designed for the first function should be specifically administered so as to induce and support self-help measures essential for securing the conditions of development progress. Such assistance should be selective in the sense that it emphasizes the promotion of strategic sectors or subsectors. It should not be based on the principle of seeking out good projects eligible for financing in terms of traditional loan standards. Rather, the selection of programs and projects for financing should be based on an assessment of the economy as a whole and should be in direct support of, and integrated with, domestic policies and programs. Although for reasons detailed in Chapter 6 I have rejected general program loans conditioned upon broad policy undertakings by the recipient, the form of economic assistance available to the aid administrators should be quite flexible. Project assistance should be provided under an arrangement whereby the amount of external financing is not necessarily determined by the direct foreign-exchange requirements associated with the project. Sector or subsector program loans might be made covering a certain proportion of the total cost of carefully formulated programs mutually agreed upon between the recipient and donor or donors. Again, the donor's contribution should not be governed by the direct foreign-exchange cost of the sectoral program. Disbursements under the program should be made as required by actual outlays for the program. Aid should be employed so as to achieve maximum leverage in terms of the domestic financial contribution to projects and programs and to induce the formulation and implementation of the largest number of high-priority projects and programs. Extensive use should be made of local industrial development banks, intermediate credit institutions, and semi-independent regional development authorities for the channeling of aid. Finally, technical assistance, including pre-investment studies, should be packaged with financial and commodity assistance to a maximum degree.

Although foreign-assistance agencies should exert strong influence on monetary, fiscal, and trade policies of the recipient countries, even to the point of suspending aid when policies are widely at variance with those required for development progress, experience has shown that general pro-

gram assistance, or total aid commitments conditioned on overall performance, has not achieved the desired objectives. Broad policy agreements are
not capable of enforcement and the sanction of aid suspension lacks credibility. On the other hand, when aid disbursements for specific programs
are closely tied to the implementation of the projects and programs, pre-
agreed conditions can be enforced more or less automatically by varying
the rate of disbursements.

Aid strategy is frequently related to an assessment of long-range development plans, with projects for assistance selected on the basis of promoting certain sectoral goals approved or favored by the foreign-assistance
agency. Development plans vary widely in quality, but most of them suffer
from a failure to relate plans to specific measures and policies for implementing them. Governmental revenues are inadequate for public-sector
projects, and budget allocations to various ministries and agencies do not
meet the requirements for activities under the plans. Industrial and agricultural outputs are projected against future demand, but insufficient attention is given to private investment incentives, productive credit, and the
availability of raw material and capital goods inputs for the plans to be
implemented. A certain rate of export growth is projected, but monetary
and exchange rate policies are inconsistent with the export goals. All too
often, foreign-assistance agencies give general approval to development
plans and then proceed to finance certain of the obviously economic and
high-priority projects consistent with the plan. This is not the strategy
which is called for in the performance of the first function of foreign aid
to countries not yet on the road to sustained development progress.

Foreign-assistance agencies should not be concerned so much with
plans as with a continual assessment of how a country is performing with
respect to the achievement of the plan goals, or, more broadly, with respect to the achievement of viability with economic progress. (This assumes of course that the long-range plans are broadly consistent and the
goals are feasible; when they are not realistic, either because of incon-
sistencies or because they are based on unrealistic assumptions with respect to external assistance, the countries should be so advised.) If, for
example, agriculture is stagnating or performing far below its potential, the
foreign-assistance agency should work out with the host government
strategies and programs for improving agriculture. If industry is lagging,
or if industrial output is concentrated in high-cost import-substituting
goods designed for a middle- and upper-class market, specific programs
should be devised for expanding and changing the direction of industry.
And if, as is so often the case, exports are lagging, financial or commodity
aid and technical-assistance programs should be directed to expanding the
export sector. Programs in each of these fields will need to be conditioned
upon, or perhaps integrated with, appropriate governmental policy meas-

ures. Since the sectoral performance failures can usually be traced to improper or inadequate policies, aid should be oriented to inducing and facilitating a change in these policies.

As regards our second function of aid, that primarily concerned with supplementing the resources of countries that have successfully mobilized their resources and adopted policies required for sustained progress, there is no special need for the application of aid strategies or for an intimate involvement by the donor with the development program of the recipient. Capital inflow may take a variety of forms and be provided by various public and private sources. Project loan assistance is well adapted to this aid function, partly because the recipient will have the advantage of the technical experience of foreign lending agencies in formulating and reviewing development projects, and partly because hard-loan agencies such as the World Bank have a preference for project financing. However, other types of financing, such as loans to domestic development banks, are quite appropriate for this second function of aid.

THE ROLE OF TRADE IN DEVELOPMENT ASSISTANCE

A satisfactory rate of export growth, in most cases at least equal to the rate of growth in GNP, is an indispensable condition for successful development. Over the longer run, aid cannot substitute for export growth unless it is made available in the form of grants in ever increasing amounts. Even then, the aid recipient would pay a high price by sacrificing productivity gains from specialization and would lose the stimulus to growth provided by export markets. Preferential trade arrangements and above-equilibrium prices for exports constitute a clumsy device for transferring aid resources, and such aid is not likely to be directed into channels that promote development. The principal advantage of preferential trade arrangements is to be found in the stimulus to export growth. I seriously doubt whether preferences to developing countries offer greater advantages than an equivalent general lowering of trade barriers. However, if developed countries are unable to eliminate or drastically reduce tariffs and other import barriers on commodities having the greatest importance for the less-developed countries, I would favor preferential tariff treatment of the products of *all* less developed countries. Of major importance also is the elimination of trade barriers on imports from other developing countries by the developing countries. Developing countries are seeking to produce many of the same industrial products; the impact of their trade barrier is often greatest on exports to one another. They tend to use all of their available exchange for imports from the developed countries, which are not normally produced in the developing countries in any case. Free trade among the developing countries would constitute at least a first step toward the establishment of open economies in the developing countries. Uneconomic import substitution, fostered by restrictive trade policies, not only contributes to a misallocation of resources in the developing countries, but is perhaps the most important constraint on the expansion of their exports.

Aid programs have been woefully negligent in stimulating export growth, and, except for the production and processing of primary commodities, the same may be said for private foreign investment. Foreign aid has frequently financed the production of high-cost import substitutes while neglecting strategies for the promotion of exports. Foreign-assistance agencies should refrain from financing, directly or indirectly, industries whose products are protected by effective rates of duty in excess of a reasonable maximum and which cannot be expected over time to become competitive in world markets, or at least in regional markets. A basic objective of aid programs should be the achievement of open economies—in the absence of which, industrial exports are unlikely to expand. Much of the program and balance-of-payments assistance has had the result of enabling recipient countries to perpetuate a regime in which internal prices bear no relation to external prices. Everything we have learned about the conditions for successful export growth in developed and developing countries alike indicates that a satisfactory rate of export growth cannot take place in such an environment.

Competitive prices of industrial goods will not assure exports, even to markets where tariffs are not a significant barrier. Modern marketing requires product standardization and quality control, and either contractual arrangements with foreign distributors, or investments abroad in warehousing, packaging, assembly plants, etc. Some attention is being given to assisting developing countries in marketing their products abroad by United Nations agencies, but not nearly enough is being done in this field. Effective action is difficult for bilateral aid agencies where the products are competitive with the products of their own nationals. Very often, bilateral assistance agencies can enlist the support of importing firms for this purpose. In any event, it is not overstating the case to say that unless foreign-assistance agencies, in cooperation with the developing and the developed countries, solve the problem of export stagnation, they will fail in their mission of creating viable economies capable of sustained development, no matter how much aid resources they have at their disposal. They will simply create relatively unproductive wards, dependent upon an ever-increasing volume of international charity.

THE TERMS OF AID

Few if any questions in the field of foreign aid have been the subject of more scholarly and non-scholarly analysis and debate than that of the terms of aid. The U.S. Congress has been steadily hardening AID's minimum terms, and the Foreign Assistance Act of 1966 narrowly escaped establishing a further increase of AID's minimum interest rate from 2.5 per cent to 3 per cent. Officials of the World Bank, the OECD, and AID have pointed with alarm to the growing debt service of the developing countries and have pleaded for softer loan terms. As noted in Chapter 4, economists have constructed models of externally financed growth in which annual debt service on hard or medium terms rises to more than ten times the initial annual capital inflow, and in some models continues to rise indefinitely. In some models, interest payments alone increase at a rate exceeding the rate of growth in GNP. Based on the results of externally financed growth models, a number of economists are questioning whether aid programs can ever be successful in achieving a condition of self-generating growth at minimum target levels on a loan basis, without most developing countries going through a period of defaults or requiring general debt forgiveness. Thus for example, in a recent study by Goran Ohlin published by the OECD Development Center (1966b), the author concludes that "probably the time is not far away when a concerted effort has to be made to put development assistance not merely on a soft, but on a grant basis."

Without prejudicing the case for softer development loan terms, it should be said that "growth-cum debt" models based on geometric progressions over long periods of time inevitably yield astronomical results. My own skepticism arises not from the arithmetic but from the relevance of the investment-savings gap models which require several decades of net external capital flow before a target rate of self-generating growth can be achieved. As I stated in Chapter 3, there is no empirical evidence to support the assumed relationship between the long-run marginal and average savings ratios on the one hand, and the growth of the national product on the other. There is also little basis for postulating a long-run export growth rate which after a few decades approaches tangentially the foreign-exchange requirements function. Nevertheless I believe that aid on very generous terms is essential for inducing and facilitating structural change in countries which have not achieved the conditions for sustained development progress.

The rationale given for aid on concessionary terms as against hard loans has usually emphasized limited debt-service capacity of aid recipients, but other reasons such as the long payout period in terms of product returns for certain types of investment such as education, or the assertion that very poor countries cannot be expected to make loan repayments with interest for a number of decades, have been advanced. In linking concessionary terms with my first function of aid, that designed to facilitate structural change rather than primarily to supplement capital resources, I have rejected the position that the terms of aid should be related solely to the balance of payments and estimated debt-servicing capacity of the recipient. One difficulty with the balance-of-payments approach is that it constitutes an incentive for a country to sustain a poor balance-of-payments performance. The practice of allocating aid to countries in relation to the magnitude and frequency of their balance-of-payments crises has been all too common. This practice has put a premium on poor financial management and disregard of the external sector. There are a number of poor countries that need external assistance for modernizing their economies and establishing the conditions for broad development progress, but which have had a history of balance-of-payments equilibrium. They should not be denied concessionary aid while reserving such aid for countries with chronic balance-of-payments difficulties created by improper policies.

There are perhaps three arguments for concessionary aid employed in connection with our first function of aid. First, such aid has important inducement effects as compared with hard-loan assistance. It is easier to induce governments to adopt programs which may be unpopular with important social groups if assistance for these programs is provided on generous terms. There are many administrative rigidities and budgetary constraints within governments that can only be overcome if temporary external assistance is provided until larger fiscal revenues are forthcoming from tax reforms, or until the programs to be financed are well established and a wide vested interest for popular support for them has been engendered. Productive enterprise may be restrained by lack of credit available from commercial banks until potentially self-sustaining development banks can be established and financed with the help of external assistance agencies. Frequently, governments will not be willing to assume hard-loan obligations for financing programs important for structural change, or hard-loan agencies (which tend to prefer assistance to infrastructure requiring substantial import components) may be unwilling to provide financing for strategic programs involving little or no direct foreign-exchange outlays.

A second argument for concessionary loans is that certain projects and programs have long payout periods and delayed impacts on the social product out of which service payments on foreign loans must be made. Concessionary loans which delay payment of interest should not be justified on the grounds that the increment to the social product arising directly or indirectly from the loan is less than the rate of interest on hard loans. Rather, the justification should lie in the lag between many types of investment and the expected increments to the social product, and in the lag between the adoption of policy measures for expanding and redirecting savings, on the one hand, and the actual employment of the savings for larger investment expenditures on the other. Lags between investment and increased output are common both in social-impact programs, such as those relating to education and health, and in infrastructure projects, such as highways and multipurpose dams. There are also lags between the enactment of fiscal reforms and the expansion of fiscal revenues. It should be cautioned, however, that our first function of aid does not envisage a rapid buildup of infrastructure and social-impact programs in advance of the ability of a country to utilize the outputs in a manner which would contribute to the expansion of the social product. Moreover the rate of capital investments in such projects and programs should not exceed the capacity of the economy for undertaking them by means of a better utilization of their own resources, except for the supplying of strategic commodities and services in temporary short supply. The importance of such foreign assistance is in facilitating the mobilization and redirection of indigenous resources. The bulk of the savings for raising the level of investment should also be expected to come from domestic sources, although capital imports can bridge the investment-savings gap during a period of structural shifts in the volume and direction of savings.

The third, and perhaps most important, argument for concessionary aid relates to the time required for changing the structure of the balance of payments. During the period when countries are making a serious effort to alter their economic structure through appropriate policy measures designed to achieve sustained development, foreign-exchange shortages are likely to be severe and of some duration. The assumption of large hard-loan obligations may impair the long-run balance-of-payments position of the country in a manner which works against the maintenance or achievement of an open economy relatively free from import restrictions. Domestic resources can more readily be mobilized by appropriate fiscal policies and incentives for reinvested earnings, but in the majority of cases it is the foreign-exchange constraint that is dominant. Much of the investment required for structural change will have the effect of raising import requirements, and even though an appropriate volume of investment is directed to industries that may become potential exporters, except for certain primary product industries, the process of expanding exports will take considerable time. Many countries cannot expect a rapid growth in their exports of primary products, but must look increasingly to exports of manufactures for raising the rate of growth in their foreign-exchange earn-

THE ECONOMICS OF FOREIGN AID

ings. Most potential export industries in the manufacturing field are initially established for the production of substitutes for imports. However well adapted these industries may be to the country's resources and comparative advantage, it generally requires considerable time before they become sufficiently competitive to enter the export market. Moreover, it is not always easy to predict which industries will in fact become successful exporters.

I have the distinct impression that aid planners have concentrated too much on programs for closing a hypothetical investment-savings gap, and not enough on the improvement of the balance of payments. There has been a tendency to minimize the latter problem by arguments for low-interest aid with 40- to 50-year amortization periods, derived from the manipulation of investment-savings gap models which call for a long period of gap-filling aid. The emphasis on the savings gap—which I believe is misplaced—tends to obscure the foreign-exchange problem. There is a real danger that this doctrine may encourage developing countries to pursue policies which will doom them to a long-run condition of nonviability and misallocation of resources. Expectations of a long period of foreign-exchange loans on concessionary terms can certainly dull the zeal of governments for policy reforms.

I would recommend that, during the period required for the structural adjustment of a developing economy with the help of concessionary aid as outlined above, no interest be charged on concessionary loans, so that annual net resource transfers are equal to annual amounts of the loans. However there should be a definite and pre-announced time limit for this period during which the conditions for sustained progress are expected to be achieved, and in most cases this period should not exceed ten years. After this period, annual interest on old loans should be charged at conventional rates, beginning with each loan as it reaches a maturity of ten years (or whatever the period of concessionary aid which is determined). Additional borrowing beyond this period should take place under conventional terms as provided by hard-loan sources. As illustrated by Table 3 in Chapter 4, interest service would rise gradually as old loans reach a maturity of, say, ten years, and additional lending at interest rates charged by hard-loan agencies took place. But the rate of rise in exports should be sufficient to cover both the slowly rising interest service and the growing volume of imports, provided the country has indeed achieved the conditions for sustained progress.

Debt-cycle models usually provide for net repayment of capital. This is unrealistic and unnecessary. A successful developing country should be able to increase its net indebtedness indefinitely so long as its interest service does not rise faster than the increments to its net national product or than the rate of increase in its exports. Developing countries should have continuous access to international financial capital markets, whether private or public, which will enable them to maintain a net inflow of capital indefinitely, so long as they are meeting the conditions outlined above. This means, in effect, that developed countries have an obligation to maintain access to their capital markets for the sale of bonds by the World Bank and other international or regional institutions, or for private flotations of the obligations of developing countries.

THE ALLOCATION OF AID

The question of aid allocation faced by any one of the major foreign-assistance agencies is partly political and administrative, only partially economic. DAC estimates of net official aid flows from DAC countries and multilateral organizations to developing countries show that in 1964, out of a total net flow of nearly $6.3 billion, Asia received $2.9 billion, Africa $1.7 billion, Latin America $1.0 billion, and Europe $0.3 billion. The bulk of U.S. bilateral aid from all sources (mainly AID, PL 480, and Export-Import Bank) went to Asia and Latin America, with only about $300 million going to Africa (Table 7). A very heavy proportion of Western Europe's aid goes to Africa, with smaller amounts to India and Pakistan. Aid disbursements of multilateral organizations are heavily concentrated in Asia and Latin America. Considering the fact that over 60 per cent of the population of the underdeveloped countries outside the Soviet bloc and Communist China lives in Asia, per capita aid to that region is relatively low. Per capita aid was highest in the case of Africa, followed by Latin America.

It is impossible to discern any economic rationale for the distribution of aid, either overall or by agency or donor country. Countries tend to distribute aid in part on the basis of their historical, political, and commercial relationships with certain areas, while various national and multilateral organizations operate under certain regional or functional constraints. Thus, the United States provides the bulk of the aid for Latin America and has made very heavy commitments to South Vietnam, Korea, and Taiwan. The IDB makes loans solely to Latin America. The World Bank and the Export-Import Bank make only hard loans, while AID and IDA are the principal soft-loan agencies.

It is impossible to discover any connection between aid per capita and per capita income among the developing countries. In 1964, Chile received aid equal to $16 per capita, while India received less than $3 per capita in aid, and Israel received over $50 in per capita aid. Yet per capita income in Chile is five times that of India, and in Israel per capita income is more than twelve times that of India. Nor does the allocation between

TABLE 7

GEOGRAPHICAL DISTRIBUTION OF NET OFFICIAL FLOWS TO
LESS-DEVELOPED COUNTRIES FROM DAC MEMBER COUNTRIES AND
MULTILATERAL ORGANIZATIONS, 1964

	Net Official Capital Flow * (In millions of dollars)	Population in 1964 (Million)	Net Official Flow per Capita (In dollars)
Total Recipient Countries	$6,257	1,546	$ 4
Asia	2,935	933	3
India	1,230	472	3
Pakistan	518	101	5
South Vietnam	246	16	15
South Korea	174	28	6
Israel	107	2	53
Philippines	94	31	3
Indonesia	85	102	0.8
Jordan	81	2	40
China (Taiwan)	52	12	4
Thailand	46	30	1.5
Iran	−1	23	......
Other	303	114	3
Africa	1,722	285	6
French Franc Area South of Sahara	447	41	11
Algeria	252	11	22
Egypt (U.A.R.)	238	29	8
Congo (Leopoldville)	115	15	8
Morocco	107	13	8
Tunisia	71	5	14
Portuguese Overseas Provinces	64	13	5
Nigeria	54	56	1
Kenya	53	9	6
Tanzania	44	10	4
Ghana	40	8	5
Malawi	32	4	8
Uganda	20	7	3
Zambia	18	4	4
Other	167	60	3
America	1,018	232	4
Brazil	233	79	3
French Overseas Departments	174	1	174
Chile	132	8	16
Colombia	103	15	7
Mexico	47	40	1
Peru	45	11	4
Bolivia	44	4	11
Other	240	74	3

Table 7 (cont.)

	Net Official Capital Flow * (In millions of dollars)	Population in 1964 (Million)	Net Official Flow per Capita (In dollars)
Europe	343	91	4
Turkey	149	31	5
Yugoslavia	136	19	7
Greece	40	9	4
Spain	−10	31	......
Other	28	1	28
Oceania	20	5	4
Unallocated	219	......	......

* Minus figures indicate net repayment.

Notes: (1) Including loans of one year or more. (2) Net official flows equal net bilateral official grants and loans received, plus grants and loans received from multilateral organizations, less capital repayments and capital subscription payments to these organizations. (3) Preliminary data complemented in some cases by Secretariat estimates.

Source: *Development Assistance Efforts and Policies, 1965 Review* (Paris: OECD, 1965) Appendix Table 7, pp. 134-35.

concessionary and hard-loan assistance appear to make much sense. Thus, many Latin American countries receive substantial amounts of both. Mexico obtains most of its assistance from hard-loan agencies and India receives most of its aid on concessionary terms, but each country receives some aid on hard terms and some on concessionary terms.

Apart from political and administrative factors, how should aid be allocated assuming that there is a fixed amount of aid? The amount of hard-loan funds available for lending has not, thus far, been an absolute constraint, and hard-loan agencies are usually eager to finance projects that meet their standards in countries with a reasonably favorable capacity for assuming additional debt service. I should hope that the supply of hard-loan capital from public external sources would continue to be sufficient to meet the demand on the basis of reasonable standards with respect to both the use of the capital and the debt-service capacity of the borrowers. As I have already indicated, I believe that the developed countries which dominate the international financial community have an obligation to maintain an environment in which long-term credit, such as that provided by the World Bank, on terms reflecting those in the international capital markets (except for the assumption of risk by the lending agency) will continue to be available in adequate amounts without the

272

need for any special rationing. This depends, of course, upon the willingness of developed countries not only to underwrite the obligations of the World Bank by increasing their callable subscriptions as needed, but to open their capital markets for the sale of World Bank obligations, along with the obligations of other hard-loan agencies, such as the Inter-American Development Bank and the new Asian Development Bank.

If hard-loan capital from public and private loan sources continues to be available in ample supply, the problem of aid allocation boils down to the allocation of aid on concessionary terms. From the standpoint of economic as opposed to political criteria, the following questions with respect to the allocation of concessionary aid appear relevant:

1) Should available aid be concentrated on those countries regarded as the most favorable candidates for the achievement of rapid development progress?

2) Should a termination date for concessionary aid be established for each recipient of concessionary aid?

3) Should preference be given to those countries with low per capita income, even though their outlook for successful development is less promising?

4) Should any concessionary aid be given to countries that have been able to achieve a condition of sustained growth but nevertheless have a relatively low per capita income?

Concentration of aid on the most promising prospects for successful development has considerable appeal from the standpoint of the allocation of resources directed toward the goal of achieving viable and progressive economies. This approach is also in line with the desire for an early termination date for concessionary aid programs, since presumably the most favorable candidates will require aid for a shorter period for realizing the objectives.[1] Two objections can be cited for this approach. First, it is not always possible to predict the successful cases in terms of development progress on the basis of existing technical and managerial skills, material resource endowments, or even efficiency and dedication of government administration. Progress in Argentina and Chile has certainly been disappointing in spite of substantial amounts of external assistance. On the other hand, considering the paucity of basic conditions regarded as favorable for growth in Jordan and in Tunisia, these countries have been mak-

1. Concentration of aid on fewer countries has been urged by members of the Senate Foreign Relations Committee partly on the economic grounds discussed here, and partly because of the view that the United States should limit its commitments to world security and economic progress. The position that the United States in its foreign relations generally is greatly overextended is one which has been frequently expressed by Senator William Fulbright.

ing significant progress. South Korea is another country that appeared to have little potential for growth and most observers viewed the large amount of economic aid extended to that country as an exercise in economic futility, whatever might be its political justification. Yet impressive results in terms of both national income and export growth are being achieved by Korea. Israel's remarkable development—which has led to a per capita income higher than that of many developed countries, together with a several-fold expansion of exports, over the past decade—indicates what can be done by a country with a high skill and motivation level, but with an extremely poor resource base. Since history is replete with surprises, it may not be wise to put all of our aid chips on a few countries regarded as the most likely candidates for success.

A second reason for not concentrating aid on a few countries is that it is just as important for countries with poor human and material resource endowments to be assisted on the road to progress as it is for relatively well-endowed countries to be assisted. Also, the amount of aid funds that can usefully be directed in mobilizing the domestic resources of poor countries toward economic progress may be considerably less than that required for facilitating structural adjustment in a relatively well-to-do country with the same population, such as Argentina. The combined aid requirements of several small countries may be less than that required for one medium-sized or large country.

It may be objected that by offering to assist too many countries with limited aid resources, an agency such as AID may become overextended, and that unfulfilled promises of adequate assistance for carrying out self-help measures will lead to frustrations and unfavorable political and economic consequences. However, there inevitably will be some countries whose performance will not warrant substantial amounts of assistance, in accordance with the principle of providing aid as it is actually used in strategic projects and subsectoral programs. The history of aid-giving is replete with instances in which more aid has been provided than could be justified in terms of the self-help measures of the recipient. What I am suggesting is that donors should pay more attention to the allocation of aid for high priority and strategic purposes within countries, than to the allocation of aid among countries, as a means of maximizing the impact of aid. There are of course political reasons for concentrating aid on certain countries rather than others, but I am not concerned with these.

There is a further reason for maintaining a minimum aid program in a number of countries, even where political conditions may not now be conducive to successful development. Political conditions frequently change, as in the case of Ghana following the overthrow of Nkrumah, and in the case of Brazil following the ouster of the Goulart government. Competent technicians and development economists with an intimate knowledge of the economy should be on hand to cooperate with a new government dedicated to formulating policies and programs necessary for development progress. Except in the most extreme cases, development-assistance relationships with countries should be maintained even when significant amounts of aid do not appear to be warranted.

The question of a termination date for concessionary aid with respect to an individual country involves both a definition of the objectives which concessionary aid is designed to achieve, and the possibility of projecting the process and time path for the objectives to be realized. Under the approach I have been suggesting, the objectives would differ considerably from country to country, depending upon the resource endowments and the economic and social structure. In broad terms, the objective is to assist the country in mobilizing its resources and changing its economic structure by means of a variety of policy instruments, so as to enable the country to achieve significant economic and social progress on a sustained basis. More concretely, it means raising its agricultural output by transforming agricultural techniques and organization; increasing investment incentives in industry and agriculture; establishing a price and credit system which will direct investment in an economical manner; increasing fiscal revenues and allocating public funds in relation to economic and social goals, including education, health, and other social services; achieving reasonable price stability so as to promote savings and a rational allocation of resources; realizing reasonably full employment with an efficient allocation of labor; and achieving structural external balance consistent with expected capita inflows and debt service. Other specific economic and social objectives might be added.

The time required for these policies and programs to become effective, and the external resources needed to implement them in the sense of meeting the temporary shortages encountered, can be estimated, but such estimates would need to be made in a disaggregated manner, in the sense that some objectives will be realized before others. The goal is a viable economy making economic and social progress to the maximum extent this can be accomplished with a country's own resources, allowing time for resource reallocation and a certain amount of necessary training and experience. The process must also be regarded as partly experimental, since it may be necessary to vary the policy instruments and readjust programs such as those related to expanding agricultural production, or encouraging investment in industry directed toward improving the trade balance. The goal of the process is not a specific target rate of growth, although there should be some positive rate of per capita growth. Just what statistical rate of GNP growth will occur and what the measurable indicators of social progress will show cannot readily be forecast. But the attainment of the structural conditions for sustained progress should be evident from certain performance criteria—such as a satisfactory rate of growth in agricultural output, a rising rate of investment, adequate fiscal revenues for financing public-sector economic and social programs consistent with the level of national product, the existence of an open economy with flexible prices responsive to internal and external demand and supply conditions, reasonable price stability, and balance-of-payments equilibrium, together with a favorable outlook for export growth in line with future import and debt-service requirements. The existence of these conditions would signal the suspension of concessionary aid, or its rapid tapering off as certain programs were completed. It should be said however that various internal and external developments may cause progress to be interrupted, requiring the reestablishment of a foreign-assistance program after the initial program has been suspended.

Since aid disbursements will be related to the implementation of specific programs designed to realize the conditions set forth above, long periods of substantial concessionary aid flow should certainly not be contemplated for countries which have already achieved a fairly advanced stage of development, for example, Brazil, Chile, or Colombia. For the African nations, the process of modernization in the sense of transforming agricultural techniques, bringing the subsistence sector into the modern economy, raising the level of education, improving public administration, and changing the social organization, as well as social attitudes and motivation, will require many decades. But establishing the basic conditions for continuous progress and social change need not require decades, given a favorable political environment. Most African nations have the material basis for economic progress. However, substantial amounts of technical assistance and a flow of financial assistance for strategic programs may in some cases be needed for many years to come. This does not mean massive amounts of concessionary aid capital for expensive infrastructure or capital-intensive industry. This would not be consistent with our first function of aid. Investment in industries producing primary commodities for export, and infrastructure (power and transportation) to support such industry, should be financed by a combination of private foreign capital and hard loans. Hard loans from public sources might also be appropriately provided for high-priority power, transportation, and other projects during the period in which concessionary aid programs are in existence.

The most difficult problems from the standpoint of aid policy are represented by India and Pakistan, especially the former. For these countries, viability, to say nothing of progress, is mainly a function of food production, the rate of population growth, and the trade balance. Massive amounts of aid have been going to these countries for keeping people alive, without contributing very much to agricultural output, and to supplying industry with raw materials and equipment, without orienting industry either to the improvement of the trade balance or to providing inputs for agriculture. Thus, most of the aid to the world's largest recipient, India, has not been contributing to development progress, but is simply a holding operation.

Nowhere is rapid structural and policy change more urgently required than in India. Recently the U.S. government expressed its intention of insisting that India employ aid for solving its agricultural problem, but the scale of the operation of transforming Indian agriculture is indeed staggering. Aid to Indian industry should also be exerting a greater influence on the direction of India's industrial investment and output, both for expanding exports and for making a contribution to agriculture by means of fertilizer production and the production of other agricultural inputs. But India's basic food problem is not something that can be solved by massive aid. Until India's structural problems are solved, much of the aid to India cannot properly be classified as development aid, but simply as a subsidy to consumption. If India fails in achieving a viable economy, ever larger amounts of commodity assistance will be required from the rest of the world just to keep her population alive and her economy running at a low level of productivity. How long the developed countries will consider it worthwhile to fill an ever widening consumption-production gap is a moot question.

The final question which I posed was whether aid on concessionary terms should be provided to countries with low but slowly rising per capita incomes simply because they are poor. Taiwan, which AID advertises as one of the "aid success stories" is a case in point. AID has announced suspension of assistance on concessionary terms to Taiwan on grounds that this country has achieved a condition of self-sustaining growth, although Chile, which continues to receive a large amount of concessionary assistance on a per capita basis, has a per capita income of nearly two-and-one-half times that of Taiwan. It is true, of course, that a country can grow faster with external capital, and while there is certainly a net advantage in receiving that capital on concessionary terms, Taiwan should obtain her external capital from private and public hard-loan sources. Although I recognize that the question of providing concessionary aid to a country simply because it is poor is mainly a humanitarian or an ethical one—I do not think that the political case has been proved—I hold to the principle that concessionary development aid should be employed solely as a means of facilitating the structural reorganization of a country for sustained progress, and not primarily as a supplement to its capital resources for achieving a higher growth rate. This conclusion is based partly on the view that concessionary assistance should be accompanied by rather exacting conditions and should be closely integrated with policy measures and programs required for rapid structural change. In my view, concessionary development assistance is not provided to countries primarily to equalize the distribution of world income, but rather to help countries make more productive use of their own resources.

THE COORDINATION OF AID

A major barrier to any rational approach to aid is the multiplicity of foreign-assistance agencies, many of them providing assistance to the same developing country. Further proliferation of these agencies is continuing with the organization of regional development institutions, such as the Asian Development Bank and the African Development Bank, which serve as intermediaries for the primary sources of external capital without providing any specialized functions or administrative economies. However, we must accept the existence of this unwieldy institutional structure, which has arisen mainly in response to political motivations, and seek to evolve measures for both a rational allocation of functions and a coordination of activities at the country level.

The most urgent need is for coordination of foreign-assistance activities in countries receiving concessionary aid designed to facilitate structural change required for sustained progress. The employment of aid for this purpose requires an intimate involvement by the foreign-assistance agency in the policies and sectoral programs of the country. Uncoordinated aid activities in these situations may very well do more harm than good. If the Finance Minister of the developing country cannot obtain the financing he wants for some politically motivated program (or cannot obtain it without appropriate internal reforms) from one source, he may obtain the financing from another source. If aid cannot be obtained on concessionary terms from one agency without agreeing to politically difficult conditions, it can be obtained on hard terms from another source. Aid coordination at the country level should involve a greater degree of cooperation than is generally found in aid consortia or consultative groups, most of whose activities are confined to the general approval of an annual external aid budget and an agreement as to what financing will be provided by each agency. What is required is the formation of a group representing all the donors, which will be in day-to-day contact with the officials of the aid-recipient country. Only in this way can the approach to aid administration suggested in Chapter 6 (and elsewhere in this chapter) be implemented.

Of particular importance is the coordination of concessionary assistance designed to facilitate self-help measures with the activities of hard-loan agencies in making project loans. There is some evidence that both hard-loan agencies and the suppliers of long-term credits (usually backed by government guarantees) base their debt-service capacity judgments on the expectation that program loans from AID or IDA will be available for an indefinite period in the future. (In fact this is the only possible explanation for continued hard loans to India.) In the absence of these program loans, some countries would be undergoing a balance-of-payments crisis which would preclude their receiving credits on hard terms. The availability of these credits removes much of the incentive for the policy changes which AID is seeking to promote under program loan agreements. Some measure of agreement among DAC members regarding the maximum level of export credits which should be extended to individual developing countries would also be highly desirable.

There is something to be said for eliminating all hard loans to countries during the period when they are undertaking major policy revisions under a program financed by concessionary aid. However, I would not go that far, since, frequently, vital infrastructure projects can be appropriately financed by long-term hard loans. I would suggest that all project loans on hard terms be carefully reviewed in advance by the agency or consortium of agencies making available concessionary aid, in order to determine the relationship of the project to the structural changes they are seeking to induce and to assess the effect of the proposed loan on the projected balance of payments. Similarly, the volume of import credits should be subject to review and included as a part of the general agreement for receiving concessionary aid. It seems evident that a program designed to achieve long-term viability with the help of concessionary aid can be thwarted by uncoordinated capital imports on hard terms. Under these conditions, concessionary aid may represent little more than an addition to the total capital inflow, with no contribution to the changes in basic structural conditions necessary for development progress and external balance.

Close coordination between the development assistance agencies and the IMF is also essential. Much of the IMF assistance going to developing countries is not related to balance-of-payments deficits which are temporary, and readily reversible in the normal course of events; nor are they readily amenable to changes in monetary and fiscal policies save at the politically unacceptable cost of unemployment and impairment of growth. Rather, the balance-of-payments difficulties tend to be structural in nature, and their elimination requires policy measures and programs directed toward a fundamental change in the character of the economy. It is worth noting that the approach to assistance to developing countries in cases of unexpected export shortfalls, recommended by the World Bank report entitled *Supplementary Financial Measures,*[2] provides for development type aid rather than the type of balance-of-payments assistance provided by the IMF. This is a sound approach, and might well be applied by the IMF in providing assistance to developing countries with chronic or structural balance-of-payments deficits, in cooperation with development assistance agencies. In this way, assistance from the IMF could be closely integrated with development programs involving participation by concessionary aid agencies and conditioned upon a broader range of policy measures than those usually included in IMF standby agreements.

A final field for aid coordination relates to private foreign investment in developing countries under AID investment guarantees, or financed by Cooley Loans out of PL 480 proceeds. Private foreign investment yields special benefits through the transfer of skills and techniques. However, not all private foreign investment is desirable from the standpoint of development. For example, most private foreign investment in industry in developing countries is designed to supply commodities only for the local market. This may be because the parent company establishing the foreign enterprise does not want to compete with its own sales in third markets, or with those of other affiliates. Alternatively, the resources of the host country may be so poorly adapted to the production of the commodity that the output can only be produced at a high cost and under a high degree of protection. In both cases, the foreign enterprise may decide to produce the commodity in order to maintain a market which would otherwise be lost to other firms willing to produce under the same conditions. Cases of uneconomical import substitution made possible for foreign enterprise are quite common. Where such operations are encouraged by guarantees provided by the capital-exporting nation, a net social loss may be sustained by both countries. Hence, proposals for special encouragement to private foreign investments should be carefully examined by the aid authorities from the standpoint of their contribution to the rational resource allocation and the balance of payments. In addition, developing countries should be encouraged to require foreign firms seeking to make investments in their economies to plan for exports either to regional or world markets.

Coordination of the activities of hard-loan agencies in countries where comprehensive assistance programs involving concessionary aid agencies are not being undertaken is less urgent, but there are certainly areas where closer coordination is needed. Foremost among these is the need for agreement with respect to the debt-servicing capacity of borrowers, together with a coordinated effort to avoid a condition of net capital repatriation through a proper timing of loan commitments and disbursements. Second,

2. The World Bank report made in response to a resolution of the United Nations Conference on Trade and Development was reviewed in Chapter 7.

an exchange of views looking toward a consensus among the lending agencies with regard to the priority of sectors and of large scale projects and programs in individual developing countries would lead to a more rational allocation of assistance. Third, a periodic exchange of views regarding economic conditions and general development progress would contribute to better advice and stronger influence exercised by lending-agency officials, and the avoidance of future difficulties and setbacks in development progress. Closer cooperation between technical assistance agencies and lending agencies for undertaking sector analyses and pre-investment studies, and for improving project formulation is also desired. Some progress along all of these lines has been made in recent years, but full coordination at the country level and joint consideration of loan proposals by all of the major foreign lending and technical agencies operating in a particular country is a highly desirable goal which is far from being realized.

HOW MUCH AID AND HOW SHOULD THE AID BURDEN BE SHARED?

In Chapter 3 I reviewed certain models for determining the total volume of aid required by developing countries to achieve a specified target rate of growth in per capita output. I have rejected this general approach on three grounds: (1) I do not accept the premise that social and economic progress is primarily determined by the flow of external resources; (2) I question the stability of the parameters employed in the growth models; and (3) I do not agree with the position that the primary purpose of concessionary aid is to achieve a specific rate of growth in per capita output.

The capital-absorptive approach as formulated by the staff of the World Bank determines total aid requirements by adding up, sector by sector, the value of the potential investment projects and programs in each country which are regarded as feasible and capable of implementation, and then calculating the *resource* gap for carrying them out. This approach does not determine the level of required investment by means of a growth model relating investment to output. Rather, it is a disaggregated method of determining how much external assistance developing countries might usefully employ, given certain technical and economic feasibility standards and given certain assumptions regarding private investment incentives and the administrative capacity of public officials for implementing planned projects. This approach has certain advantages over the investment-savings gap models for determining capital import requirements, but it avoids the question of why the calculated amount of external capital is "required," and to what ultimate purpose. The capacity to make productive use of a certain amount of capital does not establish the rationale for capital requirements as related to the objectives of those called upon to supply it. This is especially pertinent in the case of concessionary aid. A well-organized economy might be able to employ productively almost unlimited amounts of capital, provided there are no debt-service charges.

The approach to aid which I have suggested does not provide the basis for a ready calculation of aid requirements, nor do I intend to make any. As regards hard-loan capital for our second function of aid, I have indicated that there should be no limit on the amount of capital available for developing countries which may appropriately be obtained from the international capital markets either directly or indirectly through the sales of securities of multilateral hard-loan agencies. If lending agencies could agree on a quantitatively applicable standard for determining debt-servicing capacities, and assuming no net repayments, presumably they could calculate maximum global "requirements" for this type of capital. But there are no ready guidelines for calculating requirements for concessionary aid in accordance with the function of such assistance as I have outlined in the preceding paragraphs. Such determination would be possible on a highly disaggregated basis, given the programs formulated by the foreign-assistance agencies with respect to countries eligible for this type of aid. However, foreign-assistance agencies are not operating on the premises which I have recommended.

The intricate problem of equitable burden-sharing can scarcely be approached until we find a common denominator for aid in terms of some unit of net burden. As we have seen, not only do aid terms vary widely, but donors receive various commercial benefits from certain forms of bilateral credits. Perhaps DAC will find an acceptable formula for weighting bilateral aid which would make possible more realistic comparisons of the amounts of aid currently provided by each donor. When this is accomplished, a uniform percentage formula is perhaps as good as any other basis for allocating aid contributions among donors, with the percentage determined in accordance with the total aid bill. It might be noted that the one per cent formula currently employed has never been rationalized in terms of a formula for determining total aid requirements. It derives from the concept of a moral obligation to transfer income from the rich countries to the poor ones, rather than from a well-conceived notion of development promotion.

This still leaves unsettled the distribution of the burden arising from borrowing by multilateral agencies in the international capital markets. One solution would be for all developed countries to permit free access to their capital markets, at least for the securities of multilateral development agencies, although interest-rate differentials reflecting domestic monetary policies would lead the multilateral agencies to borrow in the cheapest markets.[3] Alternatively, the multilateral agencies might establish borrowing quotas for each developed member country.

Probably the best solution to the burden-sharing problem would be for all aid, hard and soft, to be administered by multilateral agencies financed by paid-in subscriptions. Concessionary aid would be financed by paid-in subscriptions yielding no return on the capital advanced by the developed country members. Hard loans would be financed by subscriptions on which dividends would be declared, and—in both cases—subscriptions should be made in convertible currencies. In this connection, the World Bank's charter authorizes the Bank to pay dividends on paid-in subscriptions actually utilized in making loans, but the Bank has never paid any dividends to its members.

3. If developed countries permitted completely free access to their capital markets from all sources, this would tend to force them to equalize interest rates; the development of an international capital market is forcing them to do this, anyway, athough they are resisting this process by the introduction of new restrictions on capital outflows and inflows.

Glossary

AID	Agency for International Development
CIAP	Inter-American Committee on the Alliance for Progress
DAC	Development Assistance Committee
EEC	European Economic Community
FAO	Food and Agricultural Organization
GATT	General Agreement on Tariffs and Trades
GDP	gross domestic product
GNP	gross national product
IBRD	International Bank for Reconstruction and Development
ICOR	incremental capital-output ratio
IDA	International Development Association
IDB	Inter-American Development Bank
IFC	International Finance Corporation
IMF	International Monetary Fund
OECD	Organization for Economic Cooperation and Development
OEEC	Organization for European Economic Cooperation
OSAS	Overseas Service Aid Scheme
PL 480	U.S. Public Law 480
PMSR	per capita marginal savings ratio
SMP	social marginal productivity
UNCTAD	United Nations Conference on Trade and Development
UNESCO	United Nations Education, Scientific, and Cultural Organization

Works Cited

ADLER, JOHN H. 1965. *Absorptive Capacity: The Concept and Its Determinants.* Washington, D.C.: The Brookings Institution.

ADLER, ROBERT W., and RAYMOND F. MIKESELL. 1966. *Public External Financing of Development Banks in Developing Countries.* Eugene: Bureau of Business and Economic Research, University of Oregon.

AGENCY FOR INTERNATIONAL DEVELOPMENT. 1965. *A Study on Loan Terms, Debt Burden, and Development.* Washington, D.C., U.S. Department of State, AID (Mimeo.)

———. OFFICE OF ENGINEERING. 1963. *Benefit-Cost Evaluations as Applied to AID-Financed Water or Related Land Use Projects* (Supplement No. 1 to *Feasibility Studies, Economic and Technical Soundness Analysis, Capital Projects*). Washington, D.C.: U.S. Department of State.

———. PROGRAM COORDINATING STAFF. 1963. *Principles of Foreign Economic Assistance.* Washington, D.C.: USGPO.

———. 1966. *Proposed Economic Assistance Programs, Fiscal Year 1967.* Washington, D.C.: USGPO.

———. PROGRAM COORDINATION STAFF. *Report to the Congress on the Mutual Security Program for the Fiscal Year 1960.* Washington, D.C.: USGPO.

——— and U.S. DEPARTMENT OF DEFENSE. 1965. *Proposed Mutual Defense and Development Programs, Fiscal Year 1966.* Washington, D.C.: USGPO.

AVRAMOVIC, DRAGOSLAV. 1958. *Debt Service Capacity and Postwar Growth in International Indebtedness.* Baltimore: Johns Hopkins Press.

———, et al. 1964. *Economic Growth and External Debt.* Baltimore: Johns Hopkins Press.

BALASSA, BELA. 1964a. *Trade Prospects for Developing Countries.* Economic Growth Center, Yale University. Homewood, Ill.: Richard D. Irwin.

———. 1964b. "The Capital Needs of the Developing Countries," *Kylos,* 18 (2): 197-206.

BANDERA, V. N. 1965. "Tied Loans and International Payments Problems," *Oxford Economic Papers,* 17 (July), 299-308.

BANFIELD, EDWARD C. 1963. *American Foreign Aid Doctrines.* Washington, D.C.: American Enterprise Institute for Public Policy Research.

BARNA, TIBOR (Ed.). 1963. *Structural Interdependence and Economic Development.* New York: St. Martin's Press.

BATOR, F. M. 1957. "On Capital Productivity, Input Allocation, and Growth," *Quarterly Journal of Economics,* 71 (February), 86-106.

BAUER, P. T., and B. S. YAMEY. 1957. *The Economics of Underdeveloped Countries.* Cambridge, England: Cambridge University Press.

BERRILL, KENNETH. 1963. "Foreign Capital and the Take-Off." In W. W. Rostow (Ed.), *The Economics of Take-Off Into Sustained Growth.* New York: St. Martin's Press.

BOWMAN, MARY JEAN. "Schultz, Denison, and the Contributions of 'Eds' to National Income Growth," *Journal of Political Economy,* 72 (October), 450-64.

BRUTON, HENRY J. 1965. *Principles of Development Economics.* Englewood Cliffs, N.J.: Prentice-Hall.

CAIRNCROSS, A. K. 1963. "Capital Formation in the Take-Off." In W. W. Rostow (Ed.), *The Economics of Take-Off into Sustained Growth.* New York: St. Martin's Press.

CENTER FOR INTERNATIONAL STUDIES, MIT. 1957. "The Objectives of United States Economic Assistance Programs," *Foreign Aid Program (Compilation of Studies and Surveys),* Special Committee to Study the Foreign Aid Program. U.S. Senate, 85th Cong., 1st sess.

CHAKRAVARTY, S. 1964. "The Use of Shadow Prices in Programme Evaluation." In P. N. Rosenstein-Rodan (Ed.), *Capital Formation and Economic Development.* Cambridge, Mass.: MIT Press.

CHENERY, HOLLIS B. 1953. "The Application of Investment Criteria," *Quarterly Journal of Economics,* 67 (February), 76-96.

————. 1955. "The Role of Industrialization in Development Programs," *American Economic Review,* 45 (May), 40-57.

————. 1960. "Patterns of Industrial Growth," *American Economic Review,* 50 (September), 634.

————. 1961. "Comparative Advantage and Development Policy," *American Economic Review,* 51 (March), 18-51.

————, and PAUL G. CLARK. 1959. *Inter-Industry Economics.* New York: John Wiley and Sons.

————, and M. BRUNO. 1962. "Development Alternatives in an Open Economy: The Case of Israel," *Economic Journal* (March), 79-103.

————, and ALAN M. STROUT. 1965. "Foreign Economic Assistance and Economic Development." (AID Discussion Paper No. 7, Office of Program Coordination.) Washington, D.C.: U.S. Department of State.

————, ————. 1966. "Foreign Assistance and Economic Development," *American Economic Review,* 56: 679-733.

CLARK, P. G. 1962. *Indicators of Self-Help*. (Policy Discussion Paper No. 1, Program Review and Coordination Staff, AID.) (Mimeo.)

CLOWER, R. W., G. DALTON, M. HARWITZ, and A. A. WALTERS. 1966. *Growth without Development: An Economic Survey of Liberia*. Evanston, Ill.: Northwestern University Press.

COHEN, BENJAMIN I. 1966. "Foreign Exchange Constraints in Economic Development and Efficient Aid Allocation: Comment," *Economic Journal*, 76 (March), 168-70.

COLLEGE OF AGRICULTURE, UNIVERSITY OF ARIZONA. 1962. *Policy for United States Agricultural Export Surplus Disposal*. (Technical Bulletin 150) Tucson: University of Arizona.

COLUMBIA UNIVERSITY SCHOOL OF LAW AND INSTITUTE OF INTERNATIONAL STUDIES AND OVERSEAS ADMINISTRATION, UNIVERSITY OF OREGON. 1963. *Public International Development Financing in Colombia*. New York: Columbia University.

————. 1964. *Public International Development Financing in Chile*. New York: Columbia University. (Mimeo.)

COMMITTEE ON FOREIGN AFFAIRS. 1964. *Staff memorandum on International Lending and Guarantee Programs*. Washington, D.C.: House of Representatives, 88th Cong., 2d sess.

COMMITTEE ON FOREIGN AFFAIRS, SUBCOMMITTEE ON FOREIGN ECONOMIC POLICY. 1965. *Utilization of Excess U.S.-Owned Foreign Currencies in Certain Countries*. (Hearings; Appendix Table I.) Washington D.C.: House of Representatives,, 89th Cong., 1st sess.

COMMITTEE ON GOVERNMENT OPERATIONS, SUBCOMMITTEE ON FOREIGN AID EXPENDITURES. 1966. *United States Foreign Aid in Action: A Case Study*. Washington, D.C.: U.S. Senate, 89th Cong., 2d sess.

COOPER, RICHARD N. 1964. "External Assistance and the Balance of Payments of Donor Countries." Geneva: UNCTAD (E/CONF./.46/P/13, March 10).

————. 1965. *A Note on Foreign Assistance and Capital Requirements for Development*. Santa Monica, Calif.: RAND Corp.

COOTNER, PAUL H. 1963. "Social Overhead Capital and Economic Growth." In W. W. Rostow (Ed.), *The Economics of Take-Off into Sustained Growth*. New York: St. Martin's Press.

DEANE, PHYLLIS, and H. J. HABAKKUK. 1963. "The Take-Off in Britain." In W. W. Rostow (Ed.), *The Economics of Take-Off into Sustained Growth*. New York: St. Martin's Press.

DENISON, E. F. 1962. *The Sources of Economic Growth in the United States and the Alternatives before Us*, Supplementary Paper No. 13. New York: Committee for Economic Development.

————. 1964. "The Unimportance of the Embodied Question," *American Economic Review*, 54 (March), 90-94.

DEPARTMENT OF AGRICULTURAL ECONOMICS, MICHIGAN STATE UNIVERSITY, and DEPARTMENT OF ECONOMICS AND SOCIAL SCIENCES, NATIONAL

UNIVERSITY OF COLOMBIA. 1964. *Public Law 480 and Colombia's Economic Development.* Medellín, Colombia: Graficas Vallejo.

DOMAR, EVSEY D. 1946. "Capital Expansion, Rate of Growth and Employment," *Econometrica,* 14 (April), 137-47.

———. 1947. "Expansion and Employment," *American Economic Review,* 37 (March), 34-35.

DOUGLAS, PAUL H. 1934. *The Theory of Wages.* New York: Macmillan.

DUNNING, J. H. 1966. "Further Thoughts on Foreign Investment," *Moorgate and Wall Street: A Review,* Autumn, 1966, 5-37.

ECKSTEIN, O. 1957. "Investment Criteria for Economic Development and the Theory of Intertemporal Welfare Economics." *Quarterly Journal of Economics,* 71 (February), 56-85.

ECONOMIC COMMISSION FOR LATIN AMERICA. 1963a. "Progress in Planning in Latin America," *Economic Bulletin for Latin America,* 8(2): 129-46.

———. 1963b. *Towards a Dynamic Policy Development for Latin America.* E/CN 12/680. Santiago, Chile.

FEI, JOHN C. H., and D. S. PAAUW. 1965. "Foreign Assistance and Self-Help: A Reappraisal of Development Finance," *Review of Economics and Statistics,* 47 (August), 251-67.

———, and GUSTAV RANIS. (Yale Growth Center) 1964. *Development of the Labor Surplus Economy: Theory and Policy.* Homewood, Ill.: Richard B. Irwin.

FEIS, HERBERT. 1964. *Foreign Aid and Foreign Policy.* New York: St. Martin's Press.

FINCH, DAVID. 1951. "Investment Service of Underdeveloped Countries." *Staff Papers.* Washington, D.C.: International Monetary Fund.

FIRST NATIONAL CITY BANK OF NEW YORK. 1967. *Monthly Economic Letter* (April).

FOOD FOR PEACE DIRECTOR. 1965. *Food for Peace, 1964 Annual Report on Public Law 480.* Washington, D.C.: USGPO.

FOREIGN RELATIONS COMMITTEE. 1965. *Foreign Assistance Act, 1965.* (Hearings; pp. 504-29) Washington, D.C.: U.S. Senate, 89th Cong., 1st sess.

FRIEDMAN, MILTON. 1958. "Foreign Economic Aid: Means and Objectives," *Yale Review,* 47 (December), 500-516.

GALENSON, W., and H. LEIBENSTEIN. 1955. "Investment Criteria, Productivity, and Economic Development," *Quarterly Journal of Economics.* 69 (August), 343-70.

GILBERT, MILTON, and ASSOCIATES. 1957. *Comparative National Products and Price Levels.* Paris: OEEC.

GOERING, THEODORE J., and LAWRENCE WITT. 1963. *United States Agricultural Surpluses in Colombia: A Review of Public Law 480.* (Technical Bulletin 289). East Lansing: Department of Agricultural Economics, Michigan State University.

GREAT BRITAIN. HER MAJESTY'S STATIONERY OFFICE. 1957. *The United Kingdom's Role in Commonwealth Development*, Cmnd. 237.

——. 1963. *Aid to Developing Countries*. Cmnd. 2147.

GROUP OF TEN. 1965. *Report of the Study Group on the Creation of Reserve Assets: Report to the Deputies of the Group of Ten*. Washington: D.C.: USGPO.

GRUBLE, HERBERT G. 1964. "The Benefits and Costs of Being a World Banker," *The National Banking Review*, 2 (December), 189-212.

GULHATI, RAVI I. 1965. "The Need for Foreign Resources, Absorptive Capacity and Debt Servicing Capacity." (Paper prepared for Round Table Conference on Capital Movements and Economic Development, sponsored by the International Economic Association.) Washington, D.C. (Mimeo.)

GULICK, CLARENCE S., and JOAN M. NELSON, 1965. "Promoting Effective Development Policies: AID Experience in the Developing Countries." (AID Discussion Paper No. 9.) Washington, D.C.: U.S. Department of State.

HAGEN, EVERETT E. 1959. "Population and Economic Growth," *American Economic Review*, 49 (June), 310-27.

——. 1962. *On the Theory of Social Change: How Economic Growth Begins*. Homewood, Ill.: Dorsey Press.

HAHN, F. H., and R. C. O. MATTHEWS. 1964. "The Theory of Economic Growth: A Survey," *The Economic Journal*, 74 (December), 779-902.

HANSEN, ALVIN H. 1939. "Economic Progress and Declining Population Growth," *American Economic Review*, 29 (March), 1-15.

HARBERGER, A. C. 1962. "A Note on the Rate of Return to Capital in Indian Industry," *Price Policy for Electricity Undertakings*. New Delhi: Planning Unit, Indian Statistical Institute.

HARBISON, FREDERICK, and CHARLES A. MYERS. 1964. *Education, Manpower, and Economic Growth: Strategies of Human Resource Development*. New York: McGraw-Hill.

HARROD, R. F. 1939. "An Essay in Dynamic Theory," *Economic Journal*, 44 (April), 14-33.

——. 1948. *Towards a Dynamic Economics*. London: Macmillan.

HAYES, J. P. 1964. "Long-Run Growth and Debt Servicing Problems." In Dragoslav Avramovic *et al.*, *Economic Growth and External Debt* (IBRD) Baltimore: Johns Hopkins Press.

HICKS, W. WHITNEY. 1963. "Estimating Foreign Exchange Cost of Untied Aid," *Southern Economic Journal*, 30 (October) 168-173.

HIGGINS, BENJAMIN. 1962. *United Nations and U.S. Foreign Economic Policy*. Homewood, Ill.: Richard D. Irwin.

——. 1965. *Economic Development*. New York: W. W. Norton.

HIRSCHMAN, ALBERT O. 1958. *The Strategy of Economy Development*. New Haven, Conn.: Yale University Press.

HOUTHAKKER, H. S. 1961. In *Proceedings of the 32nd Session of the Inter-*

national Statistics Institute, Vol. 38, Pt. 2. Tokyo: International Statistical Institute.

――――. 1962. "On Some Determinants of Saving in Developed and Under-developed Countries," Memorandum No. 20. Stanford Research Center in Economic Growth.

HOWELL, L. D. 1954. "Benefits Versus Costs of Price Supports," *Quarterly Journal of Economics*, 48 (February), 115-130.

INTERNATIONAL BANK FOR RECONSTRUCTION AND DEVELOPMENT. 1965. *Supplementary Financial Measures*. Washington, D.C.: IBRD.

JASAY, A. E. 1960. "The Social Choice between Home and Overseas Investment," *Economic Journal*, 70 (March), 105-113.

JOHNSON, HARRY G. 1962. "International Liquidity—Problems and Plans," *Malayan Economic Review*, 7 (April), 1-19.

――――. 1964. "Comments on Mr. John Vaizey's Paper," *The Residual Factor and Economic Growth*. Paris: OECD.

――――. 1965. "An Economic Theory of Protectionism, Tariff Bargaining, and the Formation of Customs Unions," *Journal of Political Economy*, 70 (June), 265-83.

――――. 1967. *Economic Policies Toward Less-Developed Countries*. Washington, D.C.: The Brookings Institution.

JOHNSON, L. L. 1965. *Problems of Industrialization in Chile*. Santa Monica, Calif.: RAND Corp.

JOHNSTON, B. F. 1962. "Agricultural Development and Economic Transformation: A Comparative Study of the Japanese Experience," *Food Research Institute Studies*. Stanford, Calif.: Stanford University Press.

JOINT ECONOMIC COMMITTEE OF THE CONGRESS OF THE UNITED STATES. 1966. *Twenty Years After: An Appeal for the Renewal of International Economic Cooperation on a Grand Scale*. (Report of Subcommittee on International Exchange and Payments.) Washington, D.C.: USGPO.

KAHN, ALFRED. 1951. "Investment Criteria in Development Programs," *Quarterly Journal of Economics*, 65 (February), 38-61.

――――. 1962. "Agricultural Aid in Economic Development: The Case of Israel," *Quarterly Journal of Economics*, 16 (November), 568-91.

KAO, CHARLES, KURT ANSCHEL, and CARL EICHER. 1964. "Disguised Unemployment in Agriculture: A Survey," *Agriculture and Economic Development* (Carl Eicher and Lawrence Witt, eds.,). New York: McGraw-Hill.

KINDLEBERGER, CHARLES P. 1956. *The Terms of Trade: A European Case Study*. New York: MIT and John Wiley.

――――. 1958. *International Economics*. (rev. ed.) Homewood, Ill.: Richard D. Irwin.

――――. 1965. *Balance of Payments Deficits and the International Market for Liquidity*. (Essays on International Finance, International Finance Section) Princeton: Princeton University Press.

KIRMAN, ALAN P., and WILSON E. SCHMIDT. 1965. "Key Currency Burdens: The U.K. Case," *The National Banking Review*, 3 (September), 101-102.

KRAVIS, IRVING B. 1957. "The Scope of Economic Activity in International Income Comparisons." In *Studies in Income and Wealth* (XX). Princeton: Princeton University Press.

———, and MICHAEL W. S. DAVENPORT. 1963. "The Political Arithmetic of International Burden Sharing," *Journal of Political Economy*, 71 (August), 309-330.

KUZNETS, SIMON. 1960. "Quantitative Aspects of the Economic Growth of Nations, V: Capital Formation Proportions: International Comparisons for Recent Years," *Economic Development and Cultural Change*, Vol. 6, Part II (July).

———. 1963. "Notes on the Take-Off." In W. W. Rostow (Ed.), *The Economics of Take-Off into Sustained Growth*. New York: St. Martin's Press.

LEGISLATIVE REFERENCE SERVICE, LIBRARY OF CONGRESS. 1966. *Some Important Issues in Foreign Aid*. (Prepared for Committee on Foreign Relations, U.S. Senate.) Washington, D.C.: USGPO.

LEIBENSTEIN, HARVEY. 1957. *Economic Backwardness and Economic Growth*. New York: John Wiley & Sons.

———. 1966. "Incremental Capital-Output Ratios and Growth Rates in the Short Run," *The Review of Economics and Statistics*, 48 (February), 20-27.

LEWIS, JOHN P. 1962. *Quiet Crisis in India*. Washington, D.C.: The Brookings Institution.

LEWIS, W. ARTHUR. 1954. "Economic Development with Unlimited Supplies of Labor." *The Manchester School of Economic and Social Studies*. Reprinted in A. N. Agarwala and S. P. Singh (Eds.), *The Economics of Underdevelopment*. New York: Oxford University Press.

———. 1964. Address at the Sixth World Conference of the Society for International Development.

LITTLE, I. M. D., and J. M. CLIFFORD. 1966. *International Aid*. Chicago: Aldine Publishing Company.

McCLELLAND, DAVID C. 1961. *The Achieving Society*. Princeton: D. Van Nostrand.

MacDOUGALL, G. D. A. 1960. "The Benefits and Costs of Private Investment from Abroad: A Theoretical Approach," *The Economic Record* (Essays in Honor of Sir Douglas Copland).

McKINNON, R. I. 1964. "Foreign Exchange Constraints in Economic Development and Efficient Aid Allocation," *Economic Journal*, 74 (June), 388-409.

———. 1966. "Rejoinder," *Economic Journal*, 76 (March), 170-171.

MARX, KARL. 1909. *Capital*. Vol. III. Chicago: Kerr and Co.

MASON, EDWARD S. 1964a. *Foreign Aid and Foreign Policy*. New York: Harper and Row.

————. 1966. "On the Appropriate Size of a Development Program" *Occasional Papers in International Affairs, No. 8.* Cambridge: Harvard University Press.

MELLOR, JOHN W., and R. D. STEPHENS. 1956. "The Average and Marginal Product of Farm Labor in Underdeveloped Countries," *Journal of Farm Economics,* 38 (August), 780-91.

MIKESELL, RAYMOND F. 1958. *Agricultural Surpluses and Export Policy.* Washington, D.C.: American Enterprise Institute.

————. 1962. "The Capacity to Service Foreign Investment." In Raymond F. Mikesell (Ed.), *U.S. Private and Government Investment Abroad.* Eugene: University of Oregon.

————. 1963a. "Commodity Agreements and Aid to Developing Countries," *Law and Contemporary Problems,* 28(2): 294-312.

————. 1963b. "International Commodity Stabilization Schemes and the Export Problems of Developing Countries," *American Economic Review,* 53 (May), 75-92.

————. 1966a. *Public Foreign Capital for Private Enterprise.* (Essays on International Finance, International Finance Section). Princeton: Princeton University Press.

————. 1966b. *Public International Lending for Development.* New York: Random House.

————. 1966c. "United States as World Banker," *The National Banking Review,* 4 (December) 145-50.

————, and JACK N. BEHRMAN. 1958. *Financing Free World Trade with the Sino-Soviet Bloc.* (Studies in International Finance) Princeton: Princeton University Press.

MILLIKAN, MAX, and WALT W. ROSTOW. 1957. *A Proposal: Key to an Effective Foreign Policy.* New York: Harper and Brothers.

MORGAN, THEODORE. 1959. "The Long-Run Terms-of-Trade Between Agriculture and Manufacturing," *Economic Development and Cultural Change,* 7 (October), 1-23.

MORGENTHAU, HANS. 1962. "A Political Theory of Foreign Aid," *American Political Science Review,* 60 (June), 405-406.

MORRIS, CYNTHIA T. 1963. *International Comparison of Domestic Savings Rates.* (Discussion Paper No. 6, Program Coordination Staff, AID.)

MURPHY, CARTER. 1960. "International Investment and the National Interest," *Southern Economic Journal,* 27 (July), 11-17.

MYRDAL, GUNNAR. 1956. *An International Economy.* New York: Harper and Brothers.

NEALE, A. D. 1961. *The Flow of Resources from Rich to Poor.* (Occasional Papers on International Affairs, No. 27.) Cambridge: Center for International Affairs, Harvard University.

NELSON, RICHARD R. 1956. "A Theory of the Low-Level Equilibrium Trap in Underdeveloped Countries," *American Economic Review,* 46 (December), 894-908.

————. 1964. "Aggregate Production Functions and Medium-Range Growth Projections," *American Economic Review,* 54 (September), 575-606.

NURKSE, RAGNER. 1957. *Problems of Capital Formation in Underdeveloped Countries.* New York: Oxford University Press.

OHLIN, GORAN. 1966a. *Foreign Aid Policies Reconsidered.* Paris: OECD Development Center.

————. 1966b. *The Relationship between Aid Requirements, Terms of Assistance, and Indebtedness of Developing Countries.* Paris: OECD Development Center.

ORGANIZATION FOR ECONOMIC COOPERATION AND DEVELOPMENT. 1965a. *Development Assistance Efforts and Policies, 1965 Review.* Paris: OECD.

————. 1965b. *The Flow of Financial Resources to Less Developed Countries, 1956-1963.* Paris: OECD.

————. 1966. *Development Assistance Efforts and Policies: 1966 Review.* Paris: OECD.

OSHIMA, HARRY T. 1958. "Underemployment in Backward Economies: An Empirical Comment," *Journal of Political Economy,* 66 (June), 259-64.

PAGLIN, MORTON. 1965. " 'Surplus' Agricultural Labor and Development: Facts and Figures," *American Economic Review,* 55 (September), 815-34.

PATTERSON, GARDNER. 1965. "Would Tariff Preferences Help Economic Development?" *Lloyd's Bank Review,* 76 (April), 18-30.

————. 1966. *Discrimination in International Trade, The Policy Issues, 1945-1965.* Princeton: Princeton University Press.

PEACOCK, A. T., and DOUGLAS DOSSER. 1959. "Input-Output Analysis in an Underdeveloped Country, A Case Study," *Review of Economic Studies,* 25 (October), 21-24.

PEPELASIS, ADAM A., and PAN A. YOTOPOULOS. 1962. *Surplus Labor and Greek Agriculture, 1953-1960.* Athens: Center of Economic Research (Monograph Series 2).

PHELPS, E. S. 1962. "The New View of Investment: A Neo-Classical Analysis," *Quarterly Journal of Economics,* 76 (November), 548-67.

PINCUS, JOHN A. 1963. "The Cost of Foreign Aid," *Review of Economics and Statistics,* 45 (November), 360-67.

————. 1965. *Economic Aid and International Cost Sharing.* Baltimore: Johns Hopkins Press.

PIZER, SAMUEL, and FREDERICK CUTLER. 1965. "U.S. Exports to Foreign Affiliates of U.S. Firms," *Survey of Current Business,* 45 (December), 12-16.

PREBISCH, RAUL. 1959. "Commercial Policies in the Underdeveloped Countries," *American Economic Review, Papers and Proceedings,* 49 (May), 251-73.

————. 1963. *Towards a Dynamic Development Policy for Latin America,* U.N. Economic Commission for Latin America (E/CN 12/680, April 14), Santiago, Chile.

PREST, A. R., and R. TURVEY. 1965. "Cost-Benefit Analysis: A Survey," *Economic Journal,* 75 (December), 683-735.

QAYUM, A. 1960. *The Theory and Policy of Accounting Prices.* Amsterdam: North Holland Press.

RICARDO, DAVID. 1821. *The Principles of Political Economy and Taxation.* (3rd ed., 1937.) New York: E. P. Dutton.

ROOSA, ROBERT V. 1965. *Monetary Reform for the World Economy.* New York: Harper and Row, for Council on Foreign Relations.

ROSENSTEIN-RODAN, PAUL N. 1943. "Problems of Industrialization of Eastern and South-Eastern Europe," *Economic Journal* 53 (June-September), 202-211.

————. 1961a. "Notes on the Theory of the 'Big Push.' " *Economic Development for Latin American.* (Proceedings of a Conference of the International Economic Association; Howard S. Ellis and Henry C. Wallich, eds.) New York: St. Martin's Press.

————. 1961b. "International Aid for Underdeveloped Countries," *Review of Economics and Statistics,* 43(2): 107-138.

ROSTOW, WALT W. 1956. "The Take-Off into Self-Sustained Growth," *Economic Journal,* 66 (March), 25-48.

————. 1961. *The Stages of Economic Growth.* Cambridge, England: Cambridge University Press.

———— (Ed.). 1963. *The Economics of Take-Off Into Sustained Growth.* (Proceedings of a conference held by the International Economic Assn.) New York: St. Martin's Press.

SALANT, WALTER S., *et al.* 1963. *The U.S. Balance of Payments in 1968.* Washington, D.C.: The Brookings Institution.

SAMUELSON, PAUL A. 1952. "The Terms of Trade under Capital Transfer When Impediments to Transport Are Absent," *Economic Journal,* 62 (June), 278-304.

SCHMEDTJE, J. K. 1965. *On Estimating the Economic Cost of Capital.* Washington, D.C.: IBRD. (Mimeo.)

SCHMIDT, WILSON E. 1964. "The Economics of Charity: Loans vs. Grants," *Journal of Political Economy,* 72 (August), 387-95.

SCHULTZ, THEODORE W. 1956. *The Economic Test in Latin America.* (New York State School of Industrial and Labor Relations, Bulletin 35). Ithaca: Cornell University Press.

————. 1961. "Education and Economic Growth." In Nelson B. Henry (Ed.), *Social Forces Influencing American Education.* Chicago: University of Chicago Press.

————. 1962. "Reflections on Investment in Man," *Journal of Political Economy Supplement,* 70 (October), 1-8.

————. 1964. *Transforming Traditional Agriculture.* New Haven: Yale University Press.

SCHUMPETER, J. A. 1949. *The Theory of Economic Development.* (Translated by R. Opie.) Cambridge: Harvard University Press.

SILVERT, K. H. 1963. "The Costs of Anti-Nationalism: Argentina." In K. H. Silvert (Ed.), *Expectant Peoples: Nationalism and Development.* New York: Random House.

SIMPSON, PAUL B. 1962. "Foreign Investment and the National Economic Advantage: A Theoretical Analysis." In Raymond F. Mikesell (Ed.), *U.S. Private and Government Investment Abroad.* Eugene: University of Oregon Press.

SINGER, H. W. 1950. "The Distribution of Gains Between Investing and Borrowing Countries," *American Economic Review,* 40 (May), 473-85.

————. 1965. "External Aid: For Plans or Projects?" *Economic Journal,* 75 (September), 539-45.

SOLOW, ROBERT M. 1960. "Investment and Technical Change." In K. Arrow, S. Karlin and P. Suppes (Eds.), *Mathematical Methods in Social Sciences.* Stanford: Stanford University Press.

————. 1962. "Technical Progress, Capital Formation, and Economic Growth," *American Economic Review,* 52 (May), 76-86.

————. 1963a. *Capital Theory and Rates of Return.* Amsterdam: North Holland Press.

———— 1963b. *Capital Theory and the Rate of Interest.* (Lecture III.) Amsterdam: North-Holland Publishing Company.

SWERLING, BORIS C. 1962. *Current Issues in Commodity Policy.* (Essays in International Finance, International Finance Section.) Princeton: Princeton University Press.

TINBERGEN, JAN. 1958. *The Design of Development.* Baltimore: Johns Hopkins Press.

TOBIN, JAMES. 1964. "Economic Growth as an Objective of Government Policy," *American Economic Review,* 54 (May), 1-20.

UNITED NATIONS. 1951. *Measures for the Economic Development of Underdeveloped Countries.* (Report by a Group of Experts Appointed by the Secretary General.) New York: United Nations.

————. 1960. *World Economic Survey, 1959.* New York: United Nations.

————. 1961. *International Compensation for Fluctuations in Commodity Trade.* (Report by a Committee of Experts Appointed by the Secretary General.) New York: United Nations.

————. 1964a. *The Economic Development of Latin American in the Post-War Period.* New York: United Nations.

————. 1964b. *United Nations World Economic Survey, 1963, Vol. I. Trade and Development: Trends, Needs, and Policies.* New York: United Nations.

————. CONFERENCE ON TRADE AND DEVELOPMENT. 1964. *Final Act, United Nations Conference on Trade and Development.* (E/CONF. 46/L28.) Recommendation A IV 2. Geneva: United Nations.

————. CONFERENCE ON TRADE AND DEVELOPMENT. 1964. "Memorandum Concerning Certain Items on the Agenda of the U.N. Conference on Trade and Development," (E/CONF/46/74, Geneva, February 26, 1964).

————. 1965. *Preferences: Review of Discussions.* (Report by the Secretary General of the Conference, U.N. Trade and Development Board. TD/AC.1/1, March 25, 1965).

UNITED STATES. DEPARTMENT OF AGRICULTURE. 1966. Food for Peace Press Release No. 579-66 (February 23).

———. DEPARTMENT OF COMMERCE. 1965. *Balance of Payments Statistics of the United States, A Review and Appraisal.* Washington, D.C.: USGPO.

———. DEPARTMENT OF COMMERCE. 1965, 1966. *The Survey of Current Business.* Washington, D.C.: USGPO.

VERNON, RAYMOND. 1966. "Comprehensive Model-Building in the Planning Process: The Case of the Less-Developed Economies." *Economic Journal,* 76 (March), 57-69.

WARRINER, DOREEN. 1948. *Land and Poverty in the Middle East.* London: Royal Institute of International Affairs.

WATERSTON, ALBERT. 1963. *Planning in Pakistan.* (Economic Development Institute, IBRD). Baltimore: Johns Hopkins Press.

———. 1965. *Development Planning: Lessons of Experience.* (Economic Development Institute, IBRD). Baltimore: Johns Hopkins Press.

WHITMAN, MARINA VON NEUMANN. 1965. *Government Risk Sharing in Foreign Investment.* Princeton: Princeton University Press.

WILSON, G. M. 1963. "World Bank Operations." (An address before the Economic Commission of the Council of Europe, Paris, December 16, 1963.) Washington, D.C.: IBRD.

WITT, LAWRENCE W. 1964. "Development Through Food Grants and Concessional Sales," *Agriculture and Economic Development.* (Carl Eicher and Lawrence Witt, eds.). New York: McGraw-Hill.

———, and CARL EICHER. 1964. *The Effects of United States Agricultural Surplus Disposal Programs on Recipient Countries.* (Research Bulletin 2). East Lansing: Agricultural Experiment Station, Department of Agricultural Economics, Michigan State University.

WOLF, CHARLES, JR. 1960. *Foreign Aid: Theory and Practice in Southern Asia.* Princeton: Princeton University Press.

———. 1965. "The Political Effects of Economic Progress: Some Indications from Latin America," *Economic Development and Cultural Change,* 14 (October), 1-20.

WOODS, GEORGE D. 1965. *Statement of George D. Woods to the Ministerial Meeting, Development Assistance Committee, Organization for Economic Cooperation and Development.* Paris: World Bank.

WRIGGINS, HOWARD. 1962. "Foreign Assistance and Political Development." In *Development of the Emerging Countries: An Agenda for Research* Washington, D.C.: The Brookings Institution, 181-214.

WRIGHT, DAVID McCORD. 1959. "Stages of Growth Versus Growth of Freedom," *Fortune,* 60 (December), 135-36, 201-209.

YOUNGSON, ALEXANDER JOHN. 1956. "Marshall on Economic Growth," *Scottish Journal of Political Economy,* 3 (February), 1-18. Reprinted in Bernard Okun and R. W. Richardson (Eds.), *Studies in Economic Development.* New York: Holt, Rinehart and Winston, 1961.

Index

Adler, John H., 100–101
Agency for International Development (AID), 3, 5, 108–109, 131, 137, 148, 150, 166, 169, 173, 174, 176, 177, 178, 180, 204, 230, 269, 276
  and program loans, 169–83
  and legislative regulations, 179–80
  and benefit-cost, 130–31
  See also Foreign aid, Foreign loans
Agricultural commodity assistance, 184–93
  and investment contribution, 185–87
  and real burden of aid, 228–29
  and valuation of aid, 229–30
  See also Public Law 480
Agricultural development, 53–57, 145–47, 187–88
Associated African Countries, 202
Avramovic, Dragoslav, 115

Balance of payments, 211–13, 246–51
  and aid tying, 248–51
  See also Balance-of-payments assistance
Balance-of-payments assistance, 164–66
  and aid tying, 248
  and compensatory aid, 211–18
  and development plans, 137
  and program loans, 171
  See also Foreign loans
Balassa, Bela, 73n., 80
Banfield, Edward D., 10
Benefit-cost analysis, 130–33
  and the burden of aid, 233–34
  and externalities, 131
  and secondary effects, 131–32
  and shadow prices, 131–32
  See also Foreign aid requirements
Brasseur Plan, 202

Burden of aid, 219–55
  and government promotion of private investment, 230–31
  and international commodity agreements, 234–36
  and PL 480, 228–29
  and social rate of return, 227–28
  and tied aid, 246–54
  measurement of, 227–36
  multilateral *vs.* bilateral aid, 254–55
  See also International burden sharing, Benefit-cost analysis, Foreign loans

Cairncross, A. K., 42
Capital, and growth; *see* Growth theories
  and private investment, 230–31
  and social rate of return, 227–28
  return on, 133–34
  See also Burden of aid, Benefit-cost analysis
Capital-absorptive capacity, 76, 99–104
  See also Foreign-aid requirements
Capital exports, 220–27
  and gains from trade, 224–27
  and rate of return, 220, 222–24
  and terms of trade, 220, 224
Capital-output ratio, 176
  See also Growth theories
Chenery, Hollis B., 62–64, 65, 82–86, 91–93, 119, 133
Chile, 165, 174–76, 178
  and letter of intent, 165–66, 174–76
Clark, P. G., 161–62
Cobb-Douglas production funetion, 30–35
  See also Growth theories
Cohen, Benjamin J., 96
Colonial Development Act, 14